HOUGHTON MIFFLIN

Quest

INVITATIONS
TO LITERACY

Houghton Mifflin Company • Boston

Atlanta • Dallas • Geneva, Illinois • Palo Alto • Princeton

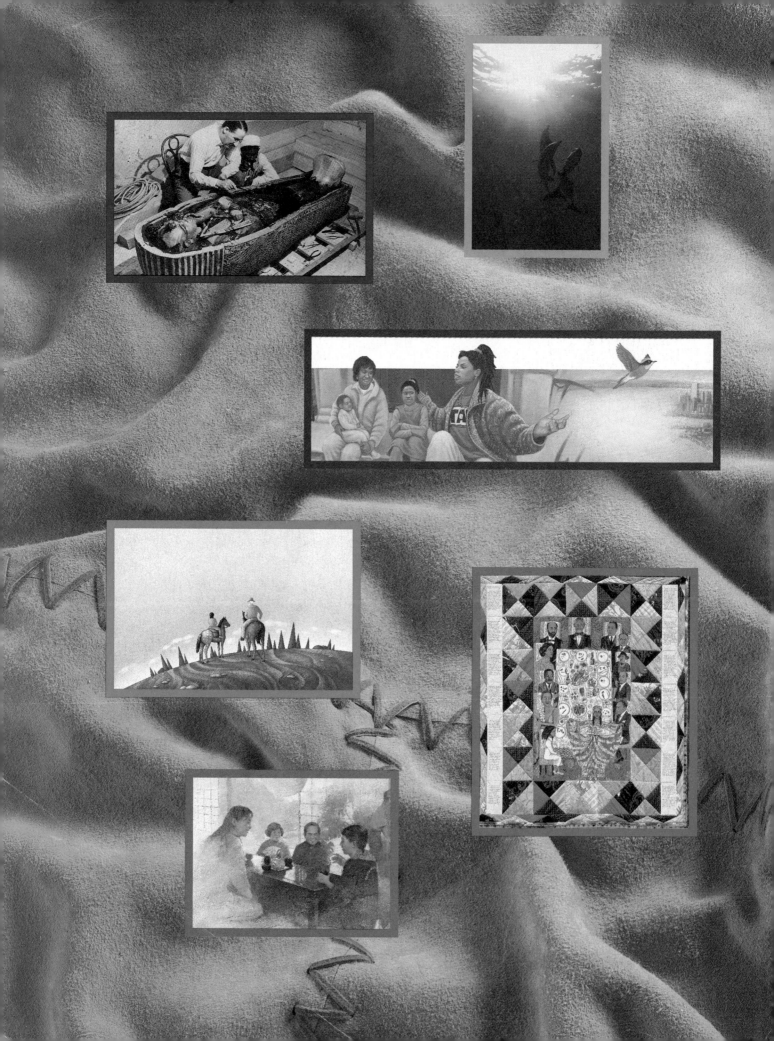

HOUGHTON MIFFLIN

Quest

Senior Authors

J. David Cooper
John J. Pikulski

Authors

Kathryn H. Au
Margarita Calderón
Jacqueline C. Comas
Marjorie Y. Lipson
J. Sabrina Mims
Susan E. Page
Sheila W. Valencia
MaryEllen Vogt

Consultants

Dolores Malcolm
Tina Saldivar
Shane Templeton

INVITATIONS TO LITERACY

Houghton Mifflin Company • Boston

Atlanta • Dallas • Geneva, Illinois • Palo Alto • Princeton

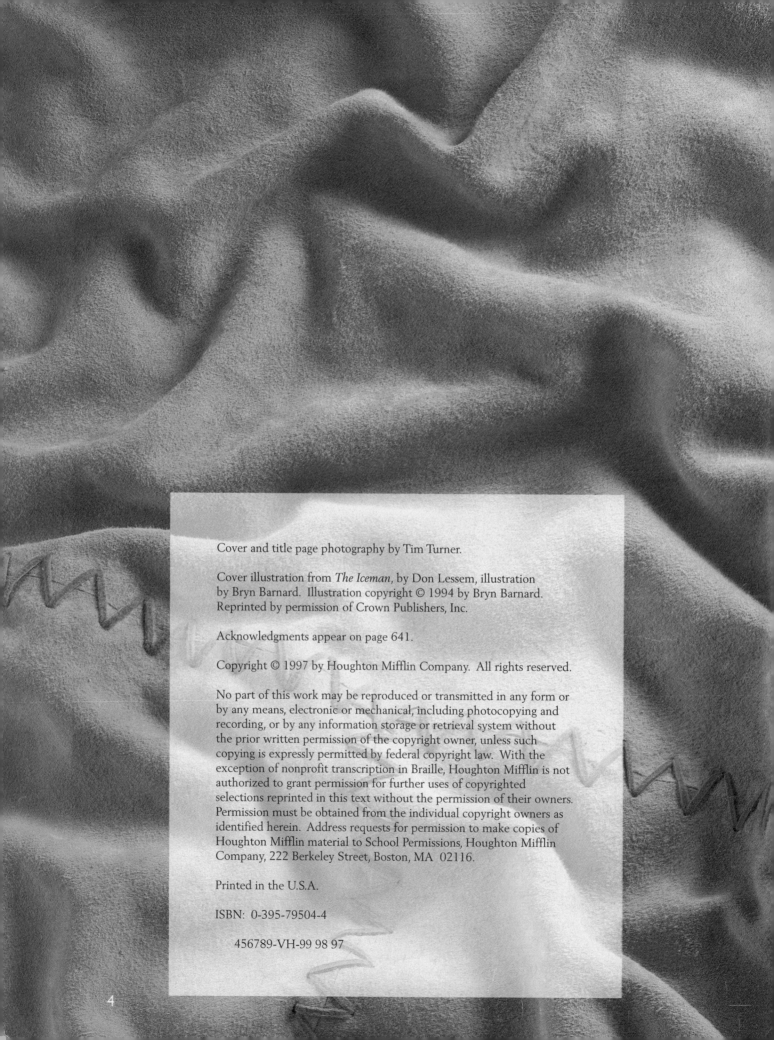

Introductory Selection

Themes

SURVIVAL!

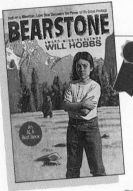

PAPERBACK **PLUS**

CONTENTS

In Search of the Real Me

PAPERBACK **PLUS**

Strider
fiction by
Beverly Cleary

In the same book . . .
more about pets and
family relationships.

A Jar of Dreams
fiction by Yoshiko Uchida

In the same book . . .
more about growing up and
fitting in.

UNWRAPPING ANCIENT MYSTERIES

Treasures from the Past

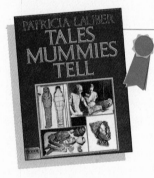

Dig and Discover

PAPERBACK **PLUS**

Zekmet the Stone Carver: A Tale of Ancient Egypt
fiction by Mary Stolz

In the same book . . .
more about the world of the Great Sphinx.

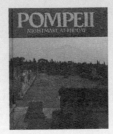

Pompeii: Nightmare at Midday
historical nonfiction by Kathryn Long Humphrey

In the same book . . .
more about the explosion from a teenage witness, victims' stories, and treasures.

CONTENTS

PAPERBACK **PLUS**

Tuck Everlasting
fantasy by
Natalie Babbitt

In the same book . . .
more facts and fiction
about being forever young.

A Young Painter: The Life
and Painting of Wang Yani,
China's Extraordinary Young
Artist
biography by Zheng Zhensun
and Alice Low

In the same book . . .
more about art and art materials.

CONTENTS

FINDING COMMON GROUND

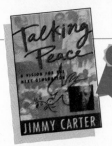

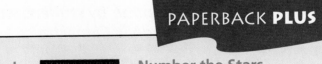

PAPERBACK **PLUS**

Mop, Moondance, and
the Nagasaki Knights
fiction by
Walter Dean Myers

In the same book . . .
looking at baseball from
different angles and cultures.

Number the Stars
fiction by Lois Lowry

In the same book . . .
more about experiences during
World War II.

CONTENTS

OCEAN QUEST

About the author

Born in Fresno, California, **Gary Soto** is a Mexican American writer who first became famous as a poet. But his stories about growing up have been widely read and enjoyed since *Living Up the Street: Narrative Recollections* was published in 1985. Soto says that his stories are extensions of his poems. "I would rather show and not tell about certain levels of poverty, of childhood; I made a conscious effort not to tell anything but just present the stories and let the reader come up with assumptions about the book — just show not tell, which is what my poetry has been doing for years." Selections from *Baseball in April and Other Stories, Pacific Crossing,* and a poem also appear in this anthology.

About the illustrator

After moving from city to city, **Scott Nash**'s family settled on Cape Cod in Massachusetts. His best advice for young artists is: "When it comes to art, don't listen to any advice that begins, 'You can't or you shouldn't.'" To sketch and take notes before starting an illustration, he goes to places where there are lots of kids. Besides illustrating and running his own design firm, Scott plays guitar and reads a lot.

SUMMER SCHOOL

SUMMER SCHOOL
SUMMER SCHOOL
SUMMER SCHOOL
SUMMER SCHOOL
Summer School

by Gary Soto

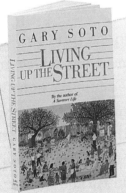

The summer before I entered sixth grade I decided to go to summer school. I had never gone, and it was either school or mope around the house with a tumbler of Kool-Aid and watch TV, flipping the channels from exercise programs to soap operas to game shows until something looked right.

My sister decided to go to summer school too, so the two of us hopped onto our bikes and rode off to Heaton Elementary, which was three miles away, and asked around until we were pointed to the right rooms. I ran off without saying good-bye to Debra.

These were the home rooms where the teachers would check roll, announce bulletins, and read us a story before we dashed off to other classes. That morning I came in breathing hard, smiling a set of teeth that were fit for an adult, and took a seat behind a fat kid named Yodelman so I couldn't be seen.

The teacher, whose name is forgotten, told us that summer school classes were all electives — that we could choose anything we wanted. She had written them on the blackboard, and from her list I chose science, history, German, and square dancing.

Little John, a friend from our street, sat across the room. I had not seen him at first, which miffed him because he thought I was playing stuck-up for some reason, and so he threw an acorn at me that bounced harmlessly off Yodelman's shoulder. Yodelman turned his head slowly, turtle-like, blinked his small dull eyes, and then turned his head back to the teacher who was telling us that we had to fill out cards. She had two monitors pass out pencils, and we hovered and strained over the card: Date of birth, address, grade, career goals. At the last one I thought for the longest time, pencil poised and somewhat worried, before I raised my hand to ask the teacher how to spell paleontology. Surprised, as if someone had presented her flowers, she opened her mouth, searched the ceiling with her eyes, and gave it a stab: p-a-y-e-n-t-o-l-o-g-y. I wrote it in uneven capitals and then wrote "bone collector" in the margin.

Little John glared at me, made a fist, and wet his lips. When class was dismissed he punched me softly in the arm and together the two of us walked out of class talking loudly, happy that we were together.

While Little John went to typing I went to science class. The teacher stood before us in a white shirt, yardstick in hand, surrounded by jars of animal parts floating in clear liquids. This scared me, as did a replica of a skeleton hanging like a frayed coat in the corner. On the first day we looked carefully at leaves in groups of threes, after which the teacher asked us to describe the differences.

"This one is dried up and this one is not so dried up," one kid offered, a leaf in each hand.

The teacher, who was kind, said that that was a start. He raised his yardstick and pointed to someone else.

From there I went to history, a class I enjoyed immensely because it was the first one ever in which I would earn an A. This resulted from reading thirty books — pamphlets to be more exact. I was a page turner, and my index finger touched each paragraph before the thumb peeled a new page, as I became familiar with Edison, Carnegie, MacArthur, Eli Whitney . . .

At the end of the five-week summer school, the teacher would call me to the front of the class to tell about the books I had read. He stood behind the lectern, looking down at his watch now and then, and beamed at me like a flashlight.

"Who was Pike?"

"Oh, he was the guy that liked to go around in the mountains."

"Who was Genghis Khan?"

"He was a real good fighter. In China."

With each answer the teacher smiled and nodded his head at me. He smiled at the class and some of the students turned their heads away, mad that I knew so much. Little John made a fist and wet his lips.

From history we were released to the playground where we played soft-ball, sucked on popsicles, and fooled around on the monkey bars. We returned to our classes sweating like the popsicles we had sucked to a rugged stick. I went to German where, for five weeks, we sang songs we didn't understand, though we loved them and loved our teacher who parad-ed around the room and closed his eyes on the high notes. On the best days he rolled up his sleeves, undid his tie, and sweated profusely as he belted out songs so loudly that we heard people pounding on the wall for quiet from the adjoining classroom. Still, he went on with great vigor:

Mein Hut der hat drei Ecken
Drei Ecken hat mein Hut
Und wenn er das nicht hatte
Dan war's auch nicht mein Hut

And we joined in every time, faces pink from a wonderful beauty that rose effortlessly from the heart.

I left, humming, for square dancing. Debra was in that class with me, fresh from science class. Even though Debra didn't want to do it, we paired off the first day. We made ugly faces at each other as we clicked our heels, swished for a few steps, and clicked again.

It was in that class that I fell in love with my corner gal who looked like Hayley Mills, except she was not as boyish. I was primed to fall in love because of the afternoon movies I watched on television, most of which were stories about women and men coming together, parting with harsh feelings, and embracing in the end to marry and drive big cars.

Day after day we'd pass through do-si-does, form Texas stars, spin, click heels, and bounce about the room, released from our rigid school children lives to let our bodies find their rhythm. As we danced I longed openly for her, smiling like a lantern and wanting very badly for her eyes to lock onto mine and think deep feelings. She swung around my arm, happy as the music, and hooked onto the next kid, oblivious to my yearning.

When I became sick and missed school for three days, my desire for her didn't sputter out. In bed with a comic book, I became dreamy as a cat and closed my eyes to the image of her allemanding left to *The Red River Valley*, a favorite of the class's, her long hair flipping about on her precious shoulders. By Friday I was well, but instead of going to school I stayed home to play "jump and die" with the neighbor kids — a game in which we'd repeatedly climb a tree and jump until someone went home crying from a hurt leg or arm. We played way into the dark.

On Monday I was back at school, stiff as new rope, but once again excited by science, history, the gutteral sounds of German, and square dancing! By Sunday I had almost forgotten my gal, so when I walked into class my heart was sputtering its usual tiny, blue flame. It picked up, however, when I saw the girls come in, pink from the afternoon heat, and line up against the wall. When the teacher clapped her

hands, announced something or another, and asked us to pair off, my heart was roaring like a well-stoked fire as I approached a girl that *looked* like my girl-friend. I searched her face, but it wasn't her. I looked around as we galloped about the room but I couldn't spot her. Where is she? Is that her? I asked myself. No, no, my girlfriend has a cute nose. Well, then, is that her? I wondered girl after girl and, for a moment in the dizziness of spinning, I even thought my sister was my girl-friend. So it was. All afternoon

I searched for *her* by staring openly into the faces of girls with long hair, and when class was dismissed I walked away bewildered that I had forgotten what the love of my life looked like. The next day I was desperate and stared even more boldly, until the teacher pulled me aside to shake a finger and told me to knock it off.

But I recovered from lost love as quickly as I recovered from jumping from trees, especially when it was announced, in the fourth week of classes, that there would be a talent show — that everyone was welcome to join in. I approached Little John to ask if he'd be willing to sing with me — *Michael Row the Boat Ashore*, *If I Had a Hammer*, or *Sugar Shack* — anything that would bring applause and momentary fame.

"C'mon, I know they'll like it," I whined at him as he stood in center field. He told me to leave him alone, and when a fly ball sailed in his direction he raced for it but missed by several feet. Two runs scored, and he turned angrily at me: "See what you did!"

I thought of square dancing with Debra, but I had the feeling that she would screw up her face into an ugly knot if I should ask. She would tell her friends and they would ride their bikes talking about me. So I decided that I'd just watch the show with my arms crossed.

The talent show was held on the lawn, and we were herded grade by grade into an outline of a horseshoe: The first and second

grades sat Indian-style, the third and fourth graders squatted on their haunches, and the fifth and sixth graders stood with their arms across their chests. The first act was two girls — sisters I guessed — singing a song about weather: Their fingers made the shape of falling rain, their arching arms made rainbows, and finally their hands cupped around smiling faces made sunshine. We applauded like rain while some of the kids whistled like wind from a mountain pass.

This was followed with a skit about personal hygiene — bathing and brushing one's teeth. Then there was a juggling act, another singing duo, and then a jazz tap dancer who, because he was performing on the grass, appeared to be stamping mud off his shoes. After each act my eyes drifted to a long table of typewriters. What could they possibly be for? I asked myself. They were such commanding machines, big as boulders lugged from rivers. Finally, just as the tap routine was

coming to an end, kids
began to show up behind
them to fit clean sheets of
paper into the rollers.
They adjusted their chairs
as they looked at one
another, whispering. A
teacher called our attention to the typewriters and we whistled like mountain wind again.

"All summer we have practiced learning how to type,"
the teacher said in a clear, deliberate speech. "Not only
have we learned to type letters, but also to sing with the
typewriters. If you listen carefully, I am sure that you will
hear songs that you are familiar with." She turned to the
kids, whose hands rested like crabs on the keys, raised a
pencil, and then began waving it around. Click — clickclick
— click — click — click, and I recognized *The Star Spangled
Banner* — and recognized Little John straining over his key-
board. Darn him, I thought, jealous that everyone was looking at him. They then played *Waltzing Matilda*, and this
made me even angrier because it sounded beautiful and
because Little John was enjoying himself. Click-click-click,
and they were playing *Michael Row the Boat Ashore*, and this
made me even more mad. I edged my way in front of Little
John and, when he looked up, I made a fist and wet my lips.
Smiling, he wet his own lips and shaped a cuss word, which
meant we would have a fight afterward, when the music was
gone and there were no typewriters to hide behind.

Write a Course Description

The Perfect Summer Class

If you could take a class in summer school, what would it be? Write a course description of the perfect summer school course. Combine your description with those of your classmates in a bulletin board or catalog. Include descriptions of the four courses taken by the narrator.

Plan a Talent Show

Possible Acts

If you and your classmates were to plan a talent show, who would do what? With a small group, brainstorm various acts that you and your classmates could perform. If possible, choose from among your ideas, add others, and hold a talent show of your own. Make it like the one in "Summer School" in some way.

Pick a Phrase

Gary Soto uses many original and sometimes funny comparisons in his story. For example, he writes that the typewriters were "big as boulders lugged from rivers." Choose a comparison you liked and turn it into a funny illustration that shows both things being compared.

One, Two, Agree

What did the narrator learn in "Summer School"? First, write a one- or two-sentence answer to this question. Then read your answer to a partner and listen to his or hers. Discuss each one. Finally, in a small group, share your answers and see if your group can write one answer that you all agree on.

29

SURVIVAL?

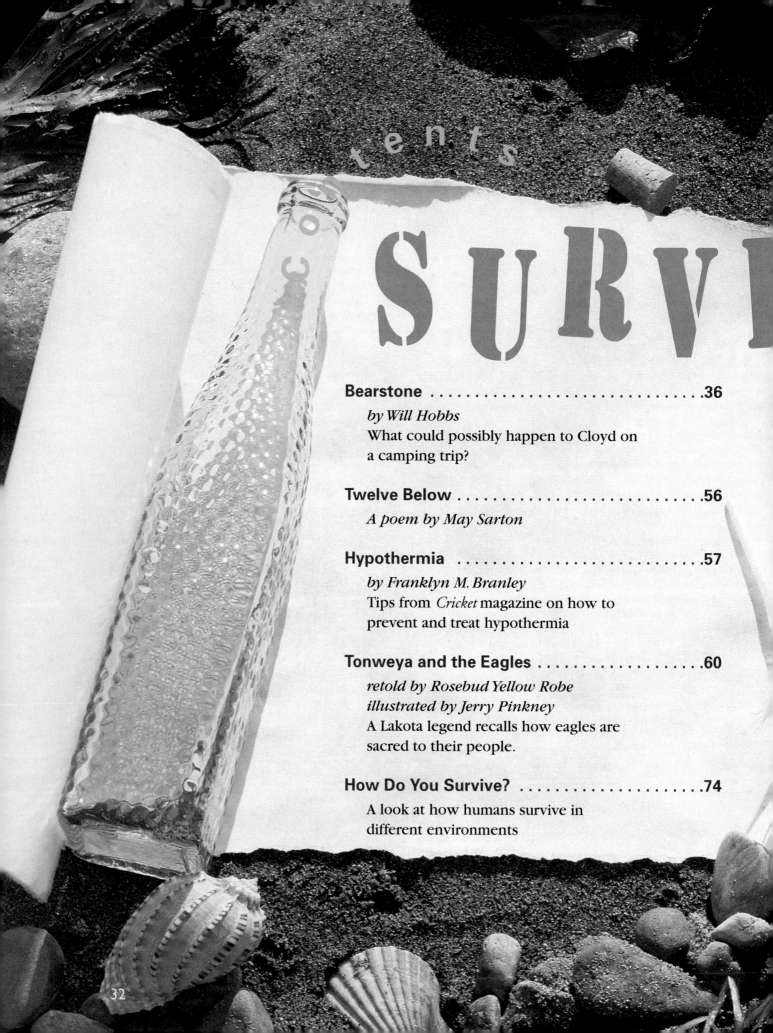

SURVI

VAL!

SURVIVAL!

Read
on Your
Own

LONG CLAWS
An Arctic Adventure

JAMES HOUSTON

PAPERBACK **PLUS**

Long Claws
written and illustrated
by James Houston
Pitohok and Upik must find
food to save their family, and
they must face Long Claws
to survive.

In the same book . . .
read about the Arctic and building
snow houses.

PAPERBACK PLUS

Hatchet
by Gary Paulsen

A small plane crashes in the Canadian wilderness, leaving a fifteen-year-old stranded — alone.

In the same book . . .
you'll learn more about navigation and tool-making.

Books to the Rescue

My Side of the Mountain
by Jean Craighead George
Sam is determined to spend the winter alone on his ancestors' land.

Adrift!
by Allan Baillie
A game of Pirates turns to terror when Flynn and his sister Sally drift helplessly out to sea.

Survive! Could You?
by Judy Donnelly and Sydelle Kramer
Do you know how to survive an earthquake? A shark attack? Or if you were caught in quicksand?

On the Long Trail Home
by Elisabeth J. Stewart
As a young girl, the author's Cherokee great-grandmother tried to find her way back to the mountains she loved.

The Hidden Children
by Howard Greenfield
During World War II, thousands of Jewish children were hidden by strangers in order to survive. Thirteen survivors tell their stories.

BEARSTONE

BY WILL HOBBS

Fourteen-year-old **Cloyd Atcitty** has run away from the group home where he'd been sent by his Ute tribe. Now he is sent to Colorado to spend the summer with **Walter Landis,** an elderly rancher. He runs again, rebelling against his new caretaker, fleeing to the mountains where he finds a small **turquoise bear** in an Indian burial cave. Cloyd returns, and sparks fly as he and the rancher get to know each other. Then their **friendship grows.** And finally, Walter takes Cloyd on a promised trip to the mountains to reopen the old man's gold mine, the "Pride of the West."

oday was the big day. Cloyd and Walter had been up since four in the morning shuttling the packhorses, mining equipment, food, and camping gear to the trailhead at the end of the road up the Pine River. It was midafternoon, and thunderclouds were gathering over the mountains. On their third and last trip to the trailhead, they stopped in Bayfield to buy a few last-minute supplies. Walter bought a fishing rod for Cloyd, and hooks and salmon eggs. "Used to be good fishing on the Pine — bet it still is. If the trout don't like the salmon eggs, you can dig worms with the camp shovel or catch grasshoppers. Maybe you can catch us some fresh dinner now and again."

They drove up the river road. Cloyd could hardly believe he was finally going to the mountains. A few miles north, Walter pulled off by the Pine River Cemetery. He told Cloyd he could wait a few minutes or come along. Cloyd looked in on the saddle horses in the gooseneck trailer, Blueboy, and the old man's sorrel mare, while Walter walked into the little cemetery. Then he caught up with the old man in front of a pair of graves.

At the far end of the plot was centered a single stone. Cloyd recognized the name *Landis*. Underneath there were two names, and one of them was Walter's.

"Why is your name on this?" Cloyd asked in undisguised confusion.

Walter scratched the thick white bristles of his beard. It was almost grown out again. "All they have to do is put the date on. Makes it easy."

Cloyd picked dandelions and piled the flowers on the grass. He thought about Walter in a box under the grass. "Do you have any relatives?"

"There's a few still around. My brother's on the Animas River down in New Mexico, and my wife's kin are back in Missouri."

Suddenly the wind began to blow. Cloyd looked up from the gravestones and saw the black clouds racing toward them from the mountains, where lightning flashed and rain hung in dark layers. He was chilled in his T-shirt, but he wanted to hear Walter talk. "Are people still alive after they die — like they say?"

"I don't know, really. Lots of folks believe there's life after death, but nobody knows for sure. Maybe your life is all there is. But that's plenty, ain't it? Make it good while you have it, is what I think, in case there ain't nothin' extra."

"Live in a good way. That's what my grandmother says."

"That's a fine way to put it."

The clouds overtook them and darkened the Pine River Valley. Thunder rumbled more frequently. A long bolt of lightning struck a few miles upriver, the concussion and unraveling thunder following behind. "Comin' our direction," Walter remarked with some anxiety.

Cloyd didn't want to cut off this talk with the old man. It was important. They could always run for the truck. "How come you stopped here — to talk to your wife?"

"Well, in a way. To tell her I'm goin' back to the mine, I guess."

"But she can't hear you."

"Prob'ly not, but it's more a matter of respect."

"How do you mean?"

"Showin' honor for her. I wouldn't do something this important without consulting her if she was alive. Matter of fact," he chuckled, "I wouldn't be doing it at all. But seeing the circumstances, she won't mind. She'd say, 'You go up there with Cloyd to that mine of yours and find your gold.'"

"But she isn't alive."

"No, that ain't right. Somehow, as long as I'm alive, she is too."

"Like she's a part of you?"

"People get like that, Cloyd. That's what's special about people."

The wind stopped abruptly, and Walter had that claustrophobic feeling he got when the air pressure was dropping fast around him. "Say, we better shake a leg," he said, and turned from the grave.

The old man wasn't much for running, but he shuffled along as briskly as he could. They were barely inside the truck when the wind and the rain struck. "Let's wait her out," Walter said. "No sense driving in this."

Cloyd reached into his jeans pocket and pulled out the bearstone, set it on the dashboard. "I want to tell you a secret about this," he said.

Walter appraised the stone up close, the turquoise bear he'd nearly destroyed in anger. "It's some piece," he said. "Forehead's dished out like a grizzly's, and this bulge here on the back, it's almost like it's a hump."

"I found it with one of the Ancient Ones — a baby — in those rocks up there, above your farm."

"In the cliffs? A burial? Why, if that ain't somethin'."

"Bears are special for Ute people — they bring strength and good luck."

"All the more reason you've got yourself something special here," Walter said. "Think how old this stone must be. This blue bear's a real treasure, Cloyd."

"When I found this, I gave myself a secret name. The Utes used to do that — they kept it secret except for one other person. You're the only one I'll ever tell my secret name to. It's Lone Bear. That's what it is — Lone Bear."

Walter conjectured what it might mean, the name Cloyd had taken for himself. It seemed like an awfully lonesome name. He wondered if the turquoise piece would bring the good luck the boy was hoping for.

"You know, Cloyd, some of that good luck just might rub off on the Pride of the West."

alter roused Cloyd when it was still dark in their camp at the trailhead.

By the light of the gas lantern they set to work sorting their gear into eight loads for the eight packhorses. After sunrise Cloyd brought the horses into camp from the meadow by the river where they'd been hobbled overnight.

The packhorses stamped their feet and shied from the wooden frames lifted toward them. The packing dragged on all morning. Cloyd could hardly believe all the gear they were taking with them. Two groups of backpackers left up the trail while they were working. Finally the last knot was tied, the riding horses saddled. Cloyd and Walter led their animals to the wooden gate between the parking lot and the beginning of the trail.

"What's this sign say?" Cloyd asked.

"Weminuche Wilderness Area. No motorized vehicles beyond this point."

Cloyd looked up the trail and saw it climb through a dense stand of pines. The trunks weren't far enough apart to allow even a jeep through. "Why do they have to say that?" he asked.

"Why, that means motorbikes, I suppose, and snowmobiles in the winter. Good thing, too. Our horses are spooky enough without having to contend with motors. That 'Weminuche' there, that's the name of the Utes who used to live up here."

"I know. My grandmother said that's us. We're the Weminuche."

"Well, now ain't that somethin'."

And then they were under way, each leading a string of four packhorses. Walter rode in front on his sorrel mare; Cloyd followed on the big blue roan.

The canyon soon narrowed, and the trail climbed well above the river. Cloyd found himself looking down hundreds of feet into pools so clear he could see the stones on the bottom. Above them, rockslide paths fell through the spruce and aspen forests from the peaks. As high as they were, these peaks weren't the towering, jagged ones he'd seen from the cliffs that first day at the farm. Before long, he would stand on top of one of the very highest and look out over the world.

The farther they worked their way up the Pine, the more Cloyd marveled at the steady gait and surefootedness of the roan. And when the horse had a chance, he'd swivel his eye back around and catch sight of the boy. There was something Cloyd had been turning over and over in his mind and now, he decided, was the time to ask the old man about it. "Is it true, like he said, that horses don't care anything about you?"

The old man hitched himself up in the saddle and halfway turned around. "You mean like Rusty said? Don't pay no mind to his talk. He just hates to agree with anybody. It's just the way he is."

"But is it true?"

"I've always puzzled on that, same as you. Horses appreciate good treatment and a steady hand, but it's a fact they don't go out of their way to fetch your slippers. Maybe some really do care. I've had one or two that made me think so, but it seems like you never know for sure. What do you think?"

"Oh, I was just wondering."

Cloyd was mostly disappointed with the old man's answer. As they rode, he continued to turn it over in his mind. He leaned forward and patted the roan. "Blueboy," he thought, "you're not just any horse. You and me, Blue, you and me."

The roan rolled an eye back and snorted loudly.

The next day the horses labored up ever-steeper grades as the river fell in leaps from the high country. Cloyd watched his string carefully as they crossed the tricky scree slides of fine rock that ran below them all the way to the river. Several times during the day they forded swift creeks that fed the Pine; with little urging, the roan crossed them easily. The others behind accepted his leadership.

Late in the afternoon they climbed out the canyon onto a large meadow, astonishingly green with knee-high grass and ringed by mountains that stabbed far above the line where the trees stopped growing. A small stream here close to the Continental Divide, the Pine River wound quietly in delicate meanders through the meadow. Walter said they'd lay over a day or two before they went up Snowslide Canyon to the mine. Cloyd was happy to make camp. As he'd been riding, he'd seen the trout darting through the riffles between the pools. They set up the sheepherder tent in the trees at the meadow's edge.

At first light Cloyd was up digging worms in the black soil underneath the trees. On the meadow, he sneaked up on a pool and let his bait drift into a likely spot. In a moment the rod came alive in his hands, and he launched the flashing trout into the air and over his head. A large cutthroat trout in its orange-red colors lay gasping in the grass. It was the first fish he'd ever caught and the beginnings of a meal for him and the old man. He remembered his grandmother saying that when the Weminuche lived in the mountains, some of the men were so skilled that they could catch fish with their bare hands. That didn't seem possible. But now he knew how they must have felt when they caught the lightning-fast trout, however they did it.

Midway up the meadow Cloyd caught his second trout, and then his third at the upper end where the stream came rushing out of the trees. He'd discovered the fishing was better if he kept trying new water than if he stayed with one hole, even if he could see plenty of trout there. It seemed they would strike pretty quick, or not at all. He decided to look upstream in the trees for another good place to fish. After walking around the rapids through a thick spruce forest, he found an even bigger, more promising meadow above.

As Cloyd began to fish the upper meadow, white clouds boiled up out of the blue sky and quickly turned dark. The wind started to blow, but he was too excited to notice the wind or the clouds — he was landing trout. Several miles from camp, at the far end of the upper meadow, he caught his seventh. As he slid the new-caught fish onto the stringer he'd fashioned from a willow branch, he shook with cold and realized the temperature had been dropping for some time. He'd been out fishing longer than he thought. Without the sun it was hard to judge the time, but it could be past noon already. He saw the clouds spill down the mountainsides toward him, dark and loaded with moisture. A few more pools, maybe one more fish, and he would collect his trout and head for camp.

Lightning broke loose and thunder rumbled, not too far off. A cold wind rushed down the meadow. He wished he'd worn more than a T-shirt, but he hadn't thought he would be out long. He knew he'd better run for it; the storm was about to break. As he picked up his stringer and started out, lightning cracked barely upstream. The shock wave and his surprise threw him to the ground. Glancing back, he saw the big spruces bending under the weight of the wind, and hail angling down with terrific speed.

Cloyd thought he could race the hail into the trees between the meadows and nestle in under a good roof of branches. He ran for the trees with the rod held high in his right hand and the stringer of trout in his left. He ran with a laughing heart because the hail was already pounding the meadow behind him, and yet at full speed he would outrun it just in time.

With no warning his right leg sank to the hip, his chest and face struck the ground, the rod and stringer of fish flew. In the tall grass, he'd failed to see the narrow trench connecting the stream with the pond where beavers had built one of their domed lodges.

Pain coursed through and through his leg. He was sure he'd hurt it badly. With his weight on his left knee, Cloyd dragged the right leg out of the beaver run and lay on his left side, watching the wall of hail advance down the meadow. He had to wait for the pain to clear. Lightning ripped the meadow simultaneously with its deafening thunder. A heartbeat later the hail struck, stinging him and bouncing all around in the grass. Within seconds he was drenched and started to shake with cold. His T-shirt and jeans clung to him; they offered no protection. The feeling went out of his fingers. He lay motionless, unable to think.

In minutes the meadow was
carpeted with a layer of hail. All of a
sudden, it was winter. Cloyd had seen hail-
storms in the high desert, but not like this one.
Here the air itself had turned freezing cold.
Shaking now from fear as well as cold, he forced
himself to think. Managing another hundred yards
to the trees meant nothing now. He had to reach
camp, the old man, and a fire — or freeze to
death. He tried the leg. It could take
some of his weight. Nothing
was broken.

Cloyd knew he had to start out immediately, but somehow it seemed important not to leave the rod and the fish behind. They couldn't be far. As he raked through the hail-flattened grass with his sneakers, he realized he couldn't feel his feet. There was the rod. He scooped it up and clamped his fingers around it. Lucky for him it wasn't broken. And here were the trout, stiff and staring.

Then he ran as best he could, shaking, tripping, falling. The hail turned to cold and steady rain. Something told him that he had no chance in the woods, the way he came up from the lower meadow. He had to find a trail. Was there a trail? He hadn't seen one all day. Maybe there would be one on the far side of the meadow, across the stream.

Cloyd couldn't feel the icy water as he plunged across the Pine River holding up his rod and reel and his fish. In fact, he'd stopped shaking and couldn't feel anything at all. His body was getting too cold, much too cold.

Across the meadow he found a trail and hastened wildly down it. After a while he was in the trees. The trail fell sharply, muddy and slick, turning this way and that. He veered through dark shapes as if in a dream. No sign of the lower meadow and the old man, and the cold was squeezing the life out of him. Through the dark trees, off the trail and down by the stream, a small patch of orange caught his eye. His mind dismissed the image, but as he stumbled forward, the idea of the orange color slowly worked its way to the surface. It was a tent. Cloyd stopped and stared through the trees at a trace of blue smoke hanging in the dark branches above the tent.

He could barely move. It took him a long time to reach the orange tent. Now he stood dumbly by the remains of a fire. There was no fire here, only a bit of blue smoke curling around the soggy stub of a log.

Cloyd faced the tent. "I need help," he said thickly.

Someone lifted the tent flap — a young man with glasses and a dark beard — and cursed in surprise. The man came out of the tent, took away the rod and the fish, and forced him to the ground and inside the small orange tent. Cursing softly, the man said not to worry. He rummaged through a sack, muttering something about long johns.

The man with the beard pulled Cloyd's wet clothes off. The boy looked curiously at his own body. It didn't seem to belong to him. He noticed he wasn't shaking anymore. He didn't even feel cold. Then the man was dressing him in different clothes. It took a long time. His elbows kept poking the tent. Everything was orange, orange all around.

The bearded man stuffed Cloyd into a sleeping bag and asked if he felt warmer. He couldn't even answer. Then he was alone. The man had left. The cold and the quiet crept into one another comfortably. The world went dark; he felt himself falling asleep. He drifted deeper and deeper into the dark, like a leaf settling into the bottom of a deep pool. It was almost perfectly peaceful. He was so close to that perfect sleep when something intruded, one faraway nagging detail. He couldn't even tell what it was. After a while it was some kind of noise, very far away. A magpie or a raven squawking, or possibly even his sister come looking for him in the canyons and calling again and again. Yes, it was a human

voice after all, nagging, calling, insisting, shouting, but it wasn't his
sister. Gradually, light seeped into his eyes, and he saw a man
with glasses and a black beard. Who was he?
　　　The world was moving. No, he was moving,
being dragged outside the orange tent into the
dark trees, sleeping bag and all.

The man's glasses were fogged up. The man lay alongside him on his elbows blowing on the wet wood, making smoke. Some coals were glowing. The man kept wheezing on them. Finally they burst into a flame and the man placed a little stick across the flame and left again.

Branches were breaking somewhere. The tiny flame was gone. The man was back with his arms full of wood, and then he was on his elbows again, blowing until his face turned purple. The flame came back. The wood started to catch. The man left; branches were breaking. After a time he was back piling branches over the fire and blowing it into stronger and stronger flames. The flames grew brighter, bigger, stronger than the rain dripping from the trees.

The bearded man with fogged-up glasses was pulling him from the sleeping bag, standing him up close to the fire, arms locked around his chest. He could begin to feel the fire spreading warmth into his body. "You're going to be all right," the man was saying. Cloyd struggled to get free of the sleeping bag. The man unzipped it, let it fall, and gained a new hold on him. Cloyd struggled again. "Hang on there," the man cautioned, "you're still medium rare. I'm gonna cook you until you're charbroiled."

Finally Cloyd's eyes cleared, and the man turned him loose. He could stand by the fire on his own. The man went for more wood. After many trips he'd built a bonfire. At its edge he boiled water in an aluminum pan and made coffee. When Cloyd drank it, he warmed from the inside out and at last became as warm as he could want to be.

"Think I'll clean your fish, if you don't mind," the man said. "They'd make a great hot meal for you, better than my freeze-dried stuff. You just stay by the fire there and make some more coffee if you like."

Cloyd nodded. The man went away through the trees to clean the fish at the stream. After he'd been gone some time, Walter rode into camp in his yellow rainslicker, leading the roan.

"Thank goodness you're okay, Cloyd," he said softly.

Walter's eyes took in the oversized clothes that weren't the boy's, a bruise below the right eye, a long scratch on his neck, the jeans and T-shirt drying by the fire. "I've been everywhere. I was afraid I wouldn't find you."

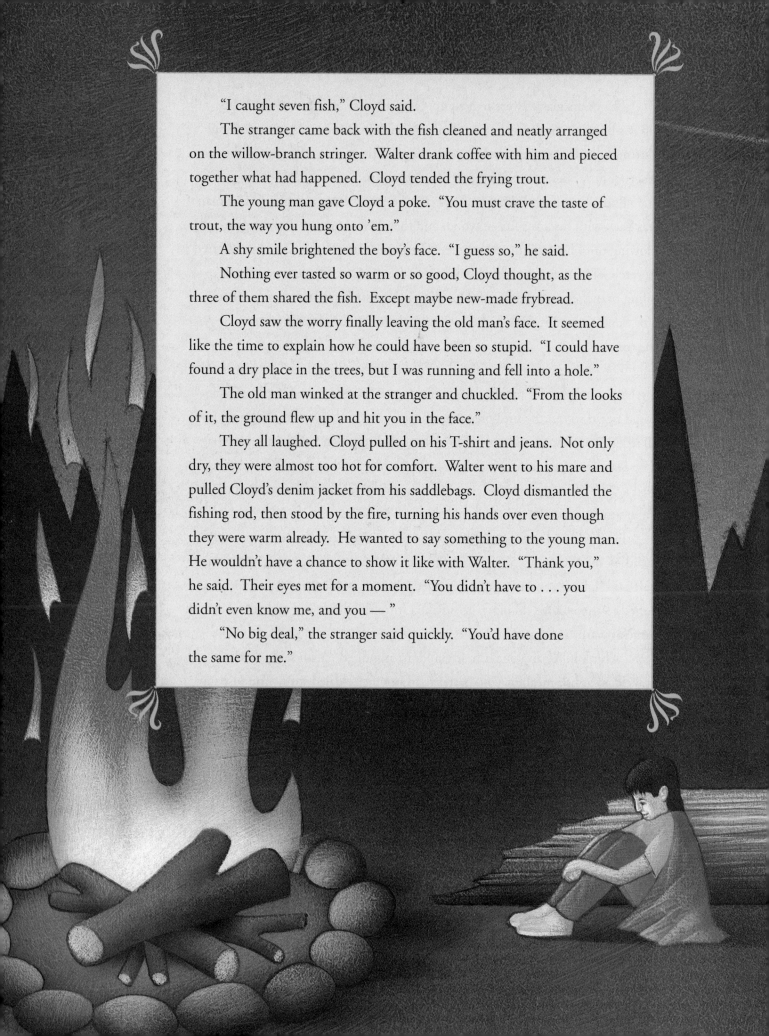

"I caught seven fish," Cloyd said.

The stranger came back with the fish cleaned and neatly arranged on the willow-branch stringer. Walter drank coffee with him and pieced together what had happened. Cloyd tended the frying trout.

The young man gave Cloyd a poke. "You must crave the taste of trout, the way you hung onto 'em."

A shy smile brightened the boy's face. "I guess so," he said.

Nothing ever tasted so warm or so good, Cloyd thought, as the three of them shared the fish. Except maybe new-made frybread.

Cloyd saw the worry finally leaving the old man's face. It seemed like the time to explain how he could have been so stupid. "I could have found a dry place in the trees, but I was running and fell into a hole."

The old man winked at the stranger and chuckled. "From the looks of it, the ground flew up and hit you in the face."

They all laughed. Cloyd pulled on his T-shirt and jeans. Not only dry, they were almost too hot for comfort. Walter went to his mare and pulled Cloyd's denim jacket from his saddlebags. Cloyd dismantled the fishing rod, then stood by the fire, turning his hands over even though they were warm already. He wanted to say something to the young man. He wouldn't have a chance to show it like with Walter. "Thank you," he said. Their eyes met for a moment. "You didn't have to . . . you didn't even know me, and you — "

"No big deal," the stranger said quickly. "You'd have done the same for me."

Meet the illustrator

As a quiet child growing up in Cincinnati, Ohio, **John Patrick** spent a lot of time playing with his older brother and the kids on their street. While studying marine biology in college, he found out that he wasn't really suited to be a research scientist. He then decided to study art and is now an illustrator. John is still interested in marine life and scuba-dives in his spare time.

Meet Will Hobbs

Like many other writers, **Will Hobbs** takes real-life experiences, mixes them up, and stirs in imagination to create his books. In 1980, Hobbs started to write a novel called *The Pride of the West*, named after a friend's gold mine. "My friend, who was the starting point for the old man in the story, was always talking about reopening his mine. I thought his chances were slim in real life; why not have a go at making it happen in a story?" As work on the novel progressed, Hobbs moved the setting to the upper Pine River — one of his own favorite places — and added a Ute boy to help the old man. By the sixth — and final — draft, the boy had become the focus of the story. *Bearstone* was published in 1989, a full nine years after Hobbs began to write it.

Hailstorm

Dear Stranger

Cloyd finds it difficult to express his gratitude at the end of this selection. Maybe if he tried to express himself in a letter, it would come more easily. Write a letter that could have been written by Cloyd to the stranger, thanking him for saving your life. Include a promise or make a resolution that shows how the experience has changed your thinking about survival.

Be a Meteorologist

Water falls to the ground in different forms: what are they? With a partner, make a poster that shows the various kinds of precipitation and the conditions in which they occur. What conditions do you think led to the dramatic hailstorm in this selection?

54

Heroics

The Ballad of Walter and Cloyd

Write an original song about what these characters experience. Remember that ballads usually rhyme, contain repeated choruses, and tell about heroic or tragic events. Here are a couple of lines to get you started: *Oh, they packed their mules and the Blueboy roan / They talked about death and the blue bearstone.* You take it from there. Perform your ballad for your classmates.

Accident or Carelessness?

Was Cloyd's near-death experience an accident or was it the result of his own carelessness? With a partner or in a small group, assign the two "sides." Find facts from the story to support the two opinions. After a fifteen-minute debate, decide which "side" you really agree with. Write your reasons in your journal.

Twelve Below

A bitter gale
Over frozen snow
Burns the skin like hail.
It is twelve below.

Too cold to live
Too cold to die
Warm animals wait
And make no cry.

Their feathers puff
Their eyes are bright
Their fur expands.
Warm animals wait.

They make no sign
They waste no breath
In this cold country
Between life and death.

by May Sarton

HYPOTHERMIA

by Franklyn M. Branley

Symptoms of Hypothermia

When exposed to wind, cold, or wet, watch for:

1. Shivering

2. Vague, slow, slurred speech

3. Memory lapses, incoherence, abnormal behavior

4. Immobile, fumbling hands

5. Undue stumbling, lurching gait

6. Drowsiness

7. Exhaustion. Too tired to get up after a rest

8. Unnoticed loss of clothing such as hat or glove

If you ski or backpack in cold weather, you've probably heard about *hypothermia*. If you haven't, it's something you should know about. The Greek word *hypo* means under, and *therm* means heat — so hypothermia means underheating, cooling, or even freezing of the body. The cooling could be fast enough to kill a person. Outside air temperature doesn't have to be very low. In fact, hypothermia can happen when the temperature is 40° or 50°F, and it often does.

Hypothermia is the chilling of the inner core of the body, as well as of the brain. When this happens, there is rapid physical and mental collapse. Memory lags, people may have trouble saying words correctly, and they may fall down or drop things because their muscles aren't working properly.

For the body to operate efficiently, its temperature must remain about 98.6°F. People produce more heat than they need, so they usually must get rid of the excess. In hypothermia, however, the body loses more heat than it produces. This condition often occurs when a person gets wet, because most insulation (such as clothing) does not work well when it is wet. The water pushes out the dead air, and water is not a good insulator. One of the deadliest accidents that can happen to a fisherman is to be washed overboard. Fishermen describe a 50-50-50 law of survival: When the water is 50°F, a person has only a 50 percent chance of surviving for 50 minutes.

Wind also speeds up heat loss because it speeds evaporation. Wet clothing exposed to the wind is dangerous. The wind cools the water. At 50°F, water is unbearably cold. If it is held against a person by sopping clothing, heat moves rapidly from the body to the water.

Whenever you're outside, keep dry. Wear rain clothes. Also, wear wool. It's the one fiber that remains an insulator, though not a good one, even when it is wet.

While you're moving — hiking or skiing, for example — your body makes a lot more heat than it does when you're resting. That's why some hikers don't realize they can suffer from hypothermia. They think they can go on and on, even though they may be wet and cold. But this is when they should be most careful. If they are in the woods, they should get out of the wind, set up camp, and build a fire.

Otherwise, they may find that once they stop hiking, their production of body heat may drop suddenly by as much as 50 percent. They may start to shiver and become unable

How to Prevent Hypothermia

Wear woolen clothing (including underwear).

Keep dry. Wear rain gear that really sheds water. (Test it in a shower to be sure it works.)

Carry a tent, windbreakers, and a stove that is sure to light. Or, if not a stove, carry fire starters that are sure to work even when wood is wet.

Remember, you don't have to be ice-cold to suffer from hypothermia. A person can die from it even when air temperature is 50°.

to control the shivering. They may slip into hypothermia; their speech will slow, they won't remember well, and they will stumble and find they cannot hold things. They may become exhausted and drowsy, but they must not sleep — or they might die.

Those suffering from hypothermia will find it difficult if not impossible to help themselves, but other people can help. In more advanced hypothermia, a person may be only semiconscious. It's important that the victim be kept awake and somehow be given warm fluids. Once stripped, the patient should be sandwiched in a large sleeping bag between two other people who are also stripped. They become heat donors to the person suffering from hypothermia.

If you are careful, you'll never suffer from hypothermia. If you ski or backpack, take precautions: keep warm, keep active but do not become exhausted, know when to quit, and keep dry. There are many things you can do to keep toasty warm, even when the temperature hovers around zero.

How to Help a Hypothermia Victim

1 Take the victim to a protected place out of the wind and rain.

2 Remove the victim's clothing immediately. (That may mean stripping completely.)

3 If the person is able to drink, warm fluids should be given.

4 Dress the victim in warm, dry clothes or put into a warm sleeping bag. *Keep the victim awake.*

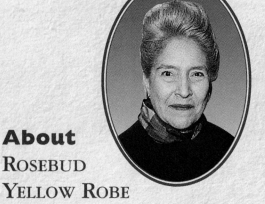

About
ROSEBUD YELLOW ROBE

Rosebud Yellow Robe was a great-grandniece of the legendary chief Sitting Bull. Because her family was so important, she got to know many famous people. She met President Calvin Coolidge and, in 1927, helped to make him an honorary Lakota Indian. She also worked on several radio shows with the actor and film-maker Orson Welles. In Welles's classic 1941 movie *Citizen Kane*, the hero's last word is "Rosebud." Did Welles get the idea for this name from Rosebud Yellow Robe? No one will ever know for sure.

About
JERRY PINKNEY

When Jerry Pinkney was growing up in Philadelphia, he was never a very good reader — but he loved to draw. "When I sat down to draw, if something didn't work, I made it work. I was assigned many projects that had to do with drawing. This made me feel special." Today, Pinkney is a well-known artist. He has illustrated children's books, designed stamps for the U.S. Postal Service, and received many awards. One reason his illustrations are so interesting is that they are full of information. To get the details right, Pinkney does a lot of library research. When he thinks about how much time he now spends reading for information, Pinkney "can't help but reflect on the little boy who wasn't a terrific reader."

Tonweya and the Eagles

AND OTHER LAKOTA TALES
retold by ROSEBUD YELLOW ROBE
pictures by JERRY PINKNEY

The boy Chano is riding to the hills with his father, Tasinagi, and his mother, Tahcawin. Suddenly two eagles circle overhead, their wing tips tinged with the color of flame. And the sight of the birds inspires the story of Tonweya, a tale of the Lakota Sioux that has passed through generations like the flight of these great birds.

61

Everyone was excited. It was the Month of Grass Appearing, and the whole camp was busy getting ready to move over the plains to a new home. They would be close to more game and they looked forward to the move. Everyone that is except Chano. He loved this camping spot and already felt lonely for the distant hills.

Tahcawin had packed the parfleche cases with clothing and food and strapped them to a travois made of two trailing poles with a skin net stretched between them. Another travois lay on the ground ready for the new tipi.

Chano was very happy when Tasinagi suggested the three of them ride up to their favorite hills for the last time.

As the three of them rode along, Tasinagi called Chano's attention to the two large birds circling overhead. They were Waŋbli, the eagle. Chano knew they were sacred to his people and that they must never be killed.

He looked at the eagle feather in his father's hair, a sign of bravery, and wondered why it was that the Lakotas as well as many other Indians held Waŋbli, the eagle, in such great respect. Someday he would ask his father about this.

The two eagles they were watching did not seem afraid of the three travelers. They flew nearer and nearer, swooping down in ever narrowing circles. They seemed to be trying to attract the attention of the travelers.

Suddenly Chano called out, "Look, Ate! The feathers on their wings are tipped with red. I never knew that Waŋbli had red feathers!"

"Are you sure of this, my son?" Tasinagi asked.

"Yes, Father. Both birds had tips of bright red on their wings."

"Tahcawin," said Tasinagi, "our son has been favored by the sight of the sacred birds of Tonweya. Few have seen them and it is a sign of good for him."

"What do you mean, Ate?" asked Chano. "What are the sacred birds of Tonweya?"

"They are the eagles who saved Tonweya's life many, many snows ago. Tonweya was a great chief and a great medicine man."

Chano immediately begged his father to tell him the story. Tasinagi motioned for Chano to ride by his side and began:

"It was the summer when the big ball of fire fell from the sky. A band of Lakotas were camping just about where we are now. Among them was a young man whose name was Tonweya. He was not only good to look upon, but he was a great runner and hunter. He was very brave in the face of danger. Everyone said that someday he would be a chief. Brave and good chiefs are always needed in every tribe.

"One day Tonweya went out hunting. He found a small herd of buffalo grazing near the hills and picking out a young fat cow sent an arrow straight into her heart. While he was skinning the buffalo, he noticed a large eagle circling above him. Watching her flight he saw that she settled on a ledge of rock projecting from a high, steep cliff about a quarter mile away. Tonweya knew there must be a nest there. He was determined to find it. If there were young eaglets, he could capture them and raise them for their feathers.

"He looked carefully at the ledge. He saw it would be impossible to climb up to it from the plain below. The only way was from above and getting down would be very dangerous. After skinning the buffalo, Tonweya cut the green hide into one long narrow strip. Then he stretched and twisted the strip through the dust until he had a long strong rope of hide.

"Coiling this about him, he made his way to the tip of the cliff right above the eagle's nest on the ledge. Fastening one end of this rawhide rope to a jack pine, he let the other fall over the ledge. Looking down he saw that it hung within a few feet of the nest. His plan was to slide down the rope and tie the eaglets to the end. Then after he had pulled himself up again, he could draw them up after him. Great honor would come to him. A pair of captive eagles would supply feathers for many warriors.

"Tonweya carefully lowered himself over the edge of the cliff and soon stood on the ledge. There were two beautiful young eaglets in the nest, full feathered, though not yet able to fly. He tied them to his rope and prepared to climb up. But just as he placed his weight on the rope, to his great surprise it fell down beside him. The green hide had been slipping at the knot where he had tied it to the tree; when he pulled on it to go up again, the knot came loose and down came the rope.

"Tonweya realized immediately that he was trapped. Only Wakan-tanka, the Great Mystery, could save him from a slow death by starvation and thirst. He looked below him. There was a sheer drop of many hundreds of feet with not even the slightest projection by which he might climb down. When he tried to climb up, he could find neither handhold nor foothold. Waŋbli had chosen well the place for a nest.

"Despite his brave heart terror gripped Tonweya. He stood looking off in the direction he knew his people to be. He cried out, 'Ma hiyopo! Ma hiyopo! Help me!' but only the echo of his own voice answered.

"As the sun was setting, the mother eagle returned to her nest. She screamed in rage when she saw a man with her eaglets. Round and round she flew. Now and then she would charge with lightning speed toward Tonweya and the young birds. The two eaglets flapped their wings wildly and called out to her. Finally in despair the mother eagle made one more swoop toward her nest, and then screaming defiantly, flew off and disappeared. Night fell and the stars came out. Tonweya was alone on the ledge with the two little birds.

"When the sun came up, Tonweya was very tired. He had not slept during the night. The ledge was so narrow, he was afraid he might roll off if he fell asleep. The sun rose high in the heavens and then started its descent into the west. Soon it would be night. Tonweya looked forward with dread to the lonely vigil he must again keep. He was very hungry and so terribly thirsty.

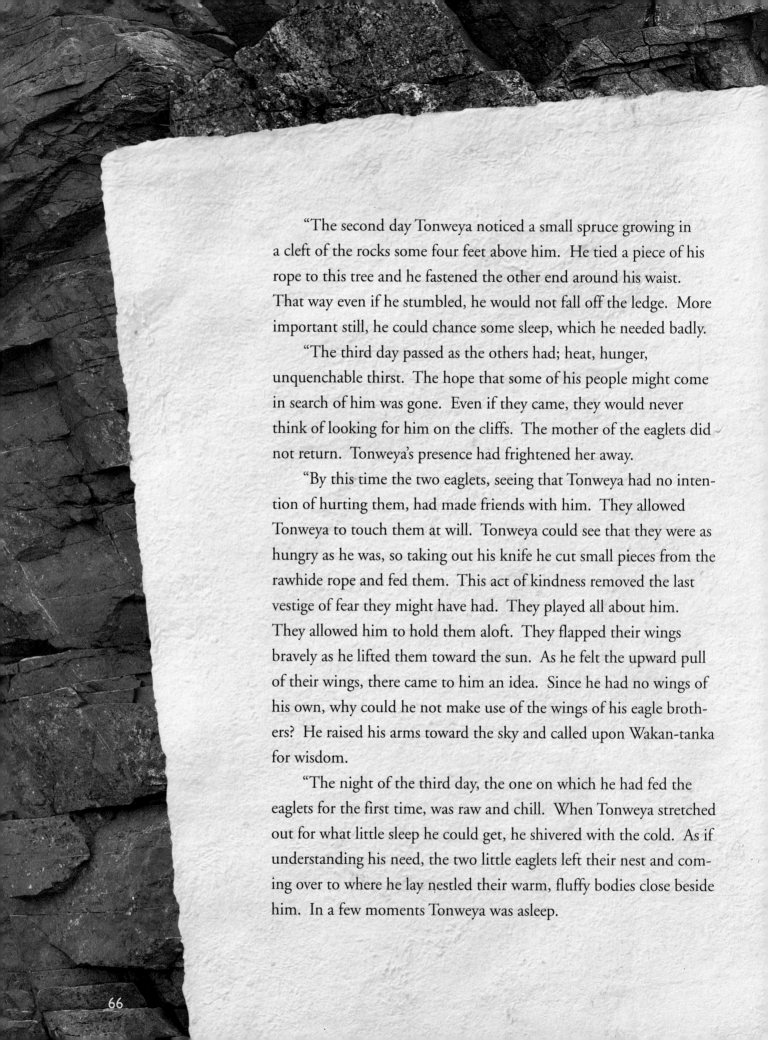

"The second day Tonweya noticed a small spruce growing in a cleft of the rocks some four feet above him. He tied a piece of his rope to this tree and he fastened the other end around his waist. That way even if he stumbled, he would not fall off the ledge. More important still, he could chance some sleep, which he needed badly.

"The third day passed as the others had; heat, hunger, unquenchable thirst. The hope that some of his people might come in search of him was gone. Even if they came, they would never think of looking for him on the cliffs. The mother of the eaglets did not return. Tonweya's presence had frightened her away.

"By this time the two eaglets, seeing that Tonweya had no intention of hurting them, had made friends with him. They allowed Tonweya to touch them at will. Tonweya could see that they were as hungry as he was, so taking out his knife he cut small pieces from the rawhide rope and fed them. This act of kindness removed the last vestige of fear they might have had. They played all about him. They allowed him to hold them aloft. They flapped their wings bravely as he lifted them toward the sun. As he felt the upward pull of their wings, there came to him an idea. Since he had no wings of his own, why could he not make use of the wings of his eagle brothers? He raised his arms toward the sky and called upon Wakan-tanka for wisdom.

"The night of the third day, the one on which he had fed the eaglets for the first time, was raw and chill. When Tonweya stretched out for what little sleep he could get, he shivered with the cold. As if understanding his need, the two little eaglets left their nest and coming over to where he lay nestled their warm, fluffy bodies close beside him. In a few moments Tonweya was asleep.

"While he was asleep, he dreamed. In his dream Wakan-tanka spoke to him. He told him to be brave, the two eaglets would save him. Tonweya awoke suddenly. The eagles were still beside him. As they felt him move, they nestled even closer to him. He placed his arms around them. He knew that his time to die had not yet come. He would once more see his people. He was no longer afraid.

"For days thereafter Tonweya fed the rawhide rope to his eagle friends. Luckily it was a long rope, for it was, of course, almost a whole buffalo hide. But while the eaglets thrived on it and grew larger and stronger each day, Tonweya grew thinner and weaker. It rained one day and water gathered in the hollows of the rocks on the ledge. Still he was very hungry and thirsty. He tried to think only of caring for the eaglets.

"Each day Tonweya would hold them up by their legs and let them try their wings. Each day the pull on his arms grew stronger. Soon it was so powerful it almost lifted him from his feet. He knew the time was coming for him to put his idea into action. He decided he must do it quickly, for weak as he was he would be unable to do it after a few more days.

"The last of the rawhide was gone, the last bit of water on the ledge was drunk. Tonweya was so weak, he could hardly stand. With an effort he dragged himself upright and called his eagle brothers to him. Standing on the edge of the ledge he called to Wakan-tanka for help. He grasped the eaglets' legs in each hand and closing his eyes he jumped.

"For a moment he felt himself falling, falling. Then he felt the pull on his arms. Opening his eyes he saw that the two eagles were flying easily. They seemed to be supporting his weight with little effort. In a moment they had reached the ground. Tonweya lay there too exhausted, too weak to move. The eagles remained by his side guarding him.

"After resting awhile Tonweya slowly made his way to a little stream nearby. He drank deeply of its cool water. A few berries were growing on the bushes there. He ate them ravenously. Strengthened by even this little food and water, he started off in the direction of the camp. His progress was slow, for he was compelled to rest many times. Always the eaglets remained by his side guarding him.

"On the way he passed the spot where he had killed the buffalo. The coyotes and vultures had left nothing but bones. However his bow and arrows were just where he had left them. He managed to kill a rabbit upon which he and his eagle friends feasted. Late in the afternoon he reached the camp, only to find that his people had moved on. It was late. He was very tired so he decided to stay there that night. He soon fell asleep, the two eagles pressing close beside him all night.

"The sun was high in the sky when Tonweya awoke. The long sleep had given him back much strength. After once more giving thanks to Wakan-tanka for his safety he set out after his people. For two days he followed their trail. He lived on the roots and berries he found along the way and what little game he could shoot. He shared everything with his eagle brothers, who followed him. Sometimes they flew overhead, sometimes they walked behind him, and now and then they rested on his shoulders.

"Well along in the afternoon of the second day he caught up with the band. At first they were frightened when they saw him. Then they welcomed him with joy.

"They were astonished at his story. The two eagles who never left Tonweya amazed them. They were glad that they had always been kind to Waŋbli and had never killed them.

"The time came when the eagles were able to hunt food for themselves and though everyone expected them to fly away, they did not. True, they would leave with the dawn on hunting forays, but when the evening drew near, they would fly back fearlessly and enter Tonweya's tipi, where they passed the night. Everyone marveled at the sight.

"But eagles, like men, should be free. Tonweya, who by now understood their language, told them they could go. They were to enjoy the life the Great Mystery, Wakan-tanka, had planned for them. At first they refused. But when Tonweya said if he ever needed their help he would call for them, they consented.

"The tribe gave a great feast in their honor. In gratitude for all they had done Tonweya painted the tips of their wings a bright red to denote courage and bravery. He took them up on a high mountain. He held them once more toward the sky and bidding them good-bye released them. Spreading their wings they soared away. Tonweya watched them until they disappeared in the eye of the sun.

"Many snows have passed and Tonweya has long been dead. But now and then the eagles with the red-tipped wings are still seen. There are always two of them and they never show any fear of people. Some say they are the original sacred eagles of Tonweya, for the Waŋbli lives for many snows. Some think they are the children of the sacred ones. It is said whoever sees the red-tipped wings of the eagles is sure of their protection as long as he is fearless and brave. And only the fearless and brave may wear the eagle feather tipped with red."

When Tasinagi finished the story, he looked to see if the red-winged eagles were still following them. They were there. He knew then that his son Chano was one of those to be blessed by great good in his life.

LOOK with Eagle Eyes

Write a Tale

Create a Special Animal

Choose an animal that you like. Write a tale about a person whose life is saved by that animal. Make your tale take place in the wilderness. Give the animal a physical characteristic — like the red-tipped wings — that makes it stand out. Give it a special name. Read your tale aloud to your friends.

Be an Illustrator

Picture a Moment

Jerry Pinkney chose to illustrate two moments of this story. As you read, you picture many more — hundreds perhaps! Choose one that is vivid in your mind and draw an illustration of that moment. Choose one sentence from the story as its caption. Display your illustration in your classroom.

Compare Animals

Eagles and Bears

"Bears are special for Ute people," Cloyd
says in *Bearstone*. In this selection, eagles are
sacred to the Lakota. Make a chart in which
you list the similarities and differences between
eagles and bears. Which one do you consider
more special or symbolic? Write a sentence
explaining your reasons.

Act Out a Scene

What Happened?

In groups of three to six, role-play the
scene in which Tonweya returns to his
family and tribe. Have one person play
Tonweya and the rest ask questions.
Make one person slow to believe his
extraordinary tale. What other reactions
can you act out?

73

1. Your brain is large and complex compared with those of other animals. Humans have the ability to ask questions and think logically. This sign of intelligence allows you to create solutions for adapting to new situations.

2. Having two eyes up front gives humans 3-D vision and the ability to judge distances. This lets you catch a moving ball and ride a bike. You can also see in full color in daylight.

3. Elbows, knees, ankles, wrists. More than 200 bones and 600 muscles work together to let you bend and move in all different ways. That's quite a symphony!

4. It's thickest (3/16") on your soles. It's clear and thin (1/500") over your eyes. It's pleated over your knuckles and joints. Your nails are tools — and shields. The hair on top of your head keeps you warm. Let's face it: your skin is a perfect all-purpose suit.

5. Noses adapt to climates. People from warm, steamy climates have shorter noses to minimize moisturizing. People from cold climates have long noses to warm the air.

6. Slicers, rippers, and crunchers live in your mouth and allow you to eat all kinds of foods. Humans are omnivorous. This means that you can eat almost anything. Your teeth also let you smile.

7. Your opposable thumbs allow you to grip and manipulate objects. This skill helps humans create and use complex tools, another sign of your ability to adapt to new environments.

8. Keeping your balance is a full-time operation. Little sensors inside your ears respond to the tiniest changes in pressure, movement, and direction.

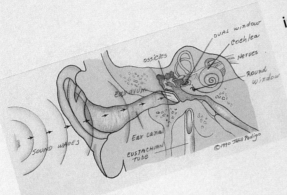

9. Lungs adapt to altitudes. People who live in high mountains develop large lung capacities and extra red blood cells to carry more oxygen.

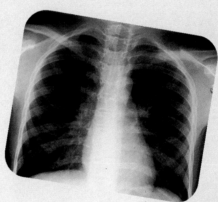

10. A drop of blood teems with 6 million cells. Red ones carry oxygen to every part of your body. White ones keep you from getting an infection if you get cut.

RED

WHITE

1. Larger livers than other humans. The diet of the Inuit of northern Canada is mainly seal meat. Large livers enable their bodies to convert protein to carbohydrates that they lack in their meals.

2. Torrential rains are common where the Yagua tribe lives in the Amazon jungle. So they build their homes on tall stilts that protect them from floods.

KEY

- AFRICA
- ASIA
- AUSTRALIA
- EUROPE
- NORTH AMERICA
- SOUTH AMERICA

3. **Reindeer provide milk and meat** to the Lapps of Finland. Since they are nomads, they live in *kata,* large tents set up around cooking areas. The floors are layers of birch twigs covered with blankets or furs.

4. **Large lungs and hearts and low blood pressure** are common to the Sherpas who live in the Himalayas. Over many generations, they have adapted to the low oxygen levels in the high altitudes.

6. **Walls aren't as important as roofs** in Indonesia. It's always warm, but it often rains heavily. Roofs are dramatic and unique. They are made of red tiles, straw, shingles, palm leaves, even carved wood.

5. **Veils called *tagilmus* protect** the eyes, nose, and lips of the Tuareg of the Sahara desert. Breathing against the cloth creates a circle of moist air and prevents the skin from cracking.

7. **A four-dog night is freezing** for the Australian Aborigines, who express temperature in terms of how many pets they need to keep warm.

77

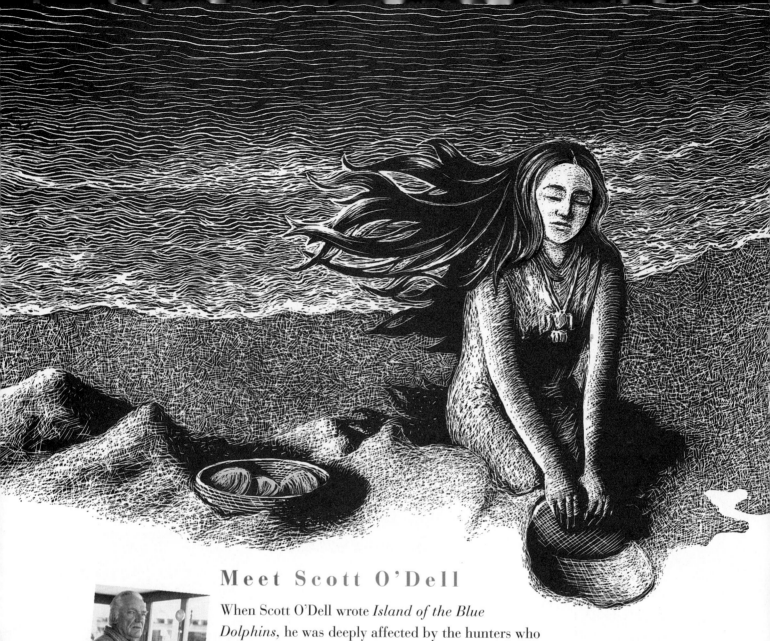

Meet Scott O'Dell

When Scott O'Dell wrote *Island of the Blue Dolphins,* he was deeply affected by the hunters who senselessly killed the wildlife near his California home. "I was angry and wished to do something about it. I considered writing a letter to the editor of the *Los Angeles Times* . . . But I realized that such a letter would be read by only a few people and would be easily dismissed. So I wrote *Island of the Blue Dolphins* about a girl who kills animals and then learns reverence for all life."

Meet the illustrator

When **Josée Morin** was young, her family lived deep in the woods of Abitibi, a region of Quebec, Canada. Her father managed a lumberjack camp, and her family's only means of communicating with the outside world was the railroad. Josée's love of animals comes from growing up with moose, bears, and porcupines.

In the early 1800s, a Native American girl named Karana lives with her people on an island off the coast of California. **After** most of the men are killed by Aleut hunters, the rest of Karana's people decide to board a ship headed for the mainland. **When** Karana discovers that her brother Ramo has been left behind, she dives off the ship and swims back to the island. **While** trying to bring them back a canoe, Ramo is killed by a pack of wild dogs, leaving Karana all alone.

Island of the Blue Dolphins

by Scott O'Dell

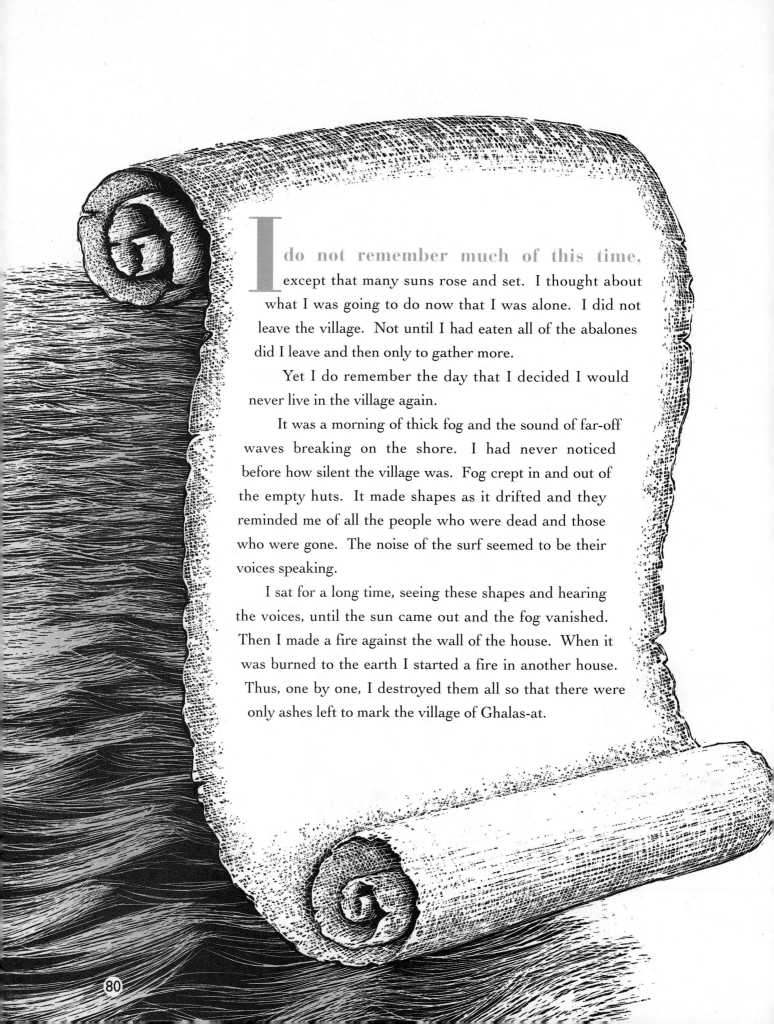

I do not remember much of this time, except that many suns rose and set. I thought about what I was going to do now that I was alone. I did not leave the village. Not until I had eaten all of the abalones did I leave and then only to gather more.

Yet I do remember the day that I decided I would never live in the village again.

It was a morning of thick fog and the sound of far-off waves breaking on the shore. I had never noticed before how silent the village was. Fog crept in and out of the empty huts. It made shapes as it drifted and they reminded me of all the people who were dead and those who were gone. The noise of the surf seemed to be their voices speaking.

I sat for a long time, seeing these shapes and hearing the voices, until the sun came out and the fog vanished. Then I made a fire against the wall of the house. When it was burned to the earth I started a fire in another house. Thus, one by one, I destroyed them all so that there were only ashes left to mark the village of Ghalas-at.

There was nothing to take away with me except a basket of food. I therefore traveled fast and before night fell I reached the place where I had decided to live until the ship returned.

This place lay on a headland a half league to the west of Coral Cove. There was a large rock on that headland and two stunted trees. Behind the rock was a clear place about ten steps across, which was sheltered from the wind, from which I could see the harbor and the ocean. A spring of water flowed from a ravine nearby.

That night I climbed onto the rock to sleep. It was flat on top and wide enough for me to stretch out. Also it was so high from the ground that I did not need to fear the wild dogs while I was sleeping. I had not seen them again since the day they had killed Ramo, but I was sure they would soon come to my new camp.

The rock was also a safe place to store the food I had brought with me and everything I should gather. Since it was still winter and any day the ship might return, there was no use to store food I would not need. This gave me time to make weapons to protect myself from the dogs, which I felt would sometime attack me, to kill them all, one by one.

I had a club I found in one of the huts, but I needed a bow and arrows and a large spear. The spear which I had taken from the slain dog was too small. It was good for spearing fish and little else.

The laws of Ghalas-at forbade the making of weapons by women of the tribe, so I went out to search for any that might have been left behind. I went first to where the village had been and sifted the ashes for spearheads, and then, finding none, to the place where the canoes were hidden, believing that weapons might have been stored there with the food and water.

I found nothing in the canoes under the cliff. Then, remembering the chest the Aleuts had brought to shore, I set out for Coral Cove. I had seen that chest on the beach during the battle but did not remember that the hunters had taken it with them when they fled.

The beach was empty except for rows of seaweed washed in by the storm. The tide was out and I looked in the place where the chest had lain.

It was just below the ledge Ulape and I had stood on while we watched the battle. The sand was smooth and I dug many small holes with a stick. I dug in a wide circle, thinking that the storm might have covered it with sand.

Near the center of the circle the stick hit something hard, which I was sure was a rock, but as I dug deeper with my hands I saw it was the black lid of the chest.

All morning I worked, moving the sand away. The chest lay deep from the washing of the waves and I did not try to dig it out, but only so I could raise the lid.

As the sun rose high the tide came rushing up the beach and filled the hole with sand. Each wave covered the chest deeper until it was completely hidden. I stood on the place, bracing myself against the waves, so that I would not have to look for it again. When the tide turned I began to dig with my feet, working them down and down, and then with my hands.

The chest was filled with beads and bracelets and earrings of many colors. I forgot about the spearheads I had come for. I held each of the trinkets to the sun, turning them so that they caught the light. I put on the longest string of beads, which were blue, and a pair of blue bracelets, which exactly fitted my wrists, and walked down the shore, admiring myself.

I walked the whole length of the cove. The beads and the bracelets made tinkling sounds. I felt like the bride of a chief as I walked there by the waves.

I came to the foot of the trail where the battle had been fought. Suddenly I remembered those who had died there and the men who had brought the jewels I was wearing. I went back to the chest. For a long time I stood beside it, looking at the bracelets and the beads hanging from my neck, so beautiful and bright in the sun. "They do not belong to the Aleuts," I said, "they belong to me." But even as I said this I knew that I never could wear them.

One by one I took them off. I also took the rest of the beads from the chest. Then I walked through the waves and flung them all far away, out into the deep water.

There were no iron spearheads in the chest. I closed the lid and covered it with sand.

I looked along the bottom of the trail, but finding nothing there that I could use, gave up my search.

For many days I did not think of the weapons again, not until the wild dogs came one night and sat under the rock and howled. They were gone at daylight, but not far. During the day I could see them slinking through the brush, watching me.

That night they came back to the headland. I had buried what was left of my supper, but they dug it up, snarling and fighting among themselves over the scraps. Then they began to pace back and forth at the foot of the rock, sniffing the air, for they could smell my tracks and knew that I was somewhere near.

For a long time I lay on the rock while they trotted around below me. The rock was high and they could not climb it, but I was still fearful. As I lay there I wondered what would happen to me if I went against the law of our tribe which forbade the making of weapons by women — if I did not think of it at all and made those things which I must have to protect myself.

Would the four winds blow in from the four directions of the world and smother me as I made the weapons? Or would the earth tremble, as many said, and bury me beneath its falling rocks? Or, as others said, would the sea rise over the island in a terrible flood? Would the weapons break in my hands at the moment when my life was in danger, which is what my father had said?

I thought about these things for two days and on the third night when the wild dogs returned to the rock, I made up my mind that no matter what befell me I would make the weapons. In the morning I set about it, though I felt very fearful.

I wished to use a sea elephant's tusk for the tip of the spear because it is hard and of the right shape. There were many of these animals on the shore near my camp, but I lacked a weapon with which to kill one. Our men usually hunted them with a strong net made of bull kelp, which they threw over an animal while it slept. To do this at least three men were needed, and even then the sea elephant often dragged the net into the sea and got away.

I used instead the root of a tree which I shaped into a point and hardened in the fire. This I bound to a long shaft, with the green sinews of a seal I killed with a rock.

The bow and arrows took more time and caused me great difficulty. I had a bowstring, but wood which could be bent and yet had the proper strength was not easy to find. I searched the ravines for several days before I found it, trees being very scarce on the Island of the Blue Dolphins. Wood for the arrows was easier to find, and also the stone for the tips and the feathers for the ends of the shafts.

Gathering these things was not the most of the trouble. I had seen the weapons made, but I knew little about it. I had seen my father sitting in the hut on winter nights scraping the wood for the shafts, chipping the stones for the tips, and tying the feathers, yet I had watched him and really seen nothing. I had watched, but not with the eye of one who would ever do it.

For this reason I took many days and had many failures before I fashioned a bow and arrows that could be used.

Wherever I went now, whether to the shore when I gathered shellfish or to the ravine for water, I carried this weapon in a sling on my back. I practiced with it and also with the spear.

The dogs did not come to the camp during the time I was making the weapons, though every night I could hear them howling.

Once, after the weapons were made, I saw the leader of the pack, the one with the gray hair and the yellow eyes, watching me from the brush. I had gone to the ravine for water and he stood on the hill above the spring, looking down at me. He stood very quiet, with only his head showing over the top of a cholla bush. He was too far away for me to reach him with an arrow.

Wherever I went during the day, I felt secure with my new weapons, and I waited patiently for the time when I could use them against the wild dogs that had killed Ramo. I did not go to the cave where they had their lair since I was sure that they would soon come to the camp. Yet every night I climbed onto the rock to sleep.

After the first night I spent there, which was uncomfortable because of the uneven places in the rock, I carried dry seaweed up from the beach and made a bed for myself.

It was a pleasant place to stay, there on the headland. The stars were bright overhead and I lay and counted the ones that I knew and gave names to many that I did not know.

In the morning the gulls flew out from their nests in the crevices of the cliff. They circled down to the tide pools where they stood first on one leg and then the other, splashing water over themselves and combing their feathers with curved beaks. Then they flew off down the shore to look for food. Beyond the kelp beds pelicans were already hunting, soaring high over the clear water, diving straight down, if they sighted a fish, to strike the sea with a great splash that I could hear.

I also watched the otter hunting in the kelp. These shy little animals had come back soon after the Aleuts had left and now there seemed to be as many of them as before. The early morning sun shone like gold on their glossy pelts.

Yet as I lay there on the high rock, looking at the stars, I thought about the ship which belonged to the white men. And at dawn, as light spread across the sea, my first glance was toward the little harbor of Coral Cove. Every morning I would look for the ship there, thinking that it might have come in the night. And each morning I would see nothing except the birds flying over the sea.

When there were people in Ghalas-at I was always up before the sun and busy with many things. But now that there was little to do I did not leave the rock until the sun was high. I would eat and then go to the spring and take a bath in the warm water. Afterwards I went down to the shore where I could gather a few abalones and sometimes spear a fish for my supper. Before darkness fell I climbed onto the rock and watched the sea until it slowly disappeared in the night.

The ship did not come and thus winter passed  and the spring.

Summer is the best time on the Island of the Blue Dolphins. The sun is warm then and the winds blow milder out of the west, sometimes out of the south.

It was during these days that the ship might return and now I spent most of my time on the rock, looking out from the high headland into the east, toward the country where my people had gone, across the sea that was never-ending.

Once while I watched I saw a small object which I took to be the ship, but a stream of water rose from it and I knew that it was a whale spouting. During those summer days I saw nothing else.

The first storm of winter ended my hopes. If the white men's ship were coming for me it would have come during the time of good weather. Now I would have to wait until winter was gone, maybe longer.

The thought of being alone on the island while so many suns rose from the sea and went slowly back into the sea filled my heart with loneliness. I had not felt so lonely before because I was sure that the ship would return as Matasaip had said it would. Now my hopes were dead. Now I was really alone. I could not eat much, nor could I sleep without dreaming terrible dreams.

The storm blew out of the north, sending big waves against the island and winds so strong that I was unable to stay on the rock. I moved my bed to the foot of the rock and for protection kept a fire going throughout the night. I slept there five times. The first night the dogs came and stood outside the ring made by the fire. I killed three of them with arrows, but not the leader, and they did not come again.

On the sixth day, when the storm had ended, I went to the place where the canoes had been hidden, and let myself down over the cliff. This part of the shore was sheltered from the wind and I found the canoes just as they had been left. The dried food was still good, but the water was stale, so I went back to the spring and filled a fresh basket.

I had decided during the days of the storm, when I had given up hope of seeing the ship, that I would take one of the canoes and go to the country that lay toward the east. I remembered how Kimki, before he had gone, had asked the advice of his ancestors who had lived many ages in the past, who had come to the island from that country, and likewise the advice of Zuma, the medicine man who held power over the wind and the seas. But these things I could not do, for Zuma had been killed by the Aleuts, and in all my life I had never been able to speak with the dead, though many times I had tried.

Yet I cannot say that I was really afraid as I stood there on the shore. I knew that my ancestors had crossed the sea in their canoes, coming from that place which lay beyond. Kimki, too had crossed the sea. I was not nearly so skilled with a canoe as these men, but I must say that whatever might befall me on the endless waters did not trouble me. It meant far less than the thought of staying on the island alone, without a home or companions, pursued by wild dogs, where everything reminded me of those who were dead and those who had gone away.

Of the four canoes stored there against the cliff, I chose the smallest, which was still very heavy because it could carry six people. The task that faced me was to push it down the rocky shore and into the water, a distance four or five times its length.

This I did by first removing all the large rocks in front of the canoe. I then filled in all these holes with pebbles and along this path laid down long strips of kelp, making a slippery bed. The shore was steep and once I got the canoe to move with its own weight, it slid down the path and into the water.

The sun was in the west when I left the shore. The sea was calm behind the high cliffs. Using the two-bladed paddle I quickly skirted the south part of the island. As I reached the sandspit the wind struck. I was paddling from the back of the canoe because you can go faster kneeling there, but I could not handle it in the wind.

Kneeling in the middle of the canoe, I paddled hard and did not pause until I had gone through the tides that run fast around the sandspit. There were many small waves and I was soon wet, but as I came out from behind the spit the spray lessened and the waves grew long and rolling. Though it would have been easier to go the way they slanted, this would have taken me in the wrong direction. I therefore kept them on my left hand, as well as the island, which grew smaller and smaller, behind me.

At dusk I looked back. The Island of the Blue Dolphins had disappeared. This was the first time that I felt afraid.

There were only hills and valleys of water around me now. When I was in a valley I could see nothing and when the canoe rose out of it, only the ocean stretching away and away.

Night fell and I drank from the basket. The water cooled my throat.

The sea was black and there was no difference between it and the sky. The waves made no sound among themselves, only faint noises as they went under the canoe or struck against it. Sometimes the noises seemed angry and at other times like people laughing. I was not hungry because of my fear.

The first star made me feel less afraid. It came out low in the sky and it was in front of me, toward the east. Other stars began to appear all around, but it was this one I kept my gaze upon. It was in the figure that we call a serpent, a star which shone green and which I knew. Now and then it was hidden by mist, yet it always came out brightly again.

Without this star I would have been lost, for the waves never changed. They came always from the same direction and in a manner that kept pushing me away from the place I wanted to reach. For this reason the canoe made a path in the black water like a snake. But somehow I kept moving toward the star which shone in the east.

This star rose high and then I kept the North Star on my left hand, the one we call "the star that does not move." The wind grew quiet. Since it always died down when the night was half over, I knew how long I had been traveling and how far away the dawn was.

About this time I found that the canoe was leaking. Before dark I had emptied one of the baskets in which food was stored and used it to dip out the water that came over the sides. The water that now moved around my knees was not from the waves.

I stopped paddling and worked with the basket until the bottom of the canoe was almost dry. Then I searched around, feeling in the dark along the smooth planks, and found the place near the bow where the water was seeping through a crack as long as my hand and the width of a finger. Most of the time it was out of the sea, but it leaked whenever the canoe dipped forward in the waves.

The places between the planks were filled with black pitch which we gather along the shore. Lacking this, I tore a piece of fiber from my skirt and pressed it into the crack, which held back the water.

Dawn broke in a clear sky and as the sun came out of the waves I saw that it was far off on my left. During the night I had drifted south of the place I wished to go, so I changed my direction and paddled along the path made by the rising sun.

There was no wind on this morning and the long waves went quietly under the canoe. I therefore moved faster than during the night.

I was very tired, but more hopeful than I had been since I left the island. If the good weather did not change I would cover many leagues be-fore dark. Another night and another day might bring me within sight of the shore toward which I was going.

Not long after dawn, while I was thinking of this strange place and what it would look like, the canoe began to leak again. This crack was between the same planks, but was a larger one and close to where I was kneeling.

The fiber I tore from my skirt and pushed into the crack held back most of the water which seeped in whenever the canoe rose and fell with the waves. Yet I could see that the planks were weak from one end to the other, probably from the canoe being stored so long in the sun, and that they might open along their whole length if the waves grew rougher.

It was suddenly clear to me that it was dangerous to go on. The voyage would take two more days, perhaps longer. By turning back to the island I would not have nearly so far to travel.

Still I could not make up my mind to do so. The sea was calm and I had come far. The thought of turning back after all this labor was more than I could bear. Even greater was the thought of the deserted island I would return to, of living there alone and forgotten. For how many suns and how many moons?

The canoe drifted idly on the calm sea while these thoughts went over and over in my mind, but when I saw the water seeping through the crack again, I picked up the paddle. There was no choice except to turn back toward the island.

I knew that only by the best of fortune would I ever reach it.

The wind did not blow until the sun was overhead. Before that time I covered a good distance, pausing only when it was necessary to dip water from the canoe. With the wind I went more slowly and had to stop more often because of the water spilling over the sides, but the leak did not grow worse.

This was my first good fortune. The next was when a swarm of dolphins appeared. They came swimming out of the west, but as they saw the canoe they turned around in a great circle and began to follow me. They swam up slowly and so close that I could see their eyes, which are large and the color of the ocean. Then they swam on ahead of the canoe, crossing back and forth in front of it, diving in and out, as if they were weaving a piece of cloth with their broad snouts.

Dolphins are animals of good omen. It made me happy to have them swimming around the canoe, and though my hands had begun to bleed from the chafing of the paddle, just watching them made me forget the pain. I was very lonely before they appeared, but now I felt that I had friends with me and did not feel the same.

The blue dolphins left me shortly before dusk. They left as quickly as they had come, going on into the west, but for a long time I could see the last of the sun shining on them. After night fell I could still see them in my thoughts and it was because of this that I kept on paddling when I wanted to lie down and sleep.

More than anything, it was the blue dolphins that took me back home.

Fog came with the night, yet from time to time I could see the star that stands high in the west, the red star called Magat which is part of the figure that looks like a crawfish and is known by that name. The crack in the planks grew wider so I had to stop often to fill it with fiber and to dip out the water.

The night was very long, longer than the night before. Twice I dozed kneeling there in the canoe, though I was more afraid than I had ever been. But the morning broke clear and in front of me lay the dim line of the island like a great fish sunning itself on the sea.

I reached it before the sun was high, the sandspit and its tides that bore me into the shore. My legs were stiff from kneeling and as the canoe struck the sand I fell when I rose to climb out. I crawled through the shallow water and up the beach. There I lay for a long time, hugging the sand in happiness.

I was too tired to think of the wild dogs. Soon I fell asleep.

A Wave

Compare and Contrast

Dolphins and Dogs

Make two cluster diagrams around
two kinds of animals: dolphins and
dogs. Include notes about their
habitats, appearances, habits, sounds,
groups, and relationships to the
narrator. When you're finished, write
a sentence about how each animal
plays a role in the girl's survival.

Role-play a Discussion

Tonweya, Karana, and Cloyd

These three characters all
survived life-threatening wilderness
experiences. What would happen
if the three sat down to share their
stories? In a group of three, assign
roles and see what happens. After
fifteen minutes or so, together try
to write one sentence about
your survival that is true
for all three of you.

# of Activity

Write a Poem

Waves, Waves, Waves

Write a poem about Karana's time in the canoe. Invent your own kind of poem or use these guidelines. Write one stanza or "wave" about her launching the boat. Write another about the green star. Write another about the leak and her decision to return to the island. Write another about the dolphins. Include one line that appears in every stanza — what will it be? Share your poem with a classmate.

SURVIVAL

AT SEA

BY ARIANE RANDALL

My trip to a resort in Haiti began at New York's La Guardia Airport, two weeks after my fourteenth birthday. All the people going to the resort had congregated around the check-in counter. While waiting around, I met Anna Rivera and Delia Clarke, who would be passengers on the doomed plane, and Delia's daughter, Krista. Anna was concerned about how she could get malaria pills.

I had a great time during my week in Haiti, waterskiing, snorkeling, swimming, and suntanning — things I don't get to do much in New York City. During the week, the Haitians went on strike a number of times to protest against the government. At the end of the week American Airlines, on which we were supposed to fly, canceled all flights to and from Haiti indefinitely because of the political unrest.

Haiti lies between Cuba and Puerto Rico in the Caribbean Sea.

The resort gave those of us who were supposed to fly home Saturday a choice: Either stay in the village for free until the airline restored service, or go by chartered airplane to Santo Domingo, in the Dominican Republic, and catch a connecting flight from there. I wanted to stay since I was having such a good time and there would be a July Fourth celebration, but my father decided that we should get out of the country while we still could. This story proves that all parents should listen to their children.

The next day, July 4, twelve guests gathered to wait for the bus. As it turned out, we wouldn't be leaving for another two hours, so I took the opportunity to sunbathe and go for a last dip in the pool. Finally the bus arrived, and I said good-bye to the friends I'd made.

At the airport the plane never came, due to engine trouble. Finally the resort chartered four small planes, and a few hours later four of us — Delia Clarke, Anna Rivera, my father, and I — boarded the last of them. It was a dinky-looking plane, a Cessna, with only three rows of seats. My father and Anna sat backward in the second row, and Delia and I faced them in the third row. Delia was slim and pretty with short brown hair. She told me she'd lost seventy pounds a few years before. (Later I guessed that kind of willpower helped give her strength after we crashed.) Anna was also nice-looking. She was going home to New York.

We took off at 8:36 P.M. It was soon after that my dad looked out the window and noticed the stars were all wrong.

From the location of the Big Dipper and other stars, he could tell that we were going west, toward Cuba, as opposed to east, toward Santo Domingo. He asked Anna, who spoke Spanish, to ask the pilot why we were going in the wrong direction, but she was reluctant. She didn't want to question authority. I don't know why I didn't use my Spanish to question him myself. The plane was getting cold, but I went to sleep for two hours, during which time, I have been told, we continued going 180 degrees in the wrong direction.

When I woke up, I noticed that we were over water, with no land in sight. The lights on the wings were not functioning properly. They started and stopped — and then stopped altogether. Most of the instruments on the dashboard were not lit up. This was something I hadn't paid too much attention to before but now scared me. The pilot was not getting a response on his radio, and Anna noticed we were running out of gas. The next thing I knew the pilot was saying, "Mayday! Mayday!" into the radio. Anna cried, "We're going to crash!" I started looking desperately for my life jacket behind and under the seat, but I couldn't find it. Anna found hers. Delia did not. The last thing I saw the pilot doing was tossing his life jacket to my father, who gave it to me and then pulled me on his lap. The plane circled three times around an oil tanker and began the swift descent, gliding toward the sea.

We hit the water, and there is a terrible crashing sound as my side of the plane breaks off and water rushes in. I climb out onto the wing. As I stand there I realize my glasses are gone. I fish around in the water and come up with half the frame. I toss it away. The plane is sinking, and my father comes out with the two ladies but no pilot. We swim away from the wreck as the tail disappears beneath the water. Now we are four people and two life jackets in the vast, dark Caribbean Sea. The pilot is nowhere to be seen.

The water is warm, and we swim together, realizing it's the safe thing to do and it's comforting. I am the least hurt, having received a blow to the head, probably from my dad's chin. He has a gash on his chin and is bleeding heavily (later we found out he'd lost a quart of blood). And he has bruises, especially on his legs. Delia seems to have broken her nose, and there is blood coming from it. She is not in pain, though. Anna has several cuts about her face, a broken arm, and a concussion that has caused partial amnesia. She keeps asking what has happened, and we tell her that the airplane has crashed. She will ask again the next minute.

> "The plane was getting cold . . . we continued going 180° in the wrong direction."

Anna and I have inflated our life jackets. They have lights on them that shine brightly. We all hold on to each other, mainly so that the two without life jackets can remain afloat but partly for security. I'm wearing boxer shorts, a T-shirt over my new red bikini, and Chinese slippers, which I keep on the whole time. My father's pants and shoes are bogging him down, so he takes them off.

We think we see a boat light, but it soon disappears. I wonder if we will ever be rescued. The thought of floating out here until I die is horrifying. I think about sharks and ask Anna and Delia not to splash about so much because it will attract "the wrong kind of fish." Sharks can smell blood a mile away, and three of us are bleeding. There is a silent agreement not to mention the pilot or sharks.

Pretty soon we are all telling each other how glad we are to be together and how much we love each other. We talk about ourselves. Anna is single (we find out later she has a sister). She works with bilingual children and has a new job waiting for her on Monday. She is worried that her job won't be kept for her if we are not rescued soon. Delia has two boys back in Connecticut, where she works in a real estate office. She's happy that her daughter, Krista, was not on our flight. My father, Francis, a Russian history professor, will be teaching in the fall. I'll be a sophomore in high school, and if I make it back, I'll have the best what-did-you-do-for-your-summer-vacation essay to hit my teachers in a long time.

All of a sudden a light appears. It looks like a boat light, and we are filled with hope. It appears to be coming steadily toward us. Delia is the only one who can really see since both my father and I have lost our glasses and Anna is fading toward unconsciousness. Anna's injuries are so serious I think she's going to die, but she seems to get better as time goes on. After a half hour (I have my waterproof watch on) the boat light starts to fade. If no boat comes, I decide that I'll swim for land in the morning . . . if there's land anywhere in sight.

We think we see another boat light, but it turns out to be the planet Venus. I feel sick and throw up a lot, which makes me feel better. I drift off into something like sleep. Around 4:30 A.M. Delia spots something that looks like land but might be mist. We wait for dawn to be certain.

When dawn comes, we see it is definitely land. We talk about what to do. Delia and Anna cannot swim well, if at all. If we all go at their pace, there is no way we will reach shore by night. We must make a decision: If my father and I swim for shore, it seems likely we'll make it and be able to tell the Coast Guard where to find Anna and Delia. Or my father might be able to find a boat

> **"Sharks can smell blood a mile away, and three of us are bleeding."**

and come back himself, and in the meantime they could continue to swim. The alternative is to stick together and hope for rescue. My father and I think that splitting up will increase our collective chances of survival. Anna and Delia are reluctant — they feel safer in a group — but they acknowledge that splitting up would be better. Anna and Delia have the better life jacket. We separate, not really saying good-bye because we expect to see each other again soon. Even after we swim far away and can't see them, we hear their voices carrying over the waves.

I keep my father posted on the time. Hours pass, and the nearer we get, the more we realize that we still have many miles to cover. We stop every twenty minutes or so for a rest break, during which I float on my back, which is not so hard to do with a life jacket. I'm not feeling very strong, and I hold on to my dad's shirttails and kick or just let him pull me.

It is noon, and we are still a good distance from land. I no longer hear the voices of Delia and Anna. Every now and then my father tells me he loves me a million, trillion times. I say I will tell him how much I love him when we get to land. I'm too tired to speak just now.

It is two o'clock. I have more energy now and a determination to get to land before dark. My dad is getting weaker but still pushes on. I get salt in my mouth all the time, and my tongue is numb from it. It also gets in my eyes, but I have learned to open them quickly

The northern coast of Haiti

afterward, and for some reason this gets rid of the sting. My hair is all matted. We have not had fresh water or food in thirteen hours, but I'm not hungry or thirsty.

It is three o'clock, and I'm starting to hallucinate. I see dolphins, seals, an occasional shark or two, sailboats, and buoys. I say to my dad, "We can do it." And he says, "Yes . . . we can do it." We keep telling each other "I love you" and that we'll make it to shore. I'm guiding my father now, because he keeps his eyes closed most of the time because of the brine and starts to go in the wrong direction unless I correct him. Two pieces of sugarcane float by us, and like the twig brought back to Noah's Ark, they seem like a sign of hope. I think I see palm trees behind me, but they are not really there. At six o'clock we are maybe a mile from shore and feel certain we will make it before nightfall.

But an hour later, with the shore in sight, the sky has become gray with thunderclouds. We think we see thousands of tiny sailboats, and my dad yells for me to swim fast to them. I try hard as the wind blows and it gets stormier. I look back. I can't see my dad. "Daddy! Where are you?" I scream. No one answers, and I'm crying for the first time. "Help! Somebody please help! Daddy, where are you?" The rain is coming down hard and fast. I stick my tongue out to see if I can get some. It doesn't work too well. I fight with the waves to keep moving toward land. I ask God why He has put this test before me. I tell Him it won't work: I will come through this with flying colors; I'll ace this test.

When the storm passes, I just want to sleep. The problem is that I then drift with the current, which seems to be going out to sea. Sea snails are biting my legs, but I don't have the strength to brush them off. I don't know what has happened to my father. I try the signal we planned — a high shriek — in case we got separated, but he doesn't answer. I fight to keep awake but slowly drift off.

All the girls I hung out with at the resort are inside my head telling me to swim this way or that. I'm trying to swim toward a hotel, where I can go to sleep. I just want to relax, but I can't because I'll drown. The straps of my life jacket are cutting into me, so I take it off and let it float away. My mouth is burning from the salt — I don't want to die now — if I have to die, can't I at least have a Coke to drink? — something nice-tasting before I drown.

I dream I am destined to drown. Everyone says so, but I'm still trying to find a way out. I dream I inhaled something that burned out my lungs and throat. Then I'm being pulled. I'm being pulled out of the water into a dugout canoe. By two men. Are they capturing me? I must get out. I pick up a piece of wood from the bottom of the boat and try to clobber one of them with it. But he stops me and hits me back.

What a nice way for me to greet my Haitian rescuers — for that's who they were. I saw that they had picked up my dad, too, in another canoe. I heard my dad asking them to start a search for Anna and Delia. The villagers of Bariadelle fed us mangoes and fresh water and crowded around us to watch. They were trying to talk to us in Creole. I could scarcely talk and was confused, but I did manage a *merci beaucoup*.

From Bariadelle we were driven to Dame Marie and deposited in a French Canadian mission station. By this time my body had gone into shock. I had a high fever, a severe sunburn, and a throat infection that made it difficult to swallow anything without coughing. We were taken to a doctor, but by morning my fever was gone. I found out that I'd lost three pounds. (What a crash diet!) My father had lost fifteen. We were driven to a hospital in Anse d'Hainault and eventually, passing through fourteen roadblocks and over sixty miles of bumpy mountain roads, to the city of Jérémie. There my father was able to phone my mother and brother and tell them that we were all right. There was still no news of Anna and Delia.

Back in New York the phone never stops ringing. People call to find out if all this really happened to us. Sometimes I ask myself the same question. But what about Anna and Delia? I think of their voices over the waves as we swam away. What happened to them? What will happen to their families?

It is a miracle my father and I survived. When people ask me what I feel about the whole experience, I say that when you've almost missed life, you see it differently. To be with my family and friends, just to be able to go shopping to replace my lost clothes, each day seems like an amazingly good thing.

Shortly after Ariane Randall and her father were rescued, the U.S. Coast Guard began the search for the two missing women and the pilot. The search continued for three days, but Delia Clarke, Anna Rivera, and the pilot, Elia Katime, were never found.

Surviving Epilepsy

A Personal Narrative
by Eric Ibell, Jr.

People have different kinds of survival experiences. Eric survived a medical emergency and wrote this true story about it and its effect on his life today.

Surviving Epilepsy

One day my mom was getting ready to go to work when she heard coughing and moaning coming from my room. She came in and found me lying on my bed with my hands in the air, my lips purple, and my body stiff. She screamed for my Dad and told him to get the car. I was unconscious. I did not know anyone or even where I was.

I don't remember waking up because I was so exhausted. All I remember is being in the hospital for three whole days. I was upset because I missed picture day at school and a test for my black belt in tae kwon do. I also was supposed to get the Student-of-the-Month Award, but I was in the hospital instead.

My room was next to the nurses' station. The nurses were very kind to me. They brought me pencils and paper to draw with and even a Nintendo game to play.

The second day my neighbors came in with a big banner they had printed on my computer that said "Get well soon, Eric!"

Three days after I was admitted to the hospital, the doctors ran a series of tests. First, a tall, thin man with a gray mustache and kind manner put sensors on my forehead to read my brain waves. Next, he put me in this big steel tube and took pictures of

Epilepsy:

Epilepsy: Questions and answers

About seizure disorder

my brain. Then the specialist, a pretty young lady with long black hair, said, "Eric, I'm going to put you on medication." Then she told my family, "Eric has epilepsy." She explained, "Epilepsy is a disorder of the nervous system, but don't worry, people with epilepsy lead perfectly normal lives. It's just like a little short circuit that occurs, but it's hard to say how often. Eric could have another seizure tomorrow or never have one again."

When I went back to school, everybody said, "Eric! We missed you! What happened?" I told them about my seizure, and after a while things went pretty much back to normal. I finally got my picture taken, received my Student-of-the-Month Award, and took my black belt test. Now I'm a junior black belt, and I can play basketball, football, and some soccer just like anyone else. I still take medicine three times a day.

I've never had another seizure — but sometimes at night when I get into bed I wonder if I'm going to have another seizure when I go to sleep. It's scary, but I can live with it.

Eric was in the sixth grade when he wrote about his seizure. He hopes he will outgrow this condition, as his mother did, who also had epilepsy.

Eric's hobbies are learning tae kwon do and drawing cartoons, which he learned from his uncle. Eric's favorite sport is football. He has one sister, Kimberly.

Eric Ibell, Jr.
Kane School
Lawrence, Massachusetts

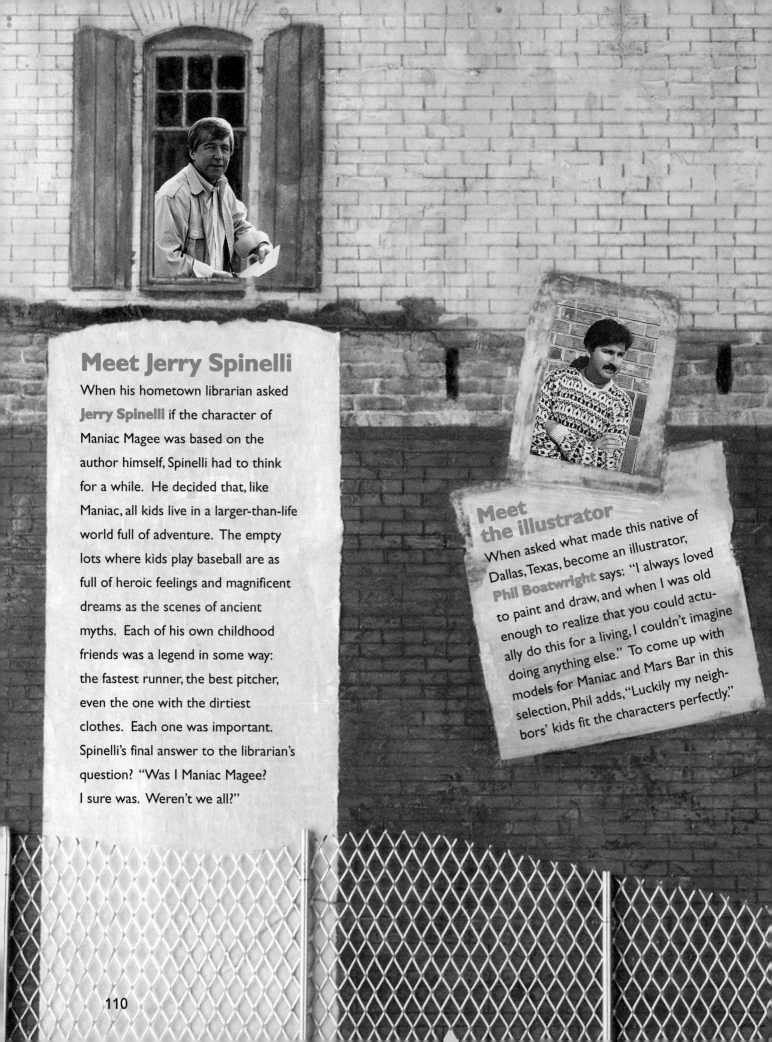

Meet Jerry Spinelli

When his hometown librarian asked **Jerry Spinelli** if the character of Maniac Magee was based on the author himself, Spinelli had to think for a while. He decided that, like Maniac, all kids live in a larger-than-life world full of adventure. The empty lots where kids play baseball are as full of heroic feelings and magnificent dreams as the scenes of ancient myths. Each of his own childhood friends was a legend in some way: the fastest runner, the best pitcher, even the one with the dirtiest clothes. Each one was important. Spinelli's final answer to the librarian's question? "Was I Maniac Magee? I sure was. Weren't we all?"

Meet the illustrator

When asked what made this native of Dallas, Texas, become an illustrator, **Phil Boatwright** says: "I always loved to paint and draw, and when I was old enough to realize that you could actually do this for a living, I couldn't imagine doing anything else." To come up with models for Maniac and Mars Bar in this selection, Phil adds, "Luckily my neighbors' kids fit the characters perfectly."

MANIAC MAGEE

by Jerry Spinelli

When Jeffrey Magee arrives at Two Mills, no one knows that he's an orphan and a runaway — everyone just knows him as Maniac Magee. The stories about his incredible feats have already turned him into a legend. But one day Jeffrey performs one legendary feat too many.

The town was buzzing. The schools were buzzing. Hallways. Lunchrooms. Streets. Playgrounds. West End. East End.

Buzzing about the new kid in town. The stranger kid. Scraggly. Carrying a book. Flap-soled sneakers.

The kid who intercepted Brian Denehy's pass to Hands Down and punted it back longer than Denehy himself ever threw it.

The kid who rescued Arnold Jones from Finsterwald's backyard.

The kid who tattooed Giant John McNab's fastball for half a dozen home runs, then circled the sacks on a bunted frog.

Nobody knows who said it first, but somebody must have: "Kid's gotta be a maniac."

And somebody else must have said: "Yeah, reg'lar maniac."

And somebody else: "Yeah."

And that was it. Nobody (except Amanda Beale) had any other name for him, so pretty soon, when they wanted to talk about the new kid, that's what they called him: Maniac.

The legend had a name.

But not an address. At least, not an official one, with numbers.

What he did have was the deer shed at the Elmwood Park Zoo, which is where he slept his first few nights in town. What the deer ate, especially the carrots, apples, and day-old hamburger buns, he ate.

He started reading Amanda Beale's book his second day in town and finished it that afternoon. Ordinarily, he would have returned it immediately, but he was so fascinated by the story of the Children's Crusade that he kept it and read it the next day. And the next.

When he wasn't reading, he was wandering. When most people wander, they walk. Maniac Magee ran. Around town, around the nearby townships, always carrying the book, keeping it in perfect condition.

This is what he was doing when his life, as it often seemed to do, took an unexpected turn.

John McNab had never in his life met a kid he couldn't strike out.
Until the runt. Now, as he thought about it, he came to two
conclusions:

    1. He couldn't stand having this blemish on his record.

    2. If you beat a kid up, it's the same as striking him out.

    So McNab and his pals went looking for the kid. They called
themselves the Cobras. Nobody messed with them. At least, nobody in the West End.

    The Cobras had heard that the kid hung around the park and the
tracks, and that's where they spotted him one Saturday afternoon, on
the tracks by the path that ran from the Oriole Street dead end to
the park. He was down by Red Hill and heading away from them,
book in hand, as usual.

    But the Cobras just stood there, stunned.

    "I don't believe it," one Cobra said.

    "Must be a trick," said another.

    "I heard about it," said another, "but I didn't believe it."

    It wasn't a trick. It was true. The kid was *running* on the rail.

    McNab scooped up a handful of track stones. He launched one.
He snarled, "He's dead. Let's get 'im!"

    By the time Maniac looked back, they were almost on him. He
wobbled once, leaped from the rail to the ground, and took off. He
was at the Oriole Street dead end, but his instincts said no, not the
street, too much open space. He stuck with the tracks. Coming
into view above him was the house on Rako Hill, where he had eaten
spaghetti. He could go there, to the whistling mother, the other kids,
be safe. They wouldn't follow him in there. Would they?

    Stones clanked off the steel rails. He darted left, skirted the
dump, wove through the miniature mountain range of stone piles and
into the trees . . . skiing on his heels down the steep bank and into
the creek, frogs plopping, no time to look for stepping rocks . . . yells
behind him now, war whoops, stones pelting the water, stinging his
back . . . ah, the other side, through the trees and picker bushes, past
the armory jeeps and out to the park boulevard, past the Italian
restaurant on the corner, the bakery, screeching tires, row houses,

streets, alleys, cars, porches, windows, faces staring, faces, faces . . . the town whizzing past Maniac, a blur of faces, each face staring from its own window, each face in its own personal frame, its own house, its own address, someplace to be when there was no other place to be, how lucky to be a face staring out from a window . . .

And then — could it be? — the voices behind him were growing faint. He slowed, turned, stopped. They were lined up at a street a block back. They were still yelling and shaking their fists, but they weren't moving off the curb. And now they were laughing. Why were they laughing?

The Cobras were standing at Hector Street. Hector Street was the boundary between the East and West Ends. Or, to put it another way, between the blacks and whites. Not that you never saw a white in the East End or a black in the West End. People did cross the line now and then, especially if they were adults, and it was daylight.

But nighttime, forget it. And if you were a kid, day *or* night, forget it. Unless you had business on the other side, such as a sports team or school. But don't be just *strolling* along, as if you *belonged* there, as if you weren't *afraid*, as if you didn't even *notice* you were a different color from everybody around you.

The Cobras were laughing because they figured the dumb, scraggly runt would get out of the East End in about as good shape as a bare big toe in a convention of snapping turtles.

Of course, Maniac didn't know any of that. He was simply glad the chase was over. He turned and started walking, catching his breath.

East Chestnut. East Marshall. Green Street. Arch Street. He had been around here before. That first day with the girl named Amanda, other days jogging through. But this was Saturday, not a school day, and there was something different about the streets — kids. All over.

One of them jumped down from a front step and planted himself right in front of Maniac. Maniac had to jerk to a stop to keep from plowing into the kid. Even so, their noses were practically touching.

Maniac blinked and stepped back. The kid stepped forward. Each time Maniac stepped back, the kid stepped forward. They traveled practically half a block that way. Finally Maniac turned and started walking. The kid jumped around and plunked himself in front again.

He bit off a chunk of the candy bar he was holding. "Where *you* goin'?" he said. Candy bar flakes flew from his mouth.

"I'm looking for Sycamore Street," said Maniac. "Do you know where it is?"

"Yeah, I know where it is."

Maniac waited, but the kid said nothing more. "Well, uh, do you think you could tell me where it is?"

Stone was softer than the kid's glare. "No."

Maniac looked around. Other kids had stopped playing, were staring.

Someone called: "Do 'im, Mars!"

Someone else: "Waste 'im!"

The kid, as you probably guessed by now, was none other than Mars Bar Thompson. Mars Bar heard the calls, and the stone got harder. Then suddenly he stopped glaring, suddenly he was smiling. He held up the candy bar, an inch from Maniac's lips. "Wanna bite?"

Maniac couldn't figure. "You sure?"

"Yeah, go ahead. Take a bite."

Maniac shrugged, took the Mars Bar, bit off a chunk, and handed it back. "Thanks."

Dead silence along the street. The kid had done the unthinkable, he had chomped on one of Mars's own bars. Not only that, but white kids just didn't put their mouths where black kids had had theirs, be it soda bottles, spoons, or candy bars. And the kid hadn't even gone for the unused end; he had chomped right over Mars Bar's own bite marks.

Mars Bar was confused. Who *was* this kid? *What* was this kid?

As usual, when Mars Bar got confused, he got mad. He thumped Maniac in the chest. "You think you bad or somethin'?"

Maniac, who was now twice as confused as Mars Bar, blinked. "Huh?"

"You think you come down here and be bad? That what you think?" Mars Bar was practically shouting now.

"No," said Maniac, "I don't think I'm bad. I'm not saying I'm an angel, either. Not even real good. Somewhere in between, I guess."

Mars Bar jammed his arms downward, stuck out his chin, sneered. "Am I bad?"

Maniac was befuddled. "*I* don't know. One minute you're yelling at me, the next minute you're giving me a bite of your candy bar."

The chin jutted out more. "Tell me I'm bad."

Maniac didn't answer. Flies stopped buzzing.

"I said, tell me I'm bad."

Maniac blinked, shrugged, sighed. "It's none of my business. If you're bad, let your mother or father tell you."

Now it was Mars Bar doing the blinking, stepping back, trying to sort things out. After a while he looked down. "What's that?"

Before Maniac answered, "A book," Mars Bar had snatched it from his hand. "This ain't yours," he said. He flipped through some pages. "Looks like mine."

"It's somebody else's."

"It's mine. I'm keepin' it."

With rattlesnake speed, Maniac snatched the book back — except for one page, which stayed, ripped, in Mars Bar's hand.

"Give me the page," said Maniac.

Mars Bar grinned. "Take it, fishbelly."

Silence. Eyes. The flies were waiting. East End vultures.

Suddenly neither kid could see the other, because a broom came down like a straw curtain between their faces, and a voice said, "*I'll* take it."

It was the lady from the nearest house, out to sweep her steps. She lowered the broom but kept it between them. "Better yet," she said to Mars Bar, "just give it back to him."

Mars Bar glared up at her. There wasn't an eleven-year-old in the East End who could stand up to Mars Bar's glare. In the West End, even high-schoolers were known to crumble under the glare. To old ladies on both sides of Hector Street, it was all but fatal. And when Mars Bar stepped off a curb and combined the glare with his super-slow dip-stride slumpshuffle, well, it was said he could back up traffic all the way to Bridgeport while he took ten minutes to cross the street.

But not this time. This time Mars Bar was up against an East End lady in her prime, and she was matching him eyeball for eyeball. And when it was over, only one glare was left standing, and it wasn't Mars Bar's.

Mars Bar handed back the torn page, but not before he crumpled it into a ball. The broom pushed him away, turned him around, and swept him up the street.

The lady looked down at Maniac. A little of the glare lingered in her eyes. "You better get on, boy, where you belong. I can't be following you around. I got things to do."

Maniac just stood there a minute. There was something he felt like doing, and maybe he would have, but the lady turned and went back inside her house and shut the door. So he walked away.

Now what?

Maniac uncrumpled the page, flattened it out as best he could. How could he return the book to Amanda in this condition? He couldn't. But he had to. It was hers. Judging from that morning, she was pretty finicky about her books. What would make her madder — to not get the book back at all, or to get it back with a page ripped out? Maniac cringed at both prospects.

He wandered around the East End, jogging slowly, in no hurry now to find 728 Sycamore Street. He was passing a vacant lot when he heard an all-too-familiar voice: "Hey, fishbelly!" He stopped, turned. This time Mars Bar wasn't alone. A handful of other kids trailed him down the sidewalk.

Maniac waited.

Coming up to him, Mars Bar said, "Where you runnin', boy?"

"Nowhere."

"You runnin' from us. You afraid."

"No, I just like to run."

"You wanna run?" Mars Bar grinned. "Go ahead. We'll give you a head start."

Maniac grinned back. "No thanks."

Mars Bar held out his hand. "Gimme my book."

Maniac shook his head.

Mars Bar glared. "Gimme it."

Maniac shook his head.

Mars Bar reached for it. Maniac pulled it away.

They moved in on him now. They backed him up. Some high-schoolers were playing basketball up the street, but they weren't noticing. And there wasn't a broom-swinging lady in sight. Maniac felt a hard flatness against his back. Suddenly his world was very small and very simple: a brick wall behind him, a row of scowling faces in front of him. He clutched the book with both hands. The faces were closing in. A voice called: "That you, Jeffrey?"

The faces parted. At the curb was a girl on a bike — Amanda! She hoisted the bike to the sidewalk and walked it over. She looked at the book, at the torn page. "Who ripped my book?"

Mars Bar pointed at Maniac. "He did."

Amanda knew better. "*You* ripped my book."

Mars Bar's eyes went big as headlights. "I did *not!*"

"You *did*. You lie."

"I *didn't!*"

"You *did!*" She let the bike fall to Maniac. She grabbed the book and started kicking Mars Bar in his beloved sneakers. "I got a little brother and a little sister that crayon all over my books, and I got a dog that eats them and poops on them and that's just inside my own family, and I'm *not* — gonna have *nobody* — else messin' — with my *books!* You under-*stand?*"

By then Mars Bar was hauling on up the street past the basketball players, who were rolling on the asphalt with laughter.

Amanda took the torn page from Maniac. To her, it was the broken wing of a bird, a pet out in the rain. She turned misty eyes to Maniac. "It's one of my favorite pages."

Maniac smiled. "We can fix it."

The way he said it, she believed. "Want to come to my house?" she said.

"Sure," he said.

When they walked in, Amanda's mother was busy with her usual tools: a yellow plastic bucket and a sponge. She was scrubbing purple crayon off the TV screen.

"Mom," said Amanda, "this is Jeffrey — " She whispered, "What's your last name?"

He whispered, "Magee."

She said, "Magee."

Mrs. Beale held up a hand, said, "Hold it," and went on scrubbing. When she finally finished, she straightened up, turned, and said, "Now, what?"

"Mom, this is Jeffrey Magee. You know."

Amanda was hardly finished when Maniac zipped across the room and stuck out his hand. "Nice to meet you, Mrs. . . . Mrs. . . ."

"Beale."

"Mrs. Beale."

They shook hands. Mrs. Beale smiled. "So you're the book boy." She started nodding. "Manda came home one day — 'Mom, there's a boy I loaned one of my books out to!' 'Loaned a *book? You?*' 'Mom, he practically *made* me. He really likes books. I met him on — '"

"Mo-om!" Amanda screeched. "I never said all *that!*"

Mrs. Beale nodded solemnly — "No, of course you didn't" — and gave Maniac a huge wink, which made Amanda screech louder, until something crashed in the kitchen. Mrs. Beale ran. Amanda and Maniac ran.

The scene in the kitchen stopped them cold: one little girl, eyes wide, standing on a countertop; one little boy, eyes wide, standing just below her on a chair; one shattered glass jar and some stringy pale-colored glop on the floor; one growing cloud of sauerkraut fumes.

The girl was Hester, age four; the boy was Lester, age three. In less than five minutes, while Mrs. Beale and Amanda cleaned up the floor, Hester and Lester and their dog Bow Wow were in the backyard wrestling and tickling and jumping and just generally going wild with their new buddy — and victim — Maniac Magee.

121

Maniac was still there when Mr. Beale came home from his Saturday shift at the tire factory.

He was there for dinner, when Hester and Lester pushed their chairs alongside his.

He was there to help Amanda mend her torn book.

He was there watching TV afterward, with Hester riding one knee, Lester the other.

He was there when Hester and Lester came screaming down the stairs with a book, Amanda screaming even louder after them, the kids shoving the book and themselves onto Maniac's lap, Amanda finally calming down because they didn't want to crayon the book, they only wanted Maniac to read. And so he read *Lyle, Lyle, Crocodile* to Hester and Lester and, even though they pretended not to listen, to Amanda and Mr. and Mrs. Beale.

And he was there when Hester and Lester were herded upstairs to bed, and Mrs. Beale said, "Don't you think it's about time you're heading home, Jeffrey? Your parents'll be wondering."

So Maniac, wanting to say something but not knowing how, got into the car for Mr. Beale to drive him home. And then he made his mistake. He waited for only two or three blocks to go by before saying to Mr. Beale, "This is it."

Mr. Beale stopped, but he didn't let Maniac out of the car. He looked at him funny. Mr. Beale knew what his passenger apparently didn't: East End was East End and West End was West End, and the house this white lad was pointing to was filled with black people, just like every other house on up to Hector Street.

122

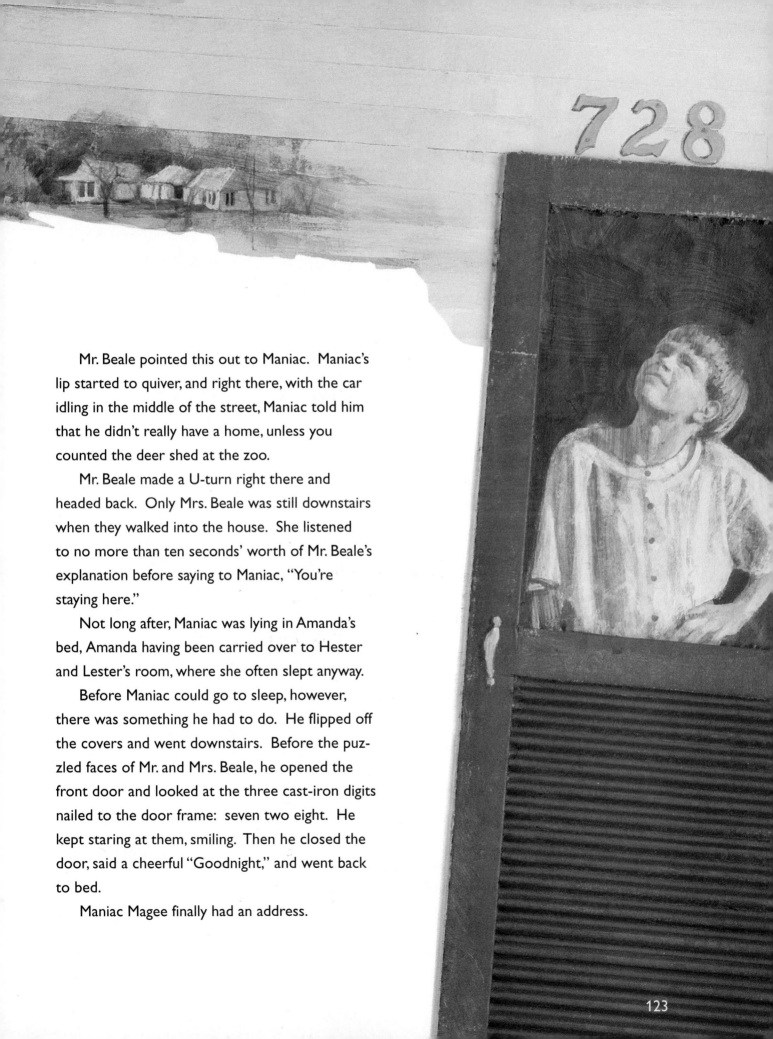

Mr. Beale pointed this out to Maniac. Maniac's lip started to quiver, and right there, with the car idling in the middle of the street, Maniac told him that he didn't really have a home, unless you counted the deer shed at the zoo.

Mr. Beale made a U-turn right there and headed back. Only Mrs. Beale was still downstairs when they walked into the house. She listened to no more than ten seconds' worth of Mr. Beale's explanation before saying to Maniac, "You're staying here."

Not long after, Maniac was lying in Amanda's bed, Amanda having been carried over to Hester and Lester's room, where she often slept anyway.

Before Maniac could go to sleep, however, there was something he had to do. He flipped off the covers and went downstairs. Before the puzzled faces of Mr. and Mrs. Beale, he opened the front door and looked at the three cast-iron digits nailed to the door frame: seven two eight. He kept staring at them, smiling. Then he closed the door, said a cheerful "Goodnight," and went back to bed.

Maniac Magee finally had an address.

Break Out

Illustrate Two Sides

East and West/ Right and Wrong

With a partner or in a small group, choose a pair of opposite images, places, people, or ideas from *Maniac Magee*. Then make a two-sided collage on both sides of a paper plate to show the two opposites. Use both pictures and words in your collage. Hang them from the ceiling so they'll spin.

Dramatic Reading

Look Out, Maniac!

Choose a paragraph or a passage from the story that you really think packs a punch. Then practice reading it aloud, using the volume, pace, and tone of your voice to show the emotional roller coaster of the action. Finally, read it aloud to a partner and listen to the paragraph he or she chose. Discuss how "hearing" a story is different from reading it to yourself.

Your IDEAS

Writing: Character's Voice

Reading Maniac's Mind

When Maniac Magee points to a house on Hector Street and says, "This is it" to Mr. Beale, what is he thinking? Write everything that could be going through his mind at that moment.

Discuss Survival

The City and The Wild

Unlike the other characters in this theme, Maniac Magee is not struggling to survive a life-threatening wilderness situation. What does "survival" mean to him as opposed to characters like Tonweya, Karana, and Cloyd? Discuss their similarities and differences with a partner or a small group.

The Rescue

by Cynthia Rylant

Running down the tracks one day,
thunder and lightning coming up on me,
and there a little girl crying
and walking,
looking at the sky.
Me scared to death of storms
crossing over:
You going home? Want me to walk with you?
And turning away from my house to walk her
through Beaver
to hers.
Lightning and thunder strong now.
So there's her mother on the porch, waving,
and she says bye to me then runs.
I turn around
and walk in the storm
slow and straight,
but inside,
a little girl crying.

Contents

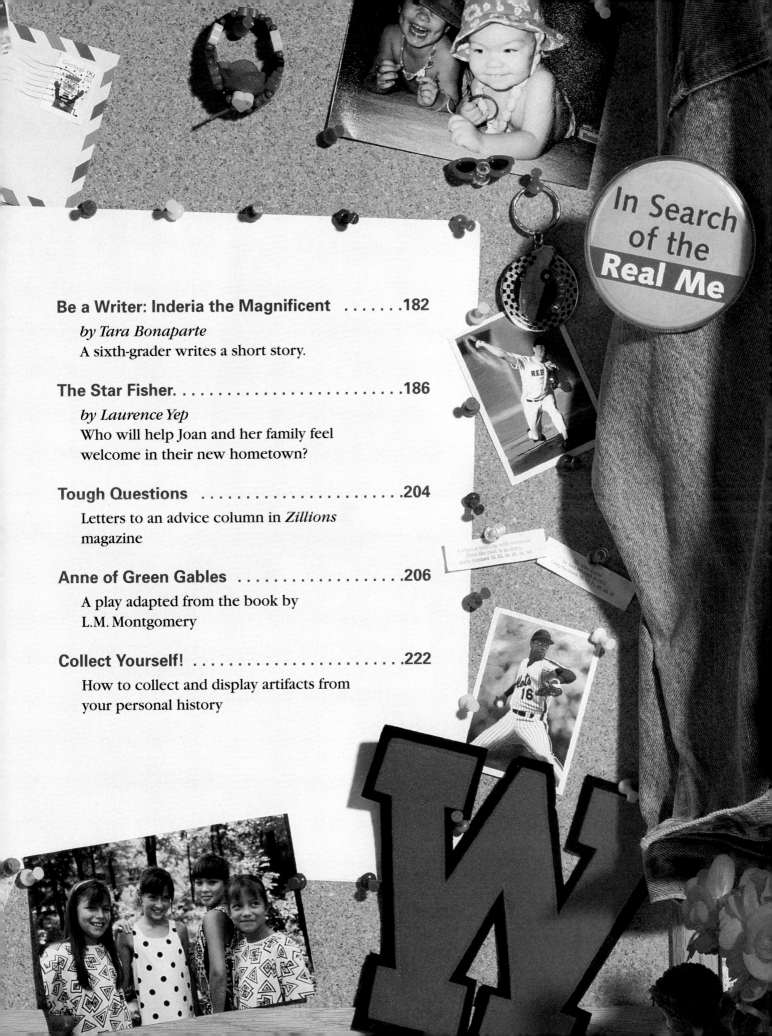

In Search of the Real Me

Read On Your Own

Beverly Cleary
STRIDER

The long-awaited sequel to the Newbery award-winning classic
Dear Mr. Henshaw

Dear Diary,

Today I read some poetry. I liked it a lot and would like to write my own poetry.

Reading Middle School Career Day!
Have you ever considered becoming a Graphic Designer?
Well... Thi

PAPERBACK **PLUS**

Strider
by Beverly Cleary
Leigh Botts finds and cares for a dog while dealing with his parents' divorce.

In the same book . . .
more about pets and family relationships.

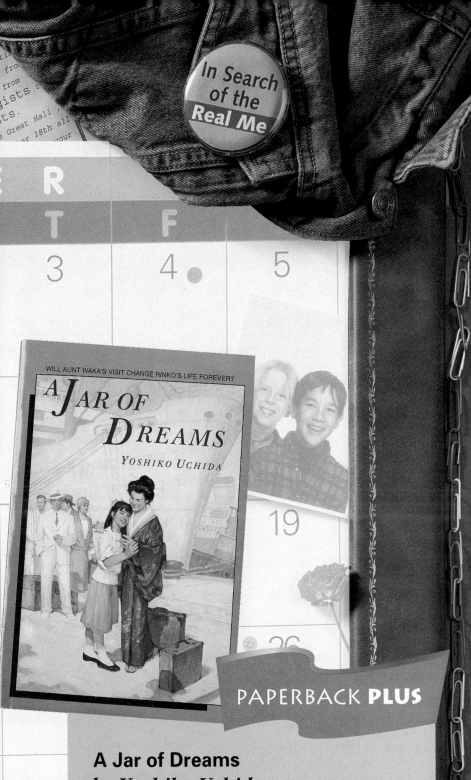

Books to Identify With

Taking Sides
by Gary Soto
After moving to the suburbs, Lincoln Mendoza practices for a basketball game against his former teammates and feels conflicting loyalties.

Pueblo Boy: Growing Up in Two Worlds
by Marcia Keegan
Timmy Roybal participates not only in contemporary life but also in the ancient Native American traditions of his ancestors.

The Summer of the Swans
by Betsy Byars
Sara feels dissatisfied with herself, especially her looks, but when her little brother is missing, she gains a new sense of herself and what's important.

My Name Is San Ho
by Jayne Pettit
San Ho survives in Saigon until his mother sends for him to join her and her American husband. Will he adjust to life in the United States?

Zeely
by Virginia Hamilton
Geeder Perry thinks Zeely is an African princess. But Zeely is not, and teaches Geeder about accepting yourself as you are.

WILL AUNT WAKA'S VISIT CHANGE RINKO'S LIFE FOREVER?

A JAR OF DREAMS
YOSHIKO UCHIDA

PAPERBACK **PLUS**

A Jar of Dreams
by Yoshiko Uchida
When her aunt from Japan comes to visit, will Rinko's life get more complicated?

In the same book . . .
more about growing up and fitting in.

Meet the Author

In many of his stories, **Gary Soto** writes about where he grew up: Fresno, California. In this place, there was a mixture of many cultures, including his own. When he was growing up, there was a popular television show called *American Bandstand* hosted by Dick Clark. It featured famous rock-and-roll bands playing their newest songs while a live audience danced in front of the TV cameras.

Meet the Illustrator

Born and raised in Brownsville, Texas, **Celina Hinojosa** was a mischievous and creative child. She once locked herself in the bathroom with her mother's lipstick and drew a perfect red ring around the room. Her family later never stopped supporting her talent. She now loves traveling in Mexico to see and visit the archeological ruins.

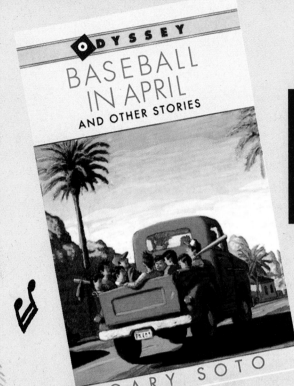

THE NO-GUITAR BLUES

by GARY SOTO

The moment Fausto saw the group Los Lobos on "American Bandstand," he knew exactly what he wanted to do with his life — play guitar. His eyes grew large with excitement as Los Lobos ground out a song while teenagers bounced off each other on the crowded dance floor.

He had watched "American Bandstand" for years and had heard Ray Camacho and the Teardrops at Romain Playground, but it had never occurred to him that he too might become a musician. That afternoon Fausto knew his mission in life: to play guitar in his own band; to sweat out his songs and prance around the stage; to make money and dress weird.

Fausto turned off the television set and walked outside, wondering how he could get enough money to buy a guitar. He couldn't ask his parents because they would just say, "Money doesn't grow on trees" or "What do you think we are, bankers?" And besides, they hated rock music. They were into the *conjunto* music of Lydia Mendoza, Flaco Jimenez, and Little Joe and La Familia. And, as Fausto recalled, the last album they bought was *The Chipmunks Sing Christmas Favorites*.

But what the heck, he'd give it a try. He returned inside and watched his mother make tortillas. He leaned against the kitchen counter, trying to work up the nerve to ask her for a guitar. Finally, he couldn't hold back any longer.

"Mom," he said, "I want a guitar for Christmas."

She looked up from rolling tortillas. "Honey, a guitar costs a lot of money."

"How 'bout for my birthday next year," he tried again.

"I can't promise," she said, turning back to her tortillas, "but we'll see."

Fausto walked back outside with a buttered tortilla. He knew his mother was right. His father was a warehouseman at Berven Rugs, where he made good money but not enough to buy everything his children wanted. Fausto decided to mow lawns to earn money, and was pushing the mower down the street before he realized it was winter and no one would hire him. He returned the mower and picked up a rake. He hopped onto his sister's bike (his had two flat tires) and rode north to the nicer section of Fresno in search of work. He went door-to-door, but after three hours he managed to get only one job, and not to rake leaves. He was asked to hurry down to the store to buy a loaf of bread, for which he received a grimy, dirt-caked quarter.

He also got an orange, which he ate sitting at the curb. While he was eating, a dog walked up and sniffed his leg. Fausto pushed him away and threw an orange peel

136

skyward. The dog caught it and ate it in one gulp. The dog looked at Fausto and wagged his tail for more. Fausto tossed him a slice of orange, and the dog snapped it up and licked his lips.

"How come you like oranges, dog?"

The dog blinked a pair of sad eyes and whined.

"What's the matter? Cat got your tongue?" Fausto laughed at his joke and offered the dog another slice.

At that moment a dim light came on inside Fausto's head. He saw that it was sort of a fancy dog, a terrier or something, with dog tags and a shiny collar. And it looked well fed and healthy. In his neighborhood, the dogs were never licensed, and if they got sick they were placed near the water heater until they got well.

This dog looked like he belonged to rich people. Fausto cleaned his juice-sticky hands on his pants and got to his feet. The light in his head grew brighter. It just might work. He called the dog, patted its muscular back, and bent down to check the license.

"Great," he said. "There's an address."

The dog's name was Roger, which struck Fausto as weird because he'd never heard of a dog with a human name. Dogs should have names like Bomber, Freckles, Queenie, Killer, and Zero.

Fausto planned to take the dog home and collect a reward. He would say he had found Roger near the freeway. That would scare the daylights out of the owners, who would be so happy that they would probably give him a reward. He felt bad about lying, but the dog *was* loose. And it might even really be lost, because the address was six blocks away.

Fausto stashed the rake and his sister's bike behind a bush, and, tossing an orange peel every time Roger became distracted, walked the dog to his house. He hesitated on the porch until Roger began to scratch the door with a muddy paw. Fausto had come this far, so he figured he might as well go through with it. He knocked softly. When no one answered, he rang the doorbell. A man in a silky bathrobe and slippers opened the door and seemed confused by the sight of his dog and the boy.

"Sir," Fausto said, gripping Roger by the collar. "I found your dog by the freeway. His dog license says he lives here." Fausto looked down at the dog, then up to the man. "He does, doesn't he?"

The man stared at Fausto a long time before saying in a pleasant voice, "That's right." He pulled his robe tighter around him because of the cold and asked Fausto to come in. "So he was by the freeway?"

"Uh — huh."

"You bad, snoopy dog," said the man, wagging his finger. "You probably knocked over some trash cans, too, didn't you?"

Fausto didn't say anything. He looked around, amazed by this house with its shiny furniture and a television as large as the front window at home. Warm bread smells filled the air and music full of soft tinkling floated in from another room.

"Helen," the man called to the kitchen. "We have a visitor." His wife came into the living room wiping her hands on a dish towel and smiling. "And who have we here?" she asked in one of the softest voices Fausto had ever heard.

"This young man said he found Roger near the freeway."

Fausto repeated his story to her while staring at a perpetual clock with a bell-shaped glass, the kind his aunt got when she celebrated her twenty-fifth anniversary. The lady frowned and said, wagging a finger at Roger, "Oh, you're a bad boy."

"It was very nice of you to bring Roger home," the man said. "Where do you live?"

"By that vacant lot on Olive," he said. "You know, by Brownie's Flower Place."

The wife looked at her husband, then Fausto. Her eyes twinkled triangles of light as she said, "Well, young man, you're probably hungry. How about a turnover?"

"What do I have to turn over?" Fausto asked, thinking she was talking about yard work or something like turning trays of dried raisins.

"No, no, dear, it's a pastry." She took him by the elbow and guided him to a kitchen that sparkled with copper pans and bright yellow wallpaper. She guided him to the kitchen table and gave him a tall glass of milk and something that looked like an *empanada*. Steamy waves of heat escaped when he tore it in two. He ate with both eyes on the man and woman who stood arm-in-arm smiling at him. They were strange, he thought. But nice.

"That was good," he said after he finished the turnover. "Did you make it, ma'am?"

"Yes, I did. Would you like another?"

"No, thank you. I have to go home now."

As Fausto walked to the door, the man opened his wallet and took out a bill. "This is for you," he said. "Roger is special to us, almost like a son."

Fausto looked at the bill and knew he was in trouble. Not with these nice folks or with his parents but with himself. How could he have been so deceitful? The dog wasn't lost. It was just having a fun Saturday walking around.

"I can't take that."

"You have to. You deserve it, believe me," the man said.

"No, I don't."

"Now don't be silly," said the lady. She took the bill from her husband and stuffed it into Fausto's shirt pocket. "You're a lovely child. Your parents are lucky to have you. Be good. And come see us again, please."

Fausto went out, and the lady closed the door. Fausto clutched the bill through his shirt pocket. He felt like ringing the doorbell and begging them to please take the money back, but he knew they would refuse. He hurried away, and at the end of the block, pulled the bill from his shirt pocket: it was a crisp twenty-dollar bill.

"Oh, man, I shouldn't have lied," he said under his breath as he started up the street like a zombie. He wanted to run to church for Saturday confession, but it was past four-thirty, when confession stopped.

He returned to the bush where he had hidden the rake and his sister's bike and rode home slowly, not daring to touch the money in his pocket. At home, in the privacy of his room, he examined the twenty-dollar bill. He had never had so much money. It was probably enough to buy a secondhand guitar. But he felt bad, like the time he stole a dollar from the secret fold inside his older brother's wallet.

Fausto went outside and sat on the fence. "Yeah," he said. "I can probably get a guitar for twenty. Maybe at a yard sale — things are cheaper."

His mother called him to dinner.

The next day he dressed for church without anyone telling him. He was going to go to eight o'clock mass.

"I'm going to church, Mom," he said. His mother was in the kitchen cooking *papas* and *chorizo con huevos*. A pile of tortillas lay warm under a dishtowel.

"Oh, I'm so proud of you, Son." She beamed, turning over the crackling *papas*.

His older brother, Lawrence, who was at the table reading the funnies, mimicked, "Oh, I'm so proud of you, my son," under his breath.

At Saint Theresa's he sat near the front. When Father Jerry began by saying that we are all sinners, Fausto thought he looked right at him. Could he know?

Fausto fidgeted with guilt. No, he thought. I only did it yesterday.

Fausto knelt, prayed, and sang. But he couldn't forget the man and the lady, whose names he didn't even know, and the *empanada* they had given him. It had a strange name but tasted really good. He wondered how they got rich. And how that dome clock worked. He had asked his mother once how his aunt's clock worked. She said it just worked, the way the refrigerator works. It just did.

Fausto caught his mind wandering and tried to concentrate on his sins. He said a Hail Mary and sang, and when the wicker basket came his way, he stuck a hand reluctantly in his pocket and pulled out the twenty-dollar bill. He ironed it between his palms, and dropped it into the basket. The grown-ups stared. Here was a kid dropping twenty dollars in the basket while they gave just three or four dollars.

There would be a second collection for Saint Vincent de Paul, the lector announced. The wicker baskets again floated in the pews, and this time the adults around him, given a second chance to show their charity, dug deep into their wallets and purses and dropped in fives and tens. This time Fausto tossed in the grimy quarter.

Fausto felt better after church. He went home and played football in the front yard with his brother and some neighbor kids. He felt cleared of wrongdoing and was so happy that he played one of his best games of football ever. On one play, he tore his good pants, which he knew he shouldn't have been wearing. For a second, while he examined the hole, he wished he hadn't given the twenty dollars away.

Man, I coulda bought me some Levi's, he thought. He pictured his twenty dollars being spent to buy church candles. He pictured a priest buying an armful of flowers with *his* money.

Fausto had to forget about getting a guitar. He spent the next day playing soccer in his good pants, which were now his old pants. But that night during dinner, his mother said she remembered seeing an old bass guitarron the last time she cleaned out her father's garage.

"It's a little dusty," his mom said, serving his favorite enchiladas, "but I think it works. Grandpa says it works."

Fausto's ears perked up. That was the same kind the guy in Los Lobos played. Instead of asking for the guitar, he waited for his mother to offer it to him. And she did, while gathering the dishes from the table.

"No, Mom, I'll do it," he said, hugging her. "I'll do the dishes forever if you want."

It was the happiest day of his life. No, it was the second-happiest day of his life. The happiest was when his grandfather Lupe placed the guitarron, which was nearly as huge as a washtub, in his arms. Fausto ran a thumb down the strings, which vibrated in his throat and chest. It sounded beautiful, deep and eerie. A pumpkin smile widened on his face.

"OK, *hijo*, now you put your fingers like this," said his grandfather, smelling of tobacco and aftershave. He took Fausto's fingers and placed them on the strings. Fausto strummed a chord on the guitarron, and the bass resounded in their chests.

The guitarron was more complicated than Fausto imagined. But he was confident that after a few more lessons he could start a band that would someday play on "American Bandstand" for the dancing crowds.

143

Make Clusters

Clusters Around Characters

Think about five of the characters: Fausto, his mother, the husband and wife (Helen), and grandfather Lupe. For each, make a cluster diagram with words, pictures, and actions from the story that show something about that character. Add your own thoughts, feelings, and opinions to your clusters. Compare and contrast your clusters with those of another reader.

Brainstorm

How Can I Get . . . ?

With a partner or a small group, discuss other ways in which Fausto could have gotten a guitar. Use details from the story to help you brainstorm possibilities. Make a list as you discuss. Then circle the ways that you think are the best and discuss why. Can you all agree?

STRIKE A CHORD

Give It a Try!

If you've never held and strummed a guitar, try it. If possible, have someone show you how to hold a guitar correctly and how to play one or two simple chords. What does it feel like? On your fingers? Your chest? What does it sound like? What do your two hands do? How is your experience like (and unlike) Fausto's? Is it something you'd like to try again? Why or why not? In your journal, write about your experience in as much detail as you can.

Write and Discuss

What Did Fausto Find?

Fausto gets something real in this story — a guitar — but he gets something more, doesn't he? What exactly does he learn or discover about himself as a result of his experience? First, write your own ideas about this question and then discuss them with another reader. Remember that there is not one right answer to this question.

Jim Abbott was born without a right hand, but he didn't let that stop him from playing sports. He became an excellent lefthanded pitcher and reached the major leagues in 1989. In December 1992, after four seasons with the California Angels, Jim was traded to the New York Yankees.

Jim told *Sports Illustrated For Kids* what his life was like when he was a kid.

When I Was a Kid

by Jim Abbott

I grew up in Flint, Michigan. My dad worked for the Anheuser-Busch company. I lived with my parents and my younger brother, Chad. During the day, my mom went to school to study law. She received her law degree and is now a lawyer in Flint.

My parents always told me not to be embarrassed by my handicap. They encouraged me to try sports and other things that interested me.

I loved sports. I played football in the fall, basketball in the winter, and baseball in the summer. I also collected baseball cards. The Detroit Tigers were my favorite team.

146

Playing sports was a way to be accepted by the kids I grew up with. Just because I was born without my right hand, I never thought to myself, "Wow, I only have one hand." I just found a way to do the same things other kids did. Sometimes kids would tease me, but I don't really remember anybody ever being cruel.

My mom and dad always let me play sports as long as I kept my grades up. I enjoyed school. I worked hard at it and took a lot of pride in getting good grades.

When I started Little League in fifth grade, I played third base and sometimes the outfield. I always had a pretty good throwing arm. I even won the softball toss in second grade! I began thinking about becoming a pitcher.

I got a chance to pitch when the starting pitcher was sick one day. After that first time, I knew I wanted to pitch again. My dad was the one who taught me how to switch my glove to my left hand after pitching so that I would be ready to field the ball.

When I was 12 years old, I started pitching quite a bit. That was the year when the first newspaper article was written about me. I still have that article at home.

When I was by myself, I practiced throwing and catching by tossing a ball against a brick wall for hours at a time. With each throw, I would move closer and closer to the wall. I had to be pretty quick because I didn't have much time to react to the rebound!

In high school, teams used to bunt on me to test my fielding abilities. I once threw out seven of the eight batters in a row who tried!

Not having a right hand didn't stop Jim from becoming a top major league pitcher.

147

Jim Abbott's baseball card from his first year in the major league (1989)

I was drafted by the Toronto Blue Jays when I finished high school. But I felt I should go to college, so I attended the University of Michigan. I had always rooted for University of Michigan teams when I was a kid. Rick Leach was the Michigan quarterback then, and he was one of my big idols. To have a chance to be a student and an athlete at Michigan was a dream come true. I had always said that if I did anything beyond that, it would be a real bonus.

As a kid, I dreamed of becoming a pro ballplayer, but I wasn't sure I was good enough. It wasn't until 1988, my junior year in college, that I realized I *was* good enough. That was the year I got to pitch for the U.S. Olympic Baseball Team at the Summer Games in Seoul, South Korea. I did well, and we won the gold medal. So far, that has been the highlight of my career.

After the Olympics, I signed a contract to play for the Angels. I left college a year early, but I didn't give up on my education. I still hope to finish my degree someday. I'd like to major in communications or history.

I'm not sure what I want to do when my playing career is over. I used to think that I would never want to coach, but now I think I might like to. Or I might want to get away from baseball completely and find something that brings a whole new set of challenges.

I've always been competitive. When people said I couldn't do something, I worked hard to prove them wrong. I guess all that hard work has paid off.

Black Kid in a New Place

by JAMES BERRY

I'm here, I see
I make a part of a little planet
here, with some of everybody now.

I stretch myself, I see
I'm like a migrant bird
who will not return from here.

I shake out colorful wings.
I set up a palmtree bluesky
here, where winter mists were.

Using what time tucked in me, I see
my body pops with dance.
Streets break out in carnival.

Rooms echo my voice. I see
I was not a migrant bird. I am
a transplanted sapling, here, blossoming.

Jacqueline Woodson feels a strong connection with the characters she creates in her books. "Ms. Dell and Hattie and Maizon and Margaret are all people I would have liked to have known in my childhood." Woodson also feels a bond with her young adult readers. Even though she is older than they are, she believes that there isn't a generation gap between them and her. "As a writer, I write remembering the child I was, am still, will always be. That is what, through literature, I hope to bring to the children."

Born on the island of Oahu in Hawaii, Lambert Davis played Little League baseball and likes beaches. Encouraged by his father, who is an architect, Lambert went to design school. He now works as an illustrator when he's not traveling the world's coastlines searching for uncrowded beaches.

LAST
SUMMER
WITH MAIZON

It is the end of a difficult summer for eleven-year-old Margaret Tory of Brooklyn, New York. Early in the summer, Margaret's father died, and now her best friend, Maizon, is leaving for boarding school. Margaret wonders how she will get along without her. Where will she find someone who understands?

"Sure wish you weren't going away," Margaret said, choking back tears for what seemed like the millionth time. They were sitting on the M train, crossing the Williamsburg Bridge, and Margaret shivered as the train passed over the water. The L train would have made the trip easier but the L didn't go over the bridge and Maizon had wanted to ride over it once more before she left.

BY JACQUELINE WOODSON

Maizon sat nervously drumming her fingers against the windowpane. "Me too," she said absently.

Margaret looked over at Mama and Grandma. Grandma stared out of her window. She looked old and out of place on the train.

"Maizon?" Margaret said, turning back toward her.

"Hmm?" Maizon frowned. She seemed to be concentrating on something in the water. It rippled and danced below them.

"Even though I wrote you those two letters, you only have to write me one back if you don't have a lot of time or something." Margaret looked down at her fingers. She had begun biting the cuticles, and now the skin surrounding her nails was red and ragged.

"I'll write you back," Maizon promised.

"Maizon . . ."

"What, Margaret!"

Margaret jumped and looked at Maizon. There was an uneasiness in her eyes she had never seen before.

"Forget it," she said.

Ms. Tory leaned over. "We'll be getting off in a few stops."

They rode the rest of the way in silence. At Delancey Street they changed for another train and a half hour later they were at Penn Station.

"I guess now we'll have to call each other to plan the same outfits," Maizon said as they waited for her train. Her voice sounded forced and fake, Margaret thought, like a grown-up trying to make a kid smile.

"I guess," Margaret said. The conductor called Maizon's train.

"I guess I gotta go," Maizon said softly, and Margaret felt a lump rise in her throat.

"I'll write you back, Margaret. Promise. Thanks for letting me keep the double-dutch trophy even if it is only second place." They hugged for a long time. Maizon sniffed loudly. "I'm scared, Margaret," she whispered.

Margaret didn't know what to say. "Don't be."

"Bye, Ms. Tory."

Margaret's mother bent down and hugged Maizon. "Be good," she said as Maizon and her grandmother made their way toward the train.

"Mama," Margaret said as they watched Maizon and her grandmother disappear into the tunnel.

"What, dear?"

"What's the difference between a best friend and an old friend?"

"I guess . . ." Her mother thought for a moment. "I guess an old friend is a friend you once had and a best friend is a friend you'll always have."

"Then maybe me and Maizon aren't best friends anymore."

"Don't be silly, Margaret. What else would you two be? Some people can barely tell you apart. I feel like I've lost a daughter."

"Maybe . . . I don't know . . . Maybe we're old friends now. Maybe this was our last summer as best friends. I feel like something's going to change now and I'm not going to be able to change it back."

Ms. Tory's heels made a clicking sound through the terminal. She stopped to buy tokens and turned to Margaret.

"Like when Daddy died?" she asked, looking worried.

Margaret swallowed. "No. I just feel empty instead of sad, Mama," she said.

Her mother squeezed her hand as they waited for the train. When it came, they took seats by the window.

Ms. Tory held on to Margaret's hand. "Sometimes it just takes a while for the pain of loss to set in."

"I feel like sometimes Maizon kept me from doing things, but now she's not here. Now I don't have any" — Margaret thought for a moment, but couldn't find the right words — "now I don't have any excuse not to do things."

When the train emerged from its tunnel, the late afternoon sun had turned a bright orange. Margaret watched it for a moment. She looked at her hands again and discovered a cuticle she had missed.

Margaret pressed her pencil to her lips and
stared out the classroom window. The school yard
was desolate and gray. But everything seemed that
way since Maizon left. Especially since a whole week
had passed now without even a letter from her.
Margaret sighed and chewed her eraser.

"Margaret, are you working on this assignment?"

Margaret jumped and turned toward Ms. Peazle.
Maizon had been right — Ms. Peazle was the crabbi-
est teacher in the school. Margaret wondered why
she had been picked to teach the smartest class.
If students were so smart, she thought, the least the
school could do was reward them with a nice teacher.

"I'm trying to think about what to write,
Ms. Peazle."

"Well, you won't find an essay on your summer vacation outside that window, I'm sure. Or is that where you spent it?"

The class snickered and Margaret looked down, embarrassed. "No, ma'am."

"I'm glad to hear that," Ms. Peazle continued, looking at Margaret over granny glasses. "And I'm sure in the next ten minutes you'll be able to read your essay to the class and prove to us all that you weren't just daydreaming. Am I right?"

"I hope so, ma'am," Margaret mumbled. She looked around the room.

It seemed everyone in 6–1 knew each other from the previous year. On the first day, a lot of kids asked her about Maizon, but after that no one said much to her. Things had changed since Maizon left. Without her, a lot of the fun had gone out of sitting on the stoop with Ms. Dell, Hattie, and Li'l Jay. Maybe she could write about that. No, Margaret thought, looking down at the blank piece of paper in front of her. It was too much to tell. She'd never get finished and Ms. Peazle would scold her — making her feel too dumb to be in 6–1. Margaret chewed her eraser and stared out the window again. There had to be something she could write about quickly.

"Margaret Tory!" Ms. Peazle warned. "Am I going to have to change your seat?"

"Ma'am? I was just . . ."

"I think I'm going to have to move you away from that window unless you can prove to me that you can sit there without being distracted."

"I can, Ms. Peazle. It helps me write," she lied.

"Then I take it you should be ready to read your essay in" — Ms. Peazle looked at her watch —"the next seven minutes."

Margaret started writing frantically. When Ms. Peazle called her to the front of the room, her sheet of notebook paper shook in her hand. She pulled nervously at the hem of the maroon dress she and Maizon had picked out for school and tried not to look out at the twenty-six pairs of eyes she knew were on her.

"Last summer was the worst summer of my life. First my father died and then my best friend went away to a private boarding school. I didn't go anywhere except Manhattan. But that wasn't any fun because I was taking Maizon to the train. I hope next summer is a lot better."

She finished reading and walked silently back to her desk and tried to concentrate on not looking out the window. Instead, she rested her eyes on the half-written page. Margaret knew she could write better than that, but Ms. Peazle had rushed her. Anyway, she thought, that *is* what happened last summer.

"I'd like to see you after class, Margaret."

"Yes, ma'am," Margaret said softly. *This is the end,* she thought. One week in the smartest class and it's over. Maizon was smart enough to go to a better *school* and I can't even keep up in this class. Margaret sighed and tried not to stare out the window for the rest of the day.

When the three o'clock bell rang, she waited uneasily in her seat while Ms. Peazle led the rest of the class out to the school yard. Margaret heard the excited screams and laughter as everyone poured outside.

The empty classroom was quiet. She looked around at the desks. Many had words carved into them. They reminded her of the names she and Maizon had carved into the tar last summer. They were faded and illegible now.

Ms. Peazle came in and sat at the desk next to Margaret's. "Margaret," she said slowly, pausing for a moment to remove her glasses and rub her eyes tiredly. "I'm sorry to hear about your father . . . "

"That's okay." Margaret fidgeted.

"No, Margaret, it's not okay," Ms. Peazle continued, "not if it's going to affect your schoolwork."

"I can do better, Ms. Peazle, I really can!" Margaret looked up pleadingly. She was surprised at herself for wanting so badly to stay in Ms. Peazle's class.

"I know you can, Margaret. That's why I'm going to ask you to do this. For homework tonight . . ."

Margaret started to say that none of the other students had been assigned homework. She decided not to, though.

"I want you to write about your summer," Ms. Peazle continued. "I want it to express all of your feelings about your friend Maizon going away. Or it could be about your father's death and how you felt then. It doesn't matter what you write, a poem, an essay, a short story. Just so long as it expresses how you felt this summer. Is that understood?"

"Yes, ma'am." Margaret looked up at Ms. Peazle. "It's understood."

Ms. Peazle smiled. Without her glasses, Margaret thought, she wasn't that mean-looking.

"Good, then I'll see you bright and early tomorrow with something wonderful to read to the class."

Margaret slid out of the chair and walked toward the door.

"That's a very pretty dress, Margaret," Ms. Peazle said.

Margaret turned and started to tell her that Maizon was wearing the same one in Connecticut, but changed her mind. What did Ms. Peazle know about best friends who were almost cousins, anyway?

"Thanks, ma'am," she said instead, and ducked out of the classroom. All of a sudden, she had a wonderful idea!

The next morning Ms. Peazle tapped her ruler against the desk to quiet the class. "Margaret," she asked when the room was silent. "Do you have something you want to share with us today?"

Margaret nodded and Ms. Peazle beckoned her to the front of the room.

"This," Margaret said, handing Ms. Peazle the sheet of looseleaf paper. It had taken her most of the evening to finish the assignment.

Ms. Peazle looked it over and handed it back to her.

"We're ready to listen," she said, smiling.

Margaret looked out over the class and felt her stomach slide up to her throat. She swallowed and counted to ten. Though the day was cool, she found herself sweating. Margaret couldn't remember when she had been this afraid.

"My pen doesn't write anymore," she began reading.

"I can't hear," someone called out.

"My pen doesn't write anymore," Margaret repeated. In the back of the room, someone exaggerated a sigh. The class chuckled. Margaret ignored them and continued to read.

"It stumbles and trembles in my hand.
If my dad were here — he would understand.
Best of all — It'd be last summer again.

But they've turned off the fire hydrants
Locked green leaves away.
Sprinkled ashes on you
and sent you on your way.

I wouldn't mind the early autumn
if you came home today
I'd tell you how much I miss you
and know I'd be okay.

Mama isn't laughing now
She works hard and she cries
she wonders when true laughter
will relieve her of her sighs
And even when she's smiling
Her eyes don't smile along
her face is growing older
She doesn't seem as strong.
I worry cause I love her
Ms. Dell says, 'where there is love,
there is a way.'

It's funny how we never know
exactly how our life will go
It's funny how a dream can fade
With the break of day.

I'm not sure where you are now
though I see you in my dreams
Ms. Dell says the things we see
are not always as they seem.

So often I'm uncertain
if you have found a new home
and when I am uncertain
I usually write a poem.

Time can't erase the memory
and time can't bring you home
Last summer was a part of me
and now a part is gone."

The class stared at her blankly, silent. Margaret lowered her head and made her way back to her seat.

"Could you leave that assignment on my desk, Margaret?" Ms. Peazle asked. There was a small smile playing at the corners of her mouth.

"Yes, ma'am," Margaret said. Why didn't anyone say anything?

"Now, if everyone will open their history books to page two seventy-five, we'll continue with our lesson on the Civil War."

Margaret wondered what she had expected the class to do. Applaud? She missed Maizon more than she had in a long time. *She would know what I'm feeling,* Margaret thought. And if she didn't, she'd make believe she did.

Margaret snuck a look out the window. The day looked cold and still. *She'd tell me it's only a feeling poets get and that Nikki Giovanni feels this way all of the time.* When she turned back, there was a small piece of paper on her desk.

"I liked your poem, Margaret," the note read. There was no name.

Margaret looked around but no one looked as though they had slipped a note on her desk. She smiled to herself and tucked the piece of paper into her notebook.

The final bell rang. As the class rushed out, Margaret was bumped against Ms. Peazle's desk.

"Did you get my note?" Ms. Peazle whispered. Margaret nodded and floated home.

Ms. Dell, Hattie, and Li'l Jay were sitting on the stoop when she got home.

"If it weren't so cold," she said, squeezing in beside Hattie's spreading hips, "it would be like old times."

"Except for Maizon," Hattie said, cutting her eyes toward her mother.

"Hush, Hattie," Ms. Dell said. She shivered and pulled Li'l Jay closer to her. For a moment, Margaret thought she looked old.

"It's just this cold spell we're having," Ms. Dell said. "Ages a person. Makes them look older than they are."

Margaret smiled. "Reading minds is worse than eavesdropping, Ms. Dell."

"Try being her daughter for nineteen years," Hattie said.

"Hattie," Margaret said, moving closer to her for warmth. "How come you never liked Maizon?"

"No one said I never liked her."

"No one had to," Ms. Dell butted in.

"She was just too much ahead of everyone. At least she thought she was."

"But she was, Hattie. She was the smartest person at P.S. 102. Imagine being the smartest person."

"But she didn't have any common sense, Margaret. And when God gives a person that much brain, he's bound to leave out something else."

"Like what?"

Ms. Dell leaned over Li'l Jay's head and whispered loudly, "Like the truth."

She and Hattie laughed but Margaret couldn't see the humor. It wasn't like either of them to say something wrong about a person.

"She told the truth . . ." Margaret said weakly.

Ms. Dell and Hattie exchanged looks.

"How was school?" Hattie asked too brightly.

"Boring," Margaret said. She would tuck what they said away until she could figure it out.

"That's the only word you know since Maizon left. Seems there's gotta be somethin' else going on that's not so *boring* all the time," Ms. Dell said.

"Well, it's sure not school. I read a poem to that stupid class and no one but Ms. Peazle liked it." She sighed and rested her chin on her hand.

"That's the chance you gotta take with poetry," Ms. Dell said. "Either everybody likes it or everybody hates it, but you hardly ever know 'cause nobody says a word. Too afraid to offend you or, worse yet, make you feel good."

Margaret looked from Ms. Dell to Hattie then back to Ms. Dell again.

"How come you know so much about poetry?"

"You're not the first li'l black girl who wanted to be a poet."

"And you can bet your dress you won't be the last," Hattie concluded.

"You wanted to be a poet, Hattie??!!"

"Still do. Still make up poems in my head. Never write them down, though. The paper just yellows and clutters useful places. So this is where I keep it all now," she said, pointing to her head.

"A poem can't exist inside your head. You forget it," Margaret said doubtfully.

"Poems don't exist, Miss Know-It-All. Poems live! In your head is where a poem is born, isn't it?"

Margaret nodded and Hattie continued. "Well, my poetry chooses to live there!"

"Then recite one for me, please." Margaret folded her arms across her chest the way she had seen Ms. Dell do so many times.

"Some poems aren't meant to be heard, smarty-pants."

"Aw, Hattie," Ms. Dell interrupted, "let Margaret be the judge of that."

"All right. All right." Hattie's voice dropped to a whisper.

"Brooklyn-bound robin redbreast followed me from down home / Brooklyn-bound robin, you're a long way from your own / So fly among the pigeons and circle the sky with your song."

They were quiet. Ms. Dell rocked Li'l Jay to sleep in her arms. Hattie looked somberly over the block in silence and Margaret thought of how much Hattie's poem made her think of Maizon. What was she doing now that the sun was almost down? she wondered. Had she found a new best friend?

"Maybe," she said after a long time. "Maybe it wasn't that the class didn't like my poem. Maybe it was like your poem, Hattie. You just have to sit quietly and think about all the things it makes you think about after you hear it. You have to let . . . let it sink in!"

"You have to feel it, Margaret," Hattie said softly, draping her arm over Margaret's shoulder.

"Yeah. Just like I felt when I wrote my poem, or you felt when you found a place for that one in your head!"

"Margaret," Ms. Dell said, "you gettin' too smart for us ol' ladies."

Margaret leaned against Hattie and listened to the fading sounds of construction. Soon the building on Palmetto Street would be finished. She closed her eyes and visions of last summer came into her head. She saw herself running down Madison Street arm in arm with Maizon. They were laughing. Then the picture faded into a new one. She and Maizon were sitting by the tree watching Li'l Jay take his first steps. He stumbled and fell into Maizon's arms. Now it all seemed like such a long time ago.

When she opened her eyes again, the moon was inching out from behind a cloud. It was barely visible in the late afternoon. The sky had turned a wintry blue and the streetlights flickered on. Margaret yawned, her head heavy all of a sudden from the long day.

"Looks like your mother's workin' late again. Bless that woman's heart. Seems she's workin' nonstop since your daddy passed."

"She's taking drawing classes. She wants to be an architect. Maybe she'll make a lot of money."

"Architects don't make a lot of money," Hattie said. "And anyway, you shouldn't be worrying your head over money."

166

"**S**he has a gift," Ms. Dell said. "All of you Torys have gifts. You with your writing, your mama with her drawings, and remember the things your daddy did with wood. Oh, that man was something else!"

"What's Li'l Jay's going to be?"

Ms. Dell stood up and pressed Li'l Jay's face to her cheek.

"Time's gonna tell us, Margaret. Now, come inside and do your homework while I fix you something to eat. No use sitting out in the cold."

Margaret rose and followed them inside.

"You hear anything from Maizon yet?" Hattie asked.

Margaret shook her head. If only Maizon were running up the block!

"I wrote her two letters and she hasn't written me one. Maybe she knows we're not really best friends anymore." Margaret sighed. She had been right in thinking she and Maizon were only old friends now, not the friends they used to be. "Still, I wish I knew how she was doing," she said, turning away so Hattie wouldn't see the tears in her eyes.

"We all do, honey," Hattie said, taking Margaret's hand. "We all do."

KEEPING IN TOUCH

WHAT IS A BEST FRIEND?

Look back through the story and find ways in which Maizon is a best friend to Margaret. Also, notice the way Margaret feels about Maizon and what the friendship means to her. Then, based on this story and your own experience, write a definition of "best friend." Write a sentence, a paragraph, or a whole essay.

WHAT SHOULD MARGARET DO?

Write a letter to Margaret in which you give her some advice about saving her friendship with Maizon, staying in Ms. Peazle's class, writing poetry, and recovering from her father's death. Be as specific as you can about what she should do. Share your letter with another reader.

Hold a Discussion

FOCUS ON FAMILIES

Both Margaret and Fausto in "The No-Guitar Blues" get help from their families. With a partner or a small group, discuss how the two families are alike and how they are different. How do both families help the two main characters? How could they help more?

Read Aloud

ALTERNATING VOICES

With a partner, read Margaret's poem aloud — each of you reading alternate verses. Read it more than once, varying your pace, rhythm, tone, and volume. What do you notice about the poem by reading it aloud that you missed by just reading it on the page?

ODE TO MY LIBRARY

by Gary Soto

It's small
With two rooms
Of books, a globe
That I once
Dropped, some maps
Of the United States and México,
And a fish tank with
A blue fish that
Is always making *jeta*.
There are tables and chairs,
And a pencil sharpener
On the wall: a crayon is stuck
In it, but I didn't do it.

It's funny, but the
Water fountain
Is cooled by a motor,
And the librarian reads
Books with her
Glasses hanging
From her neck. If she
Put them on
She would see me
Studying the Incas
Who lived two steps
From heaven, way in the mountains.

The place says, "Quiet, please,"
But three birds
Talk to us
Loudly from the window.
What's best is this:
A phonograph
That doesn't work.
When I put on the headphones,
I'm the captain of a jet,
And my passengers
Are *mis abuelitos*
Coming from a dusty ranch
In Monterrey. I want
To fly them to California,
But then walk
Them to my library.
I want to show them
The thirty books I devoured
In the summer read-a-thon.

I want to show them
The mural I helped paint.
In the mural,
An Aztec warrior
Is standing on a mountain
With a machete
And a band of feathers
On his noble head.
I made the cuts
Of muscle on
His stomach
And put a boulder
Of strength in each arm.

He could gather
Enough firewood
With one fist.
He could slice
Open a mountain
With that machete,
And with the wave of his arm
Send our enemies tumbling.

If I could fly,
I would bring
Mis abuelitos to California.
They would touch my hair
When I showed
Them my library:
The fish making *jeta*,
The globe that I dropped,
The birds fluttering
Their wings at the window.
They would stand me
Between them,
When I showed them
My thirty books,
And the cuts
On the warrior,
Our family of people.

THE SCHOLARSHIP JACKET

by Marta Salinas

The small Texas school that I attended carried out a tradition every year during the eighth grade graduation; a beautiful gold and green jacket, the school colors, was awarded to the class valedictorian, the student who had maintained the highest grades for eight years. The scholarship jacket had a big gold S on the left front side and the winner's name was written in gold letters on the pocket.

My oldest sister Rosie had won the jacket a few years back and I fully expected to win also. I was fourteen and in the eighth grade. I had been a straight A student since the first grade, and the last year I had looked forward to owning that jacket. My father was a farm laborer who couldn't earn enough money to feed eight children, so when I was six I was given to my grandparents to raise. We couldn't participate in sports at school because there were registration fees, uniform costs, and trips out of town; so even though we were quite agile and athletic, there would never be a sports school jacket for us. This one, the scholarship jacket, was our only chance.

In May, close to graduation, spring fever struck, and no one paid any attention in class; instead we stared out the windows and at each other, wanting to speed up the last few weeks of school. I despaired every time I looked in the mirror. Pencil thin, not a curve anywhere, I was called "Beanpole" and "String Bean" and I knew that's what I looked like. A flat chest, no hips, and a brain, that's what I had. That really isn't much for a fourteen-year-old to work with, I thought, as I absentmindedly wandered from my history class to the gym. Another hour of sweating in basketball and displaying my toothpick legs was coming up. Then I remembered my P.E. shorts were still in a bag under my desk where I'd forgotten them. I had to walk all the way back and get them. Coach Thompson was a real bear if anyone wasn't dressed up for P.E. She had said I was a good forward and once she even tried to talk Grandma into letting me join the team. Grandma, of course, said no.

I was almost back at my classroom's door when I heard angry voices and arguing. I stopped. I didn't mean to eavesdrop; I just hesitated, not knowing what to do. I needed those shorts and I was going to be late, but I didn't want to interrupt an argument between my teachers. I recognized the voices: Mr. Schmidt, my history teacher, and Mr. Boone, my math teacher. They seemed to be arguing about me. I couldn't believe it. I still remember the shock that rooted me flat against the wall as if I were trying to blend in with the graffiti written there.

"I refuse to do it! I don't care who her father is, her grades don't even begin to compare to Martha's. I won't lie or falsify records. Martha has a straight A plus average and you know it." That was Mr. Schmidt and he sounded very angry. Mr. Boone's voice sounded calm and quiet.

"Look, Joann's father is not only on the Board, he owns the only store in town; we could say it was a close tie and —"

The pounding in my ears drowned out the rest of the words, only a word here and there filtered through. "... Martha is Mexican ... resign ... won't do it....'" Mr. Schmidt came rushing out, and luckily for me went down the opposite way toward the auditorium, so he didn't see me. Shaking, I waited a few minutes and then went in and grabbed my bag and fled from the room. Mr. Boone looked up when I came in but didn't say anything. To this day I don't remember if I got in trouble in P.E. for being late or how I made it through the rest of the afternoon. I went home very sad and cried into my pillow that night so Grandmother wouldn't hear me. It seemed a cruel coincidence that I had overheard that conversation.

The next day when the principal called me into his office, I knew what it would be about. He looked uncomfortable and unhappy. I decided I wasn't going to make it any easier for him so I looked him straight in the eye. He looked away and fidgeted with the papers on his desk.

"Martha," he said, "there's been a change in policy this year regarding the scholarship jacket. As you know, it has always been free." He cleared his throat and continued. "This year the Board decided to charge fifteen dollars — which still won't cover the complete cost of the jacket."

I stared at him in shock and a small sound of dismay escaped my throat. I hadn't expected this. He still avoided looking in my eyes.

"So if you are unable to pay the fifteen dollars for the jacket, it will be given to the next one in line."

Standing with all the dignity I could muster, I said, "I'll speak to my grandfather about it, sir, and let you know tomorrow." I cried on the walk home from the bus stop. The dirt road was a quarter of a mile from the highway, so by the time I got home, my eyes were red and puffy.

"Where's Grandpa?" I asked Grandma, looking down at the floor so she wouldn't ask me why I'd been crying. She was sewing on a quilt and didn't look up.

"I think he's out back working in the bean field."

I went outside and looked out at the fields. There he was. I could see him walking between the rows, his body bent over the little plants, hoe in hand. I walked slowly out to him, trying to think how I could best ask him for the money. There was a cool breeze blowing and a sweet smell of mesquite in the air, but I didn't appreciate it. I kicked at a dirt clod. I wanted that jacket so much. It was more than just being a valedictorian and giving a little thank you speech for the jacket on graduation night. It represented eight years of hard work and expectation. I knew I had to be honest with Grandpa; it was my only chance. He saw me and looked up.

He waited for me to speak. I cleared my throat nervously and clasped my hands behind my back so he wouldn't see them shaking. "Grandpa, I have a big favor to ask you," I said in Spanish, the only language he knew. He still waited silently. I tried again. "Grandpa, this year the principal said the scholarship jacket is not going to be free. It's going to cost fifteen dollars and I have to take the money in tomorrow, otherwise it'll be given to someone else." The last words came out in an eager rush. Grandpa straightened up tiredly and leaned his chin on the hoe handle. He looked out over the field that was filled with the tiny green bean plants. I waited, desperately hoping he'd say I could have the money.

He turned to me and asked quietly, "What does a scholarship jacket mean?"

I answered quickly; maybe there was a chance. "It means you've earned it by having the highest grades for eight years and that's why they're giving it to you." Too late I realized the significance of my words. Grandpa knew that I understood it was not a matter of money. It wasn't that. He went back to hoeing the weeds that sprang up between the delicate little bean plants. It was a time consuming job; sometimes the small shoots were right next to each other. Finally he spoke again.

"Then if you pay for it, Marta, it's not a scholarship jacket, is it? Tell your principal I will not pay the fifteen dollars."

I walked back to the house and locked myself in the bathroom for a long time. I was angry with Grandfather even though I knew he was right, and I was angry with the Board, whoever they were. Why did they have to change the rules just when it was my turn to win the jacket?

It was a very sad and withdrawn girl who dragged into the principal's office the next day. This time he did look me in the eyes.

"What did your grandfather say?"

I sat very straight in my chair.

"He said to tell you he won't pay the fifteen dollars."

The principal muttered something I couldn't understand under his breath, and walked over to the window. He stood looking out at something outside. He looked bigger than usual when he stood up; he was a tall gaunt man with gray hair, and I watched the back of his head while I waited for him to speak.

"Why?" he finally asked. "Your grandfather has the money. Doesn't he own a small bean farm?"

I looked at him, forcing my eyes to stay dry. "He said if I had to pay for it, then it wouldn't be a scholarship jacket," I said and stood up to leave. "I guess you'll just have to give it to Joann." I hadn't meant to say that; it had just slipped out. I was almost to the door when he stopped me.

"Martha — wait."

I turned and looked at him, waiting. What did he want now? I could feel my heart pounding. Something bitter and vile tasting was coming up in my mouth; I was afraid I was going to be sick. I didn't need any sympathy speeches. He sighed loudly and went back to his big desk. He looked at me, biting his lip, as if thinking.

"Okay. We'll make an exception in your case. I'll tell the Board, you'll get your jacket."

I could hardly believe it. I spoke in a trembling rush. "Oh, thank you, sir!" Suddenly I felt great. I didn't know about adrenaline in those days, but I knew something was pumping through me, making me feel as tall as the sky. I wanted to yell, jump, run the mile, do something. I ran out so I could cry in the hall where there was no one to see me. At the end of the day, Mr. Schmidt winked at me and said, "I hear you're getting a scholarship jacket this year."

His face looked as happy and innocent as a baby's, but I knew better. Without answering I gave him a quick hug and ran to the bus. I cried on the walk home again, but this time because I was so happy. I couldn't wait to tell Grandpa and ran straight to the field. I joined him in the row where he was working and without saying anything I crouched down and started pulling up the weeds with my hands. Grandpa worked alongside me for a few minutes, but he didn't ask what happened. After I had a little pile of weeds between the rows, I stood up and faced him.

"The principal said he's making an exception for me, Grandpa, and I'm getting the jacket after all. That's after I told him what you said."

Grandpa didn't say anything, he just gave me a pat on the shoulder and a smile. He pulled out the crumpled red handkerchief that he always carried in his back pocket and wiped the sweat off his forehead.

"Better go see if your grandmother needs any help with supper."

I gave him a big grin. He didn't fool me. I skipped and ran back to the house whistling some silly tune.

About This Book

"The Scholarship Jacket" is one of the stories found in *Growing Up Chicana/o*. In this anthology, twenty Chicana/o writers write about the joys and pains of growing up Mexican American. By writing about growing up, these writers explore their search for identity. By reading this book, you have an opportunity to observe how these writers see themselves and how they feel about their world.

About The Illustrator

While growing up in El Paso, Texas, **Michael Steirnagle** played basketball and baseball when he wasn't spending a lot of time in his room drawing and painting. Michael used to draw on his school desks and then erase his work before class ended. One time he forgot and his teacher told him never to do it again. "But I could tell she really liked the drawing," he says.

Pockets
Full of Ideas

Write a Poem

In the Bean Field

Carefully read aloud the section about Martha's grandfather in the bean field. How is the field like his family? How are the small shoots like the children? Use your own ideas about farming and families to make more comparisons. Write a short poem about the grandfather in the bean field that also says something about raising children.

Pick Three Lines

Beginning, Middle, and End

Reread the story and choose three sentences that you think are the most important ones: one from the beginning, one from the middle, and one from the end. Why did you make these choices? What does each sentence show? Share your choices with another reader.

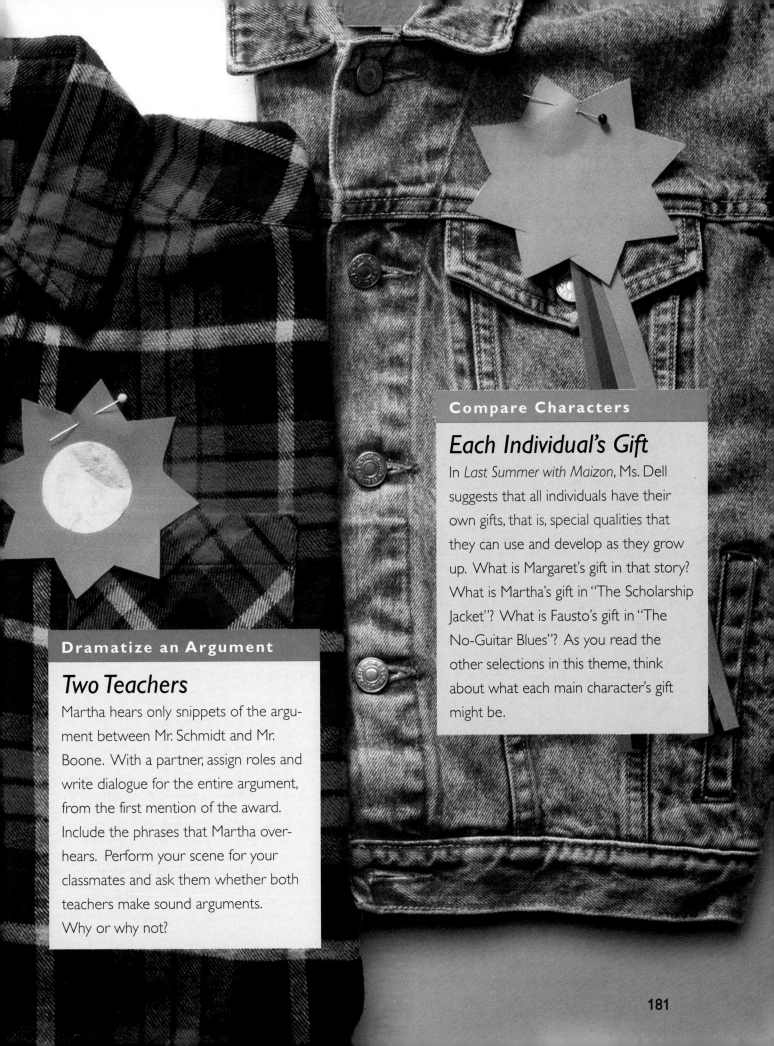

Each Individual's Gift

In *Last Summer with Maizon*, Ms. Dell suggests that all individuals have their own gifts, that is, special qualities that they can use and develop as they grow up. What is Margaret's gift in that story? What is Martha's gift in "The Scholarship Jacket"? What is Fausto's gift in "The No-Guitar Blues"? As you read the other selections in this theme, think about what each main character's gift might be.

Two Teachers

Martha hears only snippets of the argument between Mr. Schmidt and Mr. Boone. With a partner, assign roles and write dialogue for the entire argument, from the first mention of the award. Include the phrases that Martha overhears. Perform your scene for your classmates and ask them whether both teachers make sound arguments. Why or why not?

181

INDERIA THE MAGNIFICENT

A Story by Tara Bonaparte

Have you ever felt unsure of yourself?
In Tara's story, a young girl learns
to speak up and be proud
of herself.

Inderia the Magnificent

Stupid. Ugly. Untalented. Those were the names that Inderia had been called all day. As she sat in math class — smatt! — something hit her on the back of her head. She touched her head and felt a wet and soggy spitball.

She turned around and saw Tommy the bully laughing at her. "What are you looking at?" he said.

"Nothing," Inderia mumbled.

Mrs. Westmajor, the teacher, stood in front of the room. "Everyone, be quiet," she said. "Time for our math review. Tommy, how much is eleven and twenty-two?"

"Forty," he answered.

"Wrong. You had better stop talking and pay attention. Inderia, do you know the answer?"

"Yes, I do. The answer is thirty-three."

Just then Inderia heard someone call her a nerd. She was glad when the bell rang.

Inderia walked home alone, with no friends to walk with. It was late fall and the sky was smoky gray and the colorful leaves had fallen off the trees, making them look cold and naked.

Inderia saw her house and zipped up her coat because she didn't want her mother to know that her coat had been open.

As Inderia walked into her house, she heard her sister, Tammy, and her father having the same argument that they had every day.

"You can't be a dancer. You're just a high school kid. And anyway, it's not a good life for a young lady. You can't dance and that's final!"

"Fine, Dad, crush my dreams!" Tammy yelled and ran up the stairs, crying.

Later, Inderia went upstairs to find her father. She found him talking to Tammy, who wasn't crying anymore.

"Dad, I really need to talk to you. It's very important," Inderia said.

"Inderia, I'm talking to your sister. You'll just have to wait until I'm finished."

Inderia turned around and walked slowly to her room. She sat at her desk and opened her diary.

Dear Diary,

It seems like everyone is putting me off. My mother, my father, and I'm not going to even mention my sister because we don't get along as it is. Tommy the bully hit me in the back of the head with a spitball. If I wasn't so shy, I would have said something. I'm a nerd. Everyone thinks so. In school someone said, "Inderia's a nerd." I'm even starting to think that my mother and father think I'm a nerd. I've been in the same school for four months, and I haven't made one friend. Well, 'bye 'till tomorrow.

As soon as Inderia put down her diary, her parents called her. She went in their room. "Did you want to talk to me?" her father asked.

"What I want to say — it's hard to say, but do you love me anymore?"

"Of course we love you. We're your parents." Her father smiled at her.

Inderia felt like crying. "Well, why does the person who doesn't behave get the most attention, and the person who does the best gets no attention?" Inderia asked with a hurt look in her eyes.

Inderia's parents looked at each other. "Oh, Inderia, don't feel that way," her mother said. "Tammy has a lot of problems."

Her father patted her face. "How's school going?"

She stared at her shoes. "Not so good. People tease me."

Her father lifted her chin. "Tomorrow, I want you to go in that school with your head held high. I don't want you to let anyone bother you."

"We love you, Inderia," her mother said. "Come on and help me cook dinner."

Inderia walked into school the next day with her head held high. When people called her a nerd and when Tommy hit her in the back of her head with a spitball, she thought about what her father said and didn't let it bother her.

But then three o'clock came, and Inderia saw Tommy picking on a smaller boy.

"Stop, Tommy. Why do you always pick on little kids? Why are you such a bully?" demanded Inderia.

Tommy was so shocked by the new Inderia that he forgot to bully her. "The reason I act like a bully is that if I don't, people will pick on me like they pick on you," Tommy answered.

"Nobody deserves to be picked on, Tommy."

"I don't have any friends, anyway," Tommy grumbled.

Inderia smiled. "I'll be your friend, Tommy."

As Tommy and Inderia walked down the hall together, people were amazed. She'd stood up to Tommy the bully and made him a friend.

People asked Inderia to be in the most popular clubs. She turned them all down. Nobody calls Inderia stupid, ugly, and untalented anymore. Now they call her Inderia the Magnificent.

Tara Bonaparte

Charles Richard Drew Intermediate School 148
Bronx, New York

When she wrote this story in the sixth grade, Tara said that she "wanted young people like myself to see what you could do by just being yourself and being proud of yourself."

Tara likes to run track, swim, and play football, kickball, and basketball. Tara believes that you can "change the world if you put your mind to it" and plans on being a teacher, a writer, or a doctor someday.

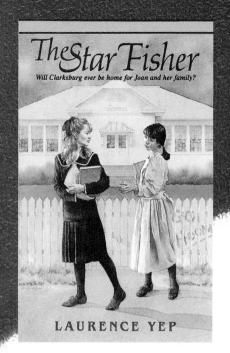

The Star Fisher
Will Clarksburg ever be home for Joan and her family?

LAURENCE YEP

MEET LAURENCE YEP

The Star Fisher is based on the life of Laurence Yep's grandmother, who really did grow up in the only Chinese American family in a small West Virginia town. Yep's grandmother was a brave and stubborn woman, who both held on to her Chinese culture and adapted to the new customs around her. "My grandmother not only learned how to speak English but how to cook and bake American dishes. Though it may sound odd nowadays, back then my grandmother's specialty was apple pies. . . . Even in her later years, my grandmother displayed a remarkable adaptability. She listened equally to traditional Chinese music and to American rock-and-roll."

MEET THE ILLUSTRATOR

Born in Brunei, Malaysia, **Simon Ng** immigrated to Canada when he was eight. Simon grew up playing street and ice hockey, a change from the beaches of Malaysia. His first "commissioned" piece of art was a painting of a mongoose on a glass jar to raise funds for a zoo. In his spare time Simon enjoys in-line skating, computers, and music.

The Star Fisher

by Laurence Yep

Fifteen-year-old Joan Lee and her
Chinese American family have opened
a laundry in a West Virginia town in
1927, and they feel out of place. Trying
to act more "American," Joan's mother
takes baking lessons from a kind neighbor and even volunteers a pie for
a church fundraiser. Joan (the
narrator), Bobby, and Emily are
worried that their mother will
humiliate the family with an
awful-tasting pie. Can Bernice,
Joan's only friend, help save
the pie social from becoming
a disaster despite the efforts of
their snobby classmate Ann?

The next day in school a new thought occurred to me that made me feel even worse: What if Ann belonged to the Reverend Bobson's congregation? Things were bad enough without giving her more ammunition. In the back of my mind, I could already hear her comments about our clumsy attempt to ape American ways.

Sometimes Bobby could get Mama to stop doing things that neither I nor Emily could. So even if I'd had a real lunch, I couldn't have let Bernice sit with us. Unfortunately — ever the optimist — she followed me out to the fence. *"It's family matters still,"* I tried to explain.

At first Bernice looked as if I had hit her in the stomach; but then her old habits came to her rescue, helping her hide her disappointment behind a polite mask. *"If you say so."*

That made me feel awful because while Ann had been Ann and her friends had been just as stuck up as ever, Bernice had made up for a lot of it. I watched her walk away proudly with an erect posture that Mama would be pleased with. Turning to the fence, I called loudly to Emily and Bobby, who reluctantly broke off their games and came to eat with me.

Quickly I told them of my new fears as I opened my lunch bag. "We're different enough without calling attention to it."

Bobby had spread his open at about the same time. "Oh, no," he groaned.

"What's the matter?" Emily asked; but when she looked into hers, she let out a little moan, too. "Apple pie."

Somehow Mama had snuck parts of last night's experiments into our lunches. Resolutely I took out my sandwich. "Throw it away later," I said.

Both Bobby and Emily chewed at their sandwiches thoughtfully, no doubt worrying about what their newfound friends might say, and occasionally glancing at the sandwich bags with their deadly contents.

"I'm open to suggestions," I said.

Bobby turned his sandwich around and around in his hand as if studying it from all angles. "You know Mama. Once she gets a notion in her head, it's like trying to stop an avalanche."

Emily made a face at her lunch bag. "We could drop her pie on the way to the social."

We considered and scrapped several plans during lunchtime, having to adjourn at the bell without reaching any solution except for Emily's suggestion. As I dumped my piece of pie into a trash can, I just hoped it wouldn't come to that.

Feeling guilty, I made sure after school to locate Bernice so I could walk with her. Outside, a worried Bobby and Emily were waiting for me. When I arched my eyebrows in silent hope, both of them shook their heads.

I let Bernice do most of the talking as we headed for home, my mind only half on what she said. Though she'd had more adventures than most of our class-mates, she was reluctant to talk about them. Instead, she wanted to talk about the books and magazines she'd read. She was a ferocious reader. I gather that the local library had a hard time keeping up with her appetite. Bernice studied the middle class like a spy studying the strange customs of a tribe because she was determined to pass herself off as one of them.

As we paused beside our laundry, ready to separate, she caught me by surprise when she asked, *"Would you like to study at the library tonight?"*

Without thinking, I shook my head apologetically. *"I wish I could, but I might have to help my mother get ready for a pie social."*

To my discomfort, Bernice said wistfully, *"Oh? I love pie."*

It was bad enough to be humiliated in front of strangers, let alone my new friend. Even if she was theater people, she was still American. Would the disaster at the pie social make her think I was too foreign?

Seeing me hesitate, the sensitive Bernice misunderstood. *"Perhaps, though, I should not eat so many sweets."*

What could I do? I was trapped. If I didn't invite her, I'd hurt her feelings twice in the same day and perhaps lose her as a friend; but if I did, I was sure I would surely go down in her estimation. With a sad shrug, I said, *"No, of course you should come. It's at the Reverend Bobson's."*

It was Bernice's turn to hesitate. *"I didn't realize it was going to be at a church."*

"I don't think you have to belong to his congregation to go," I explained. *"We don't."* In actual fact, I hoped that was the reason that would prevent Bernice from going.

There were times when Bernice sounded as if she had just read an etiquette book. *"My sister and I shall be looking forward to it,"* she said gravely.

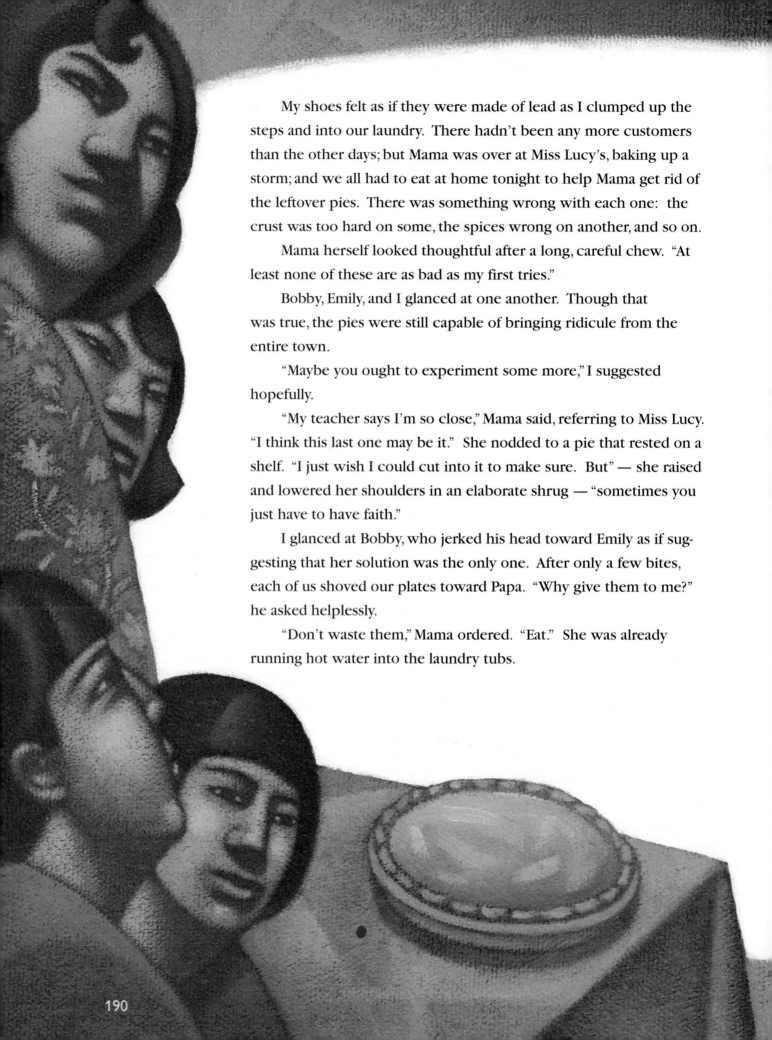

My shoes felt as if they were made of lead as I clumped up the steps and into our laundry. There hadn't been any more customers than the other days; but Mama was over at Miss Lucy's, baking up a storm; and we all had to eat at home tonight to help Mama get rid of the leftover pies. There was something wrong with each one: the crust was too hard on some, the spices wrong on another, and so on.

Mama herself looked thoughtful after a long, careful chew. "At least none of these are as bad as my first tries."

Bobby, Emily, and I glanced at one another. Though that was true, the pies were still capable of bringing ridicule from the entire town.

"Maybe you ought to experiment some more," I suggested hopefully.

"My teacher says I'm so close," Mama said, referring to Miss Lucy. "I think this last one may be it." She nodded to a pie that rested on a shelf. "I just wish I could cut into it to make sure. But" — she raised and lowered her shoulders in an elaborate shrug — "sometimes you just have to have faith."

I glanced at Bobby, who jerked his head toward Emily as if suggesting that her solution was the only one. After only a few bites, each of us shoved our plates toward Papa. "Why give them to me?" he asked helplessly.

"Don't waste them," Mama ordered. "Eat." She was already running hot water into the laundry tubs.

It seemed funny that the only things that got washed in the washroom so far were our clothes and us. The hot water only filled a few inches in the great tubs, and we shivered as we took quick sponge baths. Mama had hung sheets up over the windows for privacy. As I got dressed in my best clothes, Emily whispered to me, "You know what you have to do."

I eyed her. "Why me? Why not you or Bobby?"

"Because," she argued, "you're the only one she'd trust."

"So," I complained, "I'll be the only one who can betray that trust."

"You know I'm right," Emily insisted.

When everyone was clean and dressed, we gathered again in the kitchen. After a critical inspection and minute adjustments, Mama finally gave us her approval.

Taking a breath, I turned toward the shelf and started to stretch out my arms. "I'll carry it for you, Mama."

To my dismay, Mama elbowed me out of the way. "And have you take credit for my newest baby?"

As Mama lifted the pie lovingly from the shelf, I turned to the others and spread out my arms helplessly. Cradling the pie tin's rim against her stomach, Mama shooed us out into the rear courtyard where Miss Lucy was already waiting.

The church was a big brick building with a tall steeple and white trim. Its bell could have been heard across the whole valley. The church itself was dark, but there were stairs leading down in the basement; and light spilled from the open door like a warm, golden welcome mat. People were already streaming into the basement, their voices high with excitement; and loud, cheerful laughter boomed off the basement's low ceiling.

191

It was a large room with tables set up at one end and chairs lining the walls. There was a woman with almost silver-blue hair piled up on her head who sniffed when she saw us enter, but Miss Lucy ushered us right past her to the table where the pies were. Bobby immediately spotted two of his classmates and headed off into a corner with them. Emily met some girls she knew and darted away through the crowd as nimbly as a fish in the sea. I cringed inwardly when my worst fears proved true and I saw Ann with a pie. Havana was there, too, along with Henrietta and Florie, trailing her like two cabooses after the locomotive. However, I didn't see Bernice at all, so perhaps the disaster would not be as complete as it could have been.

I followed Miss Lucy and my parents — feeling like some odd pet that they were towing along. Miss Lucy seemed to know everyone, and she introduced us to each of them. But that only reminded me of my own isolation, so that I felt even uglier and lonelier. By the time the auction started, my head swam with names.

The Reverend Bobson stood behind the center table, tapping a little wooden hammer against the surface. Instantly the crowd grew silent.

"Now," he intoned solemnly, "we have a pie by our foremost baker." He pointed his hammer at Miss Lucy. "I know Old Jim there has been waiting all week for this." He swung his hammer toward a cheerful man with a walrus mustache.

"You bet," Jim agreed. "Fifty cents."

The Reverend waggled his hammer. "Shame on you, Jim. Trying to steal a pie like this. And in church, too. We're going to keep an eye on that bank of yours." The Reverend looked around the room. "Are you folks going to let him get away with that?"

It was corny, but everyone laughed, including the Reverend. It was a shared joke, and it was for charity. By the time he was finished, the Reverend had driven the price up to three dollars. (Jim got the pie.)

Papa leaned over toward Miss Lucy. *"You should open bake store."*

Miss Lucy tried to be modest. *"It's all for charity."* But no one else seemed surprised at the high price. Apparently, her pies always did well at the socials.

The Reverend Bobson sold several more pies — sometimes teasing, sometimes joking, but always driving the price up and up. Though when he held up Ann's pie, the Reverend didn't have to worry about driving up the price because Jim put up his hand right away. "Five dollars for that magnificent pie!"

"Oh, Daddy," Ann scolded from across the room, "give someone else a chance."

As the whole congregation burst into laughter, Ann's father sheepishly lowered his hand; but the original bid was too steep for anyone else, so he got Ann's pie — and he wound up buying two more pies.

Then the Reverend held up Mama's pie. *"And now we have an apple pie baked by our newest neighbor, Mrs. Lee."* He tapped his hammer. *"Who'll make a bid?"*

No one, not even Mr. Wood, put up a hand or said anything. To our left, I heard someone titter. I thought it sounded like Ann or one of her friends; but when I started to twist around, Mama grabbed my arm and gave me a warning pinch. "Be still."

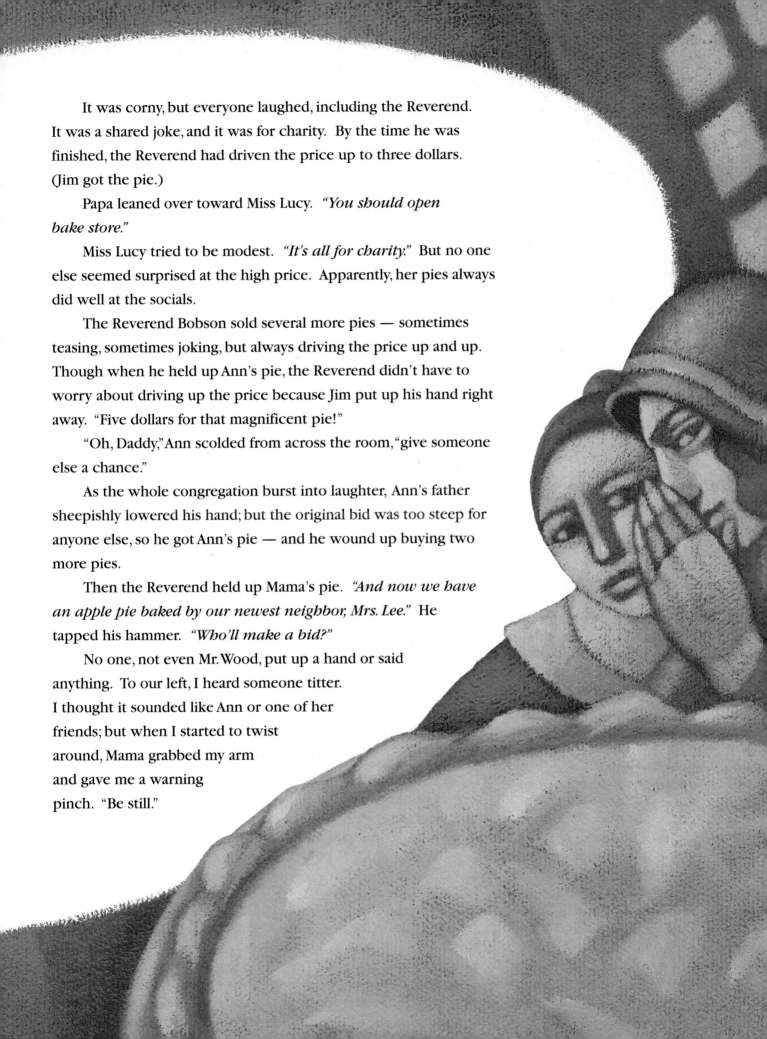

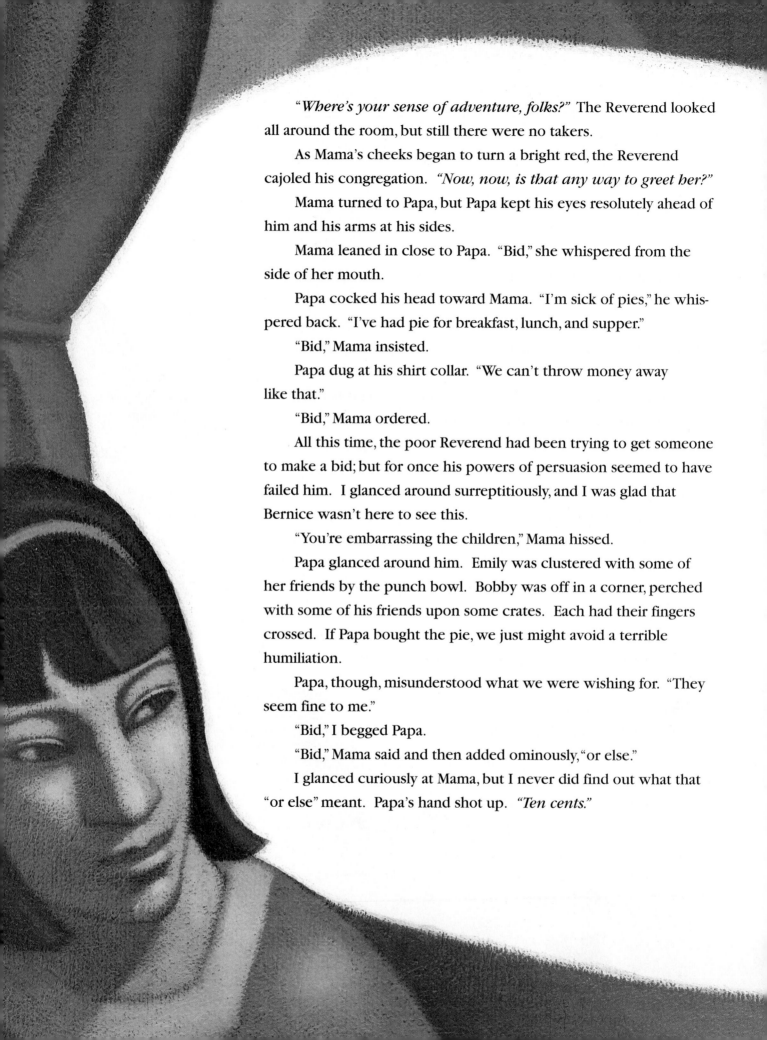

"*Where's your sense of adventure, folks?*" The Reverend looked all around the room, but still there were no takers.

As Mama's cheeks began to turn a bright red, the Reverend cajoled his congregation. "*Now, now, is that any way to greet her?*"

Mama turned to Papa, but Papa kept his eyes resolutely ahead of him and his arms at his sides.

Mama leaned in close to Papa. "Bid," she whispered from the side of her mouth.

Papa cocked his head toward Mama. "I'm sick of pies," he whispered back. "I've had pie for breakfast, lunch, and supper."

"Bid," Mama insisted.

Papa dug at his shirt collar. "We can't throw money away like that."

"Bid," Mama ordered.

All this time, the poor Reverend had been trying to get someone to make a bid; but for once his powers of persuasion seemed to have failed him. I glanced around surreptitiously, and I was glad that Bernice wasn't here to see this.

"You're embarrassing the children," Mama hissed.

Papa glanced around him. Emily was clustered with some of her friends by the punch bowl. Bobby was off in a corner, perched with some of his friends upon some crates. Each had their fingers crossed. If Papa bought the pie, we just might avoid a terrible humiliation.

Papa, though, misunderstood what we were wishing for. "They seem fine to me."

"Bid," I begged Papa.

"Bid," Mama said and then added ominously, "or else."

I glanced curiously at Mama, but I never did find out what that "or else" meant. Papa's hand shot up. "*Ten cents.*"

The Reverend Bobson instantly pounced on the bid. *"I bet Mr. Lee knows something. Who'll make it twenty-five cents?"*

Miss Lucy started to put up her hand, but Mama stopped her and shook her head. Having Papa bid was one thing — that wasn't charity — allowing her new friend to bid was another.

"Twenty-five? Twenty-five?" the Reverend asked hopefully. But when no one else put up a hand, the Reverend did a very kind thing — considering his own experience of Mama's pies. Putting down his hammer, he dug into his own pocket and counted his change. *"Well, I'll take my own advice. I'll put up twenty-five cents out of my own pocket."*

I started to slump in my chair, but Mama hissed, "Sit up straight."

Picking up his gavel again, the Reverend tried to coax some more bids and seemed disappointed when his own ploy was unsuccessful. Rapping the table, he solemnly intoned, *"Sold."* Setting Mama's pie aside, he went on to the next one.

When the auctioning was all done, people came up to pay for their pies. Taking Emily's hand, a girl who must have been her friend, Janey, pulled her toward Mr. Wood; and over in the corner, Bobby was following his friends forward to join the clumps of children hovering near Mr. Wood as he stood in line. As it turned out, his four pies weren't for him. After he had paid for them, he shared the pies with the children around him. They clamored for Miss Lucy's first; and after that, I kept hoping that Ann's pie would make people sick; but all of Mr. Wood's selections were wolfed down.

Soon Bobby's mouth was smeared with streaks of blue and purple — though he must have been sick of pie by now, he'd had nothing for supper. I saw Ann there, too, with a face just as messy as Bobby's. However, so far no one had tried Mama's pie.

Mama gave me a worried glance and nudged me. "Go on," she urged and pointed toward the mob of children around Mr. Wood.

I looked around, grateful that as yet Bernice had not shown up. I might just escape with only a partial embarrassment if we could leave soon. "No, thank you. Can we go home now?"

Mama, however, misunderstood and gave me one of her patented nudges. "You have to keep trying to make friends."

I stayed right where I was, ignoring the digging elbow as I had learned to do. "I will. It's just that I've had enough excitement for one night. Can we leave?"

Concerned, Papa put a hand to my forehead. "Now, Mama, maybe she ate something that didn't agree with her."

He'd forgotten, though, what we'd been eating all that day. Mama fairly bristled. "Are you suggesting that there was something wrong with my pies?"

Just then Bernice and Josephine stepped into the doorway, both of them dressed in their Sunday best. Holding hands, they entered the basement, looking around. They saw us just about when the Reverend Bobson did. I cringed as they all began to converge on us at the same time.

"We've been here long enough, don't you think?" I asked Papa desperately.

Mama, however, folded her arms, as immovable as a mountain until someone tried her pie. "We just got here."

The Reverend Bobson reached us first, presenting the pie to Papa with both hands. *"Mr. Lee, my conscience wouldn't let me rest unless I let you have your wife's pie."*

Before I could breathe a sigh of relief, Bernice and her sister joined us, smiling a silent hello. I tried to smile back at them bravely. Inside, I was praying that we could take the pie and escape home.

Unfortunately, Miss Lucy took a teacher's pride in her pupil and was just as determined as Mama to have the pie eaten in public. *"You ought to try a piece first, Reverend,"* she suggested.

The Reverend tried to pat his stomach with his free hand. *"Well, I've had so much pie to eat that . . ."*

Miss Lucy wasn't about to let him off the hook that easily. *"It's really one of Mrs. Lee's best."*

"All the more reason not to deprive Mr. Lee," the Reverend said meekly.

Miss Lucy folded her hands in front of her in her best school-teacherish fashion. *"No,"* she said firmly, *"you bought it. You should have at least one piece. Waste not, want not."*

The Reverend held up a hand anxiously. *"Really, no, I couldn't."*

Though Miss Lucy looked at him reproachfully, the Reverend ignored her. But just when I thought we were going to emerge from the social with some dignity, Bernice cleared her throat politely. *"May I have a slice?"* she asked in a small voice.

Everyone turned around at about the same time to stare at her and her sister, and the Reverend Bobson blinked as he tried to place them.

I thought I understood why she had asked and tried to warn her off. *"Don't feel obligated."*

Bernice gave me a small, puzzled look but persisted according to her notion of good manners. *"But I am famished."*

At that moment, the woman with silver-blue hair bustled over. *"Of all the nerve,"* she said. *"Get out."* I stared at her in shock, thinking that she meant us; but she bulled right past me and waved her hands at Bernice and her sister. *"You don't belong with respectable folk."*

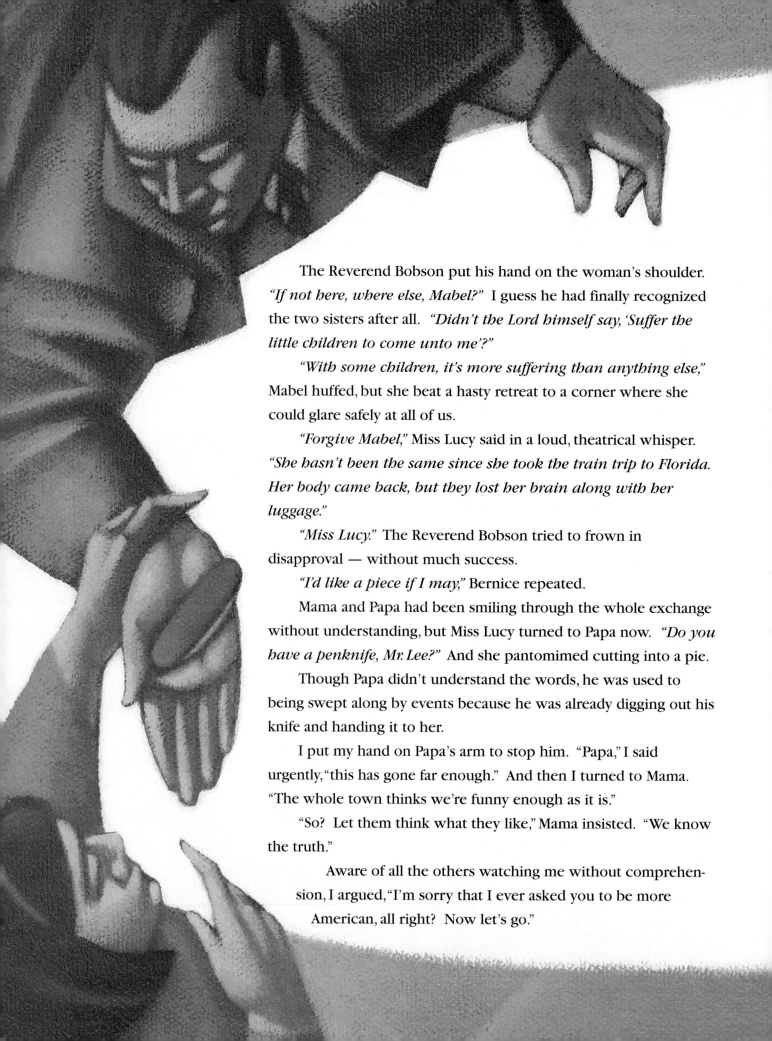

The Reverend Bobson put his hand on the woman's shoulder. *"If not here, where else, Mabel?"* I guess he had finally recognized the two sisters after all. *"Didn't the Lord himself say, 'Suffer the little children to come unto me'?"*

"With some children, it's more suffering than anything else," Mabel huffed, but she beat a hasty retreat to a corner where she could glare safely at all of us.

"Forgive Mabel," Miss Lucy said in a loud, theatrical whisper. *"She hasn't been the same since she took the train trip to Florida. Her body came back, but they lost her brain along with her luggage."*

"Miss Lucy." The Reverend Bobson tried to frown in disapproval — without much success.

"I'd like a piece if I may," Bernice repeated.

Mama and Papa had been smiling through the whole exchange without understanding, but Miss Lucy turned to Papa now. *"Do you have a penknife, Mr. Lee?"* And she pantomimed cutting into a pie.

Though Papa didn't understand the words, he was used to being swept along by events because he was already digging out his knife and handing it to her.

I put my hand on Papa's arm to stop him. "Papa," I said urgently, "this has gone far enough." And then I turned to Mama. "The whole town thinks we're funny enough as it is."

"So? Let them think what they like," Mama insisted. "We know the truth."

Aware of all the others watching me without comprehension, I argued, "I'm sorry that I ever asked you to be more American, all right? Now let's go."

Mama looked up at me challengingly. "You're a Lee. You're never going to be like the others. You can't let their laughter rule your life." And from the way she studied me, I felt just like a frayed skirt that Mama was trying to decide whether to throw out or to save.

And I found myself wondering, What if the star fisher's daughter had wanted to be like the others? She would never have flown. Impulsively I reached down and took the knife from Papa and handed it to Miss Lucy.

She took it with a polite nod and snapped out the blade. *"Let's make sure you get a nice big piece."*

Anxiously I watched Miss Lucy cut a slice of pie and put it on Bernice's open palm. Half of me realized just how terrible it was to be ashamed of Mama, but the other half — a shriller half — regretted letting Miss Lucy cut the pie.

Bernice stared around the little circle and then looked down at her dress. *"Why is everyone staring? Is there a stain on me?"*

I tried to shake my head in warning to Bernice, but Mama caught me. *"Eat,"* Mama insisted.

I held my breath, waiting for Bernice to spit it out; but when she kept on nibbling unconcernedly at her pie, Mama patted her free arm. *"Good girl, good girl,"* she murmured gratefully. And, of course, Josephine had to have a slice, too, so that Mama beamed a grateful smile at both of them. "And," Mama observed benevolently, "what good posture they both have."

With a glance at the pair who were eating in blissful ignorance, the Reverend gave a little cough. *"You know, Miss Lucy, maybe I'll try a slice after all."*

When Miss Lucy had given him one, he nodded to Mama and took a bite, chewed, paused, chewed some more; and then without saying anything more he wolfed down the rest of the piece.

"Well," he said, shaking the crumbs from his hand, *"that was the best quarter I ever spent."* He called to a passing man with sideburns like copper wire, *"Harve, try some of this. It's almost as good as Miss Lucy's."*

Miss Lucy cut the pie into slices; and when Harve tried a bite, he nodded his head approvingly. *"Not bad, Mrs. Lee. Not bad at all."*

As Harve ambled off, munching happily at his slice, Miss Lucy explained. *"Harve's the town barber and better at getting the news out than any newspaper."*

The Reverend waited for me to finish interpreting for my parents before he wagged his index finger at Mama. *"You're quite a joker, Mrs. Lee. What did I eat yesterday? One of your daughter's experiments?"*

As soon as I had translated for Mama, I waited to put her reply into English; but to my surprise her lips moved as she practiced her English words silently before she replied.

Guiltily I said to her, "I'm sorry for what I said, Mama. Let me help."

However, Mama held up a hand; and then with all the intensity of a tightrope walker on a slippery rope, she plunged ahead into the conversation all on her own. *"No, mine."* Mama hooked her arm through Miss Lucy's. *"Good cook. Good teacher, too."* She glanced at me as if to say, You see, I'll do it on my own. And inside, I silently applauded her courage. It was like trying to walk through a woods with only the sketchiest of maps.

A bearded man with a derby in one hand came over at that moment. His eyes darted around the room as if there wasn't much he was missing. When his glance fell on Bernice, I saw her cringe a little and begin to turn as if she wanted to sneak away; but I caught her hand and held it tight, and Bernice gave me a nervous smile.

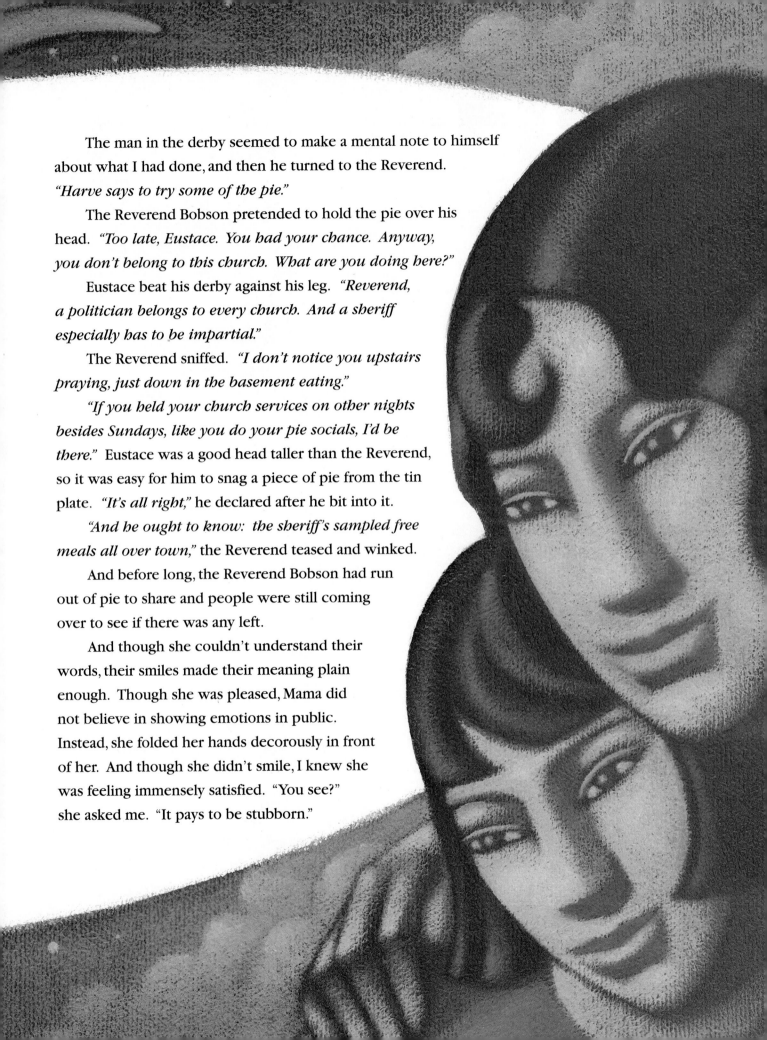

The man in the derby seemed to make a mental note to himself about what I had done, and then he turned to the Reverend. *"Harve says to try some of the pie."*

The Reverend Bobson pretended to hold the pie over his head. *"Too late, Eustace. You had your chance. Anyway, you don't belong to this church. What are you doing here?"*

Eustace beat his derby against his leg. *"Reverend, a politician belongs to every church. And a sheriff especially has to be impartial."*

The Reverend sniffed. *"I don't notice you upstairs praying, just down in the basement eating."*

"If you held your church services on other nights besides Sundays, like you do your pie socials, I'd be there." Eustace was a good head taller than the Reverend, so it was easy for him to snag a piece of pie from the tin plate. *"It's all right,"* he declared after he bit into it.

"And he ought to know: the sheriff's sampled free meals all over town," the Reverend teased and winked.

And before long, the Reverend Bobson had run out of pie to share and people were still coming over to see if there was any left.

And though she couldn't understand their words, their smiles made their meaning plain enough. Though she was pleased, Mama did not believe in showing emotions in public. Instead, she folded her hands decorously in front of her. And though she didn't smile, I knew she was feeling immensely satisfied. "You see?" she asked me. "It pays to be stubborn."

RECIPES
for Success

Pick a Phrase

Laurence Yep uses comparisons to further illustrate his characters' actions. For example, Joan sees Havana at the social "along with Henrietta and Florie, trailing her like two cabooses after the locomotive." Choose a comparison from the story and illustrate the characters and things being compared.

Are You Stubborn?

At the end, Mrs. Lee suggests that it's good to be "stubborn." What exactly does she mean? Look up the word in a dictionary. Which meaning fits Mrs. Lee's sentence? Is Mrs. Lee stubborn? Is Joan? Is it always good to be stubborn? When is it? When isn't it? Write some ideas about being stubborn in your journal.

When and Why?

Sometimes Laurence Yep uses italics for the dialogue, but not always. With a partner or small group, try to figure out when he uses this alternate type style. Once you've come up with a theory, discuss why you think he chose to write this way. Do you think it's effective? Why or why not?

Words and Images

The slice of apple pie is an important image that reflects Joan's ideas about "the real me." Draw or find a picture of a slice of apple pie. Then choose a sentence from the story to serve as a caption. Make a collage using images and captions from this and other selections in the theme. Include an image and caption that shows "the real you."

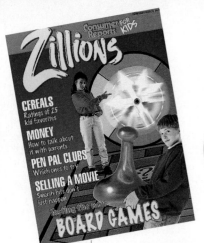

T O U G H
QUESTIONS

A Loser – NOT!

"In my school, kids judge you only by sports. I'm good at academics, but not sports. I'm considered a loser. What can I do?"

Dr. Lewit: Time is on your side. In most adult jobs, academic skills count for a lot more than sports ability. But for now, you need to lose that "loser" image so *you* don't start believing it. Sports aren't everything but they do help in making friends. Try to learn enough skills to join pickup games with regular kids (*not* the super athletes). If you can't shoot baskets, practice ball handling. Try sports that use less hand-eye coordination, such as jogging or swimming. Join activities where you use academic skills to make friends — chess club or the school paper. If you have a few friends who share your interests and do things with you, the opinions of those athletes won't seem so important.

Drifting Apart

"My best friend and I are drifting apart. It's hard to get new friends."

Dr. Lewit: Your friend may have new interests and new friends who share them. That's a main reason kids drift apart. Now you need to think about what *you* like to do and get into clubs or activities where kids do those things. That is a good way to make new friends, but you have to work at it. Ask a kid you meet at a club to do something with you, like come to your house or go to a movie. Since you already had a best friend, you have the ability to make and keep friends. Chances are you'll soon find new ones.

What a Meal!

"If you're at a friend's and you don't like what they're having for dinner, do you eat it and feel sick or not eat it and look stupid?"

Dr. Lewit: There's a way out that won't make you sick or look stupid — explain politely how you feel. If you're offered food you don't like, say, "I don't care for that, thank you." If you're urged to try it, say, "Gee, no thanks. I don't really want to." Eat other parts of the meal you do like. As you grow older, you may want to try new foods. If you're not ready yet, be honest and polite about it. Things should work out.

Who's Popular?

"What makes popular kids popular? I like things they like, but I'm not popular. Why?"

Dr. Lewit: Kids who seem very popular are the leaders in their group. They usually have a confidence that makes others look up to them. Confidence comes from knowing you're really good at something. In the social group, that may mean being really good at knowing how to make friends and what to do with them.

You may not be skilled enough at those things to be a leader in that group. But there are other groups. The group that's important now may not be so "in" later. Pick an area where you can become skilled, like music, sports, or computers. Get good at it. The confidence you develop may give you a leadership role in that group. Once you have confidence, it will carry over into other situations.

205

Anne
of Green Gables

by Lucy M. Montgomery | adapted by Jamie Turner

Plays
THE DRAMA MAGAZINE FOR YOUNG PEOPLE

MARCH • 1987

Matthew Cuthbert brings home a surprise guest.

206

CHARACTERS

Marilla Cuthbert

Matthew Cuthbert

Anne Shirley

Mrs. Rachel Lynde

Mrs. Barry

Diana Barry

Peddler

Reverend Allan

Mrs. Allan

TIME: *Early 1900's.*

SETTING: *Kitchen in Green Gables, a farm on Prince Edward Island. Dining table and chairs are center. Rocking chair, footstool, another chair and lamp are at left. Cupboard or long table across back of stage holds dishes, kitchen utensils, etc. Stove with pots on it is at right. Large window attached to back curtain shows view of trees in bloom, lake, etc. Working door is left.*

AT RISE: MARILLA CUTHBERT *sits in rocking chair, sewing.*

MARILLA (*To herself*): Where is that brother of mine? He should be back from the station by now. (*Rises and crosses to stove*) This stew will be cold if he doesn't come soon. (*After a moment,* MATTHEW CUTHBERT *and* ANNE SHIRLEY *enter,* ANNE *holding a battered suitcase.* MARILLA *turns, then gasps.*)

MARILLA (*Pointing to* ANNE): Matthew Cuthbert, who's *that*? Where's the *boy* we sent for? (*During following conversation,* ANNE *looks back and forth at* MARILLA *and* MATTHEW.)

MATTHEW: There wasn't any boy at the train station, Marilla. Just this girl.

MARILLA: But there must be a mistake. We sent word to Mrs. Spencer at the orphanage to bring us a *boy*.

MATTHEW (*Matter-of-factly*): Well, she didn't. She brought *her*, and I couldn't very well leave her at the station, mistake or not.

MARILLA (*Throwing up hands*): Well, this is a pretty state of affairs. How is a *girl* going to be able to help us with all our work on the farm?

ANNE (*With spirit*): You don't want me! You don't want me because I'm not a boy! (*Dramatically*) I might have expected it! Nobody ever did want me! I should have known all this was too good to last. Oh, what shall I do? (*Throws herself into chair, buries head in her arms and sobs loudly.*)

MARILLA (*Sharply*): Well, well, there's no need to cry about it.

ANNE (*Looking up*): Yes, there *is* need. You would cry, too, if you were an orphan and had come to a place you thought was going to be home and found they didn't want you because you're not a boy. (*Dramatically*) Oh, this is the most *tragical* thing that ever happened to me! (*More sobs*)

MATTHEW: Marilla, we'd best let her get a night's sleep. She's had a hard day.

MARILLA (*To* ANNE *a bit soothingly*): Now, now. Don't cry anymore. We're not going to turn you out of doors tonight. What's your name?

ANNE (*Wiping eyes*): Well . . . I wish my name were *Cordelia*. It's such an elegant name. But my real name is Anne — with an e on the end. A-n-n-e looks so much more distinguished than plain old A-n-n, don't you agree?

MARILLA: I don't see what difference it makes. (*Shakes head, puzzled*) Come, let's have our supper, and then you can get to bed.

ANNE: Oh, I couldn't possibly eat, thank you anyway.

MARILLA: And why not?

ANNE: Because I'm in the depths of despair. Can *you* eat when you're in the depths of despair?

MARILLA: I've never been in the depths of despair, so I can't say.

ANNE: Well, it's a very uncomfortable feeling indeed. When you try to eat, a lump comes right up in your throat and you can't swallow a thing, not even a chocolate caramel. (*Looks at pot on stove*) Everything looks extremely nice, but I still cannot eat. I hope you won't be offended.

MATTHEW: I guess she's too tired to eat, Marilla. Come on, Anne, let me show you your room. (*Exits*)

MARILLA: Good night, Anne.

ANNE (*Starting to exit*): I'm sorry, Miss Cuthbert, but I can't bear to say *good* night when I'm sure it's the very worst night I've ever had! (*Exits.* MARILLA *ladles stew from pot to bowl, sets it on table.* MATTHEW *re-enters, sits at table, and begins to eat.*)

MARILLA: Well, Matthew, this is a pretty kettle of fish! The girl will have to be sent back to the orphanage, of course.

MATTHEW (*Unhappily*): Well, yes, I suppose so.

MARILLA: You *suppose* so? Don't you *know* it?

MATTHEW (*Uneasily*): Well, she's a nice little thing, Marilla.

MARILLA (*Sharply*): Matthew Cuthbert! You don't mean to say you think we ought to keep her! We need a boy to help out on the farm. What good would she be to us?

MATTHEW (*Firmly*): We might be some good to *her*, Marilla.

MARILLA (*Crossing arms*): I can see as plain as plain that you want to let her stay.

MATTHEW: It does seem kind of a pity to send her back when she's so set on staying. (*Chuckling*) She's quite an interesting little girl, Marilla. You should have heard her talk coming home from the station.

MARILLA: Oh, she can talk, all right, but talk is . . .

MATTHEW (*Interrupting*): I can hire a boy to help out with the farm, Marilla.

MARILLA: Well, I . . . (*Exasperated*) Matthew! You're a stubborn one, for sure. (*Sighs heavily*) I can fight forever, but I may as well give in now as later. All right, Matthew. She can stay.

MATTHEW (*Smiling*): You won't regret this decision, Marilla. It will be nice to have a lively little girl on the farm.

MARILLA (*Shaking head*): Marilla Cuthbert, did you ever suppose you'd see the day when you'd be adopting an orphan girl? (*Curtain*)

Not in the depths of despair anymore, Anne welcomes the arrival of a sunny morning.

TIME: *Next morning.*

SETTING: *Same.*

AT RISE: MARILLA *is setting food on table for breakfast.* MATTHEW *is seated at table.*

MARILLA (*Calling off*): Anne! Time to be up and dressed for breakfast! (ANNE *enters.*)

ANNE: Oh, aren't mornings a wonderful thing? Though my heart is still aggrieved, I'm not in the depths of despair anymore. I'm glad it's such a sunshiny morning; it's easier to bear up under afflictions when the sun is shining, isn't it?

MARILLA (*Grumpily*): Never mind all your talk now. Let's sit down to eat. (ANNE *and* MARILLA *join* MATTHEW *at table. They start to eat.* MARILLA *puts down fork and speaks to* ANNE *in business-like tone.*) I suppose I might as well tell you that Matthew and I have decided to keep you (MATTHEW *smiles.*) — that is, if you will try to be a good little girl. (ANNE *looks disturbed.*) Why, child, whatever is the matter?

209

ANNE (*Bewildered*): I'm crying. And trembling. I can't think why. I'm as glad as glad can be. But *glad* doesn't seem the right word at all. I was glad when I saw that wild cherry tree blooming outside my window, but this — oh, Miss Cuthbert, this is something more than glad! (*Sniffs loudly, wipes eyes*)

MARILLA: Well, there's no sense in getting so worked up. I'm afraid you're too emotional for a little girl. And you must not call me Miss Cuthbert. That would make me nervous. We'll be just Marilla and Matthew.

ANNE: Oh, Miss — I mean, Marilla — I'll try ever so hard to be good — *angelically* good.

MARILLA (*Looking toward door*): Well, here comes your first opportunity. Our neighbor Mrs. Rachel Lynde is headed up the path to pay us a visit. Finish your breakfast quickly.

MATTHEW (*Standing*): I'm going out to plant the rest of my turnip seed. (*Exits right, as knock at door is heard. MARILLA rises, goes to door, and lets in MRS. RACHEL LYNDE.*)

MARILLA: Why, Rachel, you're out early this morning. (*They walk back to table.*)

MRS. LYNDE (*Sitting down with a groan*): Oh, Marilla, I'm coming down with a terrible case of the rheumatics. I can just feel myself stiffening up something fearful! (*Sighs heavily*) Well, well, life is full of suffering. (*Turns to peer over her glasses at* ANNE) Well! And who is *this*, Marilla?

MARILLA: This is Anne Shirley, Rachel. Mrs. Spencer sent her to us from the orphanage. Anne, this is Mrs. Lynde.

MRS. LYNDE: I thought you said you were getting a boy from the orphanage. She's terribly homely and skinny, Marilla. Merciful heavens, did anyone ever *see* such freckles? And hair as red as carrots!

ANNE (*Jumping to feet; angrily*): How dare you call me homely and skinny! You are a rude, impolite woman! How would you like to be told that you are fat and clumsy? You've hurt my feelings *excruciatingly*, and I shall never forgive your unkindness! Never! Never! (*Stamps foot and runs from stage, crying.* MARILLA *and* MRS. LYNDE *sit in stunned silence.*)

"Well! Did

Mrs. Lynde's remarks stir a reaction from Anne.

MRS. LYNDE: Well! Did anybody ever see such a temper? I don't envy you your job of bringing *that* up, Marilla!

MARILLA: What Anne just did was very naughty, Rachel, but I wish you hadn't called attention to her looks. (*Sighs*) I'll have to give her a good talking to.

MRS. LYNDE (*Primly*): Take my advice and do that "talking to" with a good-sized hickory switch. You'll have trouble with that child, mark my words! (*Rises and goes to the door*) Goodbye, Marilla! I'm going to look around in your garden for a few minutes before I go, if you don't mind. I want to have a word with Matthew, too. (*Exits. MARILLA turns, shakes head, and sighs.*)

MARILLA (*Calling*): Anne, come here. (ANNE *enters, head down.*) Now, aren't you ashamed of the way you spoke to Mrs. Lynde?

ANNE: She had no right to say those things.

MARILLA: And you had no right to fly into such a fury. You must ask her forgiveness.

ANNE: Oh, I can *never* do that, Marilla. (*Dramatically*) You can shut me up in a dark, damp dungeon inhabited by snakes and toads, but I *cannot* ask Mrs. Lynde to forgive me.

MARILLA (*Sternly*): Anne, disrespect in a child is a terrible thing. I'm disappointed in you. (ANNE *hangs head and is silent for a few moments.*) You did tell me that you would try to be good, didn't you?

ANNE (*Looking up*): Now that my temper has died down, I suppose I am truly sorry for speaking so to Mrs. Lynde.

MARILLA: And you will tell her so?

ANNE: Yes, Marilla. I will. (MARILLA *goes to door.*)

MARILLA (*Calling*): Rachel! Anne has something to say to you. Will you please come back in for a minute? (ANNE *is mouthing words to herself.*) What are you doing, Anne?

anybody ever see such a temper?"

ANNE: I'm imagining out what I must say to Mrs. Lynde. (MRS. LYNDE *enters, and* ANNE *approaches, falling down on her knees and extending her hands.*) Oh, Mrs. Lynde, I am *so* extremely sorry. (*In a quivering voice*) I could never express all my sorrow, no, not if I used up a whole dictionary. You must just try to *imagine* the extent of my grief. I have been dreadfully wicked and ungrateful. Oh, Mrs. Lynde, *please, please* forgive me. If you refuse, it will be a life-long sorrow to me. (MRS. LYNDE *and* MARILLA *exchange surprised glances.*)

MRS. LYNDE (*Embarrassed*): There, there, child. Get up. Of course I forgive you. I guess I was a little too harsh and outspoken.

ANNE (*Rising*): Oh, thank you, Mrs. Lynde. Your forgiveness is like a soothing ointment to my heart.

MRS. LYNDE (*Patting* ANNE *on head*): Good day, Anne. Good day, Marilla. (*Aside, to* MARILLA) She's an odd little thing, but you know, on the whole I rather like her. (*Exits. Curtain*)

"Do you think you can like me well enough to be my best friend?"

TIME: *Next day.*

SETTING: *Same.*

AT RISE: MARILLA *sweeps floor while* ANNE *dries dishes.*

MARILLA: Anne, the Barrys are coming over this morning. Mrs. Barry is going to return a skirt pattern she borrowed, and you can get acquainted with her daughter, Diana. She's about your age.

ANNE (*Dropping dish towel*): Oh, Marilla, what if she doesn't like me?

MARILLA: Now, don't get into a fluster. I guess Diana will like you well enough. Just be polite and well behaved, and don't make any of your startling speeches.

ANNE: Oh, Marilla, *you'd* be flustered too if you were going to meet a little girl who might become your best friend. I've never had a best friend in my whole life. My nerves are absolutely *frazzled* with excitement!

MARILLA: I do wish you wouldn't use such long words. It sounds funny in a little girl. (*Knock at door is heard.*) For pity's sake, calm yourself, child. (*Goes to answer door.* MRS. BARRY *and* DIANA *enter.*) Hello, Margaret. Hello Diana.

MRS. BARRY: How are you, Marilla?

MARILLA: Fine. I'd like you both to meet the little girl we've adopted. (*Gesturing*) This is Anne Shirley.

ANNE: That's "Anne" spelled with an e.

DIANA: Hello, Anne. I'm Diana.

MRS. BARRY (*Taking* ANNE's *hand*): How are you, Anne?

ANNE: I am well in body although considerably rumpled in spirit, thank you, ma'am. (*Aside, to* MARILLA) There wasn't anything startling in that, was there?

MARILLA: Anne, why don't you take Diana outside, and show her the flower garden while Mrs. Barry and I talk? (*Ladies sit down.*)

ANNE: All right, Marilla. (*Girls walk stage front, sit side by side with legs hanging over edge, looking at each other shyly.*)

MRS. BARRY (*To* MARILLA): I'm glad for the prospect of a playmate for Diana. Perhaps it will take her more out of doors. She spends too much time inside straining her eyes over books. (*Ladies continue to talk in background as focus shifts to* ANNE *and* DIANA.)

ANNE (*Fervently*): Oh, Diana, do you think . . . do you think you can like me well enough to be my best friend?

DIANA (*Laughing*): Why, I guess so. I'm glad you've come to live at Green Gables. It'll be fun to have somebody to play with.

ANNE (*Seriously*): Will you swear to be my best friend for ever and ever?

DIANA (*Gasping*): Why, it's dreadfully wicked to swear!

ANNE: Oh, no, *my* kind of swearing isn't wicked. There are two kinds, you know.

DIANA: I've heard of only one kind.

ANNE: My kind isn't wicked at all. It just means vowing and promising solemnly.

DIANA: Oh. Well, I guess it wouldn't hurt to do that. How do you do it?

ANNE: First, we stand up. (*Girls stand.*) Then we just join hands — so. (*They join hands.*) I'll repeat the oath first. (*Closes eyes*) I solemnly swear to be faithful to my best friend, Diana Barry, as long as the sun and the moon shall endure. Now you say it and put my name in.

DIANA: I solemnly swear to be faithful to my best friend, Anne Shirley, as long as the sun and moon shall endure. (*Laughs*) I can tell we're going to have lots of fun together, Anne Shirley! Will you go with me to the Sunday School picnic next week? It's going to be ever so much fun! Everyone takes a picnic basket, and we eat our lunch down by the lake and go for boat rides — and then we have *ice cream* for dessert!

ANNE: Ice cream! Oh, Diana, I would be perfectly *enraptured* if Marilla would let me go with you. I'll go ask her right now. Come on. (*Still holding hands, girls approach* MARILLA *and* MRS. BARRY.) Oh, Marilla! Diana has invited me to go to the Sunday School picnic with her next week! I've never been to a picnic, though I've dreamed of them often. Oh, and Marilla — think of it — they are going to serve *ice cream! Ice cream*, Marilla! And there will be boats on the lake and everyone will take a picnic basket — and, oh, dear Marilla, may I go, *please*, may I? I would consider my life a graveyard of buried hopes — I read that in a book once, doesn't it sound pathetic? — if I couldn't go to the picnic! *Please* say that I can go, Marilla.

MARILLA (*Shaking head and clicking tongue*): Anne, I've never seen the like for going on and on about a thing. Now, just try to control yourself. As for the picnic, I'm not likely to refuse you when all the other children are going.

ANNE (*Throwing her arms around* MARILLA): Oh, you dear, good Marilla! You are so kind to me.

MARILLA: There, there, never mind your hugging nonsense. I'll make you up a nice lunch basket when the time comes.

MRS. BARRY: Anne may ride over to the picnic with Diana if you like, and we'll bring her home, too. (*Rises*) We must be going home now, Diana. Tell Anne good-bye. Maybe you can play together tomorrow. Thank you, Marilla, for the nice visit. (BARRYS *exit.*)

ANNE: Oh, Marilla, looking forward to things is half the pleasure of them, don't you think? I do hope the weather is fine next week. I don't feel that I could endure the disappointment if anything happened to prevent me from getting to the picnic. (*Curtain*)

All of Anne's hopes rest on Marilla's permission to go.

SCENE 4

TIME: *Several days later.*

SETTING: *Same. Brooch is on floor, under chair. Loose flowers and vase are on table.*

AT RISE: ANNE *sits with patchwork in lap, daydreaming. MARILLA enters. ANNE begins stitching vigorously.*

ANNE: I've been working steadily, Marilla, but it's ever so hard when the picnic is *this very afternoon.* I keep trying to imagine what it will be like.

MARILLA (*Looking around, puzzled*): Anne, have you seen my amethyst brooch? I thought I put it right here in my pin cushion, but I can't find it anywhere.

ANNE (*Nervously*): I — I saw it last night when you were at the Ladies Aid Society. It was in the pin cushion, as you said.

MARILLA (*Sternly*): Did you touch it?

ANNE (*Uncomfortably*): Yes. I pinned it on my dress for just a minute — only to see how it would look.

MARILLA (*Angrily*): You had no business touching something that didn't belong to you, Anne. Where did you put it?

ANNE: Oh, I put it right back. I didn't have it on but a minute, and I didn't think about it being wrong at the time, but I'll never do it again. That's one good thing about me. I never do the same naughty thing twice.

MARILLA (*Sternly*): You did not put it back, or else it would be here. You've taken it and put it somewhere else, Anne. Tell me the truth at once. Did you lose it?

ANNE (*Upset*): Oh, but I *did* put it back, Marilla. I'm perfectly certain I put it back!

MARILLA (*Angrily, her voice rising*): If you had put it back, it would be here, Anne. I believe you are telling me a falsehood. In fact, I know you are.

ANNE: Oh, but, Marilla . . .

MARILLA (*Harshly*): Don't say another word unless you are prepared to tell me where the brooch is. Go to your room and stay there until you are ready to confess. (ANNE *starts to exit downcast.*)

ANNE: The picnic is this afternoon, Marilla. You *will* let me out of my room for that, won't you? I *must* go to the picnic!

"Don't say another word . . ."

MARILLA: You'll go to no picnic nor anywhere else until you've confessed, Anne Shirley. Now, *go!* (ANNE *exits*)

MATTHEW (*Entering*): Where's Anne? I wanted to show her the new geese down at the pond.

MARILLA (*Coldly*): She's in her room. The child has lost my amethyst brooch and is hiding the truth from me. She's *lied* about it, Matthew.

MATTHEW: Well now, are you certain, Marilla? Mightn't you have forgotten where you put it?

MARILLA (*Angrily*): Matthew Cuthbert, I remind you that I have kept the brooch safe for over fifty years, and I'm not likely to lose track of it now.

MATTHEW: Don't be too hasty to accuse Anne. I don't think she'd lie to you (*Exits.* MARILLA *begins to arrange flowers in vase on table as* ANNE *enters.*)

ANNE: Marilla, I'm ready to confess.

MARILLA: Well, that was mighty quick. What do you have to say, Anne?

ANNE (*Speaking quickly, as if reciting from memory*): I took the amethyst brooch, just as you said. I pinned it on my dress and then was overcome with an irresistible temptation to take it down by the Lake of Shining Waters to pretend that I was an elegant lady named Cordelia Fitzgerald. But, alas, as I was leaning over the bridge to catch its purple reflection in the water, it fell off and went down — down — down, and sank forevermore beneath the lake. Now, will you please punish me, Marilla, and have it over so that I can go to the picnic with nothing weighing on my mind?

"I've never been to a picnic, though I've

MARILLA (*Staring at* ANNE *in anger*): Anne, you must be the very wickedest girl I ever heard of to take something that wasn't yours and to lose it and then to lie about it and now to show no sign of sorrow whatever! Picnic, indeed! You'll go to no picnic! That will be your punishment, and it isn't half severe enough either for what you've done!

ANNE (*Sobbing*): Not go to the picnic! But, Marilla, that's why I confessed! Oh, Marilla, you promised! Think of the ice cream, Marilla! How can you deny me the ice cream and break my heart?

MARILLA (*Stonily*): You needn't plead, Anne. You are not going to the picnic, and that is final. (ANNE *runs to table and flings herself into a chair, sobbing and shrieking wildly.*) I believe the child is out of control. (MARILLA *walks around, wringing her hands. She suddenly catches sight of brooch under chair and picks it up with a startled cry.*) What can this mean? Here's my brooch, safe and sound! And I thought it was at the bottom of the lake! (ANNE *looks up.*) Anne, child, whatever did you mean by saying you took it and lost it?

ANNE: Well, you said you'd keep me in my room until I confessed, so I thought up an interesting confession so I could go to the picnic. But then you wouldn't let me go after all, so my confession was wasted.

MARILLA (*Trying to look stern, but finally laughing*): Anne, you do beat all! But I was wrong — I see that now. I shouldn't have doubted your word when you had never told me a lie before. Of course, you shouldn't have made up that story, but I drove you to it. So if you'll forgive me, I'll forgive you. Now, go upstairs and wash your face and get ready for the picnic.

ANNE: It isn't too late?

MARILLA: No, they'll just be getting started. You won't miss a thing — especially the ice cream. That's always last.

ANNE (*Squealing happily*): Oh, Marilla! Five minutes ago I was in the valley of woe, but now I wouldn't change places with an angel! (*Exits*)

dreamed of them often."

SCENE 5

TIME: *Next day.*
SETTING: *Same.*

AT RISE: MARILLA *is dusting furniture.*
ANNE *enters.*

ANNE: When I woke up just a while ago, Marilla, I spent a good ten minutes at my window just remembering yesterday's splendid picnic. I could hardly bear to face a plain old ordinary day after such a romantic experience. Words fail me to describe the ice cream, Marilla. I assure you it was *scrumptiously sublime.*

MARILLA: I'm glad you had a pleasant time, Anne, but you must come back down to earth. I've invited the new minister, Mr. Allan, and his wife for tea this afternoon.

ANNE (*Clasping hands*): Oh, Marilla! How divine! I think Mrs. Allan is perfectly lovely. I've watched her during sermons every Sunday since they've been here. She wears such pretty hats and has such *exquisite* dimples in her cheeks!

MARILLA: Hmph! You'd do better listening to the sermon instead of studying hats and dimples.

ANNE: Marilla, will you let me make a cake for the Allans? I'd love to do something special for them.

MARILLA: Well, I suppose you can — if you'll be very careful to measure properly and then clean up afterward.

ANNE: Oh, I will, I will — I promise! Thank you, Marilla! (ANNE *starts to measure, stir, etc. As she works, she alternately hums and talks.*) I do hope the minister and Mrs. Allan like layer cake. Diana says she has a cousin who doesn't even like ice cream. Can you *imagine*, Marilla? (*Pause*) I wonder if Mrs. Allan will ask for a second piece of cake? She's probably a dainty eater, judging from her waistline, don't you think? But then, sometimes it's hard to tell. (*Pours batter into pan*) I can eat quite a bit, and I'm awfully skinny, but Diana eats hardly anything and is ever so plump. (*Puts pan into oven*) There, now. The cake's in the oven, Marilla. Oh, I don't see how I can ever wait till this afternoon! I'm bound to *explode* before the Allans arrive.

MARILLA: Goodness, child, let's hope not. That would be quite a spectacle. Now, why don't you go outdoors and run off a little of your excitement? I'll keep a close eye on your cake and take it out when it's done.

ANNE: Thank you, Marilla! (*Exits and comes out side door,* PEDDLER *comes out other side, and they meet on floor on front of stage.* MARILLA *may work in kitchen or sew during conversation.*)

PEDDLER: Hello there, miss. Would you be interested in buying some of my wares?

ANNE: Uh — well — what kinds of things do you have?

PEDDLER (*Walking around* ANNE, *looking at her hair and shaking his head*): Well, right here in my bag, miss, I have a bottle of Mr. Roberts' Magic Hair Potion

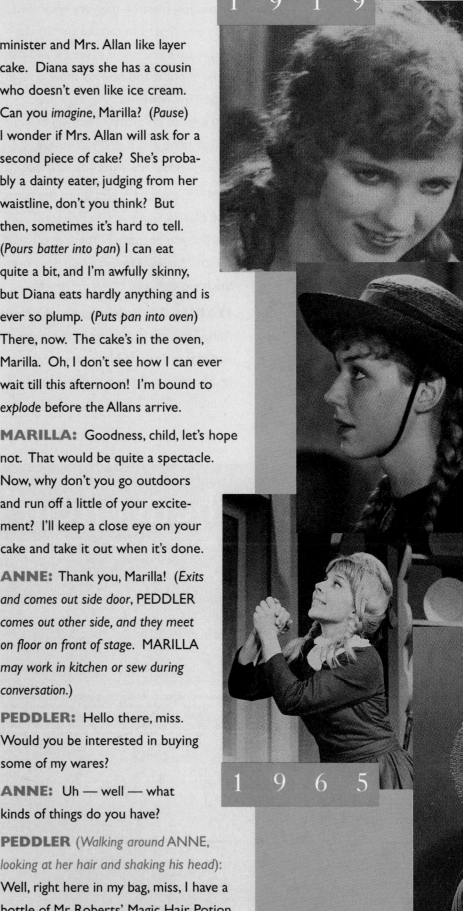

1 9 1 9

1 9 6 5

that is guaranteed to turn you into the raven-haired beauty of Prince Edward Island. (*Takes bottle from bag, holds it up*) One simple application will give your hair a glossy ebony sheen.

ANNE (*Touching her hair*): My red hair *is* a sore affliction to my soul. And I *have* always dreamed of having beautiful black hair. But I have only fifty cents. (*Fishes in pocket*)

PEDDLER: Well, now, I'll tell you what, miss. The regular price of Mr. Roberts' Magic Hair Potion is seventy-five cents, but just for today I'll give it to you for only fifty cents. (*Takes her money and gives her the bottle; exits quickly*)

1 9 3 4

1 9 9 4

1919: Mary Miles Minter in an early version of Anne of Green Gables

1934: An American production demonstrates Anne's worldwide charm.

1965: Jamie Ray on-stage in the Charlottetown Festival production on Prince Edward Island

1994: Tracy Michailidis keeps the theatrical tradition alive.

ANNE: What a kind-hearted man! (*Excited*) Now I can be the dark-haired beauty I've always wanted to be! I'll go home right now and put the magic potion on before the Allans come. With my cake and my beautiful new hair, I'm sure to impress them! (*Exits. MARILLA takes cake from oven, rearranges flowers in vase, straightens napkins at table.*)

MARILLA: Now, I must call Anne in. The Allans will be here any minute. (*Calls offstage*) It's time for tea! Anne! Anne! (MATTHEW *enters.*)

MATTHEW: I didn't see Anne outside, Marilla. (*Knock on door is heard.*)

MARILLA: Oh, dear. That must be the Allans. Now, where could Anne be? (*Goes to door.* REVEREND *and* MRS. ALLAN *enter.*) Hello, Reverend Allan. Mrs. Allan. Do come in! We're mighty glad you could come.

MRS. ALLAN: How lovely of you to invite us for tea, Marilla.

REV. ALLAN: We've been looking forward to it. (*To* MATTHEW) Hello, Matthew.

MATTHEW (*Shaking hands with* ALLANS): Welcome to our home.

MARILLA (*Gesturing to chairs*): Please have a seat. Anne will be right here to greet you.

ANNE (*Enters, wearing large, floppy hat, head down*): Here I am, Marilla.

MARILLA (*Startled*): Why, Anne, what in creation are you doing with a hat on your head?

ANNE: Uh — my head feels a little chilly, Marilla. Good day, Reverend and Mrs. Allan. It's an honor to have you come for tea. (*Curtsies with a flourish. Her hat falls off, and ANNE's hair, bright green, tumbles down.*)

MARILLA (*Stepping back; covering mouth*): Anne Shirley! What have you done to your hair?

MATTHEW (*Amused*): Well now, it looks *green*!

ANNE (*Miserably*): Oh, please don't scold me. I'm utterly wretched as it is, and scolding would only make it worse. (*Covers face with hands*) I wanted to have beautiful raven hair — the peddler promised — but . . .

MARILLA (*Sternly*): Peddler? What peddler?

MATTHEW: I saw one of those traveling peddlers around town this morning. I'll warrant he came out this way after he finished in Avonlea.

MARILLA: Anne, what did you buy from the peddler?

ANNE: Mr. Roberts' Magic Hair Potion. My hair was supposed to turn glossy black, but it turned . . . (*Holding up a strand*) green.

MARILLA (*Shaking head*): Oh, Anne, goodness only knows what's to be done with you. You can get yourself into more scrapes. It appears to me that you would run out of ideas for mischief one of these days. Now I hope you've learned . . . (MATTHEW *begins laughing quietly.*)

Matthew, what *are* you doing? (ALLANS *join in; soon everyone is laughing.*)

REV. ALLAN (*Smiling, holding hand out to* ANNE): I don't believe we've ever been greeted in such a unique fashion, Anne. We're pleased to be here.

MRS. ALLAN (*Shaking ANNE's hand*): Hello, Anne. Don't be upset. I like little girls with imagination and an adventurous spirit.

MARILLA: Well, I do hope you'll pardon us. I certainly hadn't expected to greet you in such a fashion. Anne, we'll have to try to see what we can do with your hair after tea. But for now, let's all sit down. Everything's ready. (*All sit.*) Let me serve the cake first. Anne made this all by herself.

MRS. ALLAN: My, what an accomplished girl to bake such a lovely cake!

REV. ALLAN: Yellow layer cake is my favorite, Anne. (*Everyone takes a bite at the same time. Peculiar looks cross faces; everyone begins to cough, take drinks from cups, fan faces, etc.*)

MARILLA: Anne Shirley! What did you put into that cake?

MATTHEW: Well now, it does taste a mite peculiar.

ANNE (*Forlornly*): I put in what the recipe said. Oh, it must have been that baking powder!

MARILLA: Baking powder, fiddlesticks! What flavoring did you use?

ANNE: Only vanilla.

220

MARILLA: Go and bring me the bottle of vanilla you used. (ANNE *gets up and brings back small brown bottle from cupboard.*) Mercy on us, Anne, you've gone and flavored our cake with Matthew's cough medicine! (ANNE *utters a cry of distress and runs off stage. Curtain closes. ANNE enters in front of curtain and sits down, crying dejectedly. MRS. ALLAN enters from other side and stands quietly while ANNE talks.*)

ANNE (*Crying*): Oh, I'm disgraced forever and forever. I shall never live this down, not if I live to be a hundred years old. I can never look the Allans in the face again. First my hair and then the cake — oh, I'm doomed to bounce from one tragedy to another! How can I ever tell Mrs. Allan that the cake was an innocent mistake? What if she thinks I tried to *poison* her?

MRS. ALLAN (*Stepping closer*): Oh, I doubt that she'll think that. (ANNE *looks up and rises quickly, wiping eyes.*) You mustn't cry like this, Anne. It's only a funny mistake that anybody might make.

ANNE: Oh, no, it takes me to make such a mistake, Mrs. Allan. And I so wanted to have that cake perfect for you.

MRS. ALLAN: In that case, I assure you I appreciate your kindness and thoughtfulness just as much as if it had turned out all right. Now, you mustn't cry anymore, but come down to the flower garden with me. Miss Cuthbert tells me you have a little plot all your own. I want to see it, for I love flowers. (*They begin walking across stage together.*)

ANNE: Well, I suppose there's one encouraging thing about making mistakes. There *must* be a limit to the number a person can make, and when I get to the end of them, then I'll be through with them for good. (*They exit.*)

THE END

About the Author

Lucy Maud Montgomery (1874-1942) was born and grew up on Prince Edward Island, Canada. Growing up as an only child, Maud had imaginary friends as well as real ones. Young Maud read widely and started writing at the age of nine. She became a teacher and worked on a newspaper to support her writing. In 1908, Anne of Green Gables was published. Two dozen books followed, some of them sequels to Anne of Green Gables.

Like countries, everyone has a history. It's a big part of who you are, and no one else's is like yours. It's a combination of your past and your present, likes and dislikes, good times and bad. How can you have a history?

Just ask yourself:

- When and where was I born?

- How many names do I have? What do they mean?

- Where have I lived?

- What are the ten most important things that have happened to me?

- What's my favorite food, movie, book, place, hobby, sport, color, and song?

CollEcT

To map your personal story, collect pieces of your past and your present. You might include:

PAPERS: birth certificates, letters, announcements, invitations, greeting cards, diplomas, passports, newspaper clippings, school papers, report cards

FOLKLORE: recipes, stories, customs, nicknames, special words and phrases

ARTIFACTS AND TREASURES: baby shoes, locks of hair, keys, ribbons, baby clothes, medals and awards, toys, souvenirs, coins, jewelry, books

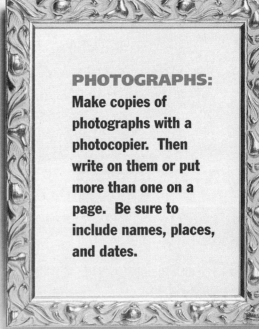

PHOTOGRAPHS: Make copies of photographs with a photocopier. Then write on them or put more than one on a page. Be sure to include names, places, and dates.

YOURSELF!

What can you do with all this stuff? If you don't keep it, it may get lost. Here are some ways to preserve and display your collection:

BOX IT OR BOOK IT.

Store things in a box, labelled, to be discovered later. Or arrange them chronologically (by date) in a scrapbook with labels.

LOOK UP THE PAST.

Many books can show you how to research, draw, or illustrate your family tree. For example, check out *The Great Ancestor Hunt* by Lila Perl or *My Backyard History Book* by David Weitzman.

LINE UP YOUR STORY.

Use photos, artifacts, or drawings to illustrate your personal time line. A time line can diagram highlights of your life from birth to the present.

TALKING HISTORY.

Use a tape recorder, video camera, or a notebook to record family stories. You don't have to be formal. Record stories told at a dinner or a celebration.

LOOK AT ME!

Display artifacts, photos, and written memories on a poster board or create a diorama.

PUBLISH A NEWSLETTER.

Relatives may love to see what you've collected. Include an ad: WANTED: MORE PHOTOS, STORIES, OR SUGGESTIONS so that your collection can grow.

WRITE AN AUTOBIOGRAPHY.

Some people turn their personal stories into full-length books. Can you find some in your library?

Your collection can be just the things in your pocket. Or it can have photographs and documents, dating back several generations. Whatever you collect, it will show someone else — and yourself — a little bit of who you are.

UNWRAPPING ANCIENT MYSTERIES

Contents

Treasures from the Past

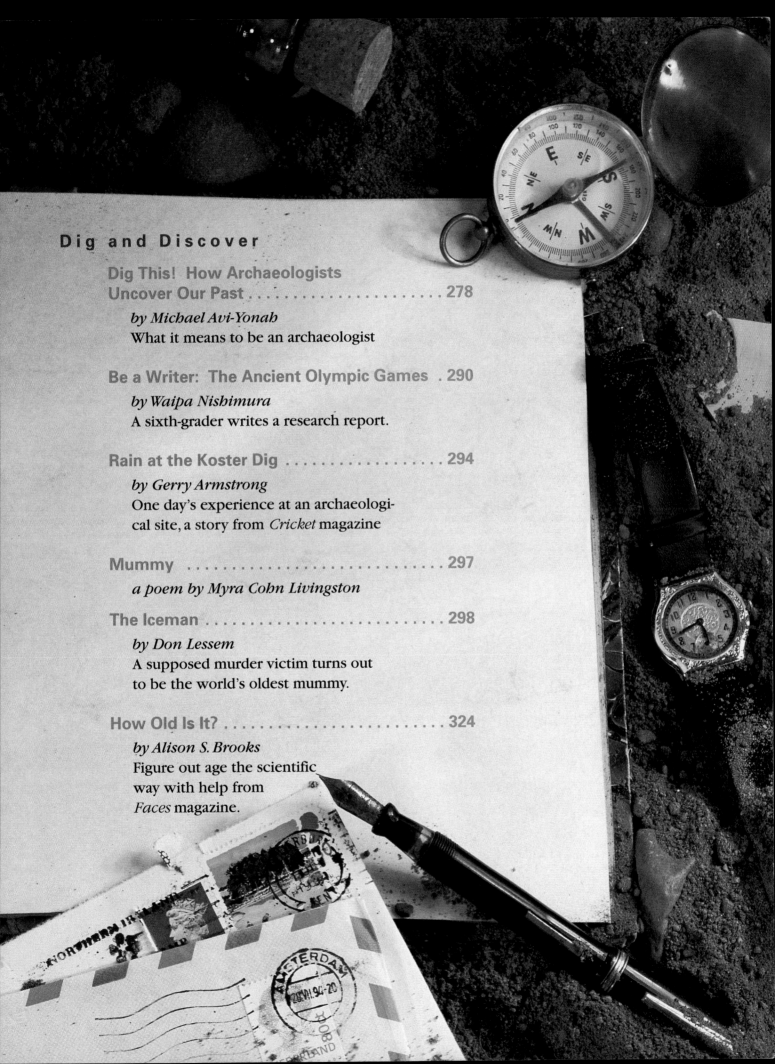

Dig and Discover

UNWRAPPING
ANCIENT
MYSTERIES

ZEKMET
THE STONE CARVER
A TALE OF ANCIENT EGYPT
BY
MARY STOLZ
ILLUSTRATED BY
DEBORAH NOURSE LATTIMORE

PAPERBACK **PLUS**

Zekmet the Stone Carver:
A Tale of Ancient Egypt
by Mary Stolz
**A poor stone mason creates the
Great Sphinx.**

In the same book . . .
More ways to understand the world of
the Great Sphinx.

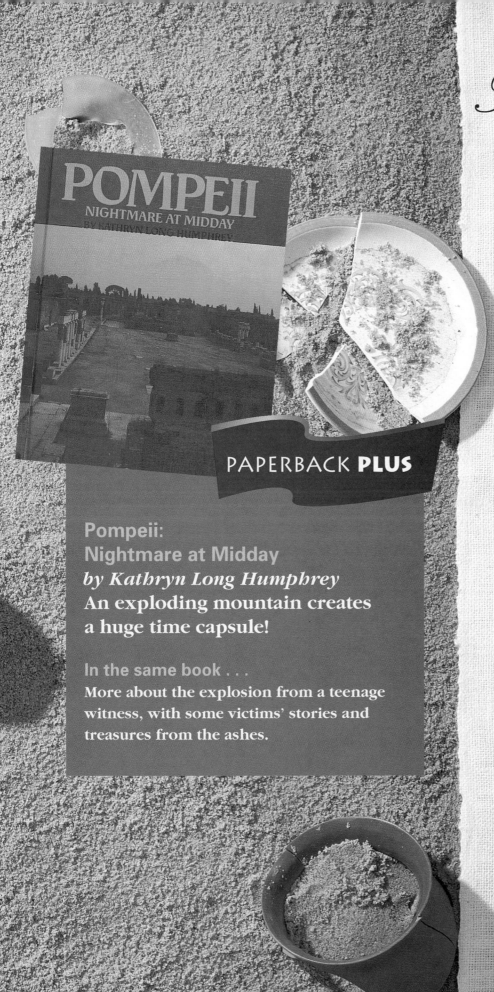

PAPERBACK **PLUS**

**Pompeii:
Nightmare at Midday**
by Kathryn Long Humphrey
**An exploding mountain creates
a huge time capsule!**

In the same book . . .
More about the explosion from a teenage
witness, with some victims' stories and
treasures from the ashes.

229

Meet Nicholas Reeves

Fourteen-year-old Nicholas Reeves was working part-time at a museum near his home, when he heard about an amazing archaeological discovery made many years earlier in Egypt. In 1922, two Englishmen, Howard Carter and Lord Carnarvon, found the undisturbed burial chamber of Egyptian king Tutankhamen, its treasures gleaming after more than 3,000 years.

Reeves became an Egyptologist, an archaeologist who specializes in ancient Egypt. In 1988, working at the British Museum, he met the grandson of Lord Carnarvon. The present Lord Carnarvon had recently

discovered ancient objects his grandfather had brought back from Egypt. When Reeves examined these treasures, he felt he was following in Howard Carter's footsteps.

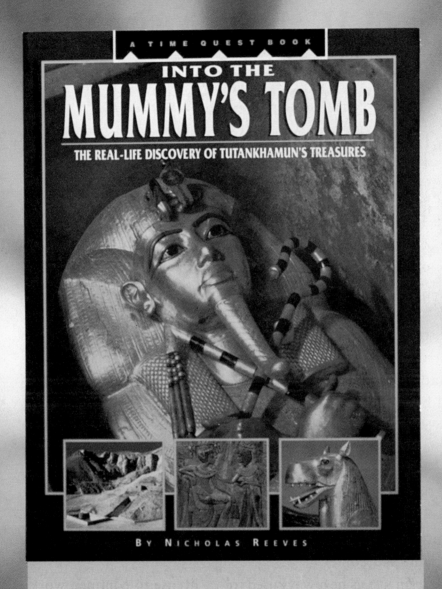

A TIME QUEST BOOK

INTO THE
MUMMY'S TOMB
THE REAL-LIFE DISCOVERY OF TUTANKHAMUN'S TREASURES

By Nicholas Reeves

In his book, Reeves retells the story of the discovery of Tutankhamen's tomb. After the outer tomb has been explored in 1922, Lord Carnarvon dies later in England. Lady Carnarvon renews his license to dig, and in 1924, Howard Carter officially opens the sarcophagus. But Carter leaves the country when Egyptian officials give him unwanted orders. Returning in 1925, he prepares to open Tutankhamen's coffin.

THE MUMMY IS REVEALED

THE VALLEY OF THE KINGS, EGYPT, 1925

"**M**r. Carter!" Reis Ahmed cried, rushing down the crowded platform of the Luxor train station.

Carter struggled to get off the train with his heavy load of luggage. He could hardly believe his eyes when he saw his loyal foreman. He had been away from Egypt for nearly a year now, yet Reis Ahmed had managed to find out when he was returning and had come to meet his train just as he always used to do.

"It's good to be back," Carter said, shaking Reis Ahmed's hand vigorously. "How's everything at the tomb?"

"Ready for us to begin work again," the foreman responded proudly.

While Carter was out of Egypt, the government had changed. A new minister was now in charge of archaeological digs, and he had renewed Lady Carnarvon's

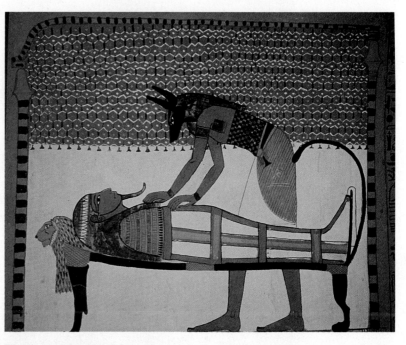

The jackal-headed Anubis, god of embalming, places a portrait mask on a mummy he has finished wrapping.

license to continue work at the tomb of Tutankhamen. Everyone had recognized that there was no archaeologist better able to do the job than Howard Carter, and there was great relief all around when he returned to Egypt.

But the clearing of the tomb would now take place under a different set of conditions. Lady Carnarvon had agreed to let all the ancient treasures remain in Egypt. And the contract which gave

The Times first news of any discovery was cancelled.

Despite Reis Ahmed's assurances that none of the precious objects in the tomb or in the lab had been damaged, Carter's stomach churned as they drove up into the valley. His time away from Egypt had been filled with nightmares about thousands of people going through the chambers, handling the artifacts, dropping and breaking the fragile alabaster, slipping smaller pieces of jewelry into pockets. Was it possible that he would find everything as he had left it?

The valley looked more beautiful than ever. The sun was sinking quickly and the hills and cliffs cast long shadows. Soon tiny stars appeared, growing brighter as the sky became a deep purple.

In near darkness Carter quickly inspected the tomb and lab. He breathed a sigh of relief when he saw that almost nothing had been touched. Outside the lab he found the ancient linen pall which had covered the second shrine. It had been left outside, and as he and Ahmed picked it up, it fell to pieces. "This is a great shame," Carter said sadly, holding the crumbling cloth in his hands, "but

When Howard Carter lifted the lid from the first coffin, he found the second coffin wrapped in a linen shroud. The second coffin had to be pulled out of the first with ropes and pulleys before its lid could be removed.

at least nothing else seems to have suffered."

Several months later, the moment Carter had waited so long for arrived. He was ready to open the gilded coffin.

Carter, Arthur Callender, and the other members of the excavation team

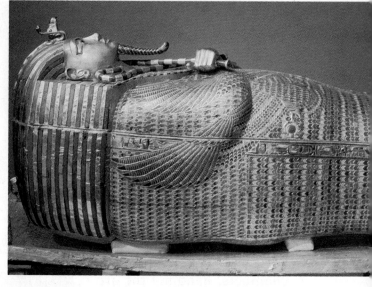

THE COFFINS OF THE BOY KING

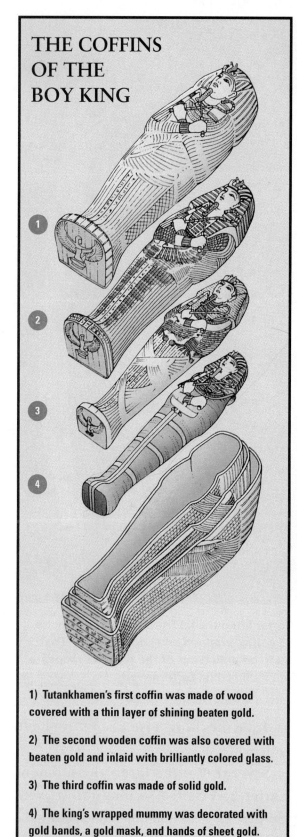

1) Tutankhamen's first coffin was made of wood covered with a thin layer of shining beaten gold.

2) The second wooden coffin was also covered with beaten gold and inlaid with brilliantly colored glass.

3) The third coffin was made of solid gold.

4) The king's wrapped mummy was decorated with gold bands, a gold mask, and hands of sheet gold.

gathered around the open sarcophagus. After attaching pulley blocks to the four silver handles on either side of the coffin lid, they slowly raised it. Inside, garlands of cornflowers, blue lotus petals, and olive and willow leaves had been strewn over a linen shroud.

Carter carefully removed these. Underneath was another coffin showing the image of a king in shining gold. It was even more magnificent than the first!

"So much care and respect for the dead pharaoh," marveled Callender. "And see how tightly the coffins fit, nestled inside one another like Russian dolls."

"They didn't leave us much elbow room, did they?" said Carter. "We'll have to lift the coffins out of the sarcophagus before we go any further, I think."

Using pulleys, they hoisted the first coffin and its contents free of the sarcophagus. It took eight men pulling on the ropes with all their strength to lift it.

(Left) The richly decorated second coffin was big enough to hold a third coffin, inside which lay the mummy of the king.

The face on the second coffin lid *(above)* was so different from the faces on the other two that Howard Carter believed it had been made for someone else.

"What on earth could make this so heavy?" said Callender in amazement, mopping his brow with his handkerchief.

Carter bent over the second gold-covered coffin and gently brushed away bits of linen from the face. Around the pharaoh's neck was a falcon collar of red, blue, and turquoise glass. The entire golden surface of the mummy-shaped coffin was decorated with an elaborate feather pattern inlaid with bright glass, but Carter noticed that some of the pieces of inlay were loose.

"That's probably due to dampness," said Callender.

"Let's just hope it hasn't damaged the mummy, too," Carter replied.

When the men removed the lid of the second coffin they saw the red linen shroud that had been carefully tucked around a third coffin. Only the burnished gold face of this coffin had been left uncovered. On top of the shroud was a collar made of glass beads, leaves, flowers, berries, and fruit. With

Before he could open the third coffin, Carter had to carefully chip away a layer of black pitch which had been poured on the coffin and left to harden for centuries.

trembling hands Carter removed the fragile collar and lifted the red linen. His heart almost stopped.

The third coffin was made of solid gold!

The men were speechless for a few moments, as they took in the sight before them. "Can you imagine how wealthy the ancient pharaohs must have been? No wonder the tombs were irresistible to thieves," Carter exclaimed. He had never even dreamed of finding anything so splendid.

"And no wonder it was so heavy," Callender added.

The third coffin was the most richly decorated of the three, with necklaces and a falcon collar inlaid with semi-precious stones. Exquisite winged goddesses decorated its body. Their outstretched arms encircled the body of the king protectively. Much of the decoration was hidden by a black pitch-like substance which had been poured over most of the coffin.

"Whatever is that?" asked Harry Burton as he moved about the chamber, setting up for the next photograph.

"It must have been some sacred oil," guessed Carter. "But it has dried as thick as tar. Unfortunately so much of it was used that this coffin seems to be stuck inside the bottom of the second one."

A hush fell over the group in the burial chamber as Callender and Carter and two other members of the team grasped the handles on the lid of the solid gold coffin, lifted it, and set it to one side.

There, inside the shell, lay the body of the king.

Carter could see that it was neatly wrapped in linen bandages. These were held in place by decorated gold bands. The mummy was covered with the same oils that they had found on the outside of the coffin.

Tutankhamen's mummy bore a magnificent mask of burnished gold, which covered its face and shoulders. Its headcloth was inlaid with blue glass. The vulture and cobra on its forehead, ready to spit fire at the pharaoh's enemies, were of solid gold. The face on Tutankhamen's mask looked sad and gentle. It was, Carter thought, the face of one who had not expected death to come so soon.

Sheet gold hands holding

The third coffin was made of solid gold and inlaid with precious stones.

the crook and the flail had been sewn onto the mummy's bandages. Across the mummy's chest lay a large golden bird, its wings spread wide as if in flight. It was a sacred image of the king's spirit. The Egyptians believed that at death the spirit flew free, but that it returned to the body when it was ready to enjoy eternal life. That was why they took care to fill tombs with everything necessary for a rich and happy afterlife. And that was why mummifying their dead was so important to them. The body had to be perfectly preserved so that the spirit would recognize it when it returned to the tomb.

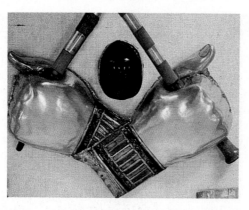

Tutankhamen's linen-wrapped mummy was decorated with gold ornaments. Hands of sheet gold *(above)* were sewn on to its chest and its head was covered with this gold mask, the most magnificent ever found *(below)*. Carter believed that the mask showed an exact likeness of the king's face.

Because the same black pitch that had covered the gold coffin had been poured over the mummy, the body as well as the mask were stuck to the inside of the casket. The men carried the heavy coffin outside, hoping that the hot sun would melt the hardened pitch, but it didn't. They would have to examine the mummy in its coffin.

The medical examination of the mummy took place on November 11, 1925. Carter had called in two anatomy experts, Dr. Derry and Dr. Hamdi, to perform the operation.

"I'm afraid it's not in very good condition," Dr. Derry warned Carter after a brief look at the bandaged form. "The skin underneath may be brittle."

Sure enough, the bandages crumbled at a touch. The two doctors decided to strengthen these wrappings with wax before making the first incision.

Carter had an uneasy feeling as the scalpel was poised above the mummy. Should we be doing this, he asked himself. From the first moment that he, Lord Carnarvon, Lady Evelyn, and Arthur Callender had entered the royal tomb he had

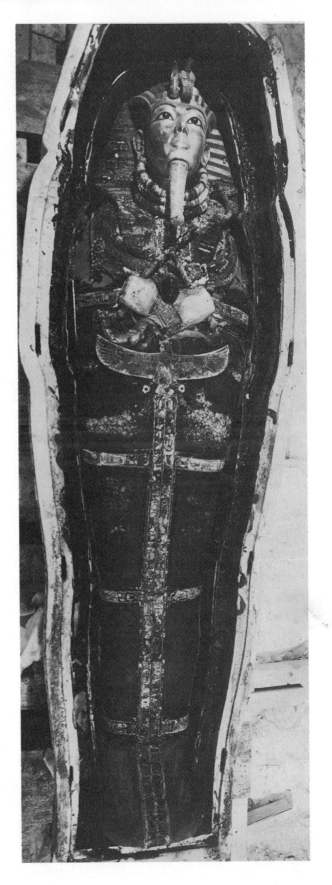

(Right) Inside the third coffin was the mummy of the king. The gold bands which surrounded the linen wrappings are inscribed with a wish for the pharaoh's safe passage into the next world.

been struck by the great care and compassion with which the ancient Egyptians had laid their young pharaoh to rest. What right had he to undo their loving work?

But at the same time Carter understood that clearing the tomb and unwrapping the mummy were vital because of what they would reveal about Egyptian life. His work over the past few years had shown the world how this ancient civilization buried their royal dead. He was adding rich knowledge to the pages of history books.

He knew, too, that once news of the treasures and the mummy reached the world they would never have been left untouched inside the tomb. Had they fallen into the hands of modern tomb robbers, they would have been lost forever or damaged beyond repair.

Dr. Derry made a shallow cut into the layers of bandages from the bottom of the gold mask down to the feet and folded the decayed wrappings back. It was impossible to remove a single piece of bandage intact.

"We won't be able to tell exactly how the mummy was bound," Carter frowned.

"No," agreed Dr. Derry. "But you can see that the fingers, toes, arms, and

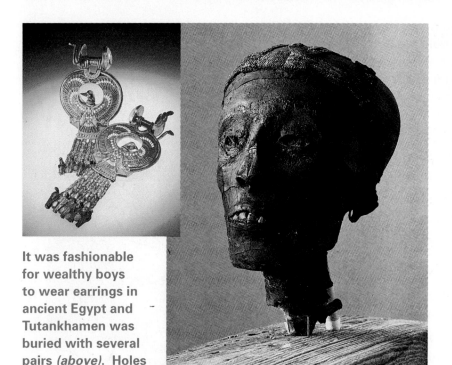

It was fashionable for wealthy boys to wear earrings in ancient Egypt and Tutankhamen was buried with several pairs *(above)*. Holes are still visible in the mummy's ears *(right)*.

were encased in gold sandals and a set of gold sheaths protected his toes. At Tutankhamen's waist was a gold-handled dagger with a blade made of iron, a metal rare in his day and prized for its strength.

When all the bandages were removed Carter could see that Tutankhamen's body was cracked and brittle. The skin was a grayish color and the limbs shrunken and thin. Carter noticed the place where the ancient embalmers had made their incision on the left side of the stomach to remove all of the king's precious internal organs.

Before the mummy's head could be examined the doctors had to remove the gold mask. Because the head was still stuck fast to the gold mask, the doctors finally had to separate the two by sliding heated knives between them. After removing a few layers of wrappings they could see that the king wore a delicate gold headband. More bandages were slowly removed — they had to be very careful with the fragile mummy.

At last Carter found himself face to face with the boy pharaoh.

In the dry and fragile skin he could read the features he had seen in the hand-

legs were all individually wrapped before being enclosed in the bandages that went around the whole body."

Carter bent down with a magnifying glass to look at the inner wrappings. To his disappointment they were like soot. Even so, he could see that the very finest linen had been used closest to the king's body.

As the men removed the brittle bandages from the body of the mummy they found more than a hundred jewels and amulets — charms whose magical powers would protect the young king from the dangers of the underworld. Around his neck were layers of collars and pendants. His folded arms were encircled by bracelets inlaid with semiprecious stones. On his fingers were two rings. His feet

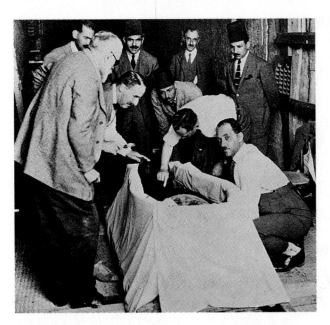

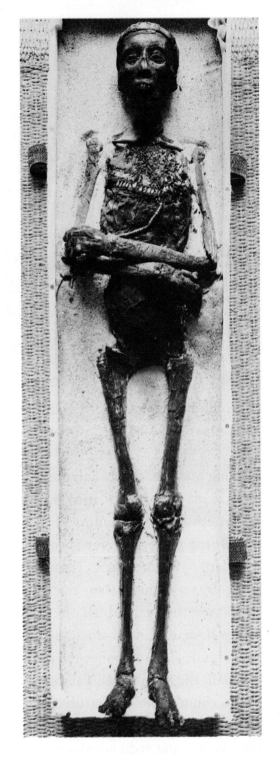

Howard Carter and the medical team *(above)* unwrapped and examined the body of King Tutankhamen *(right)*.

some gold mask. Tutankhamen wore an elaborate beaded skullcap on his shaven head. The king's eyes were open, and Carter could see that he had had long eyelashes. His nose had been flattened by the pressure of the bandages. Strong, white teeth showed through his parted lips.

After studying Tutankhamen's fragile bones, Dr. Derry and Dr. Hamdi were able to say that the young king had been 5' 5⅛" (1.65 m) tall. He had had a slight build and was about eighteen years old when he died.

"How do you think he died?" Carter asked.

"I'm not sure," Derry replied. "It does seem strange that he was so young. There's no evidence that I can see of disease. I suppose he might have had an accident . . . or maybe even have been murdered."

"We do know when he died though," said Callender. "The flowers we found in

241

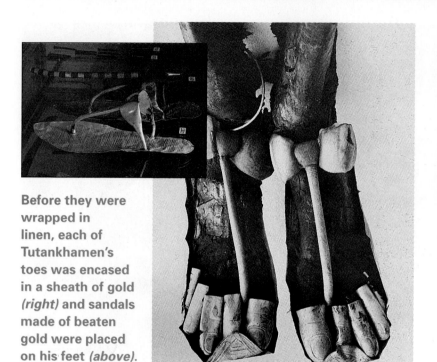

Before they were wrapped in linen, each of Tutankhamen's toes was encased in a sheath of gold *(right)* and sandals made of beaten gold were placed on his feet *(above)*.

the tomb only bloom in March or April, so it must have happened early in the year."

Long after the others had gone, Carter stood in the tomb looking down at Tutankhamen's mummy. He turned Dr. Derry's words over in his mind. Accident? Or murder? Tutankhamen had been very young when he died.

Carter thought of all the unusual things he had noticed since the clearing had begun — the fact that the tomb was so small, the simple wall paintings in the burial chamber which hardly seemed fit for a king, the fact that the shrine had been hastily put together the wrong way around and the pieces carelessly banged into place. The face on the second coffin, it now struck him, was not the same as the faces on the other two. Had it been

intended for someone else and adapted for the boy king at the last moment?

Was it possible that Tutankhamen had been murdered? Could one of his power-hungry guardians have cut short the reign of the boy king? And if so, had the tomb and burial goods been thrown together in a hurry before anyone could investigate?

As he wearily climbed the steps out of the tomb into the cool night air Carter thought of Lord Carnarvon. How sad it was that he had not been there to share the greatest moment of this discovery.

But Carter also felt that Tutankhamen had somehow escaped him. The centuries had taken their toll on the body of the king. He thought of the golden spirit bird which had been laid over the mummy. Where was Tutankhamen's spirit now, he wondered. Had it recognized the king's body when it returned to the tomb? Was Tutankhamen now pharaoh once more, surrounded by all his treasures in the afterlife? Or was his spirit without a home, soaring high in the night sky above the Valley of the Kings?

The magnificent gold death mask placed on Tutankhamen's mummy

DISCOVER YOUR IDEAS

Wanted: Experienced Workers

Howard Carter needed experienced people to help him excavate Tutankhamen's tomb. What skills do you think he was looking for in his workers? Write a want ad that describes the kinds of workers that Howard Carter might have hired.

How to Unwrap a Mummy

Find a mummy? How do you unwrap it? Use the information from the selection to create the ultimate "how-to" guide featuring step-by-step instructions on how to unwrap a mummy. Include illustrations and diagrams to help bring your guide to life!

Details, Details

Howard Carter began his career making drawings of ancient objects that archaeologists uncovered. Try your hand at drawing. Choose an artifact — or part of one — shown in *Into the Mummy's Tomb*. Draw it as exactly as you can. Then write a caption for it.

Discuss the Finding

All Wrapped Up?

Did Howard Carter and his team really solve an ancient mystery when they cleared Tutankhamen's tomb and unwrapped his mummy? Share your thoughts with a partner. Support your ideas with details from the selection.

MUMMY MAKING

The Why and the How

The ancient Egyptians believed that a new life began after death. It existed in spirit form. The spirit would regularly leave the body to receive gifts of food from living friends and family.

Every day, the spirit would return to the tomb so the body could live on. The spirit, of course, had to be able to recognize the body to which it belonged. To be sure of recognition, the Egyptians worked hard to preserve the remains of the dead.

Preparing a body, embalmers first removed various internal organs. They preserved these organs in special jars. At burial time the jars would accompany the mummy into the tomb. The heart got special treatment. It was, the Egyptians believed, the center of intelligence. It stayed inside the body.

From June 1990 issue of *National Geographic World* magazine. Copyright ©1990 by *National Geographic World*. *World* is the official magazine for Junior Members of the National Geographic Society. Reprinted by permission.

Next the embalmers packed and covered the body with natron, a kind of salt, to dry it out. The drying-out process took about 40 days.

The embalmers then covered the body with sweet-smelling oils and with a tarlike waterproofing substance. At various times a priest would read spells from a scroll.

In the final step, the body was wrapped in strips of linen and placed in a case, and then in a coffin. Both were shaped and painted in a human image. Now the mummy was ready for the tomb. The whole process, from death through burial, took about 70 days.

Life in the underworld, the Egyptians believed, went on much as it did on earth. For most, that meant hard work: tilling fields, hauling rocks, carrying water. The Egyptians found a way around that. They stocked their tombs with figurines — tiny statues — equipped with all the necessary tools. When the gods called upon a person for labor, the figurines would take on the job.

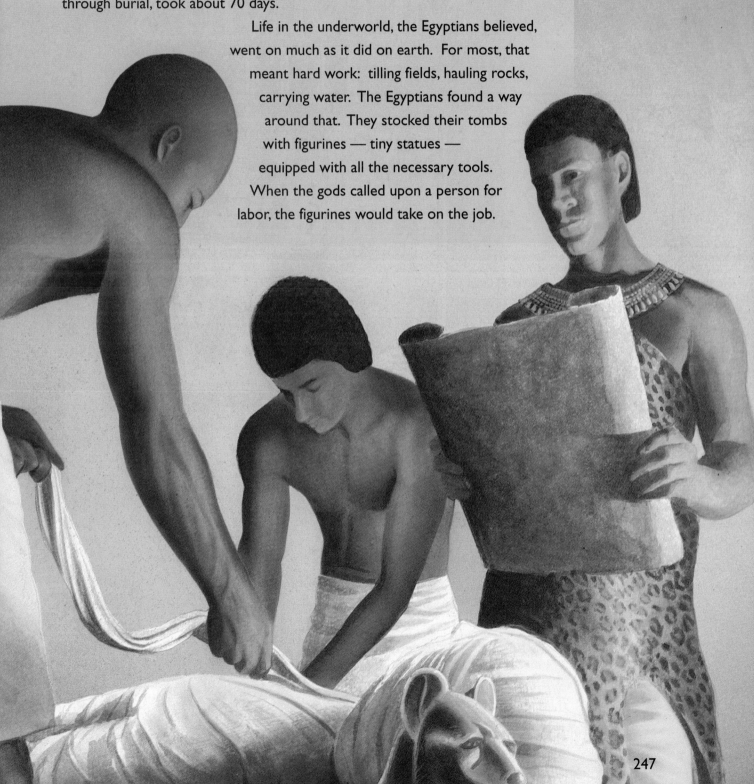

PATRICIA LAUBER
TALES
MUMMIES
TELL

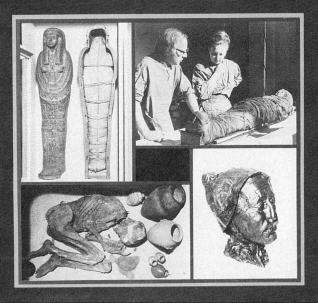

MUMMY NO. 1770:

Museums have a limited number of mummies. Every time one is unwrapped, the number grows smaller, and so autopsies are not often performed. But sometimes a museum has a mummy that is not important to its collection. This is a mummy it does not want to display and a mummy about which almost nothing is known. As it happened, the Manchester Museum in England had just such a mummy. Its wrappings were in poor condition and no one knew what period it dated from, where it was found, or who the dead person was. The mummy was known only by its museum number, 1770. This was the mummy the museum made available to a team of scientists who wanted to use modern techniques to study the wrappings and body in detail.

▼ *Mummy no. 1770 after the Manchester team removed the wrappings over the chest cover*

It was also a mummy with a mystery. X-rays taken years earlier had shown the mummy was that of a young person. The lower parts of the legs were missing, and close to the leg bones was a rounded object. The x-rays did not reveal what it was, but its shape suggested a baby's head. Was this the mummy of a mother and child? Had the mother died shortly after giving birth? Those were questions the scientists wondered about as they began their work.

After new x-rays were taken, the unwrapping began. Insect remains found in the bandages were carefully removed for later study. As pieces of cloth were lifted away, the lower part of the mask came into view. Beneath it were the bare bones of the neck and skull. These were in small pieces, but even so, once the pieces had been cleaned it was possible to see that the left side of the nose had been damaged by the iron hook the embalmers had used to remove the brain. The team was surprised to see red and blue paint on the skull bones. How and why had the bones been exposed?

Gently removing more cloth, the scientists found the mummy's arms were crossed on the chest and the hands had gold fingertip covers. The inner organs had been removed and the space filled with bandages and mud. The organs themselves were missing.

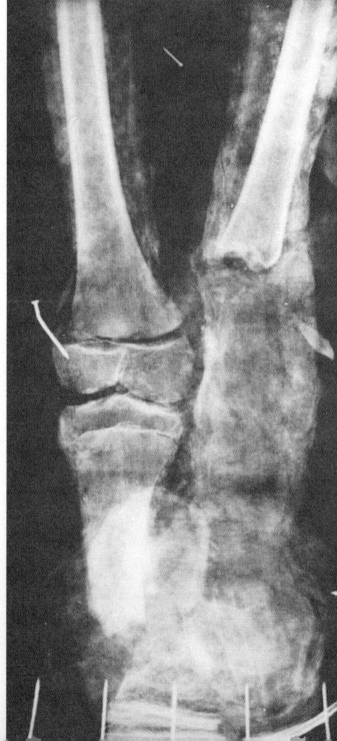

▼ X-ray pictures of 1770's legs showed a mysterious mass, which the team thought might be a baby.

250

A small, hard object that had appeared in the x-rays proved to be a Guinea worm, a parasite that is taken in with drinking water. Within a human host, the young forms of Guinea worm develop into adults. The adults mate, and the male dies. The female, which may grow three feet long, wanders through the tissues under the skin. She generally comes to rest in the legs or feet of the host. There blisters form. They burst on contact with fresh water. The female's eggs are released into the water, and the life cycle starts again. If invaded by bacteria, the blisters may form dangerous sores.

When the Manchester team unwrapped the legs of mummy 1770, they found, as the x-rays had shown, that both legs had been amputated, the left below the knee and the right above the knee. The mummy's right leg had been lengthened with a piece of wood to make it the same length as the left. The wood had been splinted to the leg bone. This meant there could not have been much, if any, flesh on the bone when the splinting was done. The feet were artificial and had gold toenail covers. The right foot was made of reeds and mud, with the ends of the reeds serving as toes. The left foot was simply a mass of reeds and mud.

By now the scientists could see that there was not even a trace of a baby. The rounded shape that had shown in the x-rays was actually a pair of beautiful slippers that had been placed on the soles of the feet.

The "baby" ▶
turned out to
be decorated
sandals placed
over false feet.

In one way mummy 1770 was disappointing — it was very poorly preserved. No one could even be certain of its sex, although members of the team came to feel that the young person had been a girl and spoke of the mummy as female. Very little skin, muscle, or soft tissue were left, and the bones of the skull and lower trunk were broken. The scientists could not tell when the fractures had occurred. In a living person, tissue called callus forms at the place where a bone is broken. It holds the bone together until the fracture heals. Callus in a recently dead person shows that the fracture occurred during life. But callus thick enough to last thousands of years would take several weeks to form. So if there is no callus in a mummy — and there was none in 1770 — there was no way to tell whether the fracture occurred after death or shortly before. The scientists suspected, however, that the bones were broken after death. The damaged mask and the lack of jewelry and charms spoke of tomb robbers and rough handling.

In other ways, mummy 1770 was both interesting and puzzling. The evidence indicated that the body had been in a state of considerable decay when the embalmers worked on it. The wooden leg was attached to bone. All the internal organs were missing and so was the left kneecap, which suggested that the ligaments holding it in place had rotted away. The red and blue paint on the skull bones was a sign that the hair and scalp had been missing.

Why had the body decayed? Why were the legs amputated? The scientific team could think of various explanations.

One had to do with the Guinea worm. Perhaps infections had cut off the flow of blood to the legs and feet. In an effort to save the girl's life, doctors had amputated her legs, but the patient died. But if that was the case, why hadn't she been promptly embalmed?

Or perhaps the legs had been cut off in an accident, such as the collapse of a building. If the girl had been buried in rubble and not found for some time, that might explain the decay.

Or suppose the girl had drowned in the Nile, where decay would set in quickly. The body might have been attacked by a hippopotamus. Although hippos are plant eaters, they are likely to attack floating objects that appear threatening. One bite from a hippo could easily cut off a pair of legs.

A crocodile was another possibility, because it would certainly attack a floating body. The problem with this idea was that crocodiles do not usually bite through bones. They are much more likely to grasp an arm or a leg in their huge jaws and shake it until it tears loose. On the other hand, a crocodile attack might explain why the embalmers went to so much trouble over a body that was hauled out of the Nile — why they made a face and chest mask, lengthened a leg, made artificial feet, applied gold covers to the fingers and toes. The ancient Egyptians, believing that crocodiles were earthly forms of gods, considered anyone who became food for them to be sacred.

As things turned out, there was another explanation for the state of the body and it took everyone by surprise. When the carbon-14 dating was completed, it showed that the mummy was far older than its wrappings. The wrappings dated to a time when the Romans ruled Egypt, around A.D. 260. The mummy's bones dated to around 1200 B.C. This meant that 1770 was a mummy that had been wrapped twice. It had been preserved and wrapped after the girl died, then rewrapped more than a thousand years later. Now some pieces of the puzzle began to fall into place.

There was no need to explain why the corpse had decayed, because it hadn't. Rather, it was the mummy that had been damaged by water and then had decayed. The soft tissues of the body were probably missing because they had stuck to the original wrappings.

The way the second embalmers had prepared the body made clear that they did not know whether they were dealing with a male or a female. This meant they did not know the mummy's identity. But the trouble they took shows that they thought they were dealing with someone of importance. The tomb from which the mummy came must have led them to that conclusion. At times in ancient Egypt royal mummies were moved to new tombs. If they had been damaged, they were repaired at the time of the move. Quite possibly 1770 was a person of royal or noble birth whose mummy was damaged when a tomb was flooded.

The Manchester team carried out many other investigations of 1770. They studied the mummy's wrappings to find out what they were made of, how they had been woven, what sort of gum had been used as an adhesive. More x-rays were taken. And the many insect remains were studied. They showed, among other things, that flies had had a chance to feed on the mummy and to breed. This finding was further evidence that the mummy had been wet before it was repaired and rewrapped.

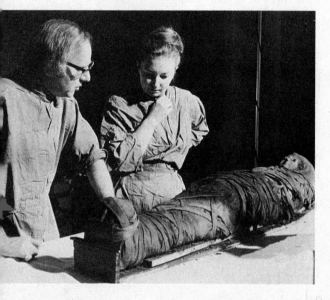

▼ *Dr. Rosalie David, leader of the Manchester University team, examines 1770 with a team member.*

Flies lay eggs, which hatch out into wormlike creatures called larvae. In time a kind of case forms around each larva. Inside, the soft matter of the larva breaks down and turns into an adult fly. If larva cases are found in mummies or their wrappings, it is a sign that flies have bred there. It is also a sign that the mummies and wrappings have been wet, because the larvae cannot eat dry food. Flies lay their eggs only on moist food sources.

While some members of the team were working with insect remains, x-rays, and wrappings, others were studying 1770's skull and teeth.

X-rays had shown that the mummy's wisdom teeth had not yet grown in, and so the girl must have been less than 20 years old. The dentist on the team now examined the roots of the second molars. Their stage of development told him that 1770 had been 13 to 14 years old. He was surprised to see that the teeth showed no sign of being worn down by sand. He also found that two teeth in the upper jaw were oddly placed. A space between them near the gum formed a trap for food particles. Usually such a trap leads to infection, which damages the bone of the jaw. But this had not happened to 1770. The lack of wear and damage suggested that her diet was soft, perhaps mostly liquid. Or she may have swallowed food without trying to chew it much. Most likely she had not been very healthy.

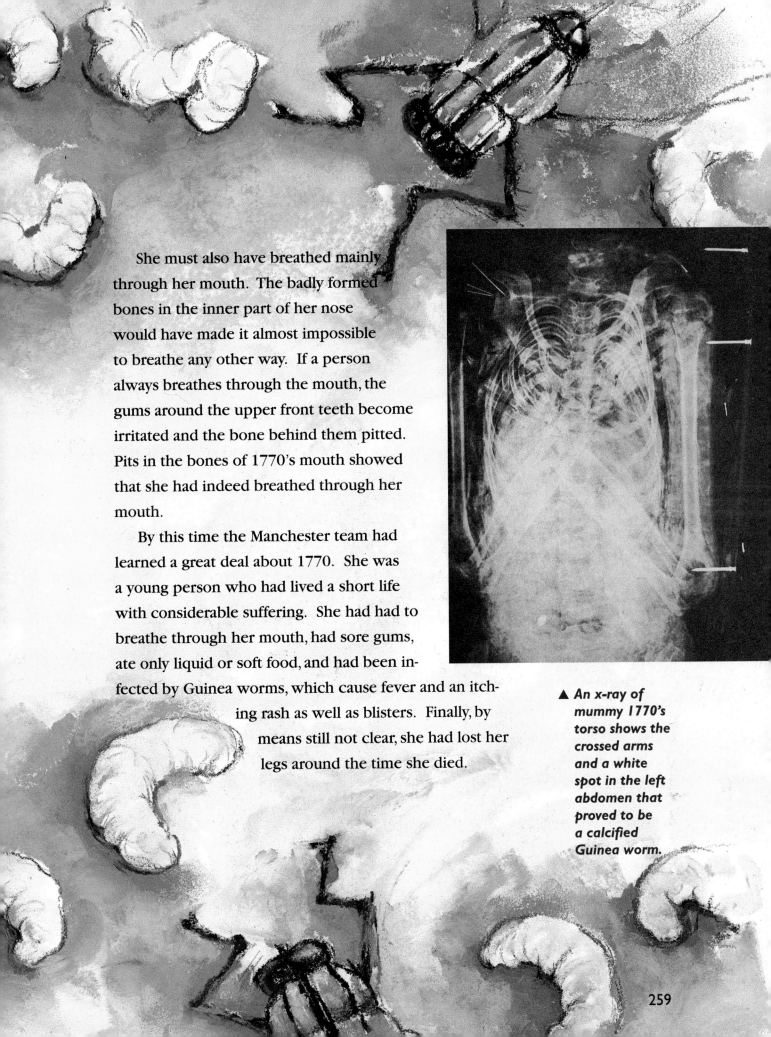

She must also have breathed mainly through her mouth. The badly formed bones in the inner part of her nose would have made it almost impossible to breathe any other way. If a person always breathes through the mouth, the gums around the upper front teeth become irritated and the bone behind them pitted. Pits in the bones of 1770's mouth showed that she had indeed breathed through her mouth.

By this time the Manchester team had learned a great deal about 1770. She was a young person who had lived a short life with considerable suffering. She had had to breathe through her mouth, had sore gums, ate only liquid or soft food, and had been infected by Guinea worms, which cause fever and an itching rash as well as blisters. Finally, by means still not clear, she had lost her legs around the time she died.

▲ An x-ray of mummy 1770's torso shows the crossed arms and a white spot in the left abdomen that proved to be a calcified Guinea worm.

One final step remained to be taken — to find out what 1770 had looked like. The skull had broken into about 30 pieces, some of them very small and fragile. The pieces lay in a jumbled heap and were mixed with mud and bandages. Once the pieces of bone had been cleaned, one member of the team made casts of them in plastic. When the plastic pieces were fitted together, much of the left side of the skull was still missing. A plaster cast was made to fill out the basic shape of the head. Now small pegs were placed in the plastic skull and cut to precise lengths. Each showed how thick the soft tissues of the face would be on a 13-year-old person. The face was then built up with modeling clay. First it took on a general human appearance. Then it took on an appearance of its own, shaped by the underlying bones. This model was used to cast the head in wax, so that changes could be made if more was learned about 1770. The wax head was painted, given glass eyes, a wig, and eyelashes. And there at last was 1770 — an attractive teenager, perhaps of royal or noble birth, who had laughed, cried, and lived 3,000 years ago.

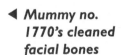

◄ Mummy no. 1770's cleaned facial bones

▼ The pegs indicate the probable thickness of soft tissues of the face.

ABOUT PATRICIA LAUBER

Patricia Lauber began to write as a child, soon after she began to read. For her, writing created a special world. And Lauber still feels this way after more than sixty published books. Like *Tales Mummies Tell*, most of her books are nonfiction, but she makes them exciting. Lauber believes young people appreciate books on science. After all, "Children are born curious, wanting and needing to know why, how, and what: the very questions that scientists ask."

Hands-on
Activities

Careful Work

The scientists who claimed 1770 wanted to learn everything they could about it. From what you've read, what special abilities did these scientists need to do their job? With a partner, discuss four or more abilities. Support your opinions with information from the selection.

A Special Mummy

Mummy no. 1770 turned out to be the mummy of a teenager, maybe a young girl. Think about all you've learned about 1770 from your reading. Then write your thoughts about her in an original poem to share or not, as you wish.

262

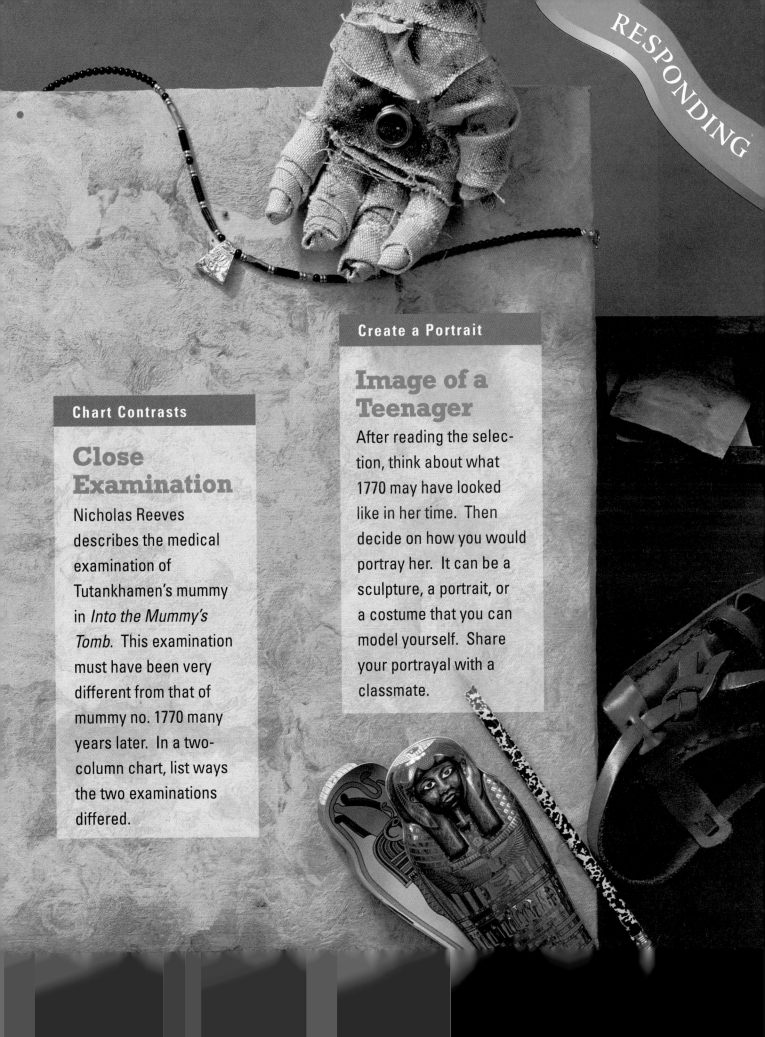

Chart Contrasts

Close Examination

Nicholas Reeves describes the medical examination of Tutankhamen's mummy in *Into the Mummy's Tomb*. This examination must have been very different from that of mummy no. 1770 many years later. In a two-column chart, list ways the two examinations differed.

Create a Portrait

Image of a Teenager

After reading the selection, think about what 1770 may have looked like in her time. Then decide on how you would portray her. It can be a sculpture, a portrait, or a costume that you can model yourself. Share your portrayal with a classmate.

PHARAOH

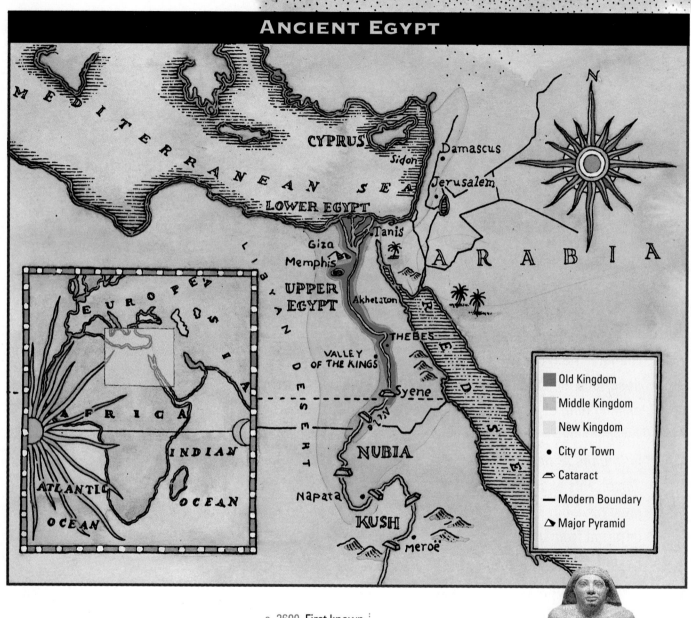

ANCIENT EGYPT

Legend:
- Old Kingdom
- Middle Kingdom
- New Kingdom
- • City or Town
- ⌂ Cataract
- — Modern Boundary
- △ Major Pyramid

Map labels: MEDITERRANEAN SEA, CYPRUS, Sidon, Damascus, Jerusalem, LOWER EGYPT, Tanis, Giza, Memphis, UPPER EGYPT, Akhetaton, ARABIA, THEBES, VALLEY OF THE KINGS, Syene, RED SEA, LIBYAN DESERT, NUBIA, Napata, KUSH, Meroë

Inset map: EUROPE, ASIA, AFRICA, ATLANTIC OCEAN, INDIAN OCEAN

Upper and Lower Egypt united

c. 2600 First known stone pyramid in ancient Egypt built for King Djoser

c. 2575-2130 Old Kingdom

c. 2524-2400 Tjenty, a scribe

Architecture and the arts flourish

c. 2500 Great Pyramid at Giza and Great Sphinx are constructed.

c. 1938-1600 Middle Kingdom

3500 B.C.   3000   2500   2000

FACTS

CRYPT NOTES

Papyrus, used in Egypt to make everything from boats to "paper," is all but extinct today. Scientists are trying to reintroduce it.

Sand buries the Great Sphinx up to its neck from time to time. King Thutmose IV cleared the sand away in the 1400s B.C. It has also been removed more "recently": in 1818, 1886, 1926, and 1938.

Ancient Egyptians' medical know-how spread to Europe through Greeks, Romans, Persians, and Arabs. Some medieval physicians believed that ground Egyptian mummy would cure most diseases!

People wore black or green eye paint to guard against dust and sand and as makeup. They also wore lip paint!

Young boys and girls were shaved bald, perhaps to protect them from head lice. Older girls often wore pigtails, and boys wore sidelocks.

c. 1479-1426 Egyptian empire reaches its height (King Thutmose III).

c. 1353 Akenaton (Amenhotep IV) becomes king of Egypt.

c. 1332 King Tutankhamen reigns.

c. 600-580 Nubian King Aspelta

| 1500 B.C. | 1000 | 500 | A.D. |

c. 1539-1075 New Kingdom

c. 1075 Egypt's decline begins.

c. 750 Nubian kingdom of Kush begins conquest of Egypt. King Kashta conquers Upper Egypt.

THE OUTSKIRTS of modern-day Cairo, the capital of Egypt, with the Pyramids of Giza in the background. The Giza Pyramids are the only one of the Seven Wonders of the Ancient World still standing.

Egypt's pyramids are the oldest stone buildings in the world. They were built nearly five thousand years ago. These ancient tombs are also among the world's largest structures. The biggest is taller than a *40-story* building and covers an area greater than that of *ten* football fields. Men built these huge structures without the help of equipment that we have today, such as cranes and bulldozers. Sometimes up to 100,000 men worked for 20 seasons on one pyramid.

More than 80 pyramids still stand today. Inside their once-smooth white limestone surfaces, there are secret passageways, hidden rooms, ramps, bridges, and shafts. Most had concealed entrances and false doors. What fun it would be to explore one!

However, the pyramids were not built for exploring. They served a very serious purpose. Ancient Egyptians had a strong belief in life after death. The kings, called pharaohs, wanted their bodies to last forever, so they had pyramids built to protect their bodies after death. Each pyramid housed a pharaoh's preserved body. It also held the goods he would need in the next life to continue living as he had when he was alive.

The pyramids of Egypt are massive monuments to the pharaohs' power. Today they are reminders of a resourceful and creative ancient civilization.

HOW HEAVY? The average weight of one of a pyramid's stone blocks is two and a half tons. That's the weight of two medium-sized cars. Some blocks, however, weigh up to 15 tons. That's as much as five elephants!

HOW TALL?
1. Eiffel Tower, 984 feet
2. **Great Pyramid at Giza, 480 feet**
3. Big Ben (Westminster Palace), 316 feet
4. Statue of Liberty, 305 feet
5. Leaning Tower of Pisa, 179 feet

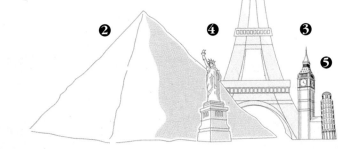

Stairway to Heaven

Egyptian tombs were not always as grand as the pyramids. The first Egyptians were buried in the desert in shallow pits. The desert's hot sand preserved the body.

Around 3000 B.C., kings and high officials began to build large, flat-topped tombs we call *mastabas* (MAS tuh buhz). Each of these tombs contained a burial chamber and rooms filled with goods.

The first pyramid was built out of stone around 2700 B.C.

It is known as the Step Pyramid. Like later pyramids, it had two purposes. It was a royal tomb. It was also a temple for worshipping the spirit of the dead king.

By 1600 B.C., robbers had ransacked many of the pyramids. Later pharaohs decided that their bodies would be safer in hidden tombs cut from solid rock. Many of these pharaohs are buried in the desolate Valley of the Kings.

Dead man • **ANUBIS,** god of mummification • Devourer of the dead

IN THE WEIGHING OF THE HEART Ceremony, a dead person's heart is weighed against an ostrich feather, the symbol of proper behavior.

How pyramids got their start

| EARLIEST TIMES | AROUND 3000 B.C. | AROUND 2700 B.C. |

EARLY EGYPTIANS BURIED THEIR DEAD UNDER a pile of rocks. Bodies were wrapped in goatskin or reed mats. Personal goods were placed around the body.

MASTABA TOMBS WERE MADE OF SUNBAKED MUD bricks, which gave protection against the harmful effects of nature. On the walls of mastabas were carved, painted scenes called *reliefs.* Some reliefs showed rows of people bringing offerings, such as ducks, food, water, wine, milk, honey, and beer.

IMHOTEP IS CREDITED WITH the invention of stone architecture and the design of Egypt's first pyramid, the Step Pyramid. It was begun as a large mastaba tomb, but after going through many changes, it ended up as a pyramid of six steps. The tomb of King Djoser lies under the Step Pyramid.

IMHOTEP

PHARAOH KHUFU

THOTH, god of wisdom

HORUS, god of the sky

OSIRIS, god of the dead

Ancient Egyptians believed that everlasting life took place in a paradise known as the Field of Reeds. To get there, the dead had to pass through an underworld filled with fearsome monsters and demons. To help insure safe passage, priests put together a collection of spells. One such collection was the Book of the Dead. A copy was placed in each tomb. No one copy contains all 200 spells.

OSIRIS, GOD OF THE DEAD, watches the ceremony along with other gods. A heavy heart meant that the person had lived a bad life. The person would then not be able to have a life after death.

PHARAOH DJOSER

AROUND 2500 B.C.

AROUND 1500 B.C.

PHARAOH TUTANKHAMEN, known as King Tut, was buried in the Valley of the Kings. The young king died when he was about 18 years old. Practically untouched by robbers, his tomb contained weapons, furniture, jewelry, musical instruments, clothing, and model boats — many of which were made of solid gold. The king's two stillborn daughters were buried with him, along with a lock of hair from his grandmother, Queen Tiya.

THE GREAT PYRAMID AT GIZA, THE LARGEST of the three Giza pyramids, is also one of the largest man-made structures in the world today. Built for Pharaoh Khufu, it was originally 480 feet high. Its base covers approximately 13 acres. The pyramid originally contained over two million blocks of limestone.

THE VALLEY OF THE KINGS CONTAINS THE TOMBS of many later pharaohs. These rulers were aware that robbers had taken the treasures from most of the earlier pyramids. So they decided to have their tombs built in these isolated cliffs near Thebes. Sixty-two tombs have been found there. However, even these tombs were robbed.

THIS IS THE BODY OF GINGER. He is named for his hair color. Buried some 5,000 years ago, his body was preserved by the hot sand. Ginger was wrapped in skins or matting and was buried with knives and pots.

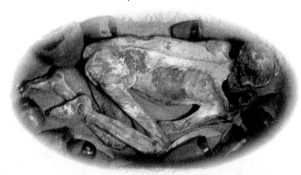

Only in Egypt

Ancient Egypt had a unique combination of ingredients for building pyramids. The country was a long, narrow, fertile strip of land in northeastern Africa. Water came from the mighty Nile River. Natural barriers protected the land from invaders. There were deserts to the east and west. There were dangerous rapids on the Nile to the south. Delta marshes lay to the north. This circle of isolation allowed the Egyptians to work in peace and security.

To build the pyramids, great supplies of raw materials were needed. Ancient Egypt had an abundance of limestone, sandstone, and granite. But these rocks had to be brought from quarries to the building sites. Egypt's most precious resource—the great Nile River—provided the means for transportation.

GIZA
MEMPHIS •
SAQQARA
DAHSHUR

• **CAIRO**

TURA
(Lime-
stone
quarry)

AFRICA

— **VALLEY OF
THE KINGS**

THE NILE RIVER IS THE longest river in the world. It flows for approximately 4,150 miles. The Nile flooded farmers' lands from July to October until the Aswan Dam was completed in 1970.

DESERTS CUT OFF ancient Egypt from the rest of the world. If you were trying to cross a desert on foot, you would need from four to six gallons of water per day. And, the more water you carried, the more water you would need!

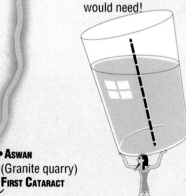

• **ASWAN**
(Granite quarry)
FIRST CATARACT

THE NILE RIVER produced fertile farmland. During the flood season, when no farming could be done, farmers paid taxes to the pharaoh in labor, by helping to build the pyramids.

ANCIENT EGYPTIANS believed that a pharaoh buried in grand style would continue to bless his people. This inspired them to work cheerfully as they built the pyramids— magnificent monuments to their kings.

THE STONES WERE levered up and hauled on board. The weighed-down boat then set off for the pyramid site. Oarsmen had to work hard, and the helmsman had to be an expert, since sandbanks could easily destroy a boat.

THINK PIECE!

Do you think a pyramid similar to those of ancient Egypt could be built today? If so, who do you think would build it? For whom might it be built? What purpose do you think it might serve?

TWO KINDS OF ROCKS were used in most pyramids— limestone and small quantities of granite. These rocks were quarried close to the banks of the Nile. They were transported on the Nile in wooden boats.

271

Traps, Mazes, and Secret Chambers

The main purpose of the pyramids was to safeguard the pharaohs' bodies. Granite doors, false passages, and fake burial chambers were constructed in an attempt to confuse and deter robbers. However, in spite of all these precautions, nearly all the pyramids were robbed of their treasures by around 1000 B.C.

Take a trip through the inside of the Great Pyramid of Giza in the illustration and see how skillfully the kings planned for their bodies' final resting places.

THE SPHINX AT GIZA is 240 feet long and carved out of limestone. Built by Pharaoh Khafre to guard the way to his pyramid, it has a lion's body and the ruler's head.

THE GRAND GALLERY in the Great Pyramid is 150 feet long and 25 feet high. After the king was buried, the entrance to the Grand Gallery was sealed off with enormous blocks that were slid down the gallery.

THE ESCAPE SHAFT let people out of the pyramid after they buried the king.

I had something a little bigger in mind.

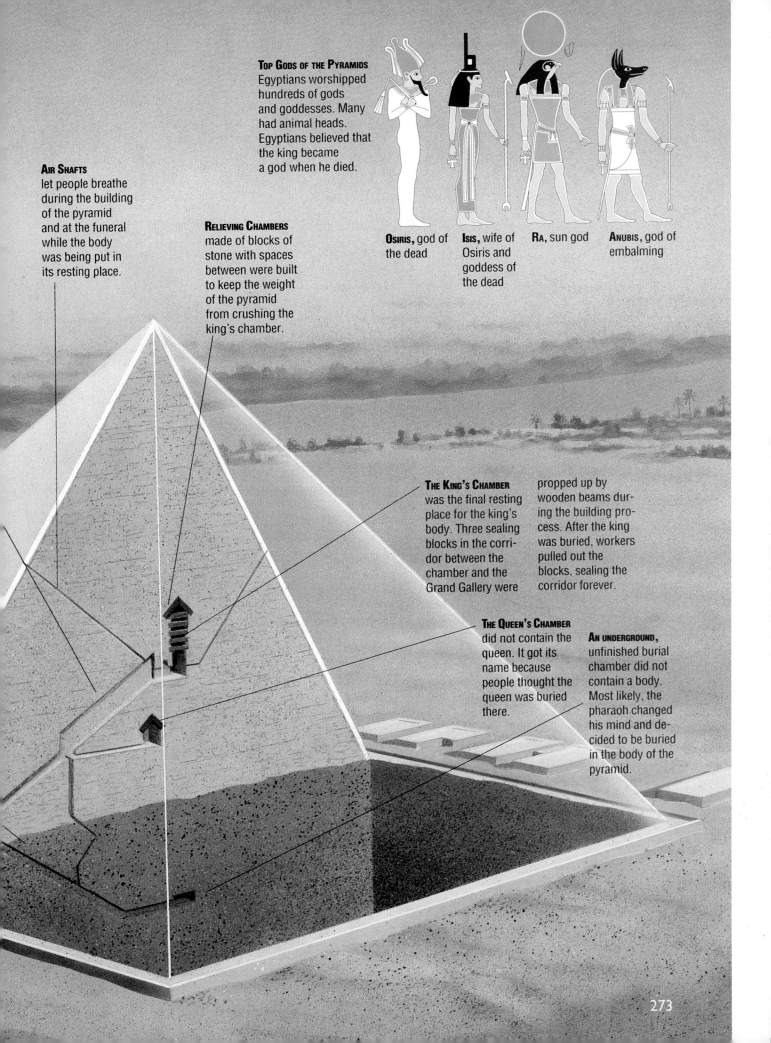

AIR SHAFTS
let people breathe
during the building
of the pyramid
and at the funeral
while the body
was being put in
its resting place.

RELIEVING CHAMBERS
made of blocks of
stone with spaces
between were built
to keep the weight
of the pyramid
from crushing the
king's chamber.

TOP GODS OF THE PYRAMIDS
Egyptians worshipped
hundreds of gods
and goddesses. Many
had animal heads.
Egyptians believed that
the king became
a god when he died.

OSIRIS, god of
the dead

ISIS, wife of
Osiris and
goddess of
the dead

RA, sun god

ANUBIS, god of
embalming

THE KING'S CHAMBER
was the final resting
place for the king's
body. Three sealing
blocks in the corri-
dor between the
chamber and the
Grand Gallery were
propped up by
wooden beams dur-
ing the building pro-
cess. After the king
was buried, workers
pulled out the
blocks, sealing the
corridor forever.

THE QUEEN'S CHAMBER
did not contain the
queen. It got its
name because
people thought the
queen was buried
there.

AN UNDERGROUND,
unfinished burial
chamber did not
contain a body.
Most likely, the
pharaoh changed
his mind and de-
cided to be buried
in the body of the
pyramid.

273

QUEENS

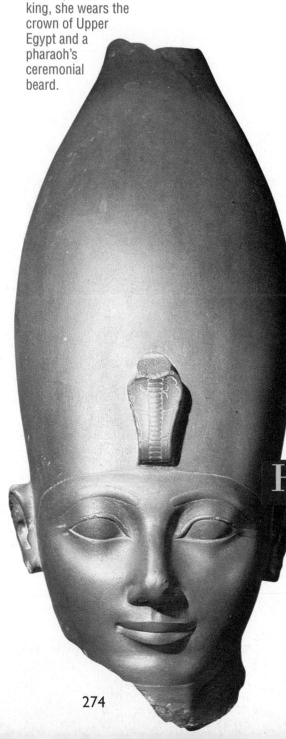

Many authorities believe this fragment of a green basalt statue represents Hatshepsut. As king, she wears the crown of Upper Egypt and a pharaoh's ceremonial beard.

In the ancient kingdoms along the Nile, women had freedom and independence. A few women even rose to positions of great power.

Strong-willed Hatshepsut, Egypt's most influential female ruler, reigned for twenty-two years in the 1400s B.C. She took a royal name and had herself depicted wearing the beard, crown, and dress of a male pharaoh.

Hatshepsut's most famous achievement was her adventurous sponsorship of a trading expedition to the far-off African kingdom of Punt. Her five ships returned safely, laden with gold, ebony, animals, and prized incense trees.

Hatshepsut is shown as a woman in this red granite statue found at Thebes.

Hatshepsut

strong-willed

adventurous

influential

of the Nile

"**Age cannot wither her, nor custom stale Her infinite variety . . .**"
From *Antony and Cleopatra* by William Shakespeare

These famous lines refer to Cleopatra, queen of Egypt from 51 B.C. to her death, at age 39, in 30 B.C. Cleopatra's charms were so "infinite" that powerful Roman leaders — first Julius Caesar, then Mark Antony — fell in love with her and obeyed her wishes.

Cleopatra has inspired playwrights, painters, and moviemakers. Ruler of one of the wealthiest kingdoms of ancient times, she was ambitious, powerful, and enchanting.

Michelangelo himself made this drawing of Cleopatra around A.D. 1533. His pencil sketch is in the Casa Buonarroti, in Florence, Italy.

Cleopatra

enchanting

powerful

ambitious

Actress Donna Croll portrays a regal Cleopatra in the Talawa Theatre Company's 1991 production of *Antony and Cleopatra.*

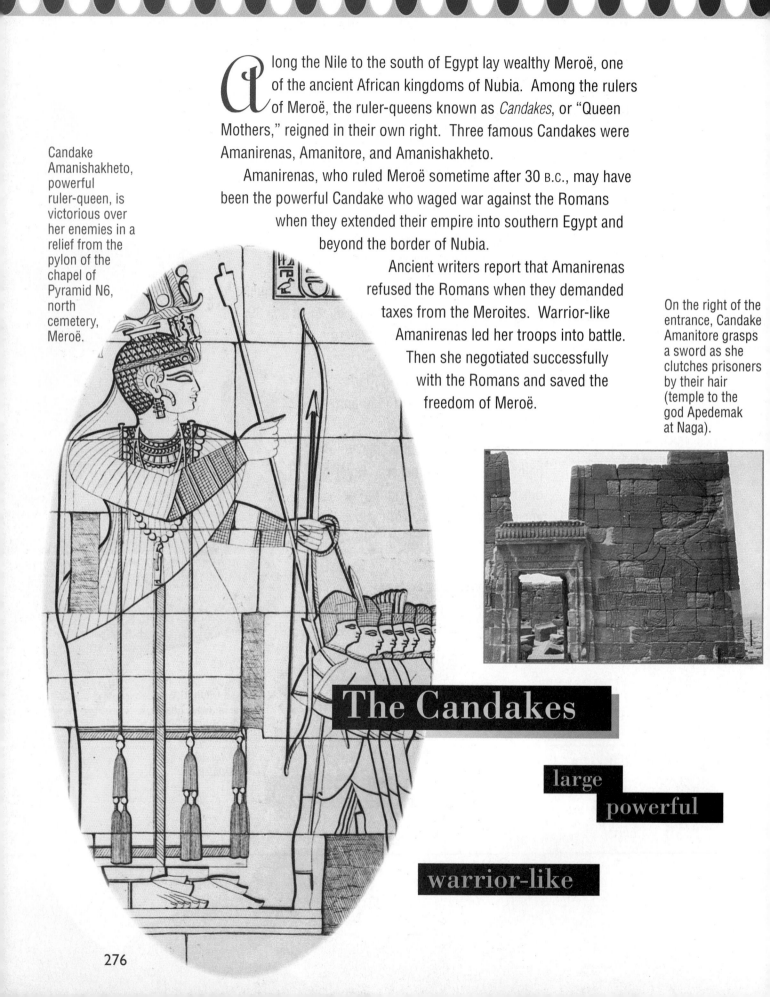

Along the Nile to the south of Egypt lay wealthy Meroë, one of the ancient African kingdoms of Nubia. Among the rulers of Meroë, the ruler-queens known as *Candakes*, or "Queen Mothers," reigned in their own right. Three famous Candakes were Amanirenas, Amanitore, and Amanishakheto.

Amanirenas, who ruled Meroë sometime after 30 B.C., may have been the powerful Candake who waged war against the Romans when they extended their empire into southern Egypt and beyond the border of Nubia.

Ancient writers report that Amanirenas refused the Romans when they demanded taxes from the Meroites. Warrior-like Amanirenas led her troops into battle. Then she negotiated successfully with the Romans and saved the freedom of Meroë.

Candake Amanishakheto, powerful ruler-queen, is victorious over her enemies in a relief from the pylon of the chapel of Pyramid N6, north cemetery, Meroë.

On the right of the entrance, Candake Amanitore grasps a sword as she clutches prisoners by their hair (temple to the god Apedemak at Naga).

The Candakes

large

powerful

warrior-like

Fit for a Queen

Designed thousands of years ago, the priceless artifacts of ancient Nubia look quite contemporary.

The handle of a Nubian bronze and gilt silver mirror from 716–701 B.C. is decorated with the figures of three goddesses and a king's sister, who was considered the earthly form of the goddesses.

This Nubian rock crystal and gold pendant from the eighth century B.C. surrounds a metal cylinder that may hold a papyrus with special words or symbols. Hathor's head in gold tops the pendant (enlarged).

A tiny gilt silver mask from Nuri represents the Kushite queen Malakaye, who reigned in the early sixth century B.C.

A hinged Meroitic bracelet of gold and enamel from the first century B.C. The goddess Hathor is featured on a panel.

The lionhead of the god Apedemak appears on the gold and enamel shield ring of Queen Amanishakheto; however, many Nubian specialists believe these objects weren't rings at all but were worn on the forehead.

Archaeologists work on site, using a paint brush and hand pick to free a Native American's skeleton from hardened earth (Illinois, United States).

Dig This!

How Archaeologists Uncover Our Past

DIG THIS!
How Archaeologists Uncover Our Past
by Michael Avi-Yonah

Humans have crafted tools, weapons, clothing, cooking utensils, and many other objects for thousands of years. When these objects broke or wore out, people usually dumped them on a garbage pile and made new things. The discarded objects were often buried under more garbage or under dust, sand, or soil.

In later times, people digging in the ground found some of the objects that were thrown away long ago. The items might be kept out of curiosity. They might be given to a collector of **artifacts** — objects that are made or modified by humans. This process of discovery and preservation is a simplified example of the science called **archaeology.** Archaeologists find, collect, study, and preserve artifacts from the past.

Brushing away four thousand years of dust from a stone artifact in ancient Nippur, Iraq

Archaeology, the Word

The word *archaeology* was first used by the Greeks more than 2,000 years ago. Its first part comes from the Greek word *archaios,* which means "ancient." The second part comes from the Greek word *logos,* which means "speech."

When historians in ancient Greece talked about the past, the discussion was called an "archaeology." Descriptions of the past are now called history, while the study of objects from the past is known as archaeology.

Why Archaeologists Dig

The goal of most archaeological expeditions is to explore and explain ancient artifacts in an effort to understand human history. But the focus of archaeology has shifted. For example, instead of asking where and when farming developed, archaeologists now ask how and why prehistoric people began to grow crops.

How Artifacts Survive

What Destroys Artifacts

Few of the objects thrown away thousands of years ago have survived. After 10 or 20 years, most objects had **decomposed** (broken down) and had mixed with the soil. After 100 years, almost everything had disappeared. The surviving artifacts were made of materials that could withstand harsh climates.

Damp weather quickly destroys cloth, writing paper, and wood. These materials almost never survive, except in the deserts where the climate is very dry. Objects made of gold and silver, however, last for hundreds or thousands of years, even when buried in soil. More common metals — such as iron, copper, or bronze — rust or corrode in the ground, but they usually have a better chance of being recovered than valuable gold or silver objects.

Above, a funeral chamber with gold jewelry, artifacts, and pottery
Inset, the gold mask of a figure at Moche site (Sipan, Peru)

What Lasts and Why?

Over the centuries, people who found objects made from precious metals often melted them down to make money or jewelry. Pottery and stone objects, on the other hand, are not very valuable and are not easily destroyed. For this reason, almost every archaeological site contains little gold but has large amounts of broken pottery called **potsherds.**

Without regular repair, even the strongest buildings eventually decayed. Wind and rain quickly destroyed wooden roofs, and earthquakes shattered the strongest stone walls. In addition, people altered buildings and made it difficult for archaeologists to determine when a structure was first inhabited. City dwellers tore down old buildings and put up new ones in the same places. Laborers often used stones and wooden beams from old buildings for new construction.

A skeleton and clay figurine vessels in a tomb at Moche site (Sipan, Peru)

281

Archaeologists and aides in a pit in Sipan, Peru

How Cities Rise Upon Trash

In ancient times, few cities had garbage collectors, so residents simply threw their trash into the street, where it decayed into the dirt of hard-packed roads. Over time, this gradual accumulation of trash raised the street level so that people walked downstairs to enter their homes. New houses were often built on top of the foundations of old houses. In the new houses, however, the ground floor was level with the street. As a result, the old ground floor lay beneath the new ground floor.

As time passed, streets continued to build up, and the process was repeated. Towns and cities rose higher and higher, forming different levels, or **strata,** of buried objects. Natural soil processes — such as

erosion, weathering, and sedimentation — also help to shape the earth's strata, which accumulate even in modern cities.

Prime Locations

Ancient cities, deeply buried tombs, and sunken ships are all places where archaeologists discover past cultures. Some of these archaeological sites were important urban areas that were abandoned or destroyed during a natural disaster or an ancient war. City dwellers who could escape often left their possessions behind. Archaeologists of a later age might find these abandoned belongings.

What Tombs Tell

Tombs and graves sometimes are the best sources of information about past cultures. Well-preserved bodies can give scientists clues about what people ate and how they died. In many ancient cultures, people buried their dead with charms and valuable possessions, believing the objects would be needed in the **afterlife.** These artifacts help archaeologists solve the puzzle of how people lived long ago.

Above, strata are revealed by foundation repairs in Mexico City, Mexico.

Where to Dig

How Archaeologists Prepare

Archaeologists can spend years finding money to fund digs or **excavations** (the process of uncovering ancient remains). Therefore, the archaeological site must contain useful and interesting artifacts. To verify this conclusion, the archaeologist reads as much as possible about the history of the region.

Archaeologists **survey** (carefully study) prospective sites before an excavation begins. They note any mounds, foundations, walls, columns, or other visible structures.

A survey also includes collecting potsherds from the surface and keeping track of where the pieces are found. By examining the broken pottery, archaeologists can determine when people last lived on the site.

As part of the survey, archaeologists also draw maps and take photographs of the entire site. These experts explore tombs, caves, or other openings in the ground. After the survey, the archaeologist is ready to decide how and where to begin the excavation.

An archaeologist surveys a prospective site.

Lascaux Cave painting (Dordogne region, France)

Luck Plays a Part

Many important archaeological finds are discovered accidentally. In 1940 four boys were exploring a forest near the town of Montignac in southwestern France. After finding a small hole in the ground, the boys scraped out a large opening with their knives and crawled through a narrow passage into a dark underground chamber.

When the boys lifted their oil lamps to look around, they were amazed to see brightly colored animals painted on the cave's white limestone walls and ceiling.

Experts believe that these paintings in Lascaux Cave are authentic **prehistoric** art from an era that predates written records.

Technology Helps Out

Some ruins have been located through aerial or satellite photographs, which can reveal the outlines of ancient cities. Archaeologists use the photographs as a guide when excavating old walls and foundations. Aerial and satellite photography has helped to locate Roman palaces and villas, ancient roads and fields, and prehistoric burial mounds and fortifications.

Oil-drilling rigs have provided another means of investigating the strata of an archaeological site. A drill is used to sample the soil and to determine its composition at different depths. After workers remove the drill, a camera and a flashlight can be lowered into the hole to take underground photographs. Archaeologists have discovered many tombs by using this method.

Organizing a Dig

Planning and Scheduling

Many preliminary arrangements are necessary before a dig can begin. Archaeologists need to get permission from the landowner — whether a government or an individual — to excavate the site.

Archaeologists must also schedule time for the work. The local climate usually determines the months that are most suitable. In hot regions, like deserts, winter is the best time to work because temperatures are cool. In rainy areas, spring or autumn may be chosen because rainfall levels are low.

Working together

Mending pottery on a dig

Gathering an Expert Team

Excavations require experts and workers who are skilled in many different areas. A surveyor diagrams the work as it progresses. A photographer takes pictures of the ruins and of any interesting objects that the dig reveals. Registrars record exact information about everything that is found.

A restorer preserves and reconstructs very delicate or valuable objects that are partly decomposed and in need of special treatment. A language expert deciphers

285

Sifting soil for pottery fragments

In addition to a team of experts, archaeologists rely on volunteers — mainly students — to assist in searching the soil for remains. The expedition provides the volunteers with food and lodging, but it does not pay them a salary. Many student volunteers participate in digs as part of their coursework.

Sifting Through the Evidence

Finding What's There

The area to be excavated is marked with stakes and string in a grid of squares. Each square — called an excavation unit — is about the size of a child's sandbox. As the earth is dug away, the markers that separate the units from each other are left standing. Dirt is carefully removed, shoveled into a basket, and carried to a dump site. Workers at a large excavation might set up conveyor belts to transport the earth.

Before it is dumped, the dirt is carefully examined for artifacts. Excavators pass the soil through a screen made of wire mesh, so that small objects are not accidentally thrown away. When a large object is discovered — such as a skull, cooking pot, or a tool — the archaeologist in charge usually removes it from the soil.

inscriptions on ancient artifacts. A physical anthropologist studies the remains of human skeletons.

Natural scientists — such as geologists, botanists, and zoologists — examine the soil, the remains of plant and animal life, and evidence of the past climates of archaeological sites. Their findings can reveal the natural environment that existed when the ruin was occupied.

Recording the Evidence

All objects collected from a certain excavation unit are put into the same basket, which is labeled with the number of the unit and the depth at which the objects were found. Materials recovered from a site are immediately recorded, bagged, and labeled. Surveyors map the locations of significant finds and label each strata. This careful process ensures that archaeologists will be able to relocate each of the thousands of objects that have been discovered.

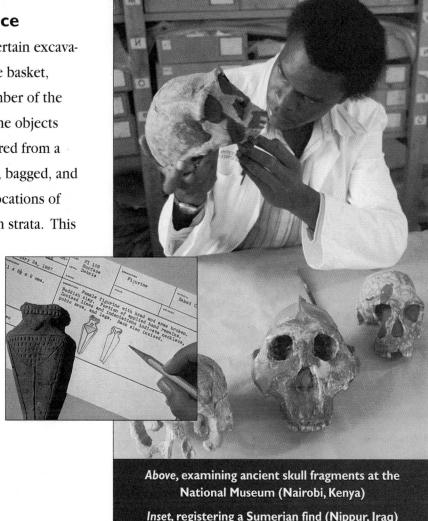

Above, examining ancient skull fragments at the National Museum (Nairobi, Kenya)

Inset, registering a Sumerian find (Nippur, Iraq)

About This Book

Dig This! How Archaeologists Uncover Our Past was revised for young American readers from a book by Michael Avi-Yonah, a famous, highly respected archaeologist. Avi-Yonah, who became a professor of archaeology and the history of art in Israel, wrote many books and articles about ancient civilizations.

This book is for you, if you are thinking of becoming an archaeologist, or want to know more about what archaeologists do.

Backyard

Back to the Future

A thousand years from now, what will people dig up? Styrofoam cups? CD players? Mountain bikes? Choose an artifact from the present. Using information from the selection, explain why this item would survive harsh climates and burial. What would future archaeologists find out about the way we live from studying this artifact?

Discuss

In Search of . . . ?

In which region would you want to dig for artifacts? Beneath New York City? In the Sahara Desert? In your own backyard? What clues on the surface would help you decide how and where to begin the excavation? Share your ideas with a partner.

Dig!

Create a Diorama

Cities Piled High on Trash

Can you imagine what the excavation site would look like of an ancient city as it's described in the selection? Create a diorama, or draw a picture, showing how one house is layered on top of another.

Role-play an Interview

You're Hired, Mr. Carter

With a partner, role-play a job interview that Howard Carter might have done before he was hired to excavate Tutankhamen's tomb. Have one person play Carter and the other the interviewer. From what you have read in this theme, what are the qualities of a good archaeologist and why is Carter qualified for the job?

THE ANCIENT OLYMPIC GAMES

A RESEARCH REPORT BY
WAIPA NISHIMURA

The Olympic Games are more than 2000 years old! Waipa learned that fact and many others when he did his research for this report.

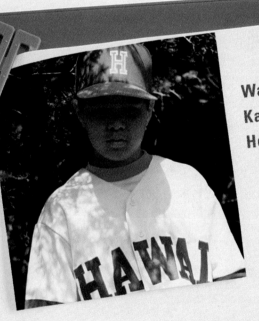

Waipa Nishimura
Kamehameha Schools
Honolulu, Hawaii

Because he likes sports, Waipa decided to research the Olympic Games when he wrote this report in the sixth grade. In addition to playing baseball and football, Waipa writes stories and poems. Waipa would like to be a politician someday.

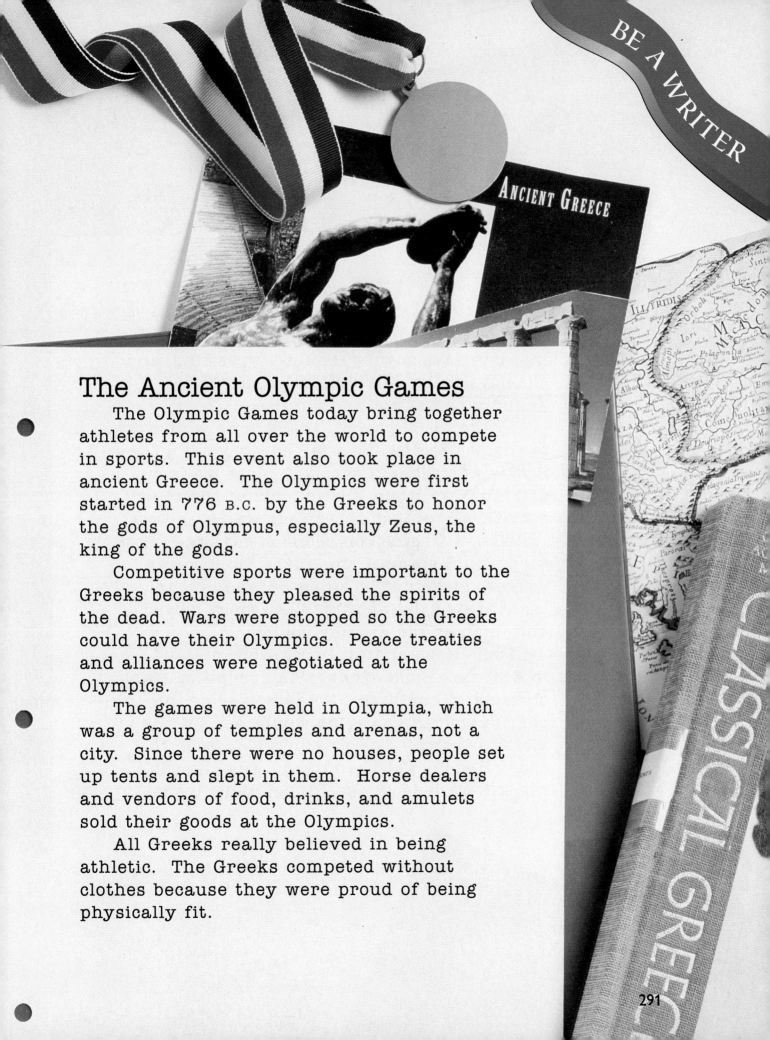

The Ancient Olympic Games

The Olympic Games today bring together athletes from all over the world to compete in sports. This event also took place in ancient Greece. The Olympics were first started in 776 B.C. by the Greeks to honor the gods of Olympus, especially Zeus, the king of the gods.

Competitive sports were important to the Greeks because they pleased the spirits of the dead. Wars were stopped so the Greeks could have their Olympics. Peace treaties and alliances were negotiated at the Olympics.

The games were held in Olympia, which was a group of temples and arenas, not a city. Since there were no houses, people set up tents and slept in them. Horse dealers and vendors of food, drinks, and amulets sold their goods at the Olympics.

All Greeks really believed in being athletic. The Greeks competed without clothes because they were proud of being physically fit.

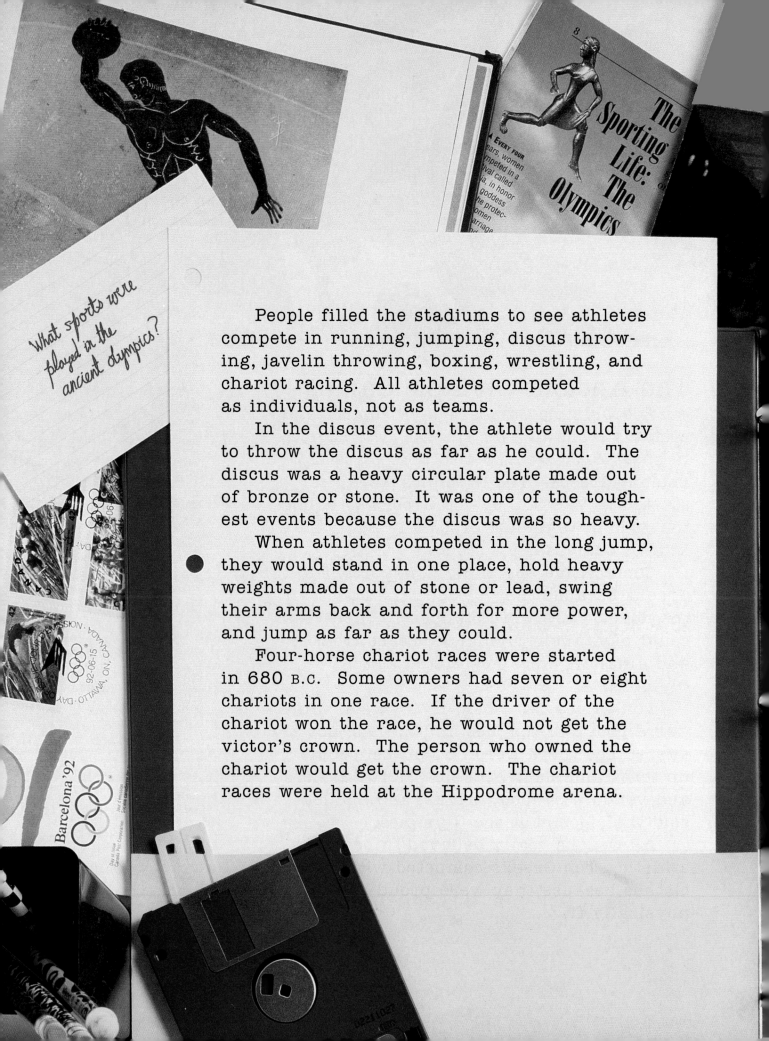

What sports were played in the ancient olympics?

The Sporting Life: The Olympics

People filled the stadiums to see athletes compete in running, jumping, discus throwing, javelin throwing, boxing, wrestling, and chariot racing. All athletes competed as individuals, not as teams.

In the discus event, the athlete would try to throw the discus as far as he could. The discus was a heavy circular plate made out of bronze or stone. It was one of the toughest events because the discus was so heavy.

When athletes competed in the long jump, they would stand in one place, hold heavy weights made out of stone or lead, swing their arms back and forth for more power, and jump as far as they could.

Four-horse chariot races were started in 680 B.C. Some owners had seven or eight chariots in one race. If the driver of the chariot won the race, he would not get the victor's crown. The person who owned the chariot would get the crown. The chariot races were held at the Hippodrome arena.

The Greeks loved it when citizen warriors carried shields and raced in a special race. This was the Greek's favorite race because it was hard to run and the participants fell a lot. It was considered funny and added to the spectators' enjoyment of the games.

The Olympics of ancient Greece brought people together in a good way. This tradition is continued today. The nations of the world send athletes to compete, and people attend to enjoy a good performance.

Works Cited:

Bowra, C. M., and the Editors of Time-Life Books. Classical Greece. New York: Time-Life Books, 1965.

"Discus," "Greece," "Olympics." The World Book Encyclopedia, Volumes 5 (p. 226), 8 (pp. 392, 395), and 14 (pp. 754–760).

"The Sporting Life: The Olympics." Kids Discover. August/September 1994: 8–9.

Rain at the Koster Dig

by Gerry Armstrong

It was broiling hot today, with no shade at all in the big field where we were digging. The sun beat down like a blast furnace, and sweat ran down my face and dripped off my nose and chin. I grinned ruefully, remembering how I had begged my parents to let me come. I'd been so happy when I was in the bunch chosen from Mrs. MacDougall's class to work here at the Koster dig near Kampsville alongside the archaeologists. There used to be an Indian town here thousands of years ago. We were finding old bones, broken pottery, and chips of flint and stone and shell. The archaeologists hoped to learn more about the ways of these ancient Indians by studying their remains.

The ground was hot to the touch where I knelt, scraping slowly at the soil. Blisters were rising on the palm of my hand, and my back ached from bending over. But I didn't slack off. I knew the other volunteers — from high school and college — hadn't been happy to have us twelve- and thirteen-year-olds share the work this year. They called us "munchkins" (the name of those little people in the Wizard of Oz story) and they said it with a sneer. All of us from Washburne Junior High wanted to prove that we could be just as good as they were. So I gritted my teeth and kept working away.

When I heard the call for lunch, I staggered to the nearby spring, sprawled in the shade, and groaned. I must have dozed off because I was suddenly aware of happy shouts. I sat up — and oh, joy! — saw churning masses of gray clouds directly overhead. Huge drops of cold rain splattered down. My friends and I welcomed the storm with wild cheers! We danced in the downpour, hugging each other and laughing insanely.

Some people were running toward the dig, so we ran, too, and discovered that the wet mud made a glorious slide. What great fun! Wheeeee!

Someone grabbed my arm. It was Gail, one of the supervisors, and she was furious. "Get the dig covered!" she screamed. "Grab this tarp!"

I caught hold of one side of it, and we scrambled up the slippery hill and dragged the covering over one of the holes. I noticed that it already had *inches* of water in it. "Hurry!" cried Gail, running down toward the shed. I slipped and slid after her, and we struggled back with another heavy tarp. I don't know how many trips we made, lugging those heavy things, but I had a stitch in my side, and my legs were shaking with exhaustion when we finally had everything covered.

I crawled into the truck with the others and sat with my head on my knees. The cold rain on my bare neck made me shiver. Or maybe it was the cold silence that chilled me. The rumbling thunder was the only sound. There was none of the usual friendly chatter as we made our way back to camp. The good feeling of being part of a team had dissolved in the rain. We kids had behaved like munchkins — goofing off while the holes at the dig filled with rainwater. We felt guilty and miserable.

I almost hoped I'd get pneumonia so I wouldn't have to attend the camp meeting that night. But I wasn't even sniffling that evening, so I trudged over to the lecture hall.

"Well, we learned something today," said Stuart Struever, director of the dig. "We learned we need a rain drill."

A few people laughed sheepishly, and Dr. Struever grinned. But then he

continued seriously, "I'm pleased with the way everyone responded today. Once you realized the problem, you worked hard to correct it. If there's anyone to blame for the damage that was done, it's me. *I* know the harm that rain can do to a dig; some of the crew had no idea. But you learned that today, so you're ahead now. We'll have a rain drill so that from now on everyone knows where the tarps are kept, which holes need protection first, when protective ditches should be dug, where tools are put to be dried later.

"All these things are vitally important to a dig, and you should have been told. I know all of you are concerned with Koster. Those holes you're digging are our tunnels into the past, the past that holds the information we're seeking about these prehistoric people. So those holes must be protected. And you worked hard today when you saw what needed to be done. I'm satisfied. Now, Gail, let's hear a report on the damage."

I sighed with relief. He wasn't going to scold. I *did* goof — all of us munchkins did — but Dr. Struever just talked about it, put it behind him, and went on to the next problem. He still wanted us. I suddenly realized I was blinking back tears. I glanced over at my best friend, and she grinned at me, but I noticed there were tears in her eyes, too. I guess we were all afraid Dr. Struever might send us home in disgrace. But everything's all right. We're still members of the team. Munchkins or not, we're archaeologists, too.

The Koster dig is now closed, but at the time this story takes place, junior-high students were actually helping archaeologists on the dig.

BY MYRA COHN LIVINGSTON

MUMMY

So small a thing
This mummy lies,
Closed in death
Red-lidded eyes,
While, underneath
The swaddled clothes,
Brown arms, brown legs
Lie tight enclosed.
What miracle
If he could tell
Of other years
He knew so well;
What wonderment
To speak to me
The riddle of
His history.

This Native American Basket Maker was found in the Canyon del Muerto, in Arizona, where the naturally dry climate had mummified him. He died around A.D. 300 to A.D. 500.

ABOUT DON LESSEM

Don Lessem is fascinated by the ways in which people try to investigate the past. When he first heard about the Iceman, Lessem was struck by the fact that "It wasn't just one or two clues that had been discovered; a whole new world was opened up." By the time he started writing his own book on the subject, "the fossil itself was off-limits, so I had to read as much as I could find, the way students do when they write a book report." When Lessem first saw color photographs of Ötzi, he was "amazed and a little grossed out" by the vivid details. However, these details helped Lessem achieve his goal of bringing the past alive.

298

THE
REMARKABLE
DISCOVERY
OF A
5,300-YEAR-
OLD MAN—
TOGETHER
WITH
HIS CLOTHES,
TOOLS, AND
WEAPONS—
FROZEN IN
AN ALPINE
GLACIER

THE ICEMAN

BY DON LESSEM

were hiking in the mountains on the border between Austria and Italy. That afternoon the Simons roamed off the path and made a startling discovery: the small head and shoulders of a human body sticking out of the ice.

At first they thought the hairless figure was an abandoned doll. Then they noticed a small hole in the back of its skull. Perhaps this was a man who had been murdered, the Simons thought. They called the Italian police, who thought it might be the body of somebody killed in a recent hiking accident. The police left without attempting to dig the body out.

The Austrian police arrived by helicopter the next day. They tried — and failed — to remove the body from the thick ice with a jackhammer, tearing its clothes in the process. The police stopped digging when their jackhammer ran out of power and their helicopter was needed elsewhere. They decided to return the following week, with an expert on corpses to supervise them.

Dr. Rainer Henn *(in light parka)* directs the recovery team. ▶

Meanwhile, news of the strange body spread quickly through the mountains. Other officials and hikers arrived and tried to free it using axes and ski poles. Some took away items belonging to the body trapped in the ice. One unsuccessful rescuer even dug at the body with a stick that was found lying nearby. Later, the stick would prove to be a valuable part of the corpse's possessions.

The people who found the body had no idea how important their discovery was. A few days later, the police flew an Austrian scientist, Rainer Henn, to the site by helicopter to inspect the body. He noticed immediately that the corpse did not have the waxy skin of someone who had died recently. Instead, it looked yellowed and dried, like a mummy.

◀ Using crude tools, including pickaxes and ski poles, the recovery team removes the Iceman from the glacier.

Dr. Henn could tell that this corpse was ancient, not modern, and for that reason it would be important to archaeologists, not the police. Archaeologists excavate their discoveries with great care to make sure nothing is overlooked, lost, or damaged. But Dr. Henn feared that the body would be further damaged by curious amateurs, so he decided to dig it out immediately and fly it to a laboratory. He had brought no tools with him, so he and his crew borrowed pickaxes and ski poles to finish the job of removing the body.

Dr. Henn wondered just how long this mummy had been preserved in the ice. Moments before the frozen body was loaded on the helicopter, a small stone knife with a wooden handle was discovered nearby. This was a primitive and very ancient tool — the first clue to the mummy's age.

More of the mummy's strange belongings were soon found, including clothes, a huge bow, and an ax. All of them would prove to be important clues to solving the mysteries of their owner's life and death. Even more important, the mummy and its possessions would turn out to give us our best view yet of the life of people in Europe thousands of years ago.

The Science of Collecting

The collecting of ancient human remains and belongings is part of the science of archaeology (ARE-key-OLL-uh-jee). Archaeologists excavate objects with great care to get all the information they can. They make a detailed map of the site and record all finds, however small. They often dig with small, specially designed tools to make sure nothing is missed or damaged.

The Iceman was not collected by archaeologists. Curious people came to the site before scientists and took some items. The mummy and its clothing were damaged because the body was removed in a hurry, without proper tools.

After scientists saw how valuable the discovery was, they returned to the site to make a more detailed search. People who had removed objects returned them. Though scientists were not the first ones at this important find, they have been able to gather a great deal of information from the Iceman and his possessions.

The mysterious body in the ice belonged to a man, soon nicknamed Ötzi (UTT-zee) by the local people, after the Ötztal, a valley near where he died. And they wondered, who was this man? Local children spoke of Ötzi as "the poor man who died alone in the snow."

Ötzi and his valuable belongings did not get proper scientific attention right away. He was flown to a village, then squeezed into a coffin for a ride to the city of Innsbruck. There Ötzi lay in a warm morgue for nearly a week, growing fungus, until an Austrian archaeologist, Dr. Konrad Spindler, was brought in to examine the corpse.

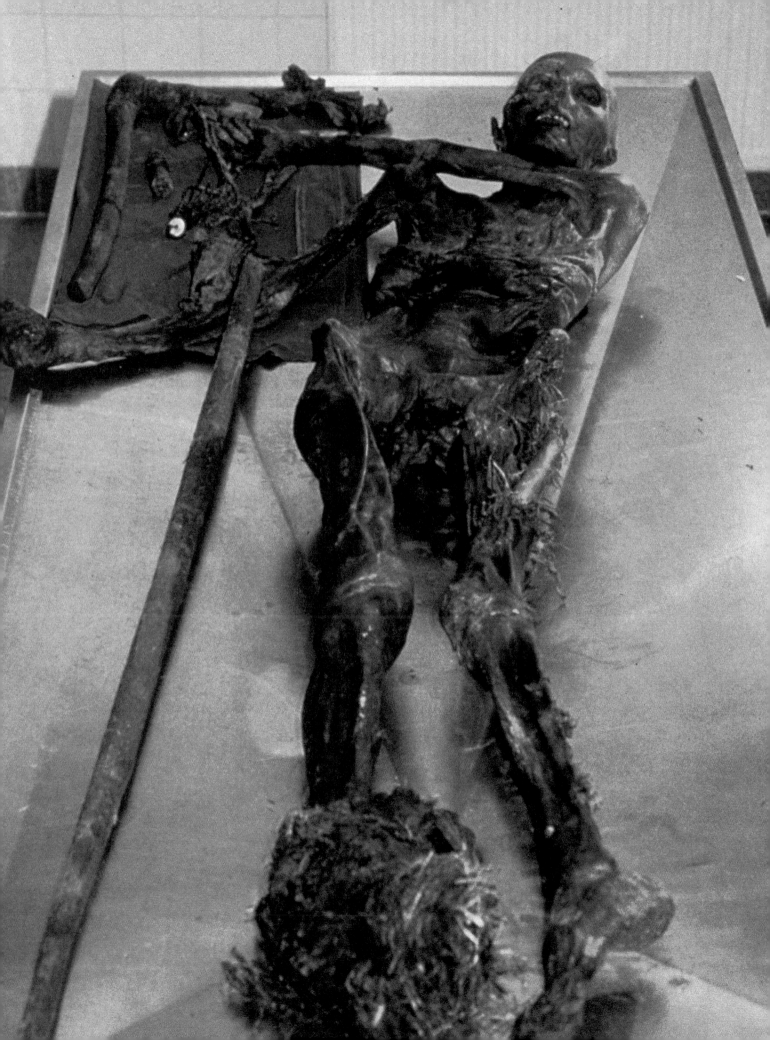

Dr. Spindler immediately guessed that Ötzi could be as much as 4,000 years old — which would make him the oldest complete mummy ever found! It was not the Iceman himself but the ax that was found with him that led Dr. Spindler to estimate Ötzi's age. Ötzi's ax was an impressive weapon, with a wedge-shaped four-inch metal blade. The blade was wrapped with cow leather and glue from the gum of birch trees. It was held tightly in an L-shaped handle made of yew wood. Dr. Spindler guessed the blade of this well-made tool was fashioned from bronze, a metal that came into use 4,000 years ago. But laboratory studies showed that Dr. Spindler's guess was wrong — and that Ötzi was even older than he had thought. The ax blade was made of almost pure copper, a metal put into use by blacksmiths almost two thousand years before bronze. Ötzi was between 5,000 and 5,500 years old and belonged to the Copper Age.

◄ Ötzi's body and belongings displayed on a table in Innsbruck. On his foot are remnants of a leather shoe stuffed with hay. Next to him are the tools and other objects that were found soon after his body was discovered, including a six-foot-long bow and an ax *(see following page).*

Who Keeps the Iceman?

The Iceman was first thought to have been found in Austria. So he was excavated by the Austrian police and taken to a laboratory in Innsbruck, Austria, for study. Researchers then learned that he had died about 100 yards across the border, in Italy. As a result, Italian officials claimed that the body belonged to Italy and requested that it be returned to them. An international agreement arranged for the Iceman to go to Italy on September 19, 1994 — three years from the day he was found.

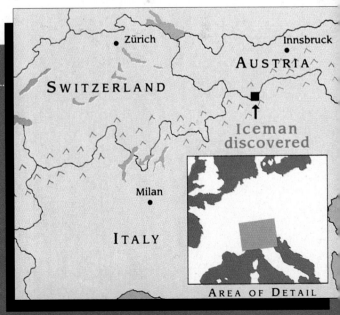

How Old Was the Iceman?

It wasn't difficult to determine how old the Iceman was when he died. The condition of his bones and teeth, which show a full-grown healthy person, indicates that he was between the ages of 25 and 40.

Figuring out how long the Iceman has been a mummy was a harder problem. His tools are similar to those found at sites known to be more than 5,000 years old. And a method called *carbon dating* verified this. All living things, and many objects, contain the element carbon. Part of that carbon is in a form that decays at a steady rate. By measuring how much of this form of carbon has decayed, scientists can estimate the age of an animal, plant, or object. Carbon dating tells us that the Iceman is 5,000 to 5,500 years old.

These wood-and-mud stilt houses were reconstructed at Lac de Chalain in eastern France by archaeologists using evidence from the remains of European Copper Age villages. Ötzi may have visited villages that looked something like this. ▶

◀ Ötzi's ax as it may have looked when he used it *(left)* and as it was found *(above)*.

There are Copper Age villages spread across the middle of Europe, including several in Switzerland, not far north of where Ötzi was found. Research has shown that these villages consisted of wood-and-mud houses built on stilts along muddy lake shores. Villagers built wheeled carts and used plows for farming. They grew barley, peas, and flax for linen clothes, and they fished and hunted for food. They raised animals: dogs, sheep, goats, pigs, and cattle. And they made whole-grain bread from the barley they grew, and butter from milk. They traded with other peoples near and far away, bartering lime-stone jewelry they made with people from the south for parsley and peppermint.

Making Copper

Copper was the first metal used by prehistoric man. It was found in rocks, including those at the base of the mountains where the Iceman died. The drawing below shows how copper was made. Coppersmiths built underground fires into which they placed rocks containing copper. They blew into the fire pit through hollowed-out sticks. When the temperature neared 2,000°F, the copper melted and separated from the rock around it. The pure copper was shaped into bars, and then re-melted and poured into molds to make tools. Copper made far sharper, stronger tools than stone did.

Copper was first used in Europe about 6,000 years ago (4000 B.C.). The Copper Age lasted until about 4,200 years ago (2200 B.C.), when copper was replaced by bronze and the Bronze Age began.

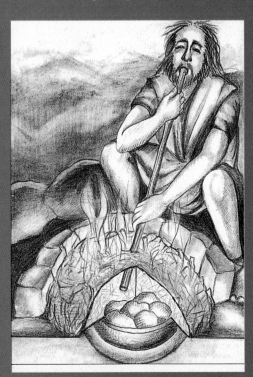

Using measurements and X-rays of Ötzi's skull and studies of Europeans today, artist John Gurche made this model showing how Ötzi might have looked. The skin is made of soft plastic and tinted red to imitate Ötzi's windburned skin. The eyes are made of glass. ▶

The remains of many Copper Age villages have been discovered and excavated, but it is Ötzi who has given archaeologists their best indication of what the people of Europe actually looked like 5,500 years ago. From his well-preserved mummy, we can tell a lot about the Iceman's appearance. He was short — about 5 feet 2 inches. But he was powerful, as the enormous bow that was found with him indicates. It was far larger than the Iceman himself and would have required great strength to draw back and fire arrows from.

Scientists are sure that Ötzi had curly brown hair. How do we know that when the hair on his body and head was not preserved? Hairs were discovered trapped in his clothes. The ends of those hairs were evenly snipped, indicating that somebody had given Ötzi a haircut.

Taking Care of the Iceman

To protect the Iceman, Dr. Spindler and his colleagues from the Institute for Prehistory and Early History in Innsbruck sprayed his body with a chemical to kill the mold that had been growing from the time the body was found. Then they placed the body in a freezer. There the temperature was kept at 21°F and the humidity at 98 percent — just the icy conditions in which Ötzi had been preserved until he was found.

Ötzi remains on ice. He is never removed from his frozen container for more than 20 minutes at a time, and then only for scientific study. Meanwhile, the investigation of Ötzi and his belongings goes on, with scientists around the world studying pieces of his skin, bones, clothes, and tools.

Investigators discovered mysterious tattoos on Ötzi's body. Four stripes, each three inches long, ran across the top of his left foot. On his left kneecap he wore a cross. And three groups of small bars lined his lower back. These weren't decorations meant for others to see, for they appeared only on parts of his body that would have

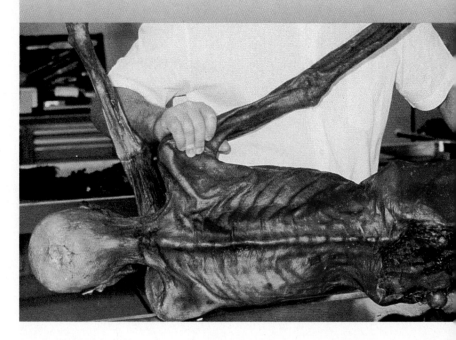

been hidden by his clothing. Maybe they were a badge of religious importance.

Ötzi may have made some of them himself, with a needle and ash or dye. But someone else had to make the tattoos on his back.

How Is an Iceman Iced?

The Iceman's remarkable preservation and his discovery occurred only because of a series of lucky events.

Many people die on icy mountains. If their bodies are not found, glaciers eventually crush them. But the Iceman died in a hollow that glaciers never reached. Light snow covered his body soon after he died and kept it from decay as it dried out. Then the snow was covered with thick layers of ice, which built up to form a glacier. Because it was in a hollow, the Iceman's body was not crushed by the ice; instead, the ice passed over him *(right)*.

In the last 70 years the weather has turned warmer, and as a result, the glaciers in the Alps have retreated. In the spring of 1991, a storm in the Sahara Desert sent clouds of dust into the air, which settled on the snow-covered mountains where the Iceman was buried. The dark dust absorbed the heat of the sun instead of reflecting it, as white snow would have. Combined with a warm summer, it helped melt the snow and ice quickly. The Iceman emerged for the first time in 5,000 years. Then, within days, his body was discovered — before the air could destroy it or snow cover it over again.

◄ Ötzi's back. In the lower part of the picture, near his spine, are three groups of tattooed lines.

SNOW

GLACIAL ICE

↑
Position of body

ROCK

From Ötzi's teeth, scientists drew conclusions about what he ate. His diet seems to have been richest in bread, for his teeth were ground down, as they could only be from eating grains for many years.

From Ötzi's body, researchers have also figured out that he died of exposure to the cold. He probably encountered an unexpected wintry storm in fall. Without sufficient clothing to keep himself warm, or food to nourish him, his body temperature dropped until he died.

But why didn't Ötzi have the strength to walk down the mountain? Perhaps the storm was too fierce. Maybe he was weak from illness, though scientists have yet to find any evidence that he was sick.

It is possible that Ötzi was suffering from a broken arm. His left arm is cracked. This injury may have been caused by his rough removal from the ice. But the skin on his arm is undamaged, suggesting that it was broken while he was still alive. Perhaps the pain of a broken arm, injured in a mountain fall, weakened this strong man.

Much of Ötzi's clothing was destroyed during the rough and sloppy excavation. But from many scraps found with the body, scientists have determined that he wore leather pants and a long-sleeved jacket made of deer, goat, and ibex hide, with the fur side turned out. The pieces of hide had been skillfully stitched together with threads made of animal sinews and grass. Rough repairs had also been made — probably by Ötzi himself — using grass thread.

He also wore a huge cape, braided from strands of grass. This heavy poncho resembled a Hawaiian grass skirt, except that it was tied around the neck, not the waist. A piece of fur discovered near Ötzi may have been a fur cap.

On Ötzi's feet were shoes — soft ovals, size six, made of leather and filled with a warm stuffing of hay. Grass laces, kept dry by a leather flap, were strung through eyeholes to keep his feet snug.

Ötzi may have worn jewelry. Near his body lay a leather string with a fringe, strung through a two-inch disk made of white stone. This mysterious object may have been Ötzi's necklace.

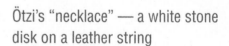

Ötzi's "necklace" — a white stone disk on a leather string

▼ Ötzi as he may have looked dressed in his hat, his braided-grass cape, his shoes, and his necklace. With him are some of the things he carried: his ax, his bow and quiver of arrows, his knife, his backpack, and his birch-bark container, which may have contained tinder for starting fires.

Ötzi's leather pouch, which he probably wore like a modern fanny pack ▶

Ötzi wasn't traveling light. In addition to his heavy cape, he was hauling a wood-frame backpack. It was a piece of this backpack that one of Ötzi's rescuers had used to try to dig him out of the ice.

Scientists can't tell what Ötzi carried in the backpack. But a soft leather pouch, like a modern fanny pack, was also found, with its contents intact. There were two pieces of flint, which could have been used for making tools and for striking sparks to start fires. There was also a four-inch-long wooden stick, like a fat pencil, with a tip made of deer antler. Ötzi may have used this tool for sharpening the chunks of flint. The pack also contained grass string and a needle-pointed awl made from a thin shaft of bone.

◀ Deer-antler-and-wood tool, which may have been used to sharpen flint

▲ Needle-pointed bone awl and grass string ▼

314

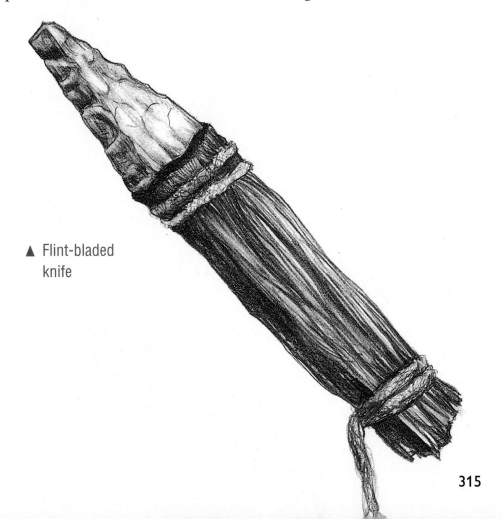

Mushrooms
threaded on a
leather string ▶

Near Ötzi's body, researchers found a
frozen sloeberry and a slice of antelope
meat, which he might have been carrying as a snack,
and two mushrooms strung on a piece of leather. Scientists know
that this kind of mushroom can be used to fight sickness; perhaps Ötzi
was carrying them as medicine. Ötzi also carried two strips of felt
and a small container made of birch bark. Scientists think he may
have used the felt as tinder for starting fires and the birch-bark
container to carry the felt in.

For cutting up leather or small animals, the Iceman carried a
tiny knife with a flint blade the size of his thumb and a handle of ash
wood. He protected this tool with a sheath woven of grass.

▲ Flint-bladed
knife

After his copper-bladed ax, the most impressive of Ötzi's possessions were his bow and arrows. The bow was nearly six feet long and made of yew, the best wood available for making bows. Ötzi's bow was new. It had not yet been notched or strung, and fresh cut marks from an ax still show on its surface.

Ötzi carried his arrows in a deerskin quiver, which also held a ball of grass string, a piece of deer antler, and a few unshaped flints. In all, there were a dozen shafts of viburnum wood for arrows Ötzi hadn't finished making.

Ötzi's arrows *(left)*, deerskin quiver *(center)*, and unstrung bow *(right)* ▶

▲ Ötzi's arrows. Two of them have
tail feathers in place.

But two arrows were complete and very well crafted. Flint, chipped perfectly into an arrowhead, had been attached to each shaft with gum made from the boiled roots of birch trees. With this glue, feathers were set at angles on the ends of the shaft to make the arrow spin and so travel straight in flight.

▲ This artist's impression of Ötzi's arrival at a lakeside village is based on what is known about daily life in the Copper Age. In the background is the mountainous terrain of the Alps. Houses built of wood and mud stand on stilts at the edge of a lake. Nearby are cultivated fields and a primitive wagon. On the lake a person is fishing from a boat.

Ötzi and the everyday objects that were found beside him are unique and wonderfully preserved clues to daily life in a time that has long been mysterious. With their help, we can imagine what life might have been like in the Copper Age and how Ötzi lived and died. We can never be certain, but it may have been something like this:

Ötzi may have been a shepherd herding sheep, a trader trading stone and metal for tools, or even a medicine man in search of messages from gods. Whatever the reason, Ötzi had hiked high into the mountains. He was strong and well equipped, perhaps a leader among his people. The tattoo lines on his knee, foot, and back may have been religious emblems or a sign of his bravery or status.

Ötzi was a welcome visitor to the villages along his route. If he was a shepherd, he would have brought the villagers meat (since wool was not yet used for clothing). If he was a trader, he would have brought them flint for tools or copper for weapons.

Ötzi may have admired the villagers' talents. They used wheeled wagons and plows to farm. They sewed linen clothes and shoes expertly. They fed him butter and other delicacies.

The villagers may have been impressed with the hard flints Ötzi had brought — wonderful stones for making daggers and knives — and with his fine ax. But Ötzi would not part with the ax. He had traveled far to the south and traded away many of his belongings to the copper workers for his ax.

Ötzi was handy and so found many uses for his ax. He had been wielding it lately to make a new bow to replace the one he'd traded away or broken. It was a huge bow, taller than he was. It took all his strength to pull the bowstring.

Ötzi had been hunting since he was a child. He had learned to feather his arrows at an angle to make them spin in flight and hold their course. After crossing the mountains, Ötzi planned to finish his new bow and arrows. Then he could hunt in the woods for ibex, deer, and boar, and kill threatening bears and wolves. But for now, his mind was on traveling across the treeless high mountains in the thin, cold air.

In the soft deerskin suit and grass cape made for him by the village tailors, Ötzi was dressed for chill mountain weather. He had stuffed his shoes with mountain grass to protect his feet from the cold. He wore a fur cap on his head.

But the autumn air turned even colder than Ötzi had expected. He huddled in the shelter of a rock hollow. He was too cold and tired to eat the last of the antelope meat and berries he had brought with him.

Ötzi tried to start a fire. He had flint to strike a spark and strips of felt to help the fire along. But far above the tree line, Ötzi could find no branches to keep a fire going. Perhaps falling snow snuffed out the few sparks he had created.

Ötzi's only hope for survival was to move on through the mountain pass and down into the valley. But he was too weak to move. Maybe he was sick or injured.

Ötzi carefully laid his belongings, including his beautiful ax, against the rocks around him. He lay down to sleep on his left side atop a large stone as the snow fell through the frigid air.

Days later, when Ötzi did not appear, other shepherds, or friends from the village, may have come looking for him. If they came upon the spot where he lay down, they would have found only a blanket of snow.

In cold isolation, Ötzi had quietly died. Five thousand years later, his snow blanket was finally removed. At last Ötzi was found, along with his treasures. Their value is beyond measure, for they give us our best view yet of the lost world of our Copper Age ancestors.

Solving Ötzi's

Design a Poster

Where's Ötzi?

Using details from the selection, write and design a missing person poster for Ötzi. Include a sketch and a description of him listing your name, stilt-house number, and a reward that could have been offered in the Copper Age.

Report a TV News Story

You Are There

As the first TV newsperson on the scene of the Iceman's discovery, prepare a report for your viewers. Include interviews with the hikers, police, and scientists. After finding out the who, what, when, where, why, and how, write and perform your newscast.

Puzzle

Make a Museum Exhibit

See It to Believe It

Prepare an item from the Iceman's
life for a classroom museum exhibit.
Create or draw an artifact and write a
brief description. Demonstrate to your
classmates your item's possible use in
the exhibit. What clues helped you
explain its use?

Make Trading Cards

Start Your Mummy Collection Today

With a partner compare and contrast the
mummies in *The Iceman*, in *Into the
Mummy's Tomb*, and in *Tales Mummies Tell*.
How were they different? What did they
have in common? Create trading cards of
each of the mummies with their pictures
and vital "stats."

How old is that pot or spearhead? When did the first humans appear? To figure out the age of an archaeological site, we need to find something that changes over time, ticking off the years since the pot was made or the bones were left in the earth. To keep good time, this "clock" has to "tick" smoothly and regularly.

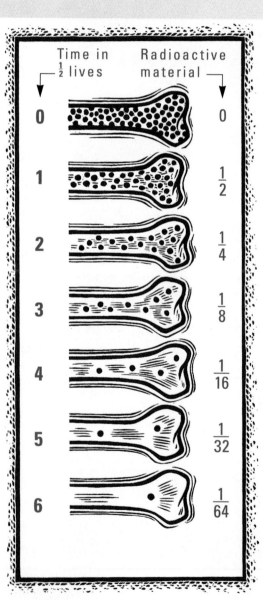

Time in ½ lives	Radioactive material
0	0
1	$\frac{1}{2}$
2	$\frac{1}{4}$
3	$\frac{1}{8}$
4	$\frac{1}{16}$
5	$\frac{1}{32}$
6	$\frac{1}{64}$

ATOMIC CLOCKS

Atomic Clocks

What kinds of buried objects change regularly over time? Some of the best archaeological clocks are atomic ones based on the slow decay of radioactive atoms.

Radioactive atoms are unstable atoms that eventually break down into more stable atoms and miscellaneous atomic particles. This breakdown happens at a known rate, called the half-life.

The half-life is the number of years it takes for half of the radioactive material to break down. For example, if the half-life is one hour, half of the original radioactive material will have decayed after one hour, half of the remaining half (or three-quarters of the original amount) will be gone after two hours, and so on.

You can easily do the math to show that after six hours, only a tiny amount ($\frac{1}{2} \times \frac{1}{2} \times \frac{1}{2} \times \frac{1}{2} \times \frac{1}{2} \times \frac{1}{2} = \frac{1}{64}$) of the original amount will be left.

If we know how much of the radioactive material was there to start with and we measure how much is left, we can tell how many half-lives have passed since decay began. To date archaeological sites, we need radioactive materials with long half-lives.

IS IT?

by Alison S. Brooks

Radiocarbon

Many ordinary objects contain tiny amounts of radioactive materials that are not dangerous to people. A very small amount of the carbon in the air (about the same as 1 grain of sand in 50 truckloads) is radioactive.

Plants absorb carbon (carbon dioxide) from the air, and animals eat the plants (and each other), taking both the normal and the radioactive plant carbon (called carbon 14) into their bodies. Once the plant or animal dies, the carbon 14 begins to decay. The half-life of carbon 14 is about 5,730 years.

By comparing the amount of carbon 14 in the things we excavate to the amount in the air, we can date things such as animal bones and plants, as well as objects made from animals and plants (leather, baskets, and charcoal, for example), that lived or were made within the past 35,000 years or so (about six half-lives).

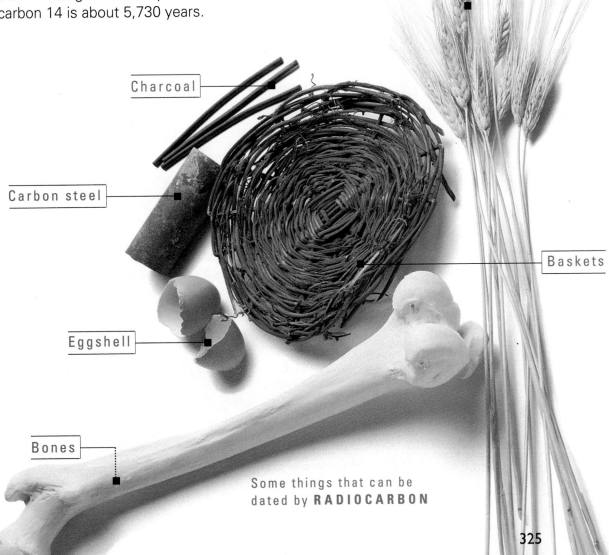

Seeds

Charcoal

Carbon steel

Baskets

Eggshell

Bones

Some things that can be dated by **RADIOCARBON**

325

Slower Clocks

What if a site is more than 35,000 years old? Or what if no objects that were once alive (organic) have survived in the ground? Another useful radioactive material is a form of potassium that is present in most of the earth's rocks.

Over a very long half-life (1.3 billion years), the small amount of radioactive potassium splits apart and turns into calcium and argon, which is a gas.

About 1 in every 10,000 atoms of potassium is radioactive, so we can figure out the amount of radioactive potassium that was there to start with from the amount of nonradioactive potassium that is still there.

If the rock is heated up in a volcano, the argon gas escapes and only potassium remains. So heating sets the clock to zero.

The amount of potassium that has decayed into argon since the explosion can tell us how much time has gone by.

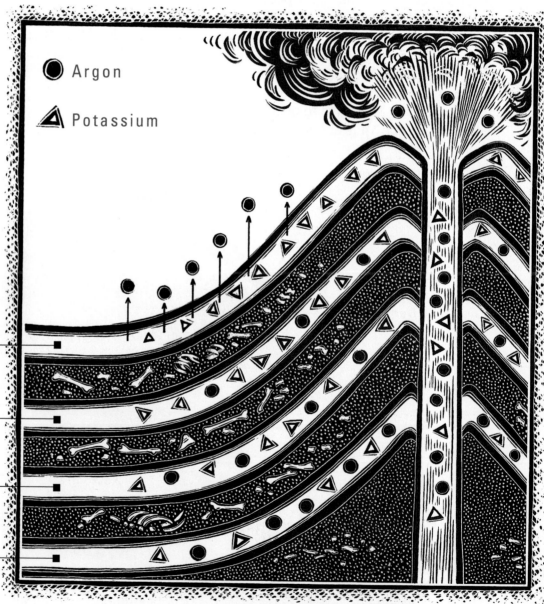

- Argon
- Potassium

0 Years
Clock Starts

2 Million
Years

10 Million
Years

20 Million
Years

POTASSIUM ARGON DATING

Protein Clocks

Another kind of clock uses the proteins in bones, teeth, and other hard animal products such as eggshells. These proteins also break down at a regular rate.

One problem is that the breakdown of proteins is faster in hotter and wetter climates. But if we can guess the ancient temperature and use a material that doesn't absorb water, like eggshells, we can use protein decay to figure out the object's age.

Thermoluminescence

When pottery, stone tools, or sand grains lie in the ground, the crystals they contain are bombarded by atomic particles (radiation) from the soil. This radiation adds energy to the atoms in the crystals. The energy is stored in tiny flaws.

Heating up the crystals makes them give up their extra energy, which is thrown off in the form of light that can be measured in a laboratory.

Even though a pot may be made from very old clay and sand grains, when it is fired in a kiln, all the stored energy is driven off and the clock is set to zero.

The amount of energy that the pot gives off when we heat it in the laboratory is related to the amount of time it has been in the ground since it was last fired.

Anything that was once heated up — fireplaces, kilns, or burned flints, for example — can be dated by this technique.

Extra energy is stored in flaws.

Heated in lab, energy comes off as light.

Soil radiation hits crystals in materials.

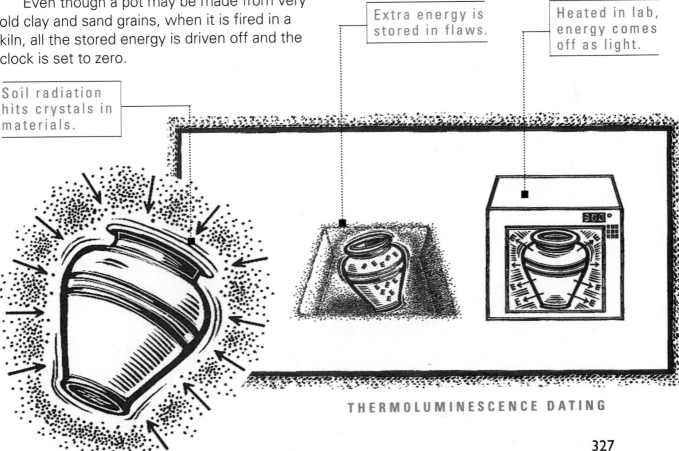

THERMOLUMINESCENCE DATING

IMAGINATION
AT
WORK

328

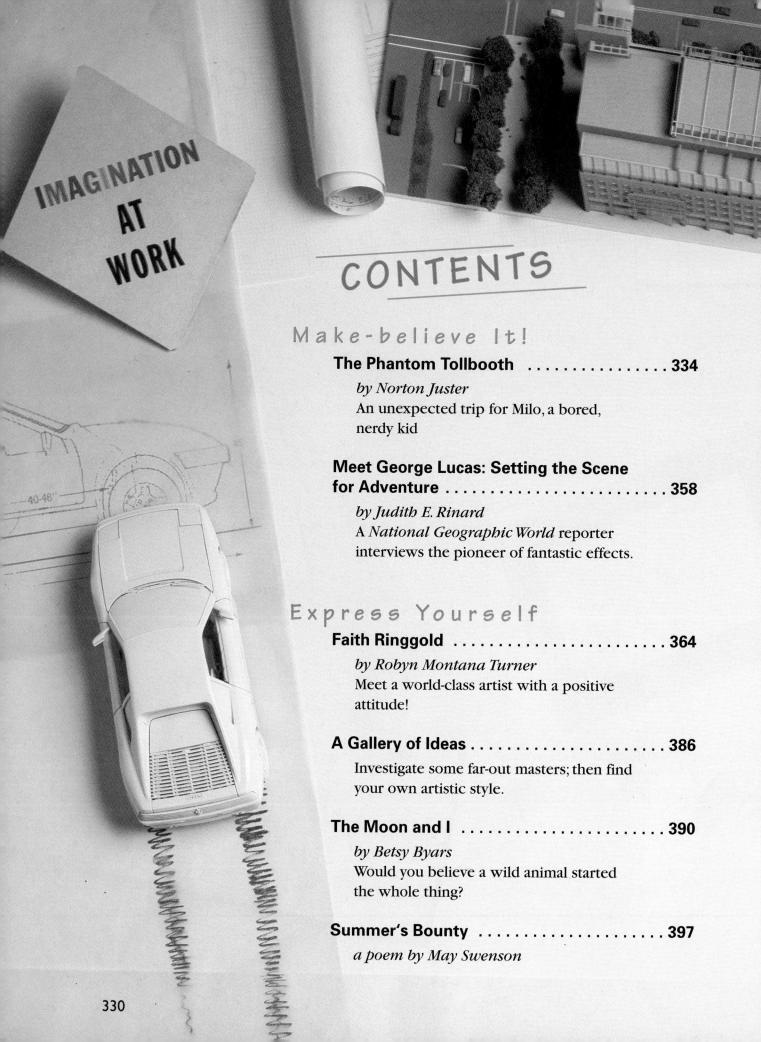

CONTENTS

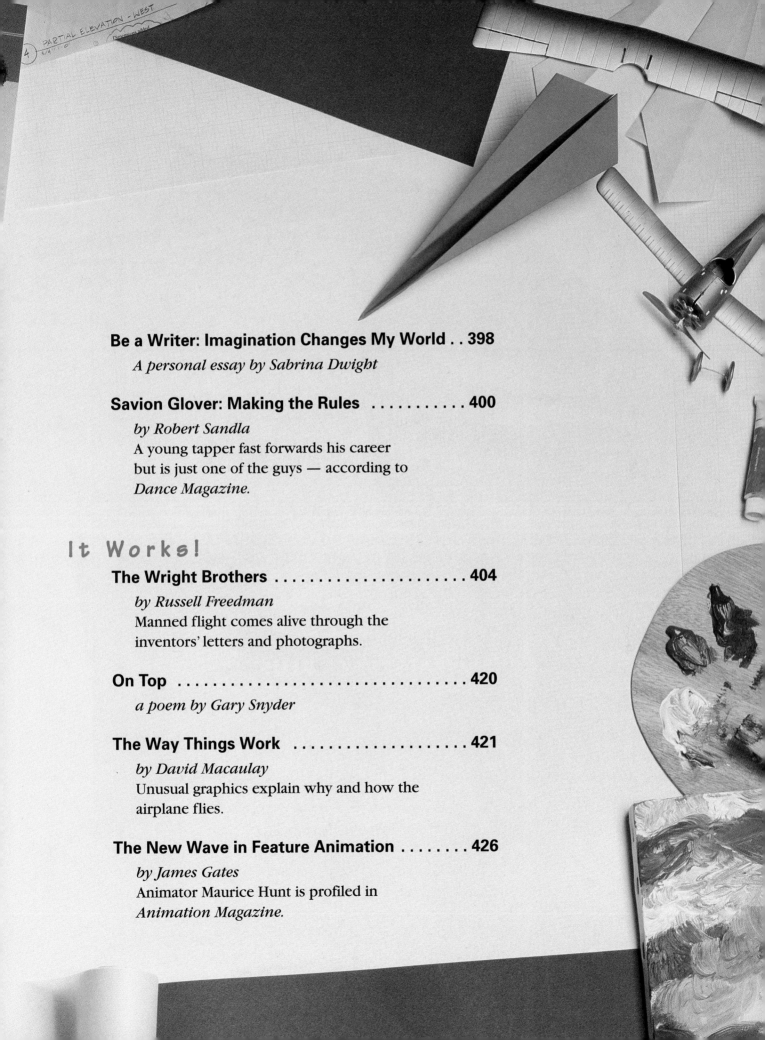

IMAGINATION
AT
WORK

NATALIE BABBITT
Tuck
Everlasting

PAPERBACK **PLUS**

Tuck Everlasting
by Natalie Babbitt
The Tucks find life's not *quite*
what they had expected.

In the same book . . .
more facts and fiction about being
forever young.

PAPERBACK PLUS

A Young Painter: The Life and Paintings of Wang Yani, China's Extraordinary Young Artist
by Zheng Zhensun and Alice Low

In the same book . . .
more about art and art materials.

333

ABOUT THE AUTHOR

NORTON JUSTER never meant to write a book. He was trained as an architect, and in 1959 he was working on an especially difficult project. For relaxation, he decided to take a little break and write a short story. "Before I knew it, it had created its own life and I was hooked. *The Phantom Tollbooth* was the result."

ABOUT THE ILLUSTRATOR

WILL TERRY says, "When it's fun for me it usually becomes a better picture." So he admires the work of children's illustrator and author Chris Van Allsburg. Terry's favorite book is also funny — *The Frog Prince Retold* by Steve Johnson. Terry's advice — "Draw as much as you can and if you like it don't worry what others say."

The Phantom Tollbooth

BY NORTON JUSTER

MILO

There was once a boy named Milo who didn't know what to do with himself — not just sometimes, but always.

When he was in school he longed to be out, and when he was out he longed to be in. On the way he thought about coming home, and coming home he thought about going. Wherever he was he wished he were somewhere else, and when he got there he wondered why he'd bothered. Nothing really interested him — least of all the things that should have.

"It seems to me that almost everything is a waste of time," he remarked one day as he walked dejectedly home from school. "I can't see the point in learning to solve useless problems, or subtracting turnips from turnips, or knowing where Ethiopia is or how to spell February." And, since no one bothered to explain otherwise, he regarded the process of seeking knowledge as the greatest waste of time of all.

335

As he and his unhappy thoughts hurried along (for while he was never anxious to be where he was going, he liked to get there as quickly as possible) it seemed a great wonder that the world, which was so large, could sometimes feel so small and empty.

"And worst of all," he continued sadly, "there's nothing for me to do, nowhere I'd care to go, and hardly anything worth seeing." He punctuated this last thought with such a deep sigh that a house sparrow singing nearby stopped and rushed home to be with his family.

Without stopping or looking up, he rushed past the buildings and busy shops that lined the street and in a few minutes reached home — dashed through the lobby — hopped onto the elevator — two, three, four, five, six, seven, eight, and off again — opened the apartment door — rushed into his room — flopped dejectedly into a chair, and grumbled softly, "Another long afternoon."

He looked glumly at all the things he owned. The books that were too much trouble to read, the tools he'd never learned to use, the small electric automobile he hadn't driven in months — or was it years? — and the hundreds of other games and toys, and bats and balls, and bits and pieces scattered around him. And then, to one side of the room, just next to the phonograph, he noticed something he had certainly never seen before.

Who could possibly have left such an enormous package and such a strange one? For, while it was not quite square, it was definitely not round, and for its size it was larger than almost any other big package of smaller dimension that he'd ever seen.

Attached to one side was a bright-blue envelope which said simply:

"FOR MILO, WHO HAS PLENTY OF TIME."

Of course, if you've ever gotten a surprise package, you can imagine how puzzled and excited Milo was; and if you've never gotten one, pay close attention, because someday you might.

"I don't think it's my birthday," he puzzled, "and Christmas must be months away, and I haven't been outstandingly good, or even good at all." (He had to admit this even to himself.) "Most probably I won't like it anyway, but since I don't know where it came from, I can't possibly send it back." He thought about it for quite a while and then opened the envelope, but just to be polite.

"**ONE GENUINE TURNPIKE TOLLBOOTH**," it stated — and then it went on:

"**EASILY ASSEMBLED AT HOME, AND FOR USE BY THOSE WHO HAVE NEVER TRAVELED IN LANDS BEYOND.**"

"Beyond what?" thought Milo as he continued to read.

"THIS PACKAGE CONTAINS THE FOLLOWING ITEMS:

"One (1) genuine turnpike tollbooth to be erected according to directions.

"Three (3) precautionary signs to be used in a precautionary fashion.

"Assorted coins for use in paying tolls.

"One (1) map, up to date and carefully drawn by master cartographers, depicting natural and man-made features.

"One (1) book of rules and traffic regulations, which may not be bent or broken."

And in smaller letters at the bottom it concluded:
"Results are not guaranteed, but if not perfectly satisfied, your wasted time will be refunded."

Following the instructions, which told him to cut here, lift there, and fold back all around, he soon had the tollbooth unpacked and set up on its stand. He fitted the windows in place and attached the roof, which extended out on both sides and fastened on the coin box. It was very much like the tollbooths he'd seen many times on family trips, except of course it was much smaller and purple.

"What a strange present," he thought to himself. "The least they could have done was to send a highway with it, for it's terribly impractical without one." But since, at the time, there was nothing else he wanted to play with, he set up the three signs,

SLOW DOWN APPROACHING TOLLBOOTH

PLEASE HAVE YOUR FARE READY

HAVE YOUR DESTINATION IN MIND

and slowly unfolded the map.

As the announcement stated, it was a beautiful map, in many colors, showing principal roads, rivers and seas, towns and cities, mountains and valleys, intersections and detours, and sites of outstanding interest both beautiful and historic.

The only trouble was that Milo had never heard of any of the places it indicated, and even the names sounded most peculiar.

"I don't think there really is such a country," he concluded after studying it carefully. "Well, it doesn't matter anyway." And he closed his eyes and poked a finger at the map.

"Dictionopolis," read Milo slowly when he saw what his finger had chosen. "Oh, well, I might as well go there as anywhere."

He walked across the room and dusted the car off carefully. Then, taking the map and rule book with him, he hopped in and, for lack of anything better to do, drove slowly up to the tollbooth. As he deposited his coin and rolled past he remarked wistfully, "I do hope this is an interesting game, otherwise the afternoon will be so terribly dull."

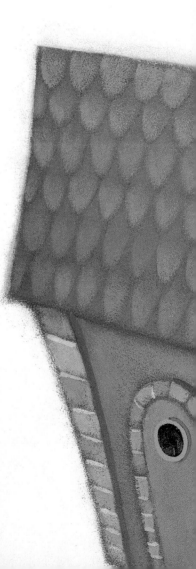

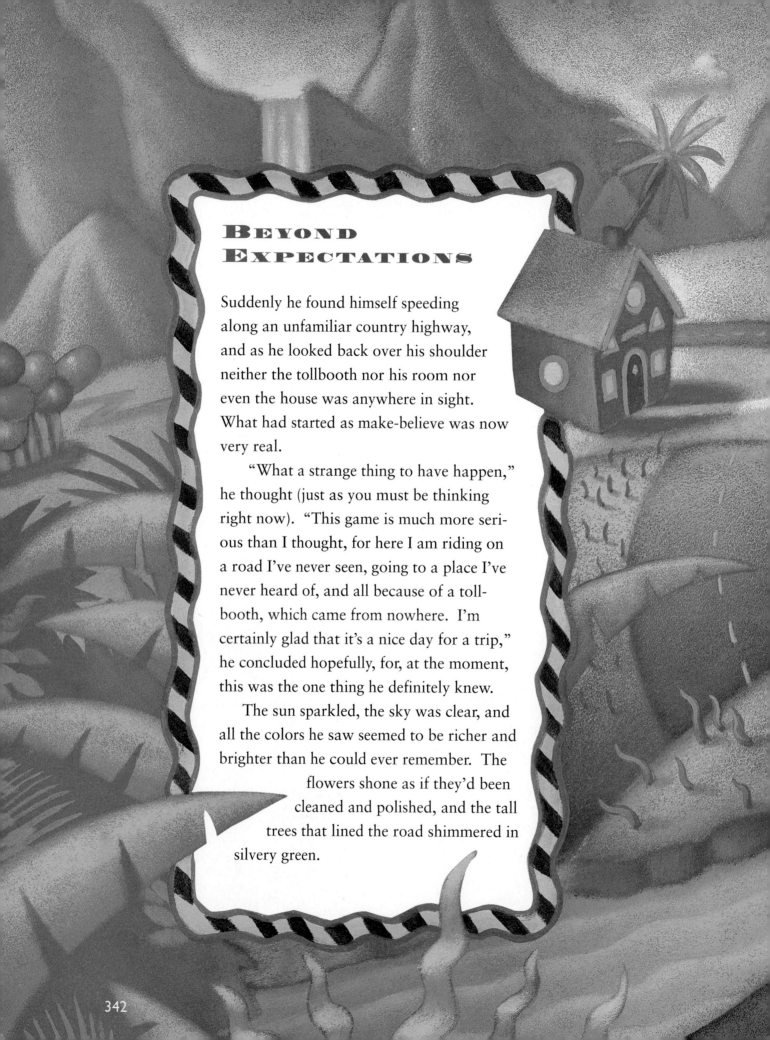

BEYOND EXPECTATIONS

Suddenly he found himself speeding along an unfamiliar country highway, and as he looked back over his shoulder neither the tollbooth nor his room nor even the house was anywhere in sight. What had started as make-believe was now very real.

"What a strange thing to have happen," he thought (just as you must be thinking right now). "This game is much more serious than I thought, for here I am riding on a road I've never seen, going to a place I've never heard of, and all because of a tollbooth, which came from nowhere. I'm certainly glad that it's a nice day for a trip," he concluded hopefully, for, at the moment, this was the one thing he definitely knew.

The sun sparkled, the sky was clear, and all the colors he saw seemed to be richer and brighter than he could ever remember. The flowers shone as if they'd been cleaned and polished, and the tall trees that lined the road shimmered in silvery green.

"WELCOME TO EXPECTATIONS," said a carefully lettered sign on a small house at the side of the road.

"INFORMATION, PREDICTIONS, AND ADVICE CHEERFULLY OFFERED. PARK HERE AND BLOW HORN."

With the first sound from the horn a little man in a long coat came rushing from the house, speaking as fast as he could and repeating everything several times:

"My, my, my, my, my, welcome, welcome, welcome, welcome to the land of Expectations, to the land of Expectations, to the land of Expectations. We don't get many travelers these days; we certainly don't get many travelers these days. Now what can I do for you? I'm the Whether Man."

"Is this the right road for Dictionopolis?" asked Milo, a little bowled over by the effusive greeting.

"Well now, well now, well now," he began again, "I don't know of any wrong road to Dictionopolis, so if this road goes to Dictionopolis at all it must be the right road, and if it doesn't it must be the right road to somewhere else, because there are no wrong roads to anywhere. Do you think it will rain?"

"I thought you were the Weather Man," said Milo, very confused.

"Oh no," said the little man, "I'm the Whether Man, not the Weather Man, for after all it's more important to know whether there will be weather than what the weather will be." And with that he released a dozen balloons that sailed off into the sky. "Must see which way the wind is blowing," he said, chuckling over his little joke and watching them disappear in all directions.

"What kind of a place is Expectations?" inquired Milo, unable to see the humor and feeling very doubtful of the little man's sanity.

"Good question, good question," he exclaimed. "Expectations is the place you must always go to before you get to where you're going. Of course, some people never go beyond Expectations, but my job is to hurry them along whether they like it or not. Now what else can I do for you?" And before Milo could reply he rushed into the house and reappeared a moment later with a new coat and an umbrella.

"I think I can find my own way," said Milo, not at all sure that he could. But, since he didn't understand the little man at all, he decided that he might as well move on — at least until he met someone whose sentences didn't always sound as if they would make as much sense backwards as forwards.

"Splendid, splendid, splendid," exclaimed the Whether Man. "Whether or not you find your own way, you're bound to find some way. If you happen to find my way, please return it, as it was lost years ago. I imagine by now it's quite rusty. You did say it was going to rain, didn't you?" And with that he opened the umbrella and walked with Milo to the car.

"I'm glad you made your own decision. I do so hate to make up my mind about anything, whether it's good or bad, up or down, in or out, rain or shine. Expect everything, I always say, and the unexpected never happens. Now please drive carefully; good-by, good-by, good-by, good . . ." His last good-by was drowned out by an enormous clap of thunder, and as Milo drove down the road in the bright sunshine he could see the Whether Man standing in the middle of a fierce cloudburst that seemed to be raining only on him.

The road dipped now into a broad green valley and stretched toward the horizon. The little car bounced along with very little effort, and Milo had hardly to touch the accelerator to go as fast as he wanted. He was glad to be on his way again.

"It's all very well to spend time in Expectations," he thought, "but talking to that strange man all day would certainly get me nowhere. He's the most peculiar person I've ever met," continued Milo — unaware of how many peculiar people he would shortly encounter.

As he drove along the peaceful highway he soon fell to daydreaming and paid less and less attention to where he was going. In a short time he wasn't paying any attention at all, and that is why, at a fork in the road, when a sign pointed to the left, Milo went to the right, along a route, which looked suspiciously like the wrong way.

Things began to change as soon as he left the main highway. The sky became quite gray and, along with it, the whole countryside seemed to lose its color and assume the same monotonous tone. Everything was quiet, and even the air hung heavily. The birds sang only gray songs and the road wound back and forth in an endless series of climbing curves.

Mile after
mile after
mile after
mile he drove, and now, gradually the car went slower and slower, until it was hardly moving at all.

"It looks as though I'm getting nowhere,"
yawned Milo, becoming very drowsy and dull.
"I hope I haven't taken a wrong turn."

Mile after

mile after

mile after

mile, and everything became grayer and more
monotonous. Finally the car just stopped altogether, and, hard as he tried, it wouldn't budge
another inch.

"I wonder where I am," said Milo in a very
worried tone.

"You're . . . in . . . the . . . Dol . . . drums,"
wailed a voice that sounded far away.

He looked around quickly to see who had
spoken. No one was there, and it was as quiet and
still as one could imagine.

"Yes . . . the . . . Dol . . . drums," yawned
another voice, but still he saw no one.

"WHAT ARE THE DOLDRUMS?" he cried loudly, and tried very hard to see who would answer this time.

"The Doldrums, my young friend, are where nothing ever happens and nothing ever changes."

This time the voice came from so close that Milo jumped with surprise, for, sitting on his right shoulder, so lightly that he hardly noticed, was a small creature exactly the color of his shirt.

"Allow me to introduce all of us," the creature went on. "We are the Lethargarians, at your service."

Milo looked around and, for the first time, noticed dozens of them — sitting on the car, standing in the road, and lying all over the trees and bushes. They were very difficult to see, because whatever they happened to be sitting on or near was exactly the color they happened to be. Each one looked very much like the other (except for the color, of course) and some looked even more like each other than they did like themselves.

"I'm very pleased to meet you," said Milo, not sure whether or not he was pleased at all. "I think I'm lost. Can you help me please?"

"Don't say 'think,'" said one sitting on his shoe, for the one on his shoulder had fallen asleep. "It's against the law." And he yawned and fell off to sleep, too.

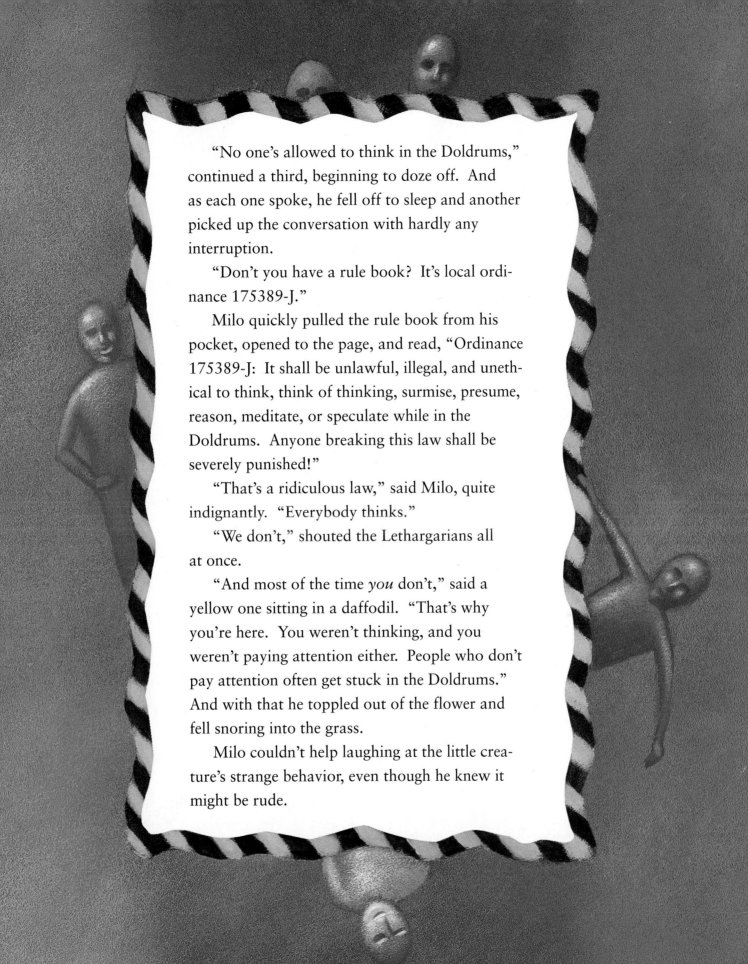

"No one's allowed to think in the Doldrums," continued a third, beginning to doze off. And as each one spoke, he fell off to sleep and another picked up the conversation with hardly any interruption.

"Don't you have a rule book? It's local ordinance 175389-J."

Milo quickly pulled the rule book from his pocket, opened to the page, and read, "Ordinance 175389-J: It shall be unlawful, illegal, and unethical to think, think of thinking, surmise, presume, reason, meditate, or speculate while in the Doldrums. Anyone breaking this law shall be severely punished!"

"That's a ridiculous law," said Milo, quite indignantly. "Everybody thinks."

"We don't," shouted the Lethargarians all at once.

"And most of the time *you* don't," said a yellow one sitting in a daffodil. "That's why you're here. You weren't thinking, and you weren't paying attention either. People who don't pay attention often get stuck in the Doldrums." And with that he toppled out of the flower and fell snoring into the grass.

Milo couldn't help laughing at the little creature's strange behavior, even though he knew it might be rude.

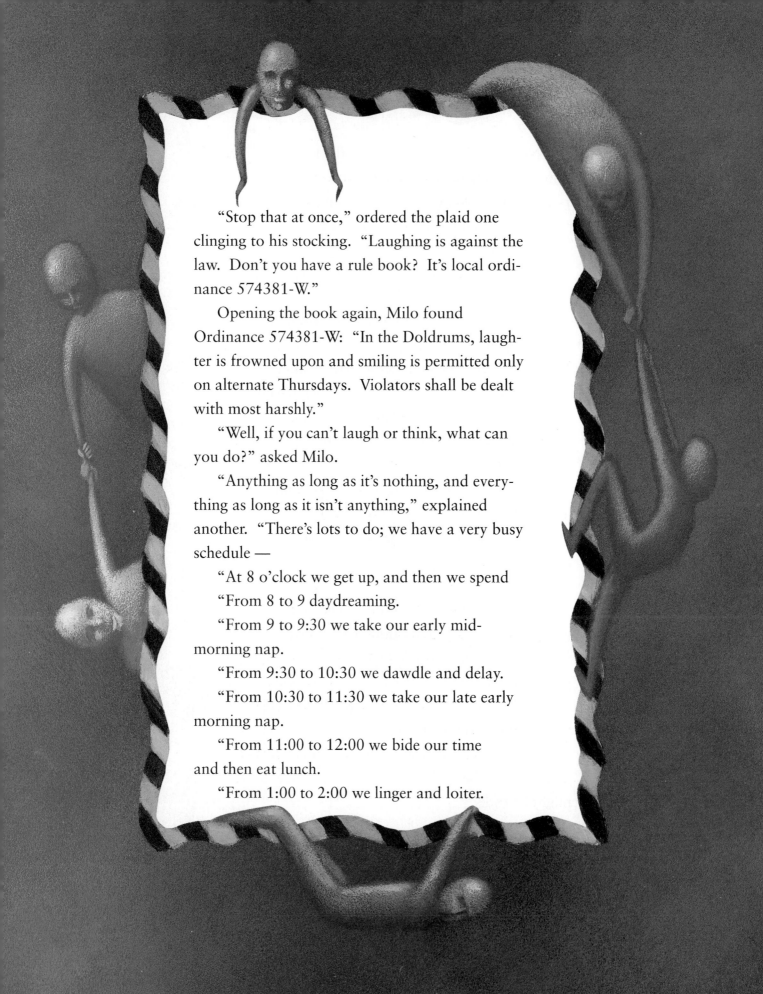

"Stop that at once," ordered the plaid one clinging to his stocking. "Laughing is against the law. Don't you have a rule book? It's local ordinance 574381-W."

Opening the book again, Milo found Ordinance 574381-W: "In the Doldrums, laughter is frowned upon and smiling is permitted only on alternate Thursdays. Violators shall be dealt with most harshly."

"Well, if you can't laugh or think, what can you do?" asked Milo.

"Anything as long as it's nothing, and everything as long as it isn't anything," explained another. "There's lots to do; we have a very busy schedule —

"At 8 o'clock we get up, and then we spend

"From 8 to 9 daydreaming.

"From 9 to 9:30 we take our early midmorning nap.

"From 9:30 to 10:30 we dawdle and delay.

"From 10:30 to 11:30 we take our late early morning nap.

"From 11:00 to 12:00 we bide our time and then eat lunch.

"From 1:00 to 2:00 we linger and loiter.

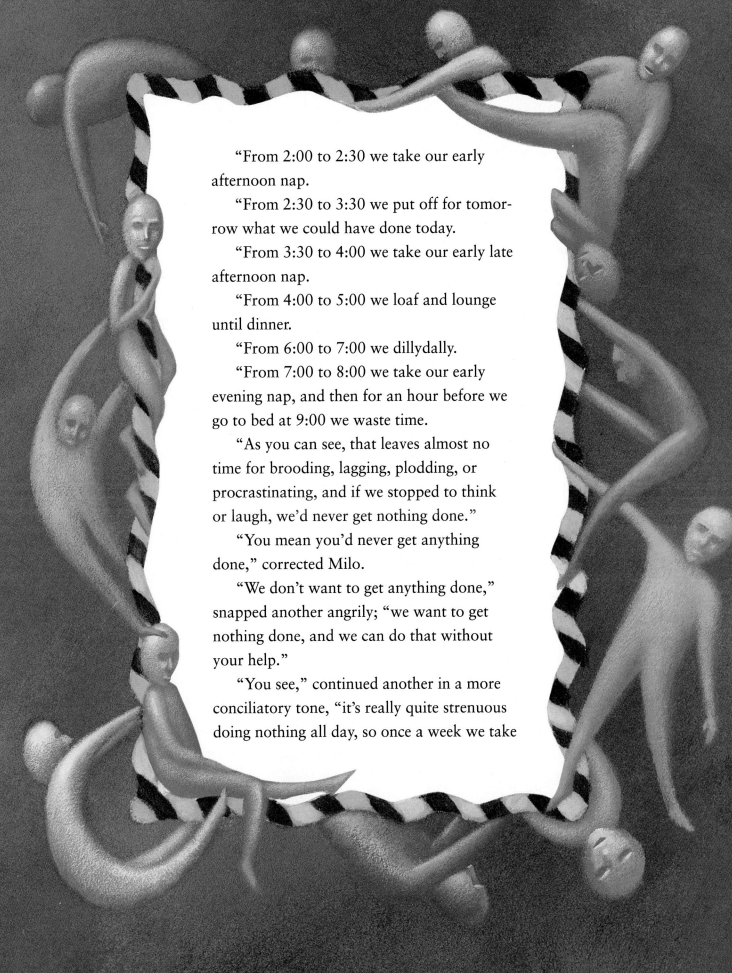

"From 2:00 to 2:30 we take our early afternoon nap.

"From 2:30 to 3:30 we put off for tomorrow what we could have done today.

"From 3:30 to 4:00 we take our early late afternoon nap.

"From 4:00 to 5:00 we loaf and lounge until dinner.

"From 6:00 to 7:00 we dillydally.

"From 7:00 to 8:00 we take our early evening nap, and then for an hour before we go to bed at 9:00 we waste time.

"As you can see, that leaves almost no time for brooding, lagging, plodding, or procrastinating, and if we stopped to think or laugh, we'd never get nothing done."

"You mean you'd never get anything done," corrected Milo.

"We don't want to get anything done," snapped another angrily; "we want to get nothing done, and we can do that without your help."

"You see," continued another in a more conciliatory tone, "it's really quite strenuous doing nothing all day, so once a week we take a holiday and go nowhere, which was just where we were going when you came along. Would you care to join us?"

"I might as well," thought Milo; "that's where I seem to be going anyway."

"Tell me," he yawned, for he felt ready for a nap now himself, "does everyone here do nothing?"

"Everyone but the terrible watchdog," said two of them, shuddering in chorus. "He's always sniffing around to see that nobody wastes time. A most unpleasant character."

"The watchdog?" said Milo quizzically.

"THE WATCHDOG," shouted another, fainting from fright, for racing down the road barking furiously and kicking up a great cloud of dust was the very dog of whom they had been speaking.

"RUN!"

"WAKE UP!"

"RUN!"

"HERE HE COMES!"

"THE WATCHDOG!"

Great shouts filled the air as the Lethargarians scattered in all directions and soon disappeared entirely.

"R-R-R-G-H-R-O-R-R-H-F-F," exclaimed the watchdog as he dashed up to the car, loudly puffing and panting.

Milo's eyes opened wide, for there in front of him was a large dog with a perfectly normal head, four feet, and a tail — and the body of a loudly ticking alarm clock.

"What are you doing here?" growled the watchdog.

"Just killing time," replied Milo apologetically. "You see — "

"KILLING TIME!" roared the dog — so furiously that his alarm went off. "It's bad enough wasting time without killing it." And he shuddered at the thought. "Why are you in the Doldrums anyway — don't you have anywhere to go?"

"I was on my way to Dictionopolis when I got stuck here," explained Milo. "Can you help me?"

"Help you! You must help yourself," the dog replied, carefully winding himself with his left hind leg. "I suppose you know why you got stuck."

"I guess I just wasn't thinking," said Milo.

"PRECISELY," shouted the dog as his alarm went off again. "Now you know what you must do."

"I'm afraid I don't," admitted Milo, feeling quite stupid.

"Well," continued the watchdog impatiently, "since you got here by not thinking, it seems reasonable to expect that, in order to get out, you must start thinking." And with that he hopped into the car.

"Do you mind if I get in? I love automobile rides."

Milo began to think as hard as he could (which was very difficult, since he

353

wasn't used to it). He thought of birds that swim and fish that fly. He thought of yesterday's lunch and tomorrow's dinner. He thought of words that begin with J and numbers that end in 3. And, as he thought, the wheels began to turn.

"We're moving, we're moving," he shouted happily.

"Keep thinking," scolded the watchdog.

The little car started to go faster and faster as Milo's brain whirled with activity, and down the road they went. In a few moments they were out of the Doldrums and back on the main highway. All the colors had returned to their original brightness, and as they raced along the road Milo continued to think of all sorts of things; of the many detours and wrong turns that were so easy to take, of how fine it was to be moving along, and, most of all, of how much could be accomplished with just a little thought. And the dog, his nose in the wind, just sat back, watchfully ticking.

WHERE TO NOW?

Make a Funny List

Wastes of Time

Milo lists a few Things That Are a Waste of Time on page 335. With a partner, brainstorm another dozen or so items for this list. Make your list varied and funny. Combine your list with Milo's and make a poster. Do you think Milo added traveling to Dictionopolis to his original list? Why or why not? Will you add reading more of *The Phantom Tollbooth* to yours?

Deliver a Monologue

Try Out a New Voice

Choose a fantasy character you enjoyed — the Whether Man or one of the Lethargarians, or the Watchdog. Choose a short speech by this character and memorize up to one minute of it. Include some of Milo's comments and rehearse it using an exaggerated voice that seems right for this character. If possible, perform your monologue for your classmates.

Write a Chapter

Where Next?

Write or outline what you imagine the next chapter of *The Phantom Tollbooth* to be. Where will Milo go next? Who will he meet? What will he learn? Put your imagination in gear and step on the gas!

Build a Booth or Draw a Map

Make It Real

Work in a pair or a small group. Using the information in this selection, build the Phantom Tollbooth and its signs. (You might try an old appliance box as a start.) OR — Draw the map referred to on page 339 with details from this selection. Show the route that Milo takes. Display your creation in your classroom.

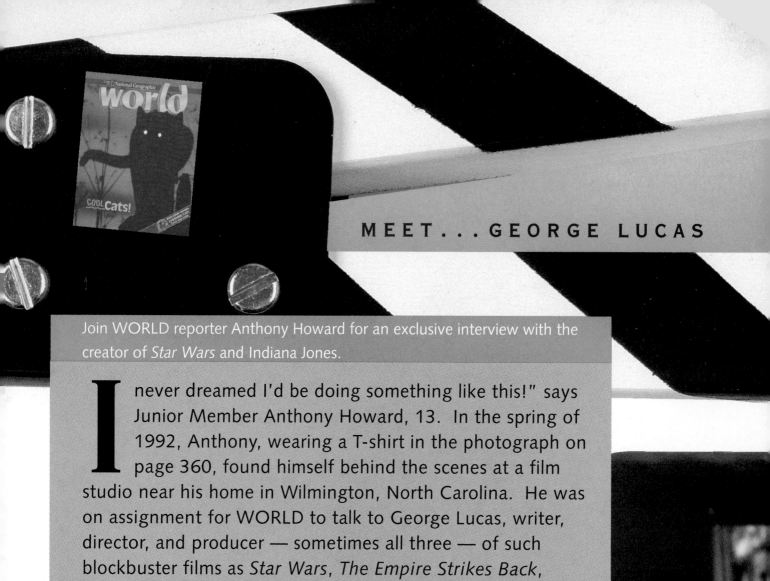

MEET...GEORGE LUCAS

Join WORLD reporter Anthony Howard for an exclusive interview with the creator of *Star Wars* and Indiana Jones.

"I never dreamed I'd be doing something like this!" says Junior Member Anthony Howard, 13. In the spring of 1992, Anthony, wearing a T-shirt in the photograph on page 360, found himself behind the scenes at a film studio near his home in Wilmington, North Carolina. He was on assignment for WORLD to talk to George Lucas, writer, director, and producer — sometimes all three — of such blockbuster films as *Star Wars*, *The Empire Strikes Back*, *Willow*, and *Raiders of the Lost Ark* and other Indiana Jones movies. Lucas was working on a TV series called *The Young Indiana Jones Chronicles*. It's about Indy's boyhood adventures traveling around the world from 1908 to 1918 and meeting famous people like President Teddy Roosevelt, inventor Thomas Edison, and Dr. Sigmund Freud.

On location in Africa. Ten-year-old actor Corey Carrier as Young Indiana Jones with a Masai on the set of *The Young Indiana Jones Chronicles*.

From October 1992 issue of *National Geographic World* magazine. Copyright ©1992 by *National Geographic World*. World is the official magazine for Junior Members of the National Geographic Society. Reprinted by permission.

SETTING THE SCENE FOR
ADVENTURE

On location. George Lucas operates a camera in Spain while filming *The Young Indiana Jones Chronicles*. This TV series was shot in 20 countries.

TAKE

To prepare for the interview, Anthony read all he could about Lucas. He learned that as a teenager, Lucas loved photography and car racing more than school. He planned to be a race car driver. Then one day when he was 17, another car slammed into his two-seater, flipping it over and nearly killing him. After the accident Lucas turned from racing itself to photographing races. At one he met a Hollywood cameraman and racing fan who urged him to go to film school. That led him to his life's work.

Today Lucas is not just making movies. He is also using his *Star Wars* technology and dazzling special effects wizardry for education. He is creating exciting videos that make history, science, and other subjects come alive for kids in the classroom.

Anthony caught up with Lucas at the busy studio during a break in shooting the TV series. "It was kind of overwhelming to meet George Lucas," he says. "At first I didn't know what to say. But he's a real personal, nice kind of guy. He put me right at ease. Pretty soon we were talking."

Spaceships charge between canyon walls in the *Star Wars* epic.

Anthony Howard, WORLD reporter, talks with George Lucas for this interview.

Young George
at 10

Q Can you tell me a little about your background?

A Well, I come from Modesto, a small town in northern California. After high school I went to a junior college for two years and then to USC (University of Southern California) and became a film student. I found I really liked it.

Q What kind of student were you before college?

A I had a very difficult time in school. I found it kind of boring. And it was hard to concentrate. It wasn't until college that I really took off and became a good student.

Q What effect did your car accident have on you?

A It's a miracle I survived. The accident made me think about my life. It made me realize I needed to get more serious about school, to try to be a better student, and do something with myself. It made me more aware of my feelings. I began to trust my instincts.

The hero Luke Skywalker and his extra-terrestrial friends make contact in Star Wars.

Q What made you become a producer and writer?

A I started out as a cameraman in school. . . . I had to learn how to become a writer so I could become a director, basically so I could edit my own films without anybody telling me what to do.

Q What do you like best about what you do?

A I love what I do, especially film editing. I love writing and telling the stories, the screenplays. I also have directed and really done all the things involved. But post-production — the cutting together of all the pictures of the scenes — is very, very exciting to me.

361

Q Do you plan to complete the *Star Wars* saga?

A Yes, I hope to do it in the next seven to eight years, after the TV series. The first ones were parts four, five, and six of *Star Wars*. Now I'll do parts one, two, and three.

Q What about Luke Skywalker? His name is Luke; yours is Lucas. Did you sort of identify with him?

A Yeah, that's pretty much what I did. Obviously, when you write a story, you identify with a character. Part of writing is pretending you're right in the story.

Q What are you doing now in your education projects?

A I'm working on a kind of experiment — to show teachers how film technology can work in the schools. I want to show what it could be like in the future.

Drama and adventure in *Return of the Jedi* **from the** *Star Wars* **trilogy**

Q What else do you like to do besides work?

A Well, I'm a father, and I'm raising two daughters. That's very important to me. And I like to have free time to read and play tennis and, you know, have fun.

Q What advice would you give kids who might want to get into filmmaking?

A Do as well as you can in school. Study things that will give you something to make movies about — like literature and history. Then get a film degree.

Q What would you say to kids to inspire them?

A I think film has an important place in our society . . . to tap in on values. It has a tremendous force for good or bad. . . . Making films is one way to help, in a small way, change the world and try to make things better.

Left, **Lucas supervises filming of his TV series.**

Right, **R2-D2 of** *Star Wars* **fame**

362

After the interview Anthony watched the actors in the cast of the TV series film a scene where young Indy solves a mystery in Thomas Edison's laboratory. "It was exciting to watch," says Anthony.

Anthony is looking forward to the next episode of his favorite Lucas story, *Star Wars* — set "a long time ago in a galaxy far away." What will Anthony do in *this* galaxy in the not too distant future? Would he be interested in making films? "Actually," he says, "after college, I want to play professional basketball. I know it will take a lot of work. But that's my dream."

Well, as Luke Skywalker might say, "Trust your instincts, Anthony. . . . And may the Force be with you."

by Judith E. Rinard

Below, **Anthony meets Sean Patrick Flanery, who starred as 17-year-old Indiana Jones, and Robyn Lively, who played a girlfriend. "They were fun!" says Anthony.**

NAME DROPPER The name of the little droid in *Star Wars* came from a note Lucas made while editing another film. His shorthand for "Reel two, Dialogue two" was R2-D2."

DOG DAYS While Lucas wrote *Star Wars*, his faithful dog, an Alaskan husky, kept him company each day. Later Lucas named a famous character after his pet. The dog's name? Indiana!

COASTER KING As a boy Lucas loved the thrilling rides of Disneyland. As an adult he created today's "Star Tours," one of Disneyland's most popular rides.

PUPIL POWER Lucas made his first major film in college — a science fiction movie called *THX–1138*. It won first prize at the 1967–68 National Student Film Festival.

MAIL CALL Lucas receives more than 20 fan letters a day, many from children.

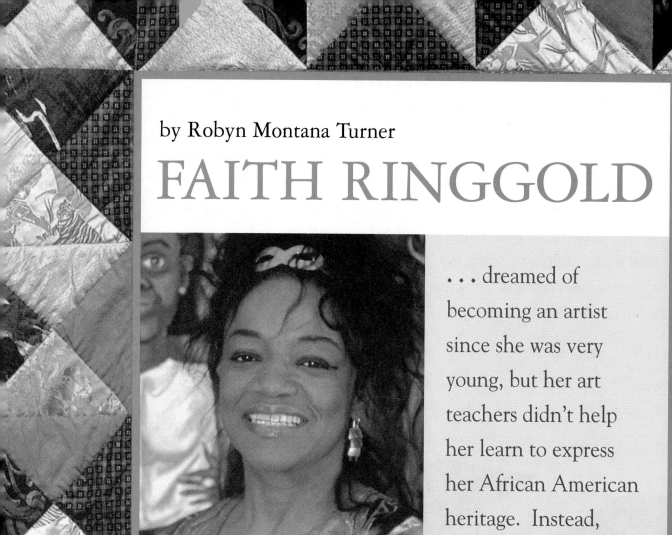

by Robyn Montana Turner

FAITH RINGGOLD

. . . dreamed of becoming an artist since she was very young, but her art teachers didn't help her learn to express her African American heritage. Instead, Faith looked to her mother and her childhood as inspiration for her art. By experimenting with fabric, beads, sculpture, and quilts, Faith Ringgold created a new art form. Today she is a famous African American artist.

FAITH RINGGOLD

ROBYN MONTANA TURNER

In 1972, something happened to take Faith Ringgold a step further toward expressing her true heritage. Teaching at Bank Street College in New York City, she was challenged by one of her students. Why did Ringgold encourage her students to create with fabric and beads — the media of African women — the student questioned, when her own artwork was made of paint on canvas?

At first Ringgold rejected the question even though she had sensed something distant and cold about the process she was using to paint. Soon she realized the worth of her student's words. Why *not* work with fabric and beads? After all, the women in her family had worked with these media for generations.

Suddenly Ringgold felt a link with her great-great-grandmother, Susie Shannon, a "house girl" who had been a slave on a plantation. Susie had taught Faith's great-grandmother, Betsy Bingham, to sew quilts. Betsy's granddaughter, Willi, had told Faith stories about watching Betsy boil and bleach flour sacks until they were as white as snow to line the quilts she made. Ringgold recalled the days when Willi, who operated powerful sewing machines in the garment district, had taught her to use the smaller sewing machines at home. Willi had taught her daughter everything about sewing. Now Ringgold knew she wanted to carry on the tradition of working with fabric and beads.

That summer, on another trip to Europe, Ringgold discovered *tankas*, cloth frames for sacred paintings from Tibet. When she returned home, she made some *tankas* for her paintings. The cloth border enhanced the images, and they could be easily rolled up and carried around. Ringgold knew she was onto something

Susie Shannon. *c. 1900.*
Susie Shannon, Ringgold's great-great-grandmother, who was part Cherokee and a former slave, lived to be 110 years old.

wonderful. Soon she asked Willi to make *tankas* as frames for her other paintings.

As much as she liked the flat *tankas*, Ringgold wanted her art to have a more human dimension. So she reflected upon her childhood in Harlem, where people had been close to each other in a friendly and beautiful place. She remembered the faces and the souls of the people — everything about them. She began to form soft sculptures in the style of African masks. These pieces featured women who had been role models to her. All of those women had a sense of themselves. They were bold, not shy. They did not hold back. They did the best they could with what they had. The subjects of her soft sculptures, such as *Mrs. Jones and Family*, also came to include children, the elderly, and heroes such as Dr. Martin Luther King, Jr.

Faith Ringgold. **Mrs. Jones and Family.** *The Family of Woman Mask Series. 1973. Sewn fabric and embroidery. 60 x 12 x 16 inches.*
Mrs. Jones and Family is a soft sculpture of Ringgold's family — Willi, Andrew, Barbara, and Faith. The mouths of the life-size mask figures are open to symbolize the rich storytelling tradition of Ringgold's culture.

In the same year that she sculpted *Mrs. Jones and Family,* Ringgold gave up teaching to be a full-time artist. Willi, who had developed a busy career as a fashion designer, continued to help her daughter by sewing *tankas* and costumes for her soft sculptures. Ringgold was so resourceful that she packed her sculptures into trunks and sent them around to college campuses to be displayed. She also traveled to give art lectures and workshops. Without the help of gallery owners or dealers, Ringgold was getting her art before the eyes of the public.

During the next few years, Ringgold's art career thrived. She began doing theatrical performances to go with her art exhibits. In 1976, on her first trip to Africa, Ringgold observed the art and the people of Ghana and Nigeria, which gave her new ideas to weave into her own style.

Ringgold's daughters, Michele and Barbara, became women during the seventies. They both graduated from college. Barbara married. Michele published a book. Life for the Ringgold family could not have been better. In 1981, however, Ringgold was suddenly faced with the saddest event of her life — the death of her mother, who was seventy-nine years old. To express her grief, Ringgold turned to a friend and companion — her art.

Perhaps because she missed working with Willi, Ringgold changed her medium and style. She painted abstract images on canvas. No longer did her subjects look familiar. Instead, she painted irregular shapes moving about in bright colors. Each shape may have been taken from an idea or a memory.

Birdie, Barbara, and Michele were surprised to see this new means of expression. They could almost feel and listen to the shapes. Ringgold explained that the images came from deep within her soul. The mysterious nature of the paintings left them nameless until

Faith Ringgold Modeling in One of Her Mother's Fashion Shows. *1950.* As a young woman, Ringgold sometimes modeled dresses that her mother had designed and sewn.

Birdie suggested calling them the Emanon series, which spells *no name* backwards, a substitute for *Untitled* in jazz circles.

The next year brought both tears and joy. The family experienced more sorrow upon the death of Faith's sister, Barbara. But their spirits were renewed with the birth of Faith's first grandchild — Baby Faith — young Barbara's daughter.

Even before Baby Faith was born, Barbara and Michele talked to her through the walls of Barbara's womb. They wanted to instill the family's rich history of language early on. So it came as no surprise that, at six months, Baby Faith pointed toward one of her grandmother's brand-new abstract paintings and said her first word: "Dah!" From that utterance came the title of a series of six abstract paintings. The Dah series expresses Faith's sorrow in losing her mother and her sister, as well as her joy in gaining a grandchild.

Faith Ringgold. **Dah #3.** *1983. Acrylic on canvas. 72 x 54 inches.*

More than twenty years had passed since Ringgold had set out to become a professional artist. On her own and with Birdie, she had developed an audience for her art across the country. Finally, in 1986, she began working with a New York art dealer who showcases the works of women and ethnic minority artists. At last she had a market for selling her art. Now Ringgold could focus strictly on *doing* art.

Just as Ringgold was experiencing newly found freedom in her career, *Groovin' High* shows jubilant movement. Dancers shift in polyrhythms, an African way of having a variety of rhythms around you at the same time. Even the figures are different sizes, moving in different directions and in different spaces. In the African tradition of the Kuba people of Zaire, Ringgold sewed her favorite motif — four triangles in a square — and quilted them together to form the border. If you look closely, you can see that she also strengthened the painted canvas by stitching rows of large squares across it. Now Ringgold would call herself "a painter who works in the quilt medium."

Faith Ringgold. **Groovin' High.** *1986. Acrylic on canvas; tie-dyed, printed, and pieced fabric. 56 x 92 inches. Collection of Barbara and Ronald Davis Balser.*

Working on her quilted paintings, Ringgold realized that she had more to say than images alone could convey. She felt a need to write down stories. After all, she had grown up listening to Willi tell family stories in the oral tradition of their heritage.

One day, Ringgold thought of a way to publish her stories through her art. She would write her stories onto her quilts. Then everyone who saw her artwork would also read her "story quilts."

The stories on Ringgold's quilts are dilemma tales. They present problems without solutions. In this way, Ringgold follows an African tradition in which the storyteller does not make judgments. Instead, she leaves the audience with questions that might have many answers.

Church Picnic tells and shows the story of an African American gathering in Atlanta, Georgia, in 1909. The event takes place during the time of Willi's childhood, a time when southern African Americans were hopeful about the future. The banner on the ground lets us know that this is a church picnic in the urban south. The picnickers sit on patterned blankets and turn their eyes to the focal point of the composition — the minister and a young woman dressed in pink.

The storyteller is the woman seated beside her son, who touches her shoulder, in the upper right of the quilt. Later, at home, the storyteller describes the picnic to her daughter, Aleathia, whom she assumes is in another room.

Ringgold wrote the words exactly as she imagined that they were said — in a southern dialect. For example, the mother says, "The Reverend and Miss Molly was sure 'nuff in love at the picnic. The way he took

her in his arms, and she look up at him so tender. They in love chile."

Midway through the story, the mother realizes her daughter is not at home after all, but nevertheless continues to talk to herself. Later, just before Aleathia returns, we learn that she too is in love with the reverend, and that she stayed away from the picnic to avoid the pain of seeing him with Miss Molly. With no solution in mind, the mother consoles herself by saying, "God don't give us no more than we can bear."

Faith Ringgold. **Church Picnic.** *1988. Acrylic on canvas; pieced fabric borders. 74½ x 75½ inches. Collection of the High Museum, Atlanta, Georgia. Gift of Don and Jill Childress through the 20th Century Art Acquisition Fund.* Ringgold wrote the story of the *Church Picnic* story quilt on cotton canvas, which she sewed onto the top and bottom of the quilt. It hangs in the permanent collection of the High Museum, in Atlanta.

To dress the characters in the *Church Picnic* story quilt, Ringgold recalled the clothes people wore to church when she was young — Sunday-best dresses, hair-ribbon bows, white socks, patent-leather shoes, starched shirts, suits, and ties. After church, families had picnics in the parks of Harlem. They brought picnic baskets, linen napkins, fine tablecloths, china plates, glasses, and sterling silverware.

Like *Church Picnic*, several of Ringgold's story quilts celebrate mealtime in the African American community. To create them, she drew from her imagination, her knowledge of historical events, and memories.

A favorite memory was of Willi's Sunday evening desserts — sweet-potato pie, pound cake, or peach cobbler. Sometimes the family would have company for this special treat. Of course, Willi's table was formally set. On Sunday evening, the children got to listen to the radio.

The elegant table setting and the dressed-up guests of *Harlem Renaissance Party* are reminders of the Sunday evening desserts and Sunday afternoon picnics from Ringgold's childhood. But this story quilt is about a fictional event and character — a deaf woman named Cee Cee Prince, who stands in a colorful African dress that she has quilted.

Even though Cee Cee comes from Ringgold's imagination, she is a lot like Ringgold in real life. They both adore quilting colorful wall hangings, coverlets, and bags. Like Ringgold, Cee Cee likes to dance and perform. Cee Cee is married to a dentist, however, who sits at the head of the table. Their daughter, Celia, seated left of Cee Cee, shrinks from embarrassment because her mother loves to dance to her own music and wear a mask in front of the distinguished dinner guests.

(Opposite page)
Faith Ringgold. **Harlem Renaissance Party.** *Bitter Nest: Part II. 1988. Acrylic on canvas; printed, tie-dyed, and pieced fabric. 94½ x 82 inches. The Harlem Renaissance Party story quilt is one among five quilts in the Bitter Nest series. Seated around the table are: Celia (left); Florence Mills (singer and comedienne); Aaron Douglass (painter); Meta Warrick Fuller (sculptor); W. E. B. Du Bois (organizer and writer); Cee Cee's husband; Richard Wright (writer); Countee Cullen (poet, novelist, playwright); Zora Neale Hurston (novelist, folklorist, anthropologist); Alain Locke (philosopher and writer); Langston Hughes (poet and writer); and Cee Cee.*

The guests are famous artists from the era of the
Harlem Renaissance. During this time, from 1919 to
1929, African American painters, sculptors, musicians,
poets, novelists, and dramatists flocked together in
Harlem. Their art left a rich cultural legacy. Indeed,
Ringgold's invention of the story quilt reflects that
same spirit of being creative and true to yourself.

Faith Ringgold. **Change:
Faith Ringgold's Over 100
Pounds Weight Loss
Performance Story Quilt.**
*1986. Photo etching on canvas.
57 x 70 inches. Detail below.*
Ringgold traveled around
the country to perform live
dramatizations of the story
and images on this quilt.

During the late 1980s, Ringgold performed *Change: Faith Ringgold's Over 100 Pounds Weight Loss Performance Story Quilt* on stages across the United States. Audiences first viewed the quilt, which features photographs of Faith's life with the story that explains how she overcame her weight problem. Then they watched her act out the story on stage.

The performance needed only a few props. As she recited the words of the story quilt, Ringgold dragged around a black plastic bag filled with a hundred pounds of water to show the heavy burden she had been carrying as body weight. "I can CHANGE. I can do it. I can do it. I can CHANGE. I can CHANGE. Now!" she chanted to the beat of African drums. The story quilt and performance remind the audience that with determination people can change their lives.

Dancing on the George Washington Bridge has a simi-lar message — that of being free and able to reach your highest goals. This story quilt is one in a series of five, which Ringgold designed to show women claiming the bridges of New York and San Francisco. Recalling her childhood fascination with the George Washington Bridge, she considered it to be a "magnificent mascu-line structure." Onto her story quilt, she now would paint fifteen women flying, dancing, laughing, and singing above that bridge and the skyline. Their colorful patterned dresses unite the canvas with the patterned cloth border.

Faith Ringgold. **Dancing on the George Washington Bridge.** *The Woman on a Bridge Series. 1988. Acrylic on canvas; pieced fabric borders. 68 x 68 inches. Collection of Roy Eaton.*
Ringgold likes the way bridges are formed because they remind her of quilts floating in air. She sees their triangles as being little quilt patches of air separated by the girders.

In 1991, Ringgold traveled to Paris to begin working on a series of story quilts called the French Collection. These twelve story quilts tell the adventures of an African American woman named Willia Marie Simone, who was born in Faith's imagination. She does things Ringgold never did but would like to have done — such as study art for years by herself in Paris. Willia's story makes us aware of the struggle that all women artists have faced in the male-centered art world.

The story starts in 1920, when sixteen-year-old Willia leaves Harlem to become an artist in Paris. Willia's mother has a sister, Aunt Melissa, who wants Willia to develop her artistic talents. So she has suggested the trip and has given Willia five hundred dollars to help with expenses. Years later, Willia will send her two children to live with Aunt Melissa because Willia is determined to become a professional artist in Paris. She eventually becomes a world-famous painter and enjoys being among the inner circles of Parisian artists.

In *Dancing at the Louvre*, Willia helps her friend Marcia take her three daughters to visit the Louvre, a historic museum in Paris. The children dance in front of the familiar painting the *Mona Lisa*, by Leonardo da Vinci.

By posing the children as dancers beneath the *Mona Lisa*, Ringgold revealed her feelings about European art. Traditionally African Americans and women were not included among the inner circles of European artists. So Ringgold depicted the figures in this piece observing European art with interest but also with lightheartedness. Even Ringgold's Mona Lisa, with her half-smile, seems to be amused at the romping and dancing below. She appears to understand Ringgold's intent for these

Leonardo da Vinci. **Mona Lisa.** *Paris, Louvre. SCALA/ ART RESOURCE, NEW YORK (K 80332).* Leonardo da Vinci was a well-known artist of the Renaissance period in Europe. He lived about five hundred years ago. His paintings are carefully preserved in museums such as the Louvre. The *Mona Lisa* is so popular that people stand in line to see it.

viewers to appreciate European art, as long as they do not take it too seriously.

As models for this story quilt, Ringgold used photographs of her own family. Marcia and her children look like Ringgold's daughter Barbara and her children, Baby Faith, Teddy, and Martha. Willia Marie resembles Ringgold's mother as a young woman. In fact, Willia's personality was inspired by Ringgold's memories of Willi. Willia Marie's story is written across the top and bottom of the quilt. A patterned border frames the brightly painted canvas.

Faith Ringgold. **Dancing at the Louvre.** *The French Collection, Part I. 1991. Acrylic on canvas; pieced fabric borders. 73½ x 80½ inches.* Ringgold used artistic freedom to reproduce the paintings that hang in the Louvre. She purposely altered the colors and frames — even the sizes of the reproductions. For example, in real life, the *Mona Lisa* is smaller than it appears on the story quilt. Perhaps Ringgold enlarged the piece because of its importance in the story.

Vincent van Gogh.
Sunflowers. *1888. Munich,
Neue Pinakothek.
SCALA/ART RESOURCE,
NEW YORK.*
Dutch painter Vincent van
Gogh (1853–1890) never
knew that his artwork would
someday become famous.
Today his paintings are popular
throughout the world.

Another quilt in the French Collection tells the story of Willia at a meeting of an imaginary group called the National Sunflower Quilters Society of America. African American women who changed history work on a quilt of sunflowers. Standing in the sunflower field is Dutch artist Vincent van Gogh, who painted many still life images of sunflowers during his lifetime.

When the sun goes down, the women finish piecing their quilt. The story reads that van Gogh "just settled inside himself, and took on the look of the sunflowers in the field as if he were one of them." In this way, Ringgold contrasts the way that some men traditionally have created art — alone with their paints — with the method of the women quilters, who work as a team.

**Diagram of #4 The
Sunflowers Quilting Bee at
Arles.** *Reprinted by permission
of Melissa McGrath.*

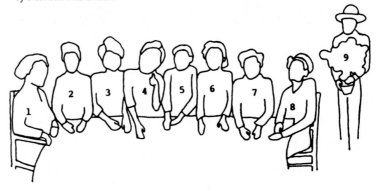

1. Madame Walker, business-woman
2. Sojourner Truth, social reformer
3. Ida Wells, journalist
4. Fannie Lou Hamer, civil rights activist
5. Harriet Tubman, abolitionist
6. Rosa Parks, civil rights activist
7. Mary McLeod Bethune, educator
8. Ella Baker, civil rights activist
9. Vincent van Gogh

Faith Ringgold. **#4 The Sunflowers Quilting Bee at Arles.** *The French Collection, Part I. 1991. Acrylic on canvas; pieced fabric. 74 x 80 inches. Private collection.*

Faith Ringgold. **Matisse's Chapel.** *The French Collection, Part I. 1991. Acrylic on canvas; pieced fabric borders. 74 x 79½ inches.*

The bright colors, flat shapes, exciting patterns, and simple lines of Matisse's chapel are present in Ringgold's story quilt. Again, she used artistic freedom to reproduce the art of a European male artist.

It is interesting to note that Ringgold painted Ralph, the brother she never knew, on Willi's lap.

The Chapel of Vence.
Photograph by Hélène Adant.
Rights reserved.
From his wheelchair, Matisse used his scissors as he would have used a chisel, carving with color the large paper shapes as designs for stained glass windows of the chapel.

As Ringgold traveled in France to gather ideas for the French Collection, she visited a chapel designed by Henri Matisse, a well-known French artist. *Matisse's Chapel* became a story quilt based on an imaginary gathering of Faith's own relatives in the chapel. In the story quilt, they are known, of course, as Willia Marie's family.

At the time that Ringgold painted *Matisse's Chapel*, everyone in the image had died. From photographs and memories, she re-created their likenesses. Their talk is of slavery. Their hearts are bitter. But their pride is still alive.

Faith Ringgold's mother, Willi Posey, with her sisters, Bessie and Edith. *c. 1920s.*

Diagram of Matisse's Chapel.
Reprinted by permission of Melissa McGrath.

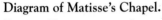

1. Ida Posey, grandmother
2. Susie Shannon, great-great-grandmother
3. Betsy Bingham, great-grandmother
4. Professor Bunyon Posey, grandfather
5. Aunt Janie, grandaunt
6. Uncle Peter, granduncle
7. Barbara Knight, sister
8. Willi Posey (Jones), mother
9. Ralph, brother who died as a baby

10. Andrew Louis Jones, Sr., father
11. Andrew Louis Jones, Jr., brother
12. Uncle Hilliard
13. Uncle Cardoza
14. Aunt Edith
15. Aunt Bessie
16. Mildred, cousin
17. Ida Mae, cousin
18. Baby Doll Hurd, grandmother
19. Rev. Jones, grandfather

Faith Ringgold's grandfather Professor Bunyon Posey. *c. 1880s.*

Faith Ringgold's uncle Cardoza Posey in his World War I uniform. *1919.*

Faith Ringgold and Baby Faith. *1989. Photograph © Lucille Tortora.* Ringgold has received six honorary doctorates from several colleges and universities. Other awards include a Caldecott Honor for her children's book *Tar Beach*, a John Simon Guggenheim Memorial Foundation Fellowship, the Coretta Scott King Award for Illustration, and the Arts Award for Painting and Sculpture from the National Endowment for the Arts. Her name was on a *New York Times* list of Ten Major Women Artists, and her artwork is published in books for both children and adults. In this portrait, she embraces her granddaughter Baby Faith.

The French Collection became the last of Ringgold's quilts with a story written on the fabric. Just as Ringgold had hoped, publishers asked her to write and illustrate her stories as children's books. Her artwork can be found in the permanent collections of many museums throughout the world. Many private collectors, including Oprah Winfrey and Bill Cosby, own her work.

Today Ringgold divides her year between teaching as a full professor and doing her art. Until recently, she had a studio in the garment district of Manhattan, where Willi Posey first taught her to sew. Reminiscing, Ringgold says, "The neighborhood has a lot of memories for me because I used to go down there, and she'd take me into factories to buy fabric by the bolt. She would get a kick out of the fact that my studio was down there for a while."

Now Ringgold enjoys a new studio and home in Englewood, New Jersey, which is across the George Washington Bridge from Harlem. Reflecting upon a time long ago when she was even too young to sew with a machine, she says with a smile, "I still love that bridge."

After I decided to be an artist, the first thing that I had to believe was that I, a black woman, could be on the art scene without sacrificing one iota of my blackness, or my femaleness, or my humanity.

— **Faith Ringgold**

ABOUT
Robyn Montana Turner

In fourth grade, Turner read a biography of Jane Addams, a social reformer from Chicago who won the 1931 Nobel Peace Prize. Addams, who had a professional career outside her home, inspired Turner's professional interests in teaching, writing, and art education. The biography of Faith Ringgold is one of Turner's series titled *Portraits of Women Artists for Children*. She says, "The series sprung from my collective experiences as mother, teacher, writer, editor, feminist, and artist. In many ways I've been researching this series all my life. There's a part of us in each of these books. I hope you find yours."

Crafting Your

Tell a Story of Your Own

Using construction paper — or cloth if you
wish — draw the design for a story quilt
that tells a story from your own life or
imagination. Like Faith Ringgold, you might
combine scraps of your life and experience
that didn't actually exist in the same time
and place. Write a short description of
what your design means and display the
design or the quilt for others to see.

First, Then, Next

Make a time line of Faith Ringgold's life by
attaching several sheets of paper length-
wise. On them, draw a long horizontal
line and divide it into five-year segments,
beginning in 1930 and continuing up to
the present. Use as many details from
the selection as possible to show the important events of Ringgold's life. Include
any major world events that you know
happened during her lifetime, too. (Like
your own birthday!) Display your time
line in your classroom.

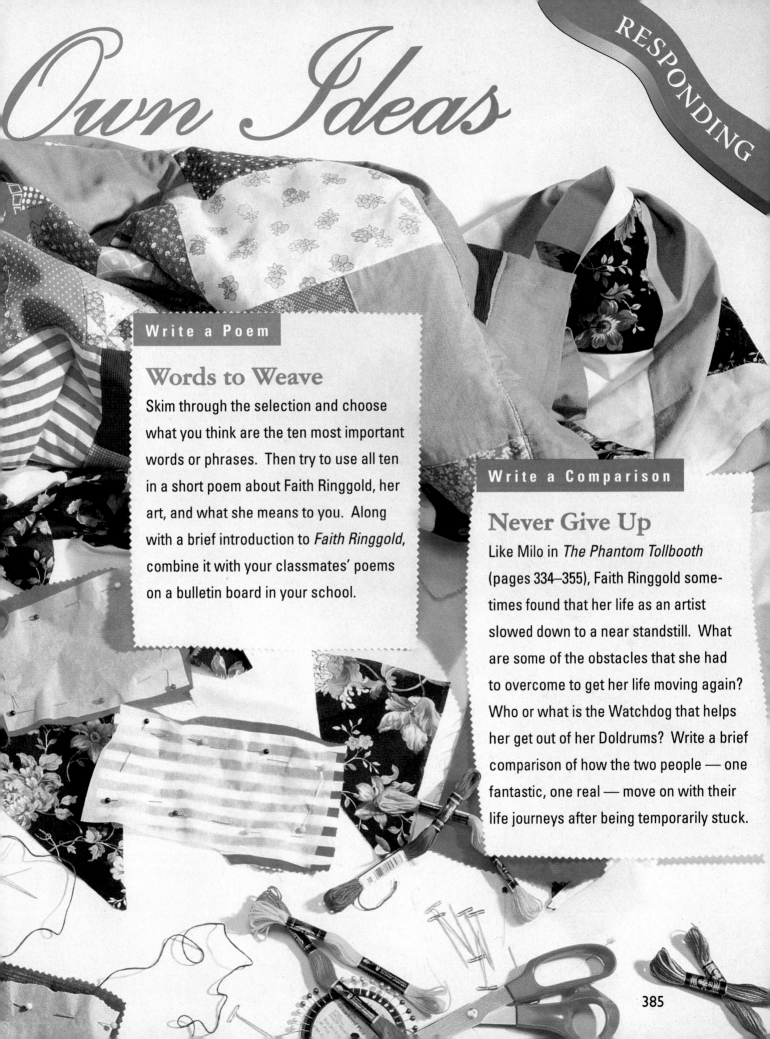

Own Ideas

Write a Poem

Words to Weave

Skim through the selection and choose what you think are the ten most important words or phrases. Then try to use all ten in a short poem about Faith Ringgold, her art, and what she means to you. Along with a brief introduction to *Faith Ringgold*, combine it with your classmates' poems on a bulletin board in your school.

Write a Comparison

Never Give Up

Like Milo in *The Phantom Tollbooth* (pages 334–355), Faith Ringgold sometimes found that her life as an artist slowed down to a near standstill. What are some of the obstacles that she had to overcome to get her life moving again? Who or what is the Watchdog that helps her get out of her Doldrums? Write a brief comparison of how the two people — one fantastic, one real — move on with their life journeys after being temporarily stuck.

A Gallery of Ideas

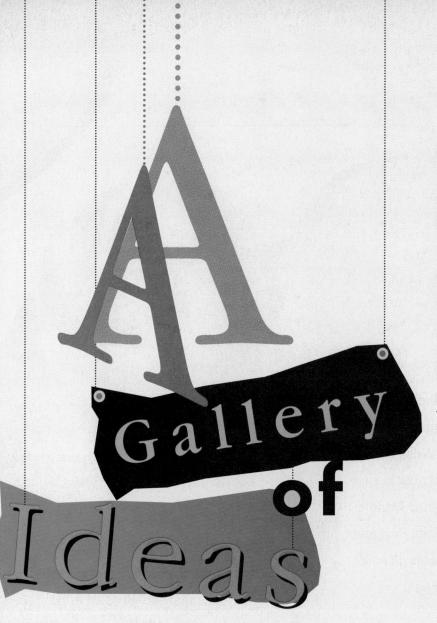

"In **art**, *freedom of the imagination is the most important act, and young people are just as good as grown-ups in this. To be able to play with colors and let what you come up with suggest your next step is to discover the wonder of making art. Later, when you grow up, the many different ways of art become revealed."*

—Mark di Suvero, sculptor

Sketch it out! Quick drawings help you to record your experiences and play out your initial thoughts and ideas.

Right, Imaginary (trompe l'oeil) windows painted by Ndebele artist Maria Msiza on an outbuilding of her family home on Witfontein farm (South Africa)

Below, Teenager Dinah Mashiana practices the art of painting taught her by Ndebele women.

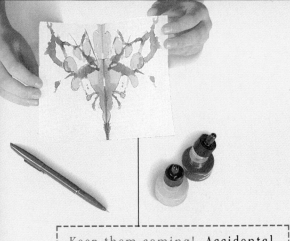

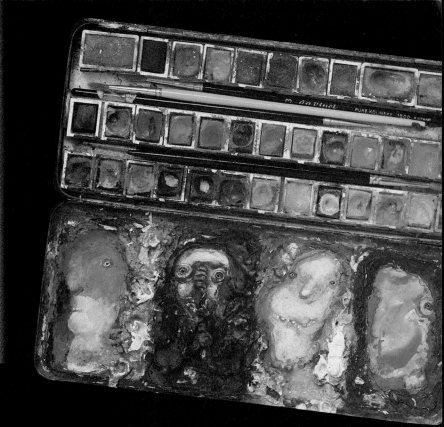

Keep them coming! Accidental results can bring meaningful surprises.

Above, Swiss artist Etienne Delessert's watercolor palette shows his remarkable doodling. Delessert, award-winning children's book illustrator, writer, publisher, and filmmaker, is seriously interested in computer-generated imagery.

"My first memory is of the brightness of light, light all around."
—Georgia O'Keeffe, painter

Right, **Claes Oldenburg.** *Floor Cone (Giant Ice-Cream Cone),* 1962. Synthetic polymer paint on canvas filled with foam rubber and cardboard boxes. The Museum of Modern Art, New York. "When you can't speak the verbal language you have to depend on your vision and on representing things —the language of seeing."

Above, **Meret Oppenheim.** *Object (Breakfast in Fur),* 1936. Overall height 2⅞". The Museum of Modern Art, New York

"*I wasn't content*
with imagining things.
I wanted to build them myself."

— **Red Grooms, sculptor**

Start a collection! Enhance your creative ideas by gathering colors, shapes, textures as they catch your eye.

Get inspired! Listen to music to expand your imagination. Draw or paint to music and ideas will come.

Left, **Alexander Calder.** *Little Clown, the Trumpeter*, 1926–31.
"Calder's art is eternally young. He plays, he amuses himself, and in so doing invests his art with life and force . . ."
—James Johnson Sweeney, art critic

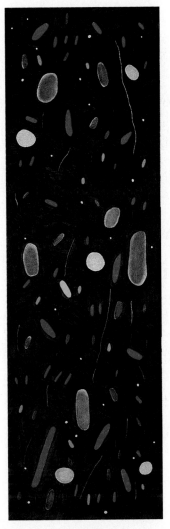

Above, **Joan Miró.** *The Song of the Vowels*. 1966. Oil on canvas, 144" x 45¼". The Museum of Modern Art, New York.
Miró uses abstract elements — line, shape, and color — to represent musical ideas and to suggest a musical range from full notes to tiny accents. The title refers to a French poem, "Vowels," by Rimbaud, which matches colors to vowels (A to black, E to white, I to red, O to blue, and U to green).

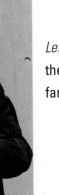

Left, Calder roars with the lion from his famous miniature circus.

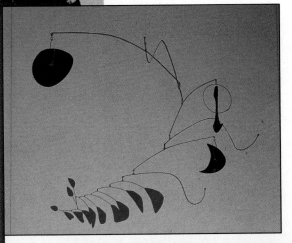

Left, **Alexander Calder.** *Red Gongs*. Mobile, 1951. Overall length approximately 12′. The Metropolitan Museum of Art, New York

Meet

Although she loved reading as a child, Betsy Byars didn't plan to be a writer and never kept a diary or wrote stories. As the mother of four children, however, Byars became fascinated by their experiences and used "thousands of things" from their lives in her books. How did her children feel about this? Apparently they didn't mind as long as Byars disguised their identities in her fiction. She commented about her children, "From age eight or nine, they began realizing these books would be in their library, and that kids they knew would read them. Now they enjoy the books because they can read about their own lives."

The Moon and I

At the log house where she does her writing, Betsy Byars discovered a big black snake and named it Moon. Inspired by her new friend, she wrote a humorous autobiography in which she blends descriptions of her writing life, advice about writing, memories of her childhood, and observations of the snake. This chapter follows eleven others such as "Moonstruck," "Moon in My Hands," and "That Lucky Old Moon."

By Betsy Byars

There is no easy way to find a blacksnake that doesn't want to be found. Blacksnakes are secretive, timid, and cautious. I accept that.

Blacksnakes hide when they are digesting food. Their prey is sometimes large and is always swallowed whole. I accept that.

Digestion — which even dissolves the victim's bones — may take a week or more. I accept that, too. Bones are definitely hard to digest.

But come on now, it couldn't take more than a few days to digest a measly lizard or frog.

So where was Moon? I had not seen the snake for over a month, and I had been actively looking for it — putting on boots and wading the length of the creek, trooping through the woods, checking every place I had ever seen it or any place that blacksnakes were known to like.

Summer is a lazy time for snakes — they mostly just hang out — but where?

I really missed Moon

As the Moon-less days passed, I kept telling myself that Moon was probably somewhere digesting, and I kept reminding myself that all the books said that snakes don't wander, that they pretty much stay in one place until it's time to hibernate, that just because you don't see a snake doesn't mean that it doesn't see you.

And most of all, I kept telling myself that with blacksnakes, like everything in nature, a person must sometimes resort to waiting patiently.

The trouble is that waiting patiently is one of the things I am terrible at. I will do anything to keep from waiting patiently. When I first began to write, it was the thing I really, really hated.

Like:

I would get one idea for a book, and I would write the book, and I would send it off. There would be rewrites and revisions and galley proof sheets to go over, but finally everything would be done, and then the only thing for me to do was to wait for the next idea.

Sometimes this waiting would go on for months. I would sit around, marking time, waiting like a tick for a dog to come by.

I would get more and more desperate because I always felt that now — now! — I had finally learned something about writing. Now — now! — I was ready to put all this self-taught, hard-earned knowledge into practice. Now I was equipped to write the best book in the entire world.

The only thing that was stopping me was that I didn't have an idea.

Finally, usually just when I had given up all hope, the idea would come, and I would be off — not, of course, writing the best book in the world but the best book I was capable of writing.

As I became more experienced, I learned that I don't need the perfect idea, with all the details in place, I just need an idea with possibilities, something that will allow my imagination to go to work. I now have more ideas than I can ever use. Indeed, I sometimes work on two manuscripts at once.

Also, I have over the years developed ways to avoid even the smallest of waits.

✴ When I finish one chapter in a manuscript and can't think of a way to start the next one.

I don't just sit around and wait for an idea to come to me. I go after it. I'm sort of like a reporter after a news item.

The first thing I do is go to the library. Then I walk along the shelves, pulling down book after book. I read the first sentence in every chapter.

Nothing.

I keep going. More books. More first lines.

Nothing.

Finally I will come to a chapter that starts with a sentence like **"The phone rang."**

I will snap the book shut. That's it! The phone is going to ring and it's going to be so-and-so, and so-and-so is going to tell what's-his-name that . . .

Before long I'm back in front of my word processor typing away.

✴ When I come to a serious stopping place in a book and can't go on.

This is usually when I, the author, have no idea what's going to happen. I can't even imagine what could happen. I'm stumped.

Once again, I don't just sit there and wait for a solution to come to me.

I sit down with my manuscript. I separate myself (mentally) from being the author of the book. I become the reader of the book.

I start reading.

What I'm looking for is this: What does the reader think is going to happen? What have I led the reader to expect will happen?

For example, I may have spent two hundred words describing a tree just because I felt like describing a tree. But what I was saying to the reader was watch out for this tree! This tree is important! I wouldn't have you read two hundred words about a tree if that tree wasn't going to fall on somebody or somebody wasn't going to fall out of it.

When I come to a fork in the road.

This doesn't happen often, but I occasionally do come to a place where I can see two completely different ways the story can go. And the result will be two completely different books.

This happened in *Cracker Jackson* when Alma and her baby, Nicole, were in the hospital. Alma was going to be all right, but Nicole was in a coma, and I couldn't decide whether Nicole would live or die.

The book would be more powerful if Nicole died — and most writers want a powerful book — but I didn't want Nicole to die.

So I stopped. And I waited.

The answer came unexpectedly. I was giving a talk at a conference, and I was sitting with another author, waiting for the meeting to begin.

Some kids came up to talk to us while we were waiting, and I could hardly concentrate on my conversation because I was listening to hers. She was saying, "I couldn't help it! I just couldn't help it!"

After the kids were gone, I turned to the other author and said, "What was that all about?"

She said, "In one of my books I had a baby that the reader came to care about, and the baby died. Kids ask me why I 'made' the baby die. I tell them I couldn't help it, but they won't accept that."

I thought to myself, Maybe *you* couldn't help it, but I think I can, and when I got home, I went back to my word processor and in the very next chapter Nicole opened her eyes.

The answers always come if I wait, but it still isn't easy for me.

Around the Writer's Block

Explore a Simile

Moon Is Like Writing

Although Byars never comes right out with it, she suggests that the blacksnake is like a writing idea. Explore this comparison by brainstorming words and phrases about snakes and then seeing how many might also be true for writing ideas. Or — Brainstorm words about writing ideas and see how many are also true for snakes. Do you think it's a good comparison? Why or why not?

Make an Advice Poster

When I Get Stuck

Byars suggests several techniques that she uses when she gets stuck as a writer. Can you think of even more? Make a poster that includes both her suggestions and yours. Give your poster a title, such as *What To Do When You Can't Write*. Make most of your suggestions serious, but throw in a couple of funny ones, too.

Draw Comparisons

"Waiting patiently"

Byars suggests that "waiting patiently" is the hardest thing for writers (and snake watchers). Think of other examples of people or characters in this theme who "wait patiently." What are they waiting for? Do they get it? How? Is "waiting patiently" difficult for all of them? Do you think it's part of any process in which the imagination is at work? Why or why not?

MAY SWENSON

Summer's Bounty

berries of Straw   nuts of Brazil
berries of Goose   nuts of Monkey
berries of Huckle   nuts of Pecan
berries of Dew   nuts of Grape

berries of Boisen   beans of Lima
berries of Black   beans of French
berries of Rasp   beans of Coffee
berries of Blue   beans of Black

berries of Mul   beans of Jumping
berries of Cran   beans of Jelly
berries of Elder   beans of Green
berries of Haw   beans of Soy

apples of Crab   melons of Water
apples of May   melons of Musk
apples of Pine   cherries of Pie
apples of Love   cherries of Choke

nuts of Pea   glories of Morning
nuts of Wal   rooms of Mush
nuts of Hazel   days of Dog
nuts of Chest   puppies of Hush

Imagination Changes My World

A Personal Essay by Sabrina Dwight

Can imagination add fun to your life? Sabrina thinks so. In this essay she shares her thoughts on using imagination to brighten a boring or a lonely day.

Sabrina Dwight

**Gertrude Scott Smith School
Aurora, Illinois**

"I like being creative," said Sabrina when she wrote this essay in the sixth grade. Sabrina also likes writing stories, reading, running, and playing the flute. In the future she would like to become a lawyer.

Imagination Changes My World

A big green ugly monster in my closet? I know there's one there, but every time my mother looks, it shrinks down to the size of a pea. My mom doesn't use her imagination; that's why she says there isn't a monster in there. (I feel sorry for her.) Because I have a strong and healthy imagination, I am very lucky. Without one, everything would be just what it really is. An imagination changes everything.

When I am bored, I talk to teddy bears or other stuffed animals. Sometimes they talk back to me. So if my sister says I'm crazy, my guess is she doesn't use her imagination enough. With an imagination, I always have someone to talk to.

When life is dull, my imagination also helps me think of funny things to do or games to play, like play Twister by myself. It is funny because I am the only person playing, and when I get all tangled up, I can't spin the spinner. With an imagination, I will never be bored again.

If I didn't have an imagination, sometimes everything would be so gray and lonely. For example, without an imagination I would get lonely when all my friends were away, sick, or just couldn't play. I would be so sad. But if all my friends are gone, I just imagine new ones. My new friends help me imagine that a plain old box is a car, and we jump in our shiny red Porsche and speed away. When I look into a mirror, I can see Ramona Quimby mischievously looking back at me; or I pretend that the same mirror is a time zone, and every time I look into it, I go back in time. If I didn't know how to use my imagination, I would need to find out. Being lonely isn't any fun at all.

I can have a lot of fun just by changing the world around me. I am not going to miss out on fun, because I know how to use my imagination to keep from being lonely and bored.

Now to all you readers, just for fun, try to figure out what this is. ⟶
(Hint: Use your imagination.)

Savion Glover

Savion Glover hunches way forward in his chair, talking about basketball. Dressed in sneakers, no-fit jeans, too-big T-shirt, and backward baseball cap, he seems primed for a quick game. But Glover isn't on the court. He's sitting in his dressing room at the Virginia Theatre on Broadway, where he costars in *Jelly's Last Jam.*

Making the Rules

by Robert Sandla

If Glover looks like the guy next door, don't be fooled: At age nineteen, he is a Broadway veteran who has literally grown up onstage, with the kind of rock-solid, so-fast-you're-not-sure-you're-hearing-it-right tap technique that has even blasé dancers racing to catch up. He's a brilliant, even avant-garde tapper, kicking up sparks, rattling out torrents of sound dense with rhythm, sailing through more pointe work than Pavlova. What makes Glover a star is that he makes tap look so easy.

Savion Glover as young Jelly Roll Morton, the famous composer, taps up sparks in *Jelly's Last Jam.*

Jelly's Last Jam tells the life story of Jelly Roll Morton, the African American pianist and composer who wrote a slew of popular tunes in the 1920s and eventually claimed to have "invented" jazz all by himself. Glover plays Morton as a smug young man growing up in New Orleans, where he is raised in a high-class Creole household but rediscovers his ethnic heritage in the music and culture of Africa. He shares the role with Gregory Hines, who plays Morton as a tortured adult and won a Tony Award for his performance.

Glover made his Broadway debut in *The Tap Dance Kid* when he was twelve; by the time he was fifteen, the *New York Times* had proclaimed him a "tap dance master." In 1989 he starred in the long-running revue *Black and Blue,* where he

401

more than held his own with such tap greats as Bunny Briggs, Lon Chaney, and Jimmy Slyde. The previous year he had appeared in the film *Tap* with Hines, who has said of him: "I call Savion 'The Man' because he is certainly the one who is going to take tap into the future. *He* is where tap dance is going."

If he is the future, Glover carries on one tap tradition that endures among the elite: He doesn't take class. A loose, highly improvisational form handed down from dancer to dancer in easygoing camaraderie, tap evolves as it gets passed along. In fact, Glover carries on the aesthetic philosophy articulated — shouted, actually — by a character in *Jelly's Last Jam* when young Jelly proudly asserts that he can play *Il Trovatore*: "That ain't no music. The notes is written out telling you what's going to come next. That's like waking up in the morning knowing you going to be alive at the end of the day."

A young Savion plays around on a photo shoot for a national magazine.

"Every night Gregory and I have an improvisation that we do together," Glover says about a showstopping competition number with Hines. "Gregory, Ted Levy, and I made the dance together, and we came up with so many steps, so many ideas, that we had to cut a lot. So I'm glad we're not nailed down to the same steps every performance. A lot of the time, I don't even like to work with a band. I like everything to be spontaneous. If it's going to happen, let it happen."

Has he *ever* been nervous?

"No." He pauses. "Actually, I was nervous twice: When I did my first performance in *The Tap Dance Kid;* and once when Gregory called me on stage at the Apollo Theater to dance with him. We decided what to do as we went along."

Though Glover doesn't take class, he teaches where he was taught, at Broadway

402

Dance Center. "It was supposed to be a nice, slow class, but I don't have patience," he says. "I like things to be done yesterday. I'm giving my students stuff that I do when I perform instead of the basic stuff."

Glover now plans to attend New York University, but he was once torn between tap and sports: "I had wanted to go to college in Syracuse so bad, just to play basketball. I gave it some thought and if I was to stop dancing for a basketball season — well, I chose not to. Staying in New York City, I can perform and go to college."

Though he's starring in a Broadway show, Glover lives with his family in New Jersey. The one tangible measure of his success is that he has moved from Newark, a city with a tough reputation, to the comparatively bucolic Montclair. "People say, 'You're out of Newark,' but I am there every day, playing basketball with the same friends in the same playground. I was born and raised there. People think once you get a certain amount of money you're going to move up on a hill and not be bothered. I think if I was to do that I'd go crazy. My house in Montclair is so quiet, sometimes I'll say, 'Where's the buses? Where's the trucks making noise?' I really wanted to get my mom out of Newark so she can chill out. Newark can be hard."

Glover's five-year plan makes him sound like the hoofer next door: "Hopefully, my girlfriend will be coming out of college. I really want to get married, start a family, and I want to keep performing. I'll be acting, singing, making movies — directing. I'll be happy, just living."

Left, Savion and Jimmy Slyde improvise on stage in a December 1992 performance of *Ted Levy and Friends* at the New School in New York City.

Below, In the same performance, Savion holds his own with the legends of tap.

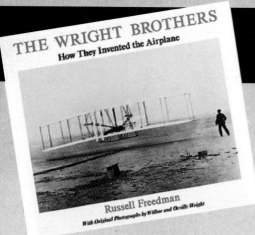

THE WRIGHT BROTHERS
How They Invented the Airplane

Russell Freedman

With Original Photographs by Wilbur and Orville Wright

MEET RUSSELL FREEDMAN

While reading *The New York Times* one day, Russell Freedman learned that Orville and Wilbur Wright had taken photographs of their first flights. Intrigued, Freedman tracked down the original negatives in the Library of Congress. The images so fascinated Freedman that he decided to write about the famous aviators. "While I was working on my book, I visited their hometown, Dayton, Ohio, where I had a chance to examine the reconstructed 1905 Wright Flyer at Carillon Park and work the controls myself.... It helped me understand (and explain to my readers) exactly how the pilot navigated that early airplane."

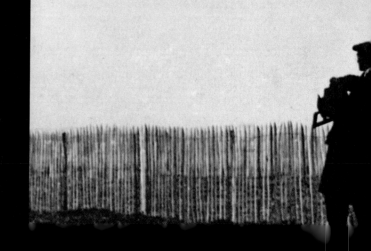

HOW THEY INVENTED THE AIRPLANE

In 1899, Orville and Wilbur Wright, hard-working brothers from Dayton, Ohio, began to study bird flight, aviation, and early gliding experiments. First they made tests on kites and tethered gliders. Then in 1901, they made manned test glides at their camp at windy Kitty Hawk on North Carolina's Outer Banks and in Ohio. But when their glider continued to spin out of control, they closed their Kitty Hawk camp early and returned sadly to Dayton. At this point Wilbur doubted that a successful manned flight would take place in his lifetime.

BACK TO THE DRAWING BOARD

Wilbur and Dan Tate launch the 1902 glider with Orville at the controls.

The experiments that Wilbur and Orville had carried out with their latest glider in 1901 were far from encouraging. Reflecting on their problems, Wilbur observed: "We saw that the calculations upon which all flying machines had been based were unreliable, and that all were simply groping in the dark. Having set out with absolute faith in the existing scientific data, we were driven to doubt one thing after another, till finally, after two years of experiment, we cast it all aside, and decided to rely entirely on our own investigations."

In the gaslit workroom behind their bicycle shop, Wilbur and Orville began to compile their own data. They wanted to test different types of wing surfaces and obtain accurate air-pressure tables. To do this, they built a wind tunnel — a wooden box 6 feet long with a glass viewing window on top and a fan at one end. It wasn't the world's first wind tunnel, but it would be the first to yield valuable results for the construction of a practical airplane.

The materials needed to make model wings, or *airfoils,* and the tools to shape them were right at hand. Using tin shears, hammers, files, and a soldering iron, the brothers fashioned as many as two hundred miniature wings out of tin, galvanized iron, steel, solder, and wax. They made wings that were thick or thin, curved or flat, wings with rounded tips and pointed tips, slender wings and stubby wings. They attached these experimental airfoils to balances made of bicycle spokes and old hacksaw blades. Then they tested the wings in their wind tunnel to see how they behaved in a moving airstream.

For several weeks they were absorbed in painstaking and systematic lab work — testing, measuring, and calculating as they tried to unlock the secrets of an aircraft wing. The work was tedious. It was repetitious. Yet they would look back on that winter as a time of great excitement, when each new day promised discoveries waiting to be made. "Wilbur and I could hardly wait for morning to come," Orville declared, "to get at something that interested us. *That's* happiness."

The Wrights knew that they were exploring uncharted territory with their wind-tunnel tests. Each new bit of data jotted down in their notebooks added to their understanding of how an airfoil works. Gradually they replaced the calculations of others with facts and figures of their own. Their doubts vanished, and their faith in themselves grew. When their lab tests were finally completed, they felt confident that they could calculate in advance the performance of an aircraft's wings with far greater accuracy than had ever before been possible.

A replica of the Wrights' pioneering wind tunnel.

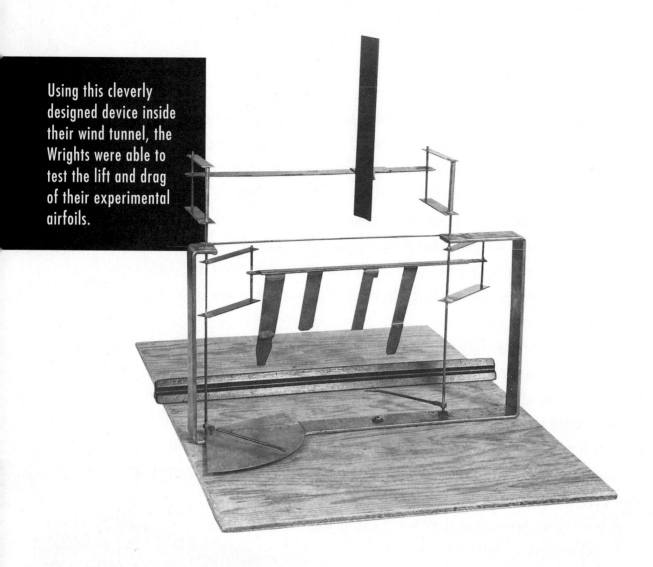

Armed with this new knowledge, they designed their biggest glider yet. Its wings, longer and narrower than before, measured 32 feet from tip to tip and 5 feet from front to rear. For the first time, the new glider had a tail — two 6-foot-high vertical fins, designed to help stabilize the machine during turns. The hip cradle developed the year before to control wing warping was retained. The craft weighed just under 120 pounds.

With growing anticipation, Wilbur and Orville prepared for their 1902 trip to the Outer Banks. "They really ought to get away for a while," Katharine wrote to her father. "Will is thin and nervous and so is Orv. They will be all right when they get down in the sand where the salt breezes blow. . . . They think that life at Kitty Hawk cures all ills, you know.

"The flying machine is in process of making now. Will spins the sewing machine around by the hour while Orv squats around marking the places to sew [the cotton wing covering]. There is no place in the house to live but I'll be lonesome enough by this time next week and wish I could have some of their racket around."

The brothers reached the Outer Banks at the end of August with their trunks, baggage, and crates carrying the glider parts. At Kill Devil Hills, they found that their wooden shed from the year before had been battered by winter storms. They set to work making repairs and remodeling the building, so they could use it instead of a tent as their new living quarters.

"We fitted up our living arrangements much more comfortably than last year," Wilbur reported. "Our kitchen is immensely improved, and then we have made beds on the second floor and now sleep aloft. It is an improvement over cots. We also have a bicycle which runs much better

"Our kitchen is immensely improved. . . ."

. . . and we have made beds on the second floor and now sleep aloft."

over the sand than we hoped, so that it takes only about an hour to make the round trip to Kitty Hawk instead of three hours as before. There are other improvements . . . so we are having a splendid time."

By the middle of September they had assembled their new glider and were ready to try it out. This year they took turns in the pilot's position, giving Orville a chance to fly for the first time. To begin with, they were very cautious. They would launch the machine from the slope on Big Hill and glide only a short distance as they practiced working the controls. Steering to the right or left was accomplished by warping the wings, with the glider always turning toward the lower wing. Up-and-down movements were controlled by the forward elevator.

In a few days they made dozens of short but successful test glides. At this point, things looked more promising than ever. The only mishap occurred one afternoon when Orville was at the controls. That evening he recorded the incident in his diary:

"I was sailing along smoothly without any trouble . . . when I noticed that one wing was getting a little too high and that the machine was slowly sliding off in the opposite direction. . . . The next thing I knew was that the wing was very high in the air, a great deal higher than before, and I thought I must have worked the twisting apparatus the wrong way. Thinking of nothing else . . . I threw the wingtips to their greatest angle. By this time I found suddenly that I was making a descent backwards

Flying the 1902 glider as a kite.

toward the low wing, from a height of 25 or 30 feet. . . . The result was a heap of flying machine, cloth and sticks in a heap, with me in the center without a bruise or scratch. The experiments thereupon suddenly came to a close till repairs can be made. In spite of this sad catastrophe we are tonight in a hilarious mood as a result of the encouraging performance of the machine."

A few days' labor made the glider as good as new. It wasn't seriously damaged again during hundreds of test glides, and it repeatedly withstood rough landings at full speed. Wilbur and Orville became more and more confident. "Our new machine is a very great improvement over anything we had built before and over anything anyone has built," Wilbur told his father. "Everything is so much more satisfactory that we now believe that the flying problem is really nearing its solution."

And yet the solution was not yet quite at hand. As they continued their test flights, a baffling new problem arose. On most flights, the glider performed almost perfectly. But every so often — in about one flight out of fifty — it would spin out of control as the pilot tried to level off after a turn.

"We were at a loss to know what the cause might be," wrote Wilbur. "The new machine . . . had a vertical tail while the earlier ones were tailless; and the wingtips were on a line with the center while the old machines had the tips drawn down like a gull's wings. The trouble might be due to either of these differences."

First they altered the wingtips and went back to Big Hill for more test flights. Again, the glider spun out of control during a turn. Then they focused their attention to the machine's 6-foot-high double-vaned tail, which was fixed rigidly in place. They had installed this tail to help stabilize the glider during turns, but now, it seemed, something was wrong.

Lying in bed one sleepless night, Orville figured out what the problem was. The fixed tail worked perfectly well most of the time. During some turns, however — when the airspeed was low and the pilot failed to level off soon enough — pressure was built up on the tail, throwing the glider off balance and into a spin. That's just what happened to Orville the day of his accident. The cure was to make the tail movable — like a ship's rudder or a bird's tail.

412

The next morning at breakfast, Orville told Wilbur about his idea. After thinking it over for a few minutes, Wilbur agreed. Then he offered an idea of his own. Why not connect the new movable tail to the wing-warping wires? This would allow the pilot to twist the wings and turn the tail at the same time, simply by shifting his hips. With the wings and tail coordinated, the glider would always make a smooth banked turn.

They removed the original tail and installed a movable single-vaned tail 5 feet high. From then on, there were no more problems. The movable tail rudder finally gave the Wright brothers complete control of their glider. "With this improvement our serious troubles ended," wrote Wilbur, "and thereafter we devoted ourselves to the work of gaining skill by continued practice."

As the brothers worked on their glider, their camp was filling up with visitors again. Their older brother Lorin arrived at the end of September to see what Wilbur and Orville were up to. Then Octave Chanute showed up again, along with two other gliding enthusiasts. Now six bunks were jammed into the narrow sleeping quarters up in the rafters. At night, the sounds of Wilbur's harmonica, Orville's mandolin, and a chorus of male voices drifted across the lonely dunes.

Lorin Wright took this photo of his brothers and their visitors at Kill Devil Hills in October, 1902.

From left: Octave Chanute,

"When the wind rose to 20 miles an hour, gliding was a real sport. . . ."

With their movable tail rudder, the Wrights felt confident that their glider could master the winds. They practiced flying at every opportunity, staying on at their camp until late in October, long after all their visitors had left. "Glides were made whenever weather conditions were favorable," Wilbur recalled. "Many days were lost on account of rain. Still more were lost on account of light winds. Whenever the breeze fell below six miles an hour, very hard running was required to get the machine started, and the task of carrying it back up the hill was real labor . . . but when the wind rose to 20 miles an hour, gliding was a real sport, for starting was easy and the labor of carrying the machine back uphill was performed by the wind."

One day they had a wind of about 30 miles an hour and were able to glide in it without any trouble. "That was the highest wind a gliding machine was ever in, so that we now hold all the records!" Orville wrote home. "The largest machine ever handled . . . the longest distance glide (American), the longest time in the air, the smallest angle of descent, and the highest wind!!! Well, I'll leave the rest of the 'blow' till we get home."

That season the Wrights had designed, built, and flown the world's first fully controllable aircraft. The three-dimensional system of aircraft control worked out by the brothers is the basic system used even today in all winged vehicles that depend on the atmosphere for support.

Except for an engine, their 1902 glider flew just as a Boeing 747 airliner or a jet fighter flies. A modern plane "warps" its wings in order to turn or level off by moving the ailerons on the rear edges of the wings. It makes smooth banking turns with the aid of a movable vertical rudder. And it noses up or down by means of an elevator (usually located at the rear of the plane).

Wilbur and Orville made hundreds of perfectly controlled glides in 1902. They proved that their laboratory tests were accurate. The next step was to build a powered airplane. "Before leaving camp," Orville wrote, "we were already at work on the general design of a new machine which we proposed to propel with a motor."

Wilbur making a right turn in the 1902 glider.

417

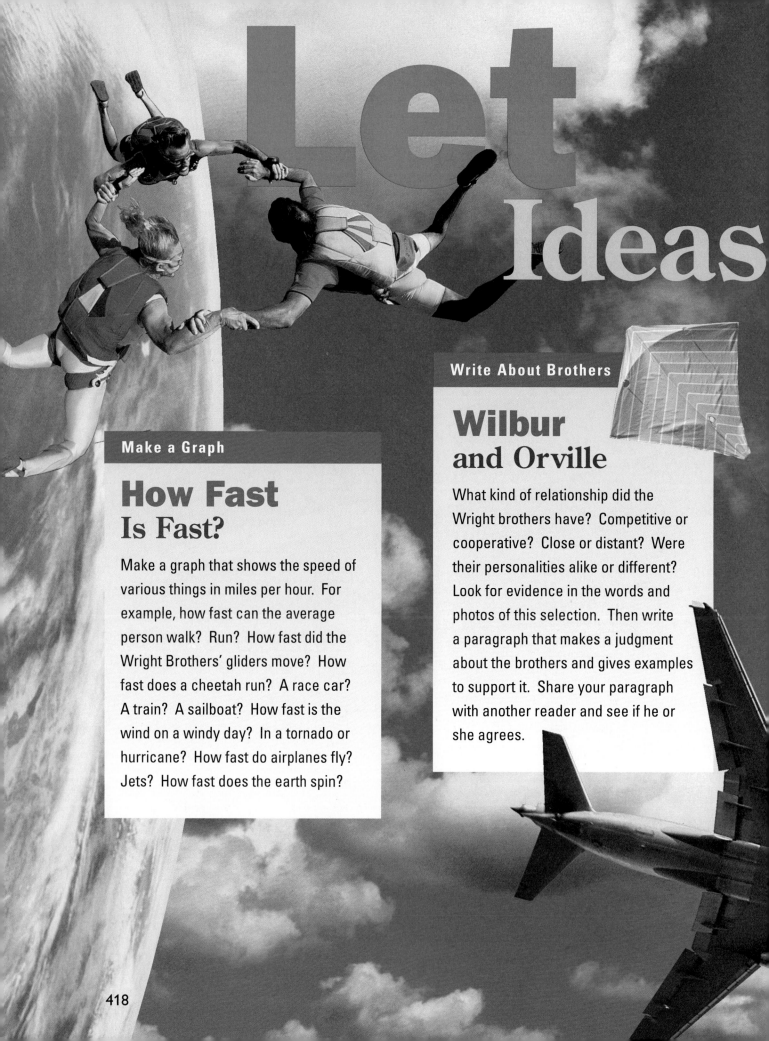

Let Ideas

Make a Graph

How Fast Is Fast?

Make a graph that shows the speed of various things in miles per hour. For example, how fast can the average person walk? Run? How fast did the Wright Brothers' gliders move? How fast does a cheetah run? A race car? A train? A sailboat? How fast is the wind on a windy day? In a tornado or hurricane? How fast do airplanes fly? Jets? How fast does the earth spin?

Write About Brothers

Wilbur and Orville

What kind of relationship did the Wright brothers have? Competitive or cooperative? Close or distant? Were their personalities alike or different? Look for evidence in the words and photos of this selection. Then write a paragraph that makes a judgment about the brothers and gives examples to support it. Share your paragraph with another reader and see if he or she agrees.

Fly!

Write a Description

The Wonder of Flight

Now that you've read this chapter about the Wright Brothers' glider, observe a plane or a bird in flight and write about what you see, hear, and experience. Take notes as you watch. Try to include some words from this selection. Turn your notes into a descriptive paragraph or a poem that you share with your classmates.

Bulletin Board Display

The Imagination at Work

Think about the old saying, "If at first you don't succeed, try, try again." As a class or group, make a bulletin board with the saying as its headline. With words and pictures, show how various people and characters from this theme are good examples of this piece of advice. Feel free to include people and characters from other themes in this book, too. Let them inspire you to try, try again when you use *your* imagination.

ON TOP

by Gary Snyder

All this new stuff goes on top
turn it over   turn it over
wait   and water down.
From the dark bottom
turn it inside out
let it spread through, sift down,
even.
Watch it sprout.

A mind like compost.

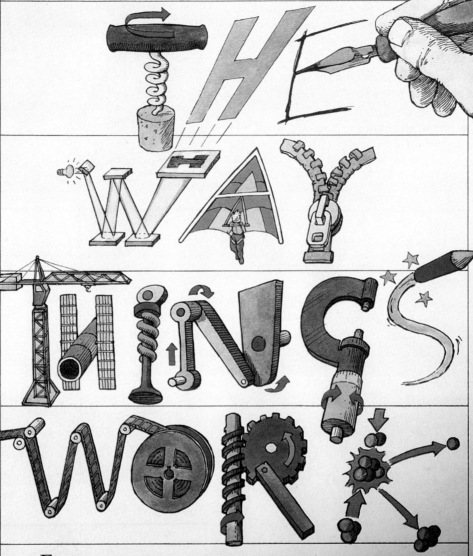

DAVID MACAULAY

THE WAY THINGS WORK

FROM LEVERS TO LASERS, CARS TO COMPUTERS-
A VISUAL GUIDE TO THE WORLD OF MACHINES

David Macaulay invites you to have serious fun as he uses
the Great Wooly Mammoth to explain the principles behind
inventions and how things work.

FLYING

ON THE ADVENT OF AIRFREIGHT

*O*ne day I chanced upon a delivery mammoth from a local awning manufacturer sighing under the weight of a large wooden frame over which was stretched a piece of canvas. Apparently waiting for its driver, the mammoth was tethered to a tree with the awning firmly secured to its back. Suddenly the wind picked up, lifting the startled beast dramatically into the sky. I noticed that as long as the wind blew and the rope between tree and mammoth held, the creature remained airborne. . .

. . .but when the wind abruptly died, the mammoth returned to the ground without ceremony, destroying not only the awning but also the manufacturer's entire premises.

HEAVIER-THAN-AIR-FLIGHT

In the struggle to overcome its not inconsiderable weight and launch itself into the air, the mammoth becomes in turn a kite, a glider and finally a powered aircraft. These are three quite different ways by which an object that is heavier than air can be made to fly.

Like balloons and airships, heavier-than-air machines achieve flight by generating a force that over comes their weight and which supports them in the air. But because they cannot float in air, they work in different ways to balloons.

Kites employ the power of the wind to keep them aloft, while all winged aircraft, including gliders and helicopters, make use of the airfoil and its power of lift. Vertical take-off aircraft direct the power of their jet engines downward and heave themselves off the ground by brute force.

The two principles that govern heavier-than-air flight are the same as those that propel powered vessels — action and reaction, and suction. When applied to flight, suction is known as lift.

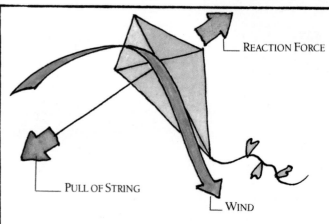

KITE

A kite flies only in a wind, and it is held by its string so that it deflects the wind downward. The wind provides the force for flight. It exerts a reaction force that equals the pull of the string and supports the kite in the air.

During my own experiments with awning delivery, I discovered that by securing a slightly curved awning to a volunteer mammoth's back, the danger and considerable expense of crash landings could be greatly reduced. Should the wind speed drop or the rope break, the mammoth would usually glide back to Earth in a gentle spiral. I planned one further improvement in which friction-reducing foot-gear would enable the mammoth to leave the ground simply by blowing backward with its trunk.

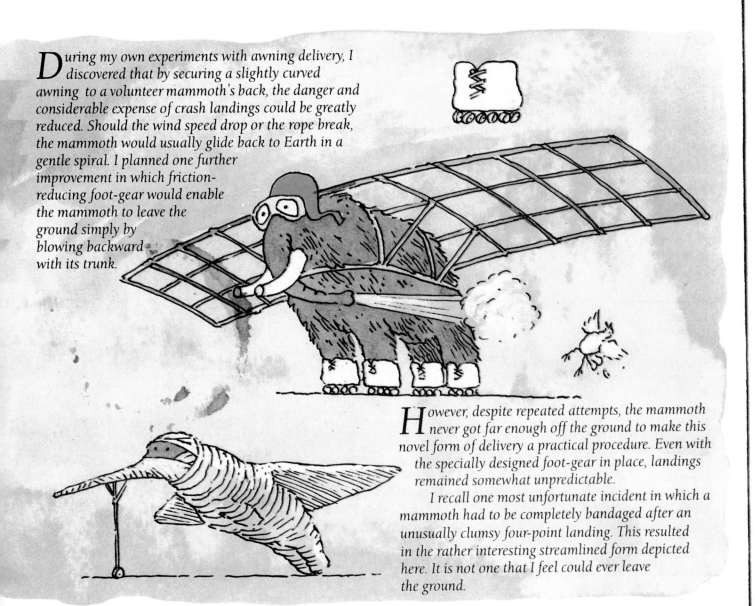

However, despite repeated attempts, the mammoth never got far enough off the ground to make this novel form of delivery a practical procedure. Even with the specially designed foot-gear in place, landings remained somewhat unpredictable.

I recall one most unfortunate incident in which a mammoth had to be completely bandaged after an unusually clumsy four-point landing. This resulted in the rather interesting streamlined form depicted here. It is not one that I feel could ever leave the ground.

AIRFOIL

The cross-section of a wing has a shape called an airfoil. As the wing moves through the air, the air divides to pass around the wing. The airfoil is curved so that air passing above the wing moves faster than air passing beneath. Fast-moving air has a lower pressure than slow-moving air. The pressure of the air is therefore greater beneath the wing than above it. This difference in air pressure forces the wing upward. The force is called lift.

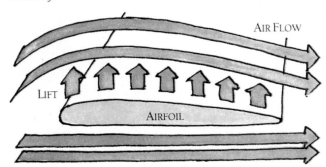

GLIDER

A glider is the simplest kind of winged aircraft. It is first pulled along the ground until it is moving fast enough for the lift generated by the wings to exceed its weight. The glider then rises into the air and flies. After release, the glider continues to move forward as it drops slowly, pulled by a thrust force due to gravity. Friction with the air produces a force called drag that acts to hold the glider back. These two pairs of opposing forces — lift and weight, thrust and drag — act on all aircraft.

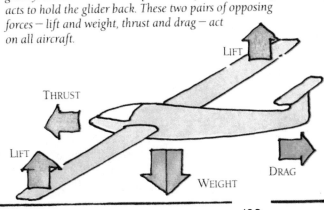

THE AIRPLANE

Adding an engine to a flying machine gives it the power to dispense with winds and air currents that govern the flight of unpowered craft such as balloons and gliders. In order to steer an airplane, a system of flaps is used. These act just like the rudder of a boat. They deflect the air flow and turn or tilt the airplane so that it rotates around its center of gravity, which in all airplanes lies between the wings.

Airplanes usually have one pair of wings to provide lift, and the wings and tail have flaps that turn or tilt the aircraft in flight. Power is provided by a propeller mounted on the nose, or by several propellers on the wings, or by jet engines mounted on the wings, tail, or inside the fuselage.

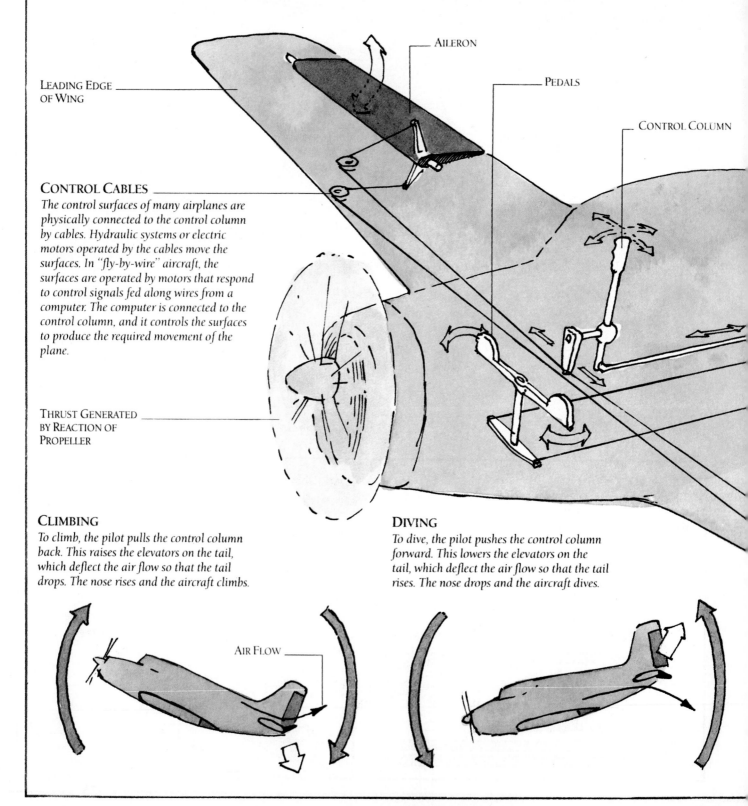

AILERON

PEDALS

CONTROL COLUMN

LEADING EDGE OF WING

CONTROL CABLES

The control surfaces of many airplanes are physically connected to the control column by cables. Hydraulic systems or electric motors operated by the cables move the surfaces. In "fly-by-wire" aircraft, the surfaces are operated by motors that respond to control signals fed along wires from a computer. The computer is connected to the control column, and it controls the surfaces to produce the required movement of the plane.

THRUST GENERATED BY REACTION OF PROPELLER

CLIMBING

To climb, the pilot pulls the control column back. This raises the elevators on the tail, which deflect the air flow so that the tail drops. The nose rises and the aircraft climbs.

DIVING

To dive, the pilot pushes the control column forward. This lowers the elevators on the tail, which deflect the air flow so that the tail rises. The nose drops and the aircraft dives.

AIR FLOW

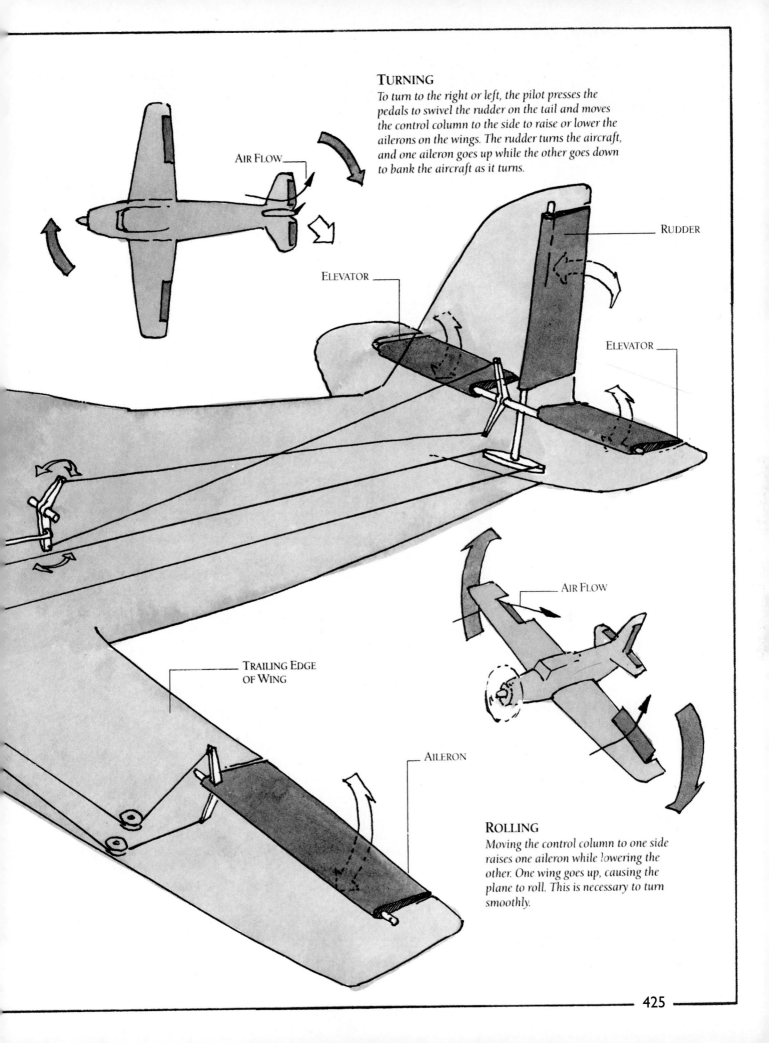

TURNING

To turn to the right or left, the pilot presses the pedals to swivel the rudder on the tail and moves the control column to the side to raise or lower the ailerons on the wings. The rudder turns the aircraft, and one aileron goes up while the other goes down to bank the aircraft as it turns.

AIR FLOW

RUDDER

ELEVATOR

ELEVATOR

TRAILING EDGE OF WING

AILERON

AIR FLOW

ROLLING

Moving the control column to one side raises one aileron while lowering the other. One wing goes up, causing the plane to roll. This is necessary to turn smoothly.

The New **WAVE** in

A Monster Hit *from* Nickelodeon *and* Klasky Csupo

AAAHH! REAL MONSTERS

Special Guide: Animating on the Macintosh

Feature Animation

"Ever since I was six years old I wanted to get into animation," Maurice Hunt explains. "I saw a clip of *Sleeping Beauty* (1959) and wanted to know how it was done."

His parents took him down to the local library where, after being given a quick lesson on the card catalogue, he devoured every book on the subject. Hunt's efforts have paid off considerably as he finds himself relaxing in his office at Turner Feature Animation, fresh off co-directing his first feature, *The Pagemaster,* for Turner Pictures Inc., in association with Twentieth Century Fox.

The Pagemaster is the story of a young boy's journey from reality into imagination when he takes refuge in an empty library one stormy evening and is literally swept into the books and a world of fantasy.

With animation screen time clocking in at 55 minutes, compared to 16 minutes of live action, Hunt had his hands full bringing to life an animated world that had the young boy Richard, played by Macaulay Culkin, wandering through a slew of classic literary scenes ranging from *Moby Dick* to *Dr. Jekyll and Mr. Hyde*. It was the transitions from live action to animation and back that presented some of the greatest challenges for Hunt.

"The Wave"

Young Richard has wandered into an enormous room in which a colorful mural, containing a drawing of *The Pagemaster* (played by Christopher Lloyd) and several of the other animated characters he is soon to meet, is painted on the ceiling. Paint from the mural drips down onto the unsuspecting Richard, slowly at first and then in torrents. The kaleidoscope of puddles on the floor gather to form a giant, raging wave of paint that chases Richard through the aisles of bookshelves, turning everything that it splashes against into animation — including Richard who, upon the discovery of his new state, promptly declares in half wonder, half disgust, "I'm a cartoon!"

"I want to stretch myself
     to the max, each and
every time I put pencil
     or pen
     or paintbrush to paper..."
he says with a laugh,
     ". . . or to computer!"

Hunt encourages young animators to obtain a command of the basics of traditional animation and a thorough understanding of the principles of creating a personality out of a human or an inanimate object.

"Personality is what appeals to people," he explains. Then one can move on to computers and combine knowledge of both worlds with limitless results.

by James Gates

429

FINDING
COMMON
GROUND

431

FINDING COMMON GROUND

CROSSING BOUNDARIES

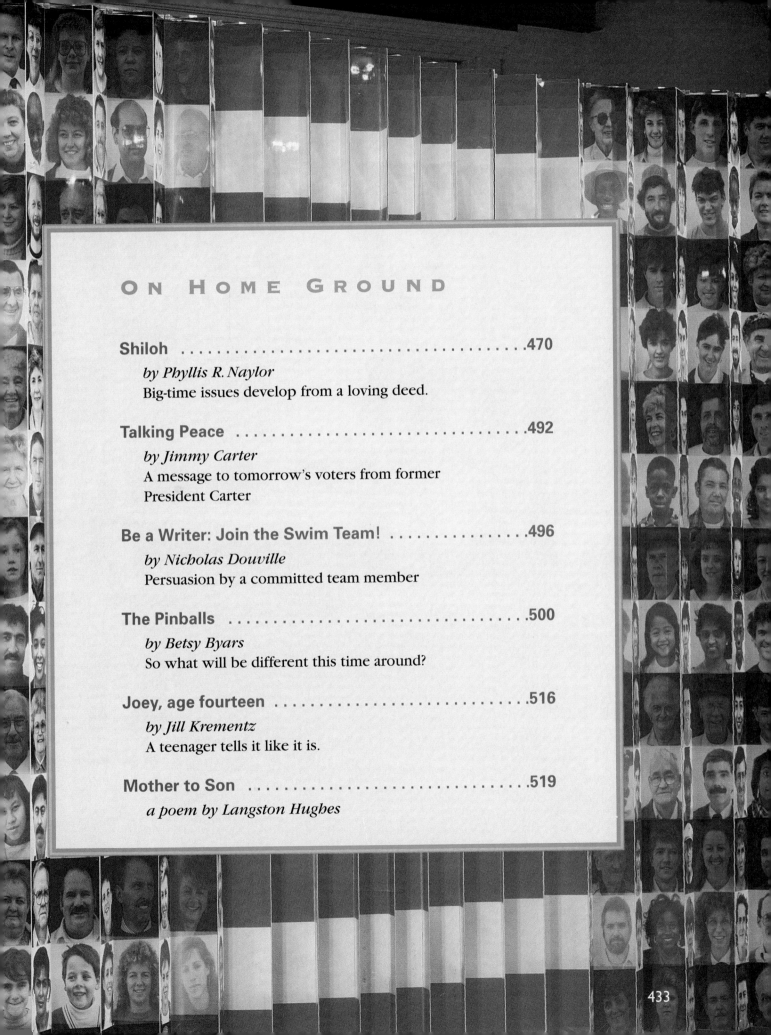

ON HOME GROUND

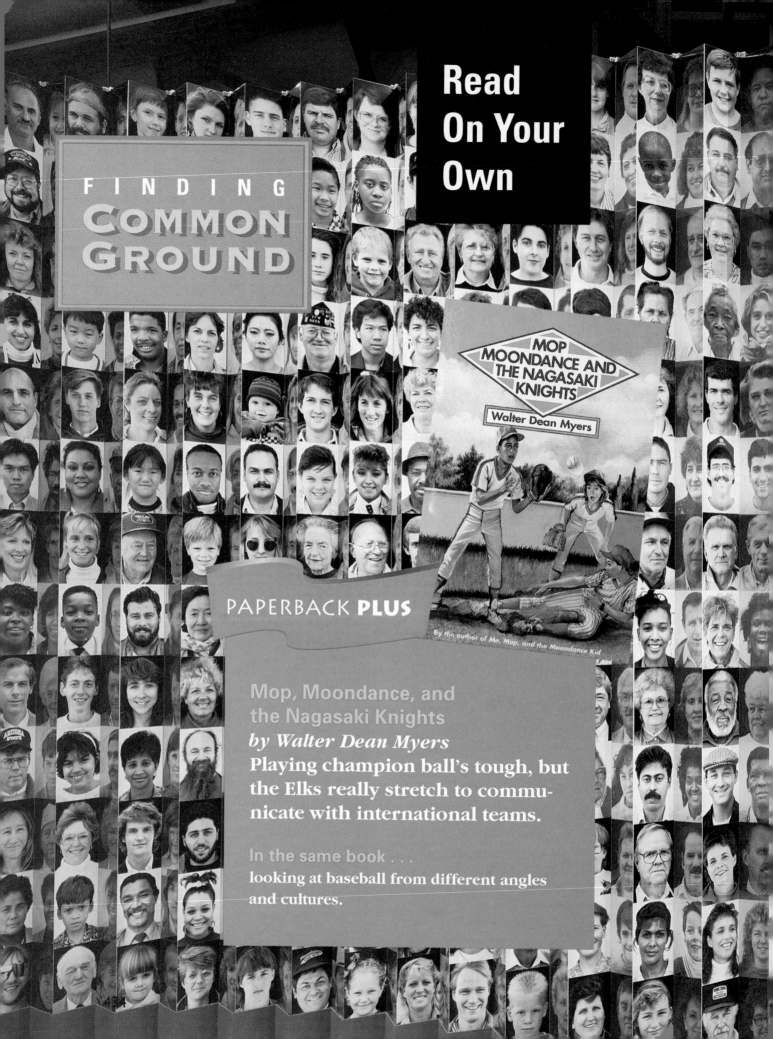

FINDING
COMMON
GROUND

MOP
MOONDANCE AND
THE NAGASAKI
KNIGHTS
Walter Dean Myers

By the author of Me, Mop, and the Moondance Kid

PAPERBACK **PLUS**

Mop, Moondance, and
the Nagasaki Knights
by Walter Dean Myers
**Playing champion ball's tough, but
the Elks really stretch to communicate with international teams.**

In the same book . . .
looking at baseball from different angles
and cultures.

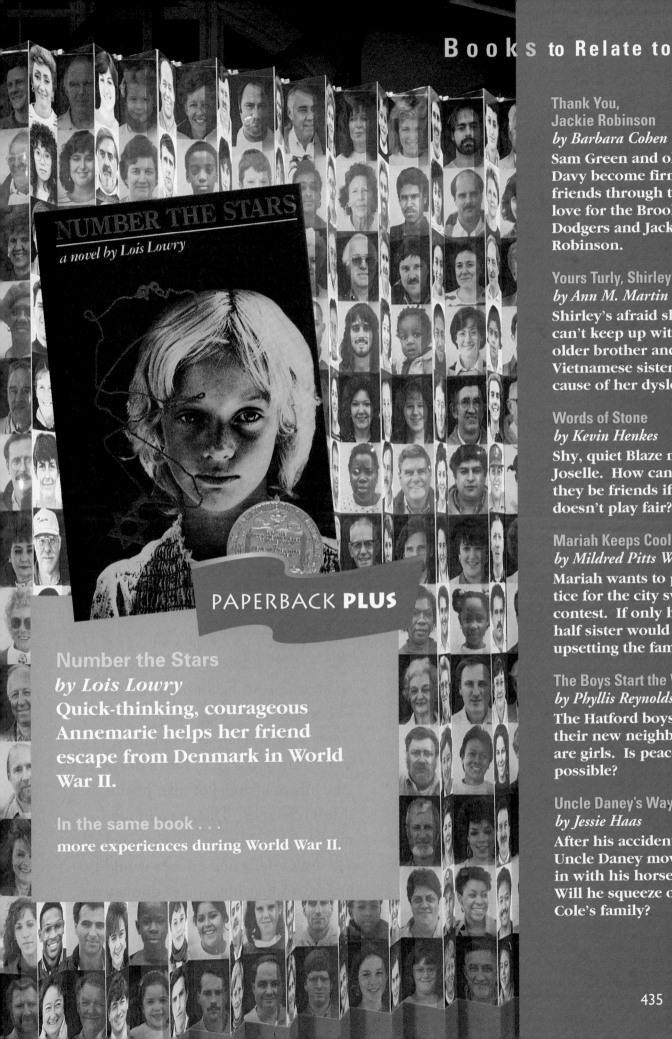

NUMBER THE STARS

a novel by Lois Lowry

PAPERBACK **PLUS**

Number the Stars
by Lois Lowry
**Quick-thinking, courageous
Annemarie helps her friend
escape from Denmark in World
War II.**

In the same book . . .
more experiences during World War II.

**Thank You,
Jackie Robinson**
by Barbara Cohen
Sam Green and old
Davy become firm
friends through their
love for the Brooklyn
Dodgers and Jackie
Robinson.

Yours Turly, Shirley
by Ann M. Martin
Shirley's afraid she
can't keep up with her
older brother and new
Vietnamese sister be-
cause of her dyslexia.

Words of Stone
by Kevin Henkes
Shy, quiet Blaze meets
Joselle. How can
they be friends if she
doesn't play fair?

Mariah Keeps Cool
by Mildred Pitts Walter
Mariah wants to prac-
tice for the city swim
contest. If only her
half sister would stop
upsetting the family!

The Boys Start the War
by Phyllis Reynolds Naylor
The Hatford boys learn
their new neighbors
are girls. Is peace
possible?

Uncle Daney's Way
by Jessie Haas
After his accident,
Uncle Daney moves
in with his horse.
Will he squeeze out
Cole's family?

ABOUT THE AUTHOR

It was **Gary Soto**'s two-and-a-half year study of *shorinji kempō* that sparked the writing of *Pacific Crossing*. Because Japan is the birthplace of this martial art, Soto wanted to set his story there. "Because so few Mexican American kids have the opportunity to travel, I wanted to use martial arts as a vehicle for Lincoln to go to Japan." When asked what he hopes students will get from reading *Pacific Crossing*, Soto says, "Literature allows kids to travel through the use of their imagination."

ABOUT THE ILLUSTRATOR

"I grew up in Guangzhou, China, a kind of naughty but smart kid," says **Hui Han Liu**. "At twenty I was accepted into Guangzhou Art School. Then I decided to become an artist." When he illustrates a book, Han Liu continues, "I do some library research; I do a drawing study from a model or take photos as a detail reference. This time, I found a model with a Hispanic background." Liu draws daily and advises would-be artists "to love life, and to do sketches from life or memories."

PACIFIC CROSSING

Because of his interest in martial arts, fourteen-year-old Lincoln Mendoza has been chosen to spend a summer with a host family in Japan. Mitsuo is his Japanese "brother." It's the first full day of his visit.

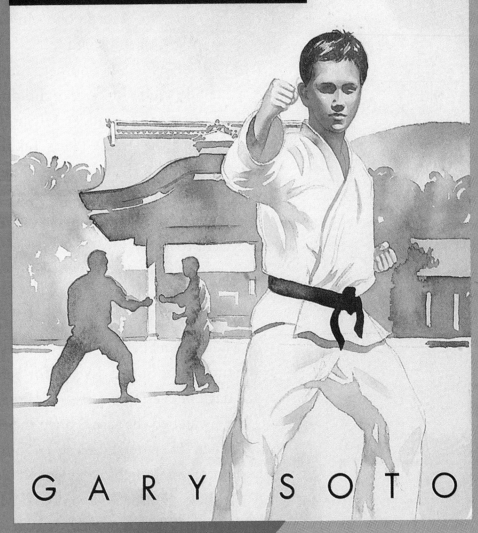

GARY SOTO

MITSUO pointed to a wooden building with slat windows. "I took judo there but quit." A wind chime banged in the breeze.

"You took judo?" Lincoln asked, excited. "That's bad."

"No, judo is good."

"No, I mean bad. In California, if you like something a lot, then it's bad."

Mitsuo gave Lincoln another strange look. He said, "In Japan, everyone takes judo or *kempō*. I didn't like judo. For me, it was not 'bad.' Baseball is 'bad.'" Mitsuo then pointed to a round man walking down the street. "He's Takahashi-*sensei*. He's OK, but his assistant is mean. He was mean to me because I lost a match at a tournament."

"You went to tournaments? Sounds fun."

"I went to a few, but I wasn't very good."

"Sure you were."

"No, really."

Lincoln let the subject drop because he knew how sensitive he was when a defeat came up in conversation. He recalled the basketball games back home. Except for basketball at school, he had to work hard at everything, even spelling.

They watched the *sensei* open the dojo with a key as large as a can opener. He entered, his shoes in his hand. The door closed behind him, and a light went on.

"I'll show you the *kempō* dojo," Mitsuo said.

"All right!" Lincoln cried.

They hurried through an alley and down three blocks, their mouths full of pumpkin seeds. When Mitsuo stopped, Lincoln nearly bumped into him.

"There," Mitsuo said, pointing.

"Where?" Lincoln asked, confused. He was facing a cement driveway with a border of wild grass.

"There."

"Where?"

"There, Lincoln-kun!"

"You mean this *driveway?*"

"Yes, they practice there and on the lawn. I think they practice at the university in winter."

Lincoln's image of a cleanly swept dojo evaporated like rain on a hot sidewalk. He was disappointed. He had come to Japan expecting to practice on tatami mats in a templelike dojo.

"They practice on concrete," he whispered.

When Mitsuo and Lincoln returned home, Mitsuo's father and mother were sitting with a woman on the *engawa*. The woman sat erect, her face composed. All three were drinking iced tea, Mrs. Ono cooling herself with a fan that showed a picture of a baseball team.

Mitsuo gave the woman a short bow and greeted her in Japanese. Lincoln bowed, too.

"Lincoln-kun, this is Mrs. Oyama," the father said. He raised his glass, sipped, and put it down by his feet. "You and Mitsuo worked hard. The field looks tidy."

After a moment of silence, Mrs. Oyama asked, "So, Lincoln, you practice *shorinji kempō?*" Her face was turned away, as if she were asking Mr. Ono.

"Yes," Lincoln answered, his back straight.

"You must be very good. You're so young and strong," Mrs. Oyama said, a smile starting at the corner of her mouth. She was still looking in the direction of Mr. Ono.

"Well, I guess so," Lincoln said, flattered, tightening his fist so that a rope of muscle showed in his forearm. He tried to hold back a smile. "I'm *sankyu* rank."

"*Sankyu*. Very good for your age," Mrs. Oyama said, an eyebrow lifted. She turned to Mrs. Ono and said, "Such a strong boy."

"Oh yes, he worked so hard in the garden today," Mrs. Ono said, fanning the cool air in Lincoln's direction.

He sat straight up, his chest puffed out a little. "Well, I am pretty good. That's what *Nakano-sensei* says. I'll be a black belt when I'm fifteen."

"I'm impressed." Mrs. Oyama beamed, pressing her hands together. "I'm so happy to hear that in America we have dedicated youth."

The telephone rang in the living room. Mitsuo jumped to his feet. Lincoln started to follow, but the adults told him to stay.

"Mitsuo will answer it," Mr. Ono told Lincoln. "Lincoln-kun, what does your mother do?"

"She's sort of an artist. She has her own company." Lincoln bit his lower lip as he tried to think of what she actually did for a living. "She's a commercial artist. She does work for computer firms."

Mr. Ono shook his head, sighing, "Ah yes."

"And your father?" Mrs. Ono asked.

Lincoln had known this was coming. He had known ever since he'd boarded the jet to come to Japan that he would be asked this question. "He's a police officer," Lincoln said, not adding that he hadn't seen his father in six years. His parents had been divorced since Lincoln was seven, a hurt that had never healed.

The adults looked at each other, nodding their heads. They sipped tea and stirred the air with newspaper shaped into fans.

440

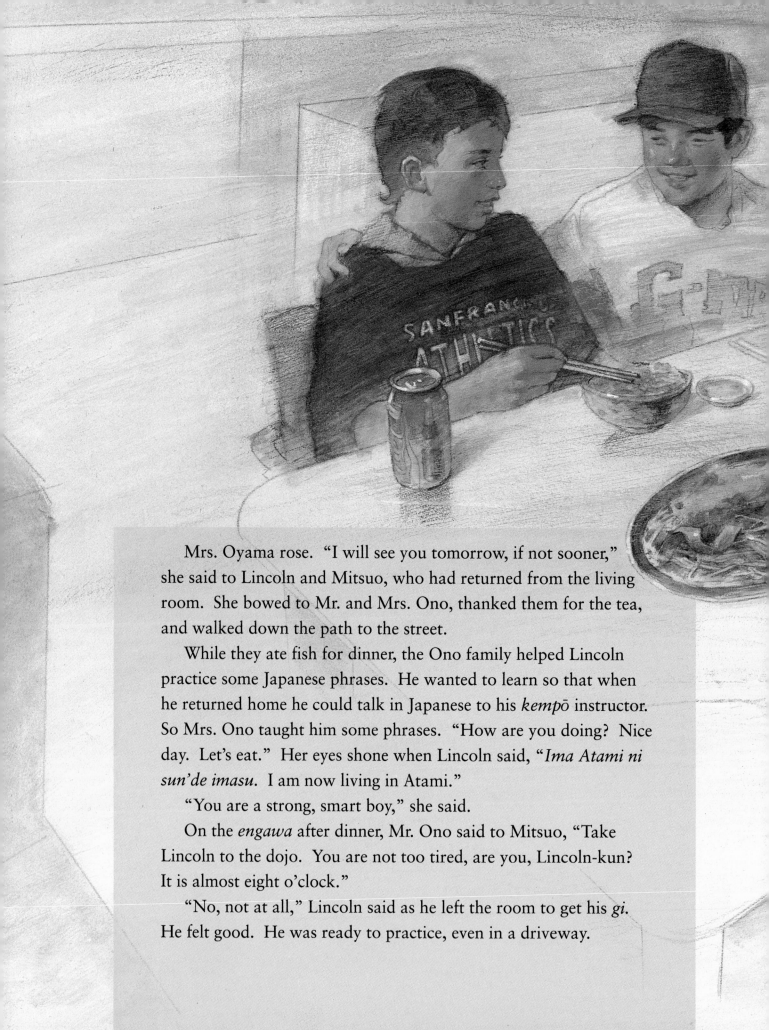

Mrs. Oyama rose. "I will see you tomorrow, if not sooner," she said to Lincoln and Mitsuo, who had returned from the living room. She bowed to Mr. and Mrs. Ono, thanked them for the tea, and walked down the path to the street.

While they ate fish for dinner, the Ono family helped Lincoln practice some Japanese phrases. He wanted to learn so that when he returned home he could talk in Japanese to his *kempō* instructor. So Mrs. Ono taught him some phrases. "How are you doing? Nice day. Let's eat." Her eyes shone when Lincoln said, "*Ima Atami ni sun'de imasu. I am now living in Atami.*"

"You are a strong, smart boy," she said.

On the *engawa* after dinner, Mr. Ono said to Mitsuo, "Take Lincoln to the dojo. You are not too tired, are you, Lincoln-kun? It is almost eight o'clock."

"No, not at all," Lincoln said as he left the room to get his *gi*. He felt good. He was ready to practice, even in a driveway.

Mr. Ono spoke to Mitsuo in Japanese, and Mitsuo turned away, almost laughing.

"What is *Chichi* joking about?" Lincoln asked, smiling as well.

"He is glad you are here," Mitsuo said as he slipped on his *geta*. "I'll take you to *kempō*."

They walked four blocks in silence, and when they arrived at the driveway, Mitsuo turned away, a smile starting on his face. "I will see you in one hour. Have fun."

Puzzled at Mitsuo's smile, Lincoln watched him hurry away, *geta* ringing on the stone walk. Lincoln shrugged his shoulders as he entered the driveway with a fistful of yen, his monthly dues. On his way down the driveway, Lincoln stopped to *gasshō* — salute — to three black belts who were stretching on the lawn, sweat already soaking into the backs of their *gi*s. They rose to their feet, saluted to Lincoln, and pointed to the side of the building. Lincoln went around and saw two others changing, a father and son. He changed there as well, folding his clothes neatly and placing his *geta* along the wall. He took off his watch, which glowed in the dark: 8:10.

Everyone was speaking in Japanese. No one paid Lincoln any attention as he joined the others on the lawn. He looked skyward at a plane cutting across the sky, and at that moment he wished he were on that plane.

A light lit the yard, reflecting off a small kidney-shaped pond, set among reeds and bamboo. Lincoln went and looked at the pond. He saw the reflection of his face in the murky water, rippling from long-legged water bugs.

He rejoined the others on the lawn and began stretching and practicing punches and kicks. His chest rose and fell, and his breathing became shallow. In the warm summer air, sweat was already starting to run from his body.

The *sensei* came out of the house, hands raised in a *gasshō*. She smiled and welcomed everyone as they formed two lines.

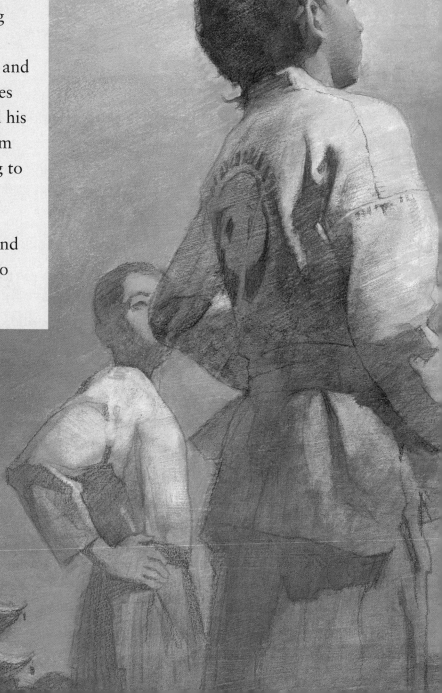

444

Lincoln's mouth fell open. It was Mrs. Oyama, whom he had met just before dinner — Oyama-*sensei*! He found a place at the back of the line, his face twisted with worry. Only an hour ago he had been bragging that he was *sankyu* rank, that he was as strong as any kid in the world.

After a formal salute to the spirit of *kempō*, some meditation, and warm-ups, the group finally started basic exercises. Only after basics did Oyama-*sensei* point to Lincoln, and everyone looked in his direction.

Lincoln forced a toothy smile. He hated life at that moment. He wished that he were on that plane, going back home to San Francisco. He promised himself this would be the last time he bragged.

"Lincoln, please," Oyama-*sensei* called, her outstretched hand gesturing for him to come up to the front. "Please tell us about yourself."

I'm a loudmouthed braggart, Lincoln thought; that's what I could tell you about myself.

Sweat streamed down his face, more from embarrassment than from the workout. He walked to the front, where he gave a *gasshō* and told his fellow practitioners — all eight of them — that he was from San Francisco and that he was staying with the Ono family for the summer. When they smiled at him, he felt a little better.

They practiced *juhō* — grabs and pinning techniques — and *embu* — planned attacks. He tried his best. He didn't want these adult black belts to think he was sorry, just because he was from America and a fourteen-year-old brown belt. His punches and kicks snapped against his *gi*. His arm locks were executed quickly, but not with the ease of the adults'.

Lincoln had never worked out on grass before. In San Francisco, he had practiced on linoleum. He liked the way the grass tickled the bottoms of his feet. He also liked having the grass to cushion his falls; he fell a lot when he practiced with the advanced belts. He was thrown and twisted into painful holds, his face pressed harshly against the grass. He got up quickly when they let go, and he didn't let on that his arm felt like a drumstick being torn from the body of a chicken.

When class ended at 9:30, Oyama-*sensei* called him aside. "Lincoln-kun, you are a good boy. Strong."

"I'm not that strong," he said, this time not wanting to brag about himself. He was still warm from the workout, and his chest was rising and falling. Grass clung to his *gi* and his tousled hair.

"You are very good. In six weeks, if you practice hard, we will see about a promotion." One side of her face was hidden in the dark; the other side glowed in the porch light. Her eyes gave away nothing.

446

Lincoln started to walk away, but she called him back. "Lincoln-kun, you must shave your hair."

"My hair?" he asked, touching the hair around his ears.

"Yes, it must be gone."

Lincoln changed from his *gi* to his street clothes and was greeted by Mitsuo, who was waiting in the driveway.

"How come you didn't tell me?" Lincoln asked. "She's the *sensei*, and you didn't tell me. That was cold."

"Sorry, Lincoln, but Father wanted to make a joke. He likes you." Mitsuo thought for a moment, then asked, "What is 'cold'?"

" 'Cold' is, is — I don't know how to explain it. But that was a 'cold' shot," Lincoln said as the two of them walked down the street, their *geta* ringing in unison. "Yeah, your dad is a wise guy."

"Yes, he is sometimes very wise," Mitsuo agreed.

Lincoln stopped in his tracks and was about to explain "wise guy" and the Three Stooges, but he was too tired. It had been a long day in Japan.

The stores were closed. A few cars passed in the street, silent as cats. Only a small neon light glowed in a bar window. They tiptoed over and looked inside, where men sat playing *go*, an ancient board game similar to checkers, or talking in dark corners.

"Just like California," Lincoln said.

"Really?"

"Yeah."

"My father used to come here, but he doesn't anymore. He likes it better at home."

Lincoln wanted to tell Mitsuo about his father — about his lack of a father — but didn't know how. In the United States, it was not uncommon to come from a broken home. But in Japan families all seemed to be intact — father, mother, children, all walking down the street together. In the *sentō*, fathers scrubbed their children, and, in turn, the children scrubbed their fathers with all their might. It wasn't Lincoln's fault that his parents' marriage hadn't worked out. Still, at times he felt lonely and embarrassed.

They walked home. Lincoln showered and then went out to the *engawa* to join Mitsuo, who was relacing his baseball mitt after having taken out some of the padding.

"This is my favorite mitt," Mitsuo said proudly. "My grandfather gave it to me."

"Nice." The night was quiet. A cat strode the thin rail of a bamboo fence, his tail waving in the moonlight. The neighbors were watching television. The vegetable garden rustled in the breeze. Lincoln felt tired but happy. He was already feeling at home.

A BLACK BELT IN READING

Make a Poster

Japanese Words and Phrases

Look through this selection and list all the Japanese words and phrases. Find out what each one means, either from context or from a Japanese-English dictionary. Make a poster or bulletin board that shows the words and their meanings — including illustrations if possible — and display it in your classroom or library.

Listen to a Japanese Speaker

"Ima Atami ni sun'de imasu."

Invite a Japanese speaker to your classroom. Before he or she visits, prepare a list of questions. Ask the speaker to read some of the words from this selection and to teach you a few Japanese phrases, as Mrs. Ono did for Lincoln. What are the biggest differences between Japanese and English?

Discuss Surprises

I Didn't Expect That!

Work in a pair or a small group. Look through the selection and list all the surprises that Lincoln experiences — or that you experienced as you read. Then circle the three that you think are the most important. For each, decide why it was a surprise. Together, write a sentence that expresses the reason. Share your three sentences with another pair or group.

Write a Letter Home

Dear Mom

Put yourself in Lincoln's place and write a letter home to your mother after your first day in Japan. What is the best thing that happened? The worst? How do you feel about what's happened so far? What are you fearful of? Looking forward to? Share your letter with another reader.

451

Coming

UPDATE spoke to four teens — two Americans and two Japanese — who had gone to live in the others' country. As you'll see, sometimes the little things about each culture taught them the most.

Tomoko Ishibashi, 18

Tomoko is a Tokyo native attending Potsdam High School in Camden, New York, as an exchange student with American Field Service (AFS).

In Japan, high school students are prohibited from doing many things. We must wear uniforms, we cannot wear makeup, we cannot grow our nails — even our hairstyles are determined by our schools. But in America, you can find your own way of wearing clothes, of expressing yourself. Since American students have opportunities to express themselves in many ways, they are very different from each other. Japanese students are very similar to each other.

In homeroom, on my first day in an American high school, all of a sudden everybody stood up and started reciting something. I was very confused, until I noticed that they were standing towards the Star Spangled Banner. We don't have flags in our classrooms in Japan. Japanese students say next to nothing about our national problems, or about being proud of being Japanese. But Americans are very proud of their country.

One of the most shocking things for me in America was that boys were in my classes. In Japan I went to a private girls school for six years, and I wasn't used to studying with boys. But it's not the boys themselves that are the shocking thing — it's that the girls talk mostly about boys. Before I told my American girlfriends that I liked certain boys, they were somewhat closed to me. But after I told them that I thought some boys were cute, they suddenly opened their minds to me. I thought, "Oh, this is the easiest way to make friends with American girls."

Here,

Kengo Wakabayashi, 17

Kengo hails from Shimosuwa, a small town in central Japan. He currently attends Yorktown High School in Arlington, Virginia, living with an American family through the Youth for Understanding exchange program.

On my first night in America, my host family took me to Bob's Big Boy Restaurant to have dinner. The waitress was very friendly. Here in America, people I don't know talk to me in the street and in stores. They'll say, "Hi, how are you?" In Japan we talk a lot with friends, but not with people we don't know.

Japanese people like Americans very much. But it is said in Japan that some Americans don't like Japan. It's said that some Americans hated Japan for not participating in the Gulf War, and because Japan doesn't like to import American beef and oranges.

Japan does this to protect Japanese farmers.

Now that I'm here, I don't think Americans hate Japan. I've never heard people speak ill of Japan. One of my friends said to me he liked Japan very much because Japan produced many good things — like Japanese cars and stereos. He said the things Japan makes are great.

I don't think Americans understand Japan. Some of my American friends ask me if all Japanese study very hard and are really smart. I don't think

so. I think Americans work harder than Japanese in classes. In some Japanese high schools, students don't study hard at all.

Also, there is more homework in the U.S. than in Japan. In my Japanese high school, teachers give us homework, but it's not related to our grades. So most of our high school students don't do homework. And some of them fall asleep in class.

Going

Sky Tandberg, 17

Sky has been to Japan twice. This past summer, he lived and went to high school in Matsue, a small city near Kyoto, on an AFS exchange program. Sky is currently a senior at Torrey Pines High School in San Diego, California.

I went to Japan because I felt it was one of the most foreign places I could go. There's a kind of a mystery about the Orient, and I wanted to see it firsthand.

The way people interact there is quite a bit different from the way we do it in the West. The focus is on the group, rather than the individual. When people introduced themselves to me, they'd tell me their name, and then they'd tell me what group they belonged to. For instance, if they went to high school, they'd say, "Hello, my name is Shimata, and I go to this high school, and I'm from this room in this high school."

There are a lot of formalities and standards for correct behavior in Japanese society. I kept forgetting to bow in the beginning. On my first day of school, before my homeroom teacher took me to meet the principal, he reminded me, "Remember to bow!" But I forgot. Then they gave me a desk in my homeroom class.

I was sitting there when the teacher walked in. Everyone stood up and bowed — except me. But I learned after a while.

One thing that startled me was that Japanese people slurp their noodles. On my first day in Japan I went into a noodle shop. Everybody all around me was slurping noodles like crazy. I thought, wow, this is really bad manners. But in Japan, it's good manners — a sign of a healthy appetite. They even slurp spaghetti.

There

Rena Richardson, 18

Rena attended a Japanese high school in Fukuyama as an AFS exchange student during the summer of 1990. A native of Chicago, she is now a freshman at Xavier University in New Orleans.

One of the hardest changes was going to school six days a week. The schedule is really rigorous. Education is put before everything else in Japan. Students go to school at 8 in the morning and don't get home until about 7 o'clock. Right after dinner, it's time to go to sleep. My host sister, who was a junior in high school like I was, would get up at 1 o'clock in the morning and study until it was time to get ready for school.

One reason why there are so many Japanese products in the U.S. is because of all the hard work that they're taught to do in school. Once a Japanese friend made me an *origami* (paper) bridge. I thought it was really nice. But instead of praising it, his friends ridiculed it: it should have been this way, it should have been that way, he should have used this type of paper to make it sturdier.

I didn't understand why they were doing it, but then they told me they were always pressed to do their best. I figure that's why they're always making bigger and better things than the other countries. They keep on trying until they make the best, most efficient product.

America could benefit by adopting some Japanese customs. But I think Americans are stubborn and we're not going to change. A lot of people say, "Why try to be like the Japanese? We're sticking to our own ideas." I think we should put our ideas together to come up with new ways of working things. But we haven't gotten to that point yet.

MEET NICHOLASA MOHR

Nicholasa Mohr began her creative life as a visual artist. In 1972, a publisher who collected her artwork asked Mohr to write about her experiences "growing up Puerto Rican and female" in New York City. At first Mohr wasn't interested, but when her agent asked how many such books she had read, she reacted strongly. "I was well aware that there were *no* books published about Puerto Rican girls, or boys either for that matter. . . . I was also reminded that when I was growing up, I'd enjoyed reading about the adventures of many boys and girls, but I had never really seen myself, my brother, and my family in those books. We just were not there." To fill the need for such a book, Mohr began to write.

MEET ROSANNE KALOUSTIAN

"Growing up in the apartment above my parents' dry cleaning store, I always loved to draw and paint and I accompanied my book reports with illustrations and drawings. Later I was awarded a scholarship to the National Academy of Art in New York City. Being an artist just came naturally. I try to feel what the characters are experiencing and express their emotions . . . to capture the mood of the story." Kaloustian's favorite illustrator, Norman Rockwell, "captures life in America wonderfully." She advises, "Keep on drawing and painting everything that inspires you. Study the great master artists and don't give up. . . . Just follow your dreams!"

The WRONG Lunch Line

by NICHOLASA MOHR

Early Spring 1946

The morning dragged on for Yvette and Mildred. They were anxiously waiting for the bell to ring. Last Thursday the school had announced that free Passover lunches would be provided for the Jewish children during this week. Yvette ate the free lunch provided by the school and Mildred brought her lunch from home in a brown paper bag. Because of school rules, free-lunch children and bag-lunch children could not sit in the same section, and the two girls always ate separately. This week, however, they had planned to eat together.

Finally the bell sounded and all the children left the classroom for lunch. As they had already planned, Yvette and Mildred went right up to the line where the Jewish children were filing up for lunch-trays. I hope no one asks me nothing, Yvette said to herself. They stood close to each other and held hands. Every once in a while one would squeeze the other's hand in a gesture of reassurance, and they would giggle softly.

The two girls lived just a few houses away from one another. Yvette lived on the top floor of a tenement, in a four-room apartment which she shared with her parents, grandmother, three older sisters, two younger brothers, and baby sister. Mildred was an only child. She lived with her parents in the three small rooms in back of the candy store they owned.

During this school year, the two girls had become good friends. Every day after public school, Mildred went to a Hebrew school. Yvette went to catechism twice a week, preparing for her First Communion and Confirmation. Most evenings after supper, they played together in front of the candy store. Yvette was a

frequent visitor in Mildred's apartment. They listened to their favorite radio programs together. Yvette looked forward to the Hershey's chocolate bar that Mr. Fox, Mildred's father, would give her.

The two girls waited patiently on the lunch line as they slowly moved along toward the food counter. Yvette was delighted when she saw what was placed on the trays: a hard-boiled egg, a bowl of soup that looked like vegetable, a large piece of cracker, milk, and an apple. She stretched over to see what the regular free lunch was, and it was the usual: a bowl of watery stew, two slices of dark bread, milk, and cooked prunes in a thick syrup. She was really glad to be standing with Mildred.

"Hey Yvette!" She heard someone call her name. It was Elba Cruz, one of her classmates. "What's happening? Why are you standing there?"

"I'm having lunch with Mildred today," she answered, and looked at Mildred, who nodded.

"Oh, yeah?" Elba said. "Why are they getting a different lunch from us?"

"It's their special holiday and they gotta eat that special food, that's all," Yvette answered.

"But why?" persisted Elba.

"Else it's a sin, that's why. Just like we can't have no meat on Friday," Yvette said.

"A sin. . . . Why — why is it a sin?" This time, she looked at Mildred.

"It's a special lunch for Passover," Mildred said.

"Passover? What is that?" asked Elba.

"It's a Jewish holiday. Like you got Easter, so we have Passover. We can't eat no bread."

"Oh. . . ."

"You better get in your line before the teacher comes," Yvette said quickly.

"You're here!" said Elba.

"I'm only here because Mildred invited me," Yvette answered. Elba shrugged her shoulders and walked away.

"They gonna kick you outta there. . . . I bet you are not supposed to be on that line," she called back to Yvette.

"Dumbbell!" Yvette answered. She turned to Mildred and asked, "Why can't you eat bread, Mildred?"

"We just can't. We are only supposed to eat matzo. What you see there." Mildred pointed to the large cracker on the tray.

"Oh," said Yvette. "Do you have to eat an egg too?"

"No . . . but you can't have no meat, because you can't have meat and milk together . . . like at the same time."

"Why?"

"Because it's against our religion. Besides, it's very bad. It's not supposed to be good for you."

"It's not?" asked Yvette.

"No," Mildred said. "You might get sick. You see, you are better off waiting like a few hours until you digest your food, and then you can have meat or the milk. But not together."

"Wow," said Yvette. "You know, I have meat and milk together all the time. I wonder if my mother knows it's not good for you."

By this time the girls were at the counter. Mildred took one tray and Yvette quickly took another.

"I hope no one notices me," Yvette whispered to Mildred. As the two girls walked toward a long lunch table, they heard

giggling, and Yvette saw Elba and some of the kids she usually ate lunch with pointing and laughing at her. Stupids, thought Yvette, ignoring them and following Mildred. The two girls sat down with the special lunch group.

Yvette whispered to Mildred, "This looks good!" and started to crack the eggshell.

Yvette felt Mildred's elbow digging in her side. "Watch out!" Mildred said.

"What is going on here?" It was the voice of one of the teachers who monitored them during lunch. Yvette looked up and saw the teacher coming toward her.

"You! You there!" the teacher said, pointing to Yvette. "What are you doing over there?" Yvette looked at the woman and was unable to speak.

"What are you doing over there?" she repeated.

"I went to get some lunch," Yvette said softly.

"What? Speak up! I can't hear you."

"I said . . . I went to get some lunch," she said a little louder.

"Are you entitled to a free lunch?"

"Yes."

"Well . . . and are you Jewish?"

Yvette stared at her and she could feel her face getting hot and flushed.

"I asked you a question. Are you Jewish?" Another teacher Yvette knew came over and the lunchroom became quiet. Everyone was looking at Yvette, waiting to hear what was said. She turned to look at Mildred, who looked just as frightened as she felt. Please don't let me cry, thought Yvette.

"What's the trouble?" asked the other teacher.

"This child," the woman pointed to Yvette, "is eating lunch here with the Jewish children, and I don't think she's Jewish. She doesn't — I've seen her before; she gets free lunch, all right. But she looks like one of the — " Hesitating, the woman went on, "She looks Spanish."

"I'm sure she's not Jewish," said the other teacher.

"All right now," said the first teacher, "what are you doing here? Are you Spanish?"

"Yes."

"Why did you come over here and get in that line? You went on the wrong lunch line!"

Yvette looked down at the tray in front of her.

"Get up and come with me. Right now!" Getting up, she dared not look around her. She felt her face was going to burn up. Some of the children were laughing; she could hear the suppressed giggles and an occasional "Ooooh." As she started to walk behind the teacher, she heard her say, "Go back and bring that tray." Yvette felt slightly weak at the knees but managed to turn around, and going back to the table, she returned the tray to the counter. A kitchen worker smiled nonchalantly and removed the tray full of food.

"Come on over to Mrs. Ralston's office," the teacher said, and gestured to Yvette that she walk in front of her this time.

Inside the vice-principal's office, Yvette stood, not daring to look at Mrs. Rachel Ralston while she spoke.

"You have no right to take someone else's place." Mrs. Ralston continued to speak in an even-tempered, almost pleasant voice. "This time we'll let it go, but next time we will notify your parents and you won't get off so easily. You have to learn, Yvette, right from wrong. Don't go where you don't belong. . . ."

Yvette left the office and heard the bell. Lunchtime was over.

Yvette and Mildred met after school in the street. It was late in the afternoon. Yvette was returning from the corner grocery with a food package, and Mildred was coming home from Hebrew school.

"How was Hebrew school?" asked Yvette.

"Okay." Mildred smiled and nodded. "Are you coming over tonight to listen to the radio? 'Mr. Keene, Tracer of Lost Persons' is on."

"Okay," said Yvette. "I gotta bring this up and eat. Then I'll come by."

Yvette finished supper and was given permission to visit her friend.

"Boy, that was a good program, wasn't it, Mildred?" Yvette ate her candy with delight.

Mildred nodded and looked at Yvette, not speaking. There was a long moment of silence. They wanted to talk about it, but it was as if this afternoon's incident could not be mentioned. Somehow each girl was afraid of disturbing that feeling of closeness they felt for one another. And yet when their eyes met they looked away with an embarrassed smile.

"I wonder what's on the radio next," Yvette said, breaking the silence.

"Nothing good for another half hour," Mildred answered. Impulsively, she asked quickly, "Yvette, you wanna have some matzo? We got some for the holidays."

"Is that the cracker they gave you this afternoon?"

"Yeah. We can have some."

"All right." Yvette smiled.

Mildred left the room and returned holding a large square cracker. Breaking off a piece, she handed it to Yvette.

"It don't taste like much, does it?" said Yvette.

"Only if you put something good on it," Mildred agreed, smiling.

"Boy, that Mrs. Ralston sure is dumb," Yvette said, giggling. They looked at each other and began to laugh loudly.

"Old dumb Mrs. Ralston," said Mildred, laughing convulsively. "She's scre . . . screwy."

"Yeah," Yvette said, laughing so hard tears began to roll down her cheeks. "Dop . . . dopey . . . M . . . Mi . . . Mrs. Ra . . . Ral . . . ston. . . ."

GET IN LINE

Role-playing Characters

What Happened Today?

Work in groups of four. Assign these roles: Yvette, Yvette's mother (or father), Mildred, Mildred's mother (or father). In pairs, role-play that each parent asks his or her child, "What happened at school today?" Each child tells what happened. Parents ask questions; children give answers. Take turns.

Write a Two-Part Poem

Yvette and Mildred

Write two short poems that mirror each other, one about Yvette and one about Mildred. Then write a couplet (two rhyming lines) about the two girls' friendship. Read your poem aloud to someone else who has read the story.

Show Common Ground

Four Cultures, Four Characters

Yvette and Mildred from this story and Lincoln and Mitsuo from *Pacific Crossing* represent four cultures. Divide a poster board into four parts and write each character's name in each quarter. Make an eight-inch circle in the middle that overlaps each quarter. Then make a collage of words, phrases, and pictures around each character's name. In the center, write two or three words or phrases that are true for all four, that show their "common ground." Display your collage in your classroom.

Subway Rush Hour
by Langston Hughes

Mingled
breath and smell
so close
mingled
black and white
so near
no room for fear

Phyllis Reynolds Naylor

was inspired to write *Shiloh* by a stray dog she encountered during a visit with friends in West Virginia. Returning home, she began writing as a way to deal with the pain she felt over the abandoned animal. A few weeks later, Naylor got a note from her friends saying that they had adopted the dog and named it Clover. "So why didn't I put my manuscript aside and say, 'Fine. It's settled then'? Because I got hooked on that dog, as Marty would say . . . I felt I owed it more." Eventually, Naylor saw the novel as more than just a plea for animals like Clover. She wanted her young readers to see, maybe for the first time, just how complicated questions of right and wrong can be.

About the Illustrator

Jo Ellen McAllister Stammen

was raised as one of ten children in a small farm community in western New York. She describes her home as "always hectic, crowded, and chaotic . . . but most of all our house was loving." Stammen adds, "I've always loved to draw from day one, but it wasn't until I had my own children that I decided on children's book illustration. I see it as a way to get fine art out to a great number of people." Already familiar with *Shiloh*, Stammen used her son and husband as the models for the illustrations. She says, "I love animals, so I have true feeling for the story."

SHILOH

by Phyllis Reynolds Naylor

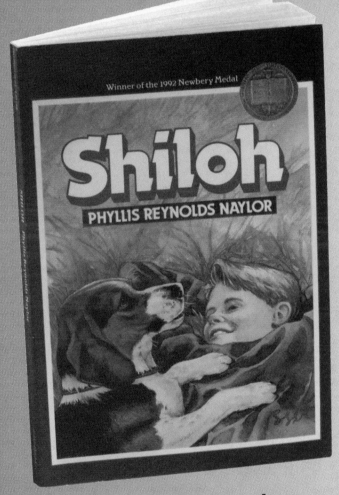

It's summer in Friendly, West Virginia, and eleven-year-old Marty Preston loves walking up in the hills behind his home. One afternoon on the road near the Shiloh schoolhouse, he rescues a dog from mean Judd Travers and secretly keeps the animal. Then his mother discovers "Shiloh."

I can't move. Seems as if the sky's swirling around above me, tree branches going every which way. Ma's face even looks different from down on the ground. Shiloh, of course, goes right over, tail wagging, but all the steam's gone out of me.

"How long have you had this dog up here?" she asks. Not one trace of a smile on her face.

I sit up real slow and swallow. "'Bout a week, I guess."

"You've had Judd's dog up here a week, and you told him you didn't know where it was?"

"Didn't say I didn't know. He asked had I seen him, and I said I hadn't seen him in our yard. That much was true."

Ma comes around to the trunk of the pine tree, unfastens the wire that holds the fencing closed, and lets herself in. She crouches down in the soft pine needles and Shiloh starts leaping up on her with his front paws, licking at her face.

I can't tell at first how she feels about him, the way she leans back, away from his dripping tongue. Then I see her hand reach out, with its short, smooth fingers, and stroke him.

"So we've got ourselves a secret," she says at last, and when I hear her say "we," I feel some better. Not a lot, but some.

"How come you to follow me up here tonight?" I want to know.

Now I can tell for sure her eyes are smiling, but her lips are still set. "Well, I had my suspicions before, but it was the squash that did it."

"The squash?"

"Marty, I never knew you to eat more'n a couple bites of squash in your life, and when you put away a spoonful of that to eat later, I knew for sure it wasn't you doing the eating. And then

the way you've been sneaking off every night . . ." She stops stroking Shiloh and turns on me. "I wish you'd told me."

"Figured you'd make me give him back."

"This dog don't belong to you."

"Mine more than Judd's!" I say hotly. "He only paid money for him. I'm the one who loves him."

"That doesn't make him yours. Not in the eyes of the law, it doesn't."

"Well, what kind of law is it, Ma, that lets a man mistreat his dog?"

Ma just sighs then and starts stroking Shiloh's head. Shiloh wiggles a few inches closer to her on his belly, rests his nose against her thigh, tail going *whick, whack, whick, whack*. Finally Ma says, "Your dad don't know about him?"

I shake my head. More silence. Then she says: "I never kept a secret from your dad in the fourteen years we've been married."

"You ain't going to tell him?"

"Marty, I've got to. He ever finds out about this dog and knows I knew but didn't tell him, how could he trust me? If I keep this one secret from him, he'll think maybe there are more."

"He'll make me give him back to Judd, Ma!" I could hear my voice shaking now. "You *know* he will!"

"What else can we do?"

I can feel hot tears in my eyes now and try to keep them from spilling out. I turn my head till they go away. "Judd Travers ever comes here to get his dog, he'll have to fight me to get it."

"Marty. . . ."

"Listen, Ma, just for one night, promise you won't tell Dad so I can figure out something."

Can tell she's thinking on it. "You aren't fixing to run off with this dog, are you? Marty, don't you *ever* run away from a problem."

I don't answer, because that very thing crossed my mind.

"I can't promise not to tell your dad tonight if you can't promise not to run off."

"I won't run off," I say.

"Then I won't tell him tonight."

"Or in the morning, neither," I add. "I got to have at least one day to think." Don't know what good it will do, though. Have already thought till my brains are dry.

Ma puts out both hands now and scratches behind Shiloh's ears, and he licks her all up and down her arms.

"His name's Shiloh," I tell her, pleased.

After a while Ma gets up. "You coming back to the house now?"

"In a bit," I answer.

It's hard to say how I feel after she leaves. Glad, in a way, that somebody knows: that I don't have to carry this whole secret on my head alone. But more scared than glad. Have me just one day to think of what to do, and not any closer to an answer than I'd been before. I'd spent all my can money on stuff to feed Shiloh. Only money I have now to my name is a nickel I'd found out by the road. Judd won't sell me Shiloh's spit for a nickel.

My first thought is to give him to somebody else and not tell them whose dog it is, then tell Ma that Shiloh had run off. But that would be two more lies to add to the pack. Word would get out somehow or other, and Judd would see David Howard or Mike Wells walking his dog, and then the war would really start.

All I can think of is to take Shiloh down to Friendly the next day, draw me up a big sign that says FREE: WORLD'S BEST DOG or something, and hold it up along the road to Sistersville, hoping that some stranger driving along will get a warm spot in his heart for Shiloh, stop his car, and take him home. And I won't ask him where home is, neither, so when Ma asks me where the dog is, I can tell her honest I don't know.

When I get back to the house, Dad's just washing up at the pump, using grease to get the oil off his arms. He's yelling at Dara Lynn and Becky, who are playing in the doorway, screen wide open, letting in the moths.

I go inside and Ma's putting the dishes away in the kitchen, lifting them out of the drain rack and stacking the plates on the shelf. She's got the radio on and is humming along with a country music song:

> *It's you I wanna come home to,*
> *It's you to bake my bread. . . .*

She sort of blushes when she sees me there by the refrigerator, listening to her sing.

I know I'm not going to sleep much that night. I sit on the couch staring at the TV, but not really watching, while Ma gives Becky her bath. Then I wait till Dara Lynn is out of the bathroom so I can take my own bath. Don't know if I soaped up or not. Don't even know if I washed my feet. I go back in the living room, and Ma has my bed made up there on the sofa. The house gets dark, the doors close, and then just the night sounds come from outside.

Know there's a piece of cardboard somewhere out in the shed I can print on. There won't be any trouble getting Shiloh to Friendly, either. I'll put that rope on his collar, and he'll follow along good as anything. We won't take the main road, though, in case Judd's out in his truck. Take every back road I can find.

Then I'll plant myself on the road to Sistersville, holding that sign, Shiloh waiting beside me wondering what it is we're going to do next. What *am* I fixing to do, anyway? Give him to the first car that stops? Don't even know the person driving? Might even be I'll give Shiloh to somebody who'll treat him worse than Judd Travers. Now that Shiloh's come to trust me, here I am getting ready to send him off again. I feel like there's a tank trunk sitting on my chest: can't hardly breathe. Got one day to decide what to do with Shiloh, and nothing I think on seems right.

I hear Shiloh making a noise up on the far hill in his pen. Not now, Shiloh! I whisper. You been good as gold all this time. Don't start now. Can it be he knows what I'm fixing to do?

Then I hear a yelp, a loud yelp, then a snarl and a growl, and suddenly the air is filled with yelps, and it's the worst kind of noise you can think of. A dog being hurt.

I leap out of bed, thrust my feet in my sneakers, and with shoelaces flying, I'm racing through the

kitchen toward the back door. A
light comes on. I can hear Dad's
voice saying, "Get a flashlight," but
I'm already out on the back porch,
then running up the hill.

There are footsteps behind me;
Dad's gaining on me. Can hear
Shiloh howl like he's being torn in
two, and my breath comes shorter
and shorter, trying to get there in time.

By the time I reach the pen, Dad's
caught up with me, and he's got the flashlight
turned toward the noise. The beam searches out the pine tree, the
fencing, the lean-to. . . . And then I see this big German shepherd, mean as nails, hunched over Shiloh there on the ground.
The shepherd's got blood on his mouth and jaws, and as Dad
takes another step forward, it leaps over the fence, same way it got
in, and takes off through the woods.

I unfasten the wire next to the pine tree, legs like rubber,
hardly holding me up. I kneel down by Shiloh. He's got blood
on his side, his ear, a big open gash on one leg, and he don't move.
Not an inch.

I bend over, my forehead against him, my hand on his head.
He's dead, I know it! I'm screaming inside. Then I feel his body
sort of shiver, and his mouth's moving just a little, like he's trying
to get his tongue out to lick my hand. And I'm bent over there in
the beam of Dad's flashlight, bawling, and I don't even care.

Dad's beside me, holding the flashlight up to Shiloh's eyes.
Shiloh's still alive.

"This Judd Travers's dog?"

I sit back on my heels and nod. Wipe one arm across my face.

Dad looks around. "Take those gunnysacks over there and put 'em in the back of the Jeep," he says, and then, still holding the flashlight in one hand, he slips his arms under Shiloh and picks him up. I can see Shiloh wince and pull back on his leg where it hurts.

The tears are spilling out of my eyes, but Dad can't see 'em in the dark. He can probably tell I'm crying, though, 'cause my nose is clogged. "Dad," I say, "*please* don't take him back to Judd! Judd'll take one look at Shiloh and shoot him!"

"Take those gunnysacks to the Jeep like I said," Dad tells me, and I follow behind as we go down the hill. I keep my mouth open to let the breath escape, crying without making a sound. Just like Shiloh.

Ma's watching from inside, the screen all covered with June bugs where they been buzzing about the light. Dara Lynn's up, standing there in her nightshirt, watching.

"What *is* it? What's he got?" Dara Lynn says, pestering Ma's arm.

"A dog," says Ma. And then she calls out, "Ray, is it alive?"

"Just barely," says Dad.

I put the gunnysacks in the Jeep, and Dad carefully lays Shiloh down. Without waiting to ask, I crawl in the Jeep beside Shiloh, and Dad don't say no. He goes in the house for his trousers and his keys, and then we're off.

"I'm sorry, Shiloh," I whisper, over and over, both hands on him so's he won't try to get up. The blood's just pouring from a rip in his ear. "I'm so sorry! So help me, I didn't know Bakers' dog could leap that fence."

When we get to the bottom of the lane, instead of going up the road toward Judd's place, Dad turns left toward Friendly, and halfway around the first curve, he pulls in Doc Murphy's driveway. Light's still on in a window, but I think old doc was in bed, 'cause he come to the door in his pajamas.

"Ray Preston?" he says when he sees Dad.

"I sure am sorry to bother you this hour of the night," Dad says, "but I got a dog here hurt bad, and if you could take a look at

him, see if he can be saved, I'd be much obliged. We'll pay. . . ."

"I'm no vet," says Doc Murphy, but he's already standing aside, holding the screen open with one hand so we can carry Shiloh in.

The doc's a short man, round belly, don't seem to practice what he preaches about eating right, but he's got a kind heart, and he lays out some newspapers on his kitchen table.

I'm shaking so hard I can see my own hands tremble as I keep one on Shiloh's head, the other on a front paw.

"He's sure bleeding good, I can tell you that," Doc Murphy says. He puts on his stethoscope and listens to Shiloh's heart.

Then he takes his flashlight and shines it in the dog's eyes, holding each eye open with his finger and thumb. Finally he looks at the big, ugly wound on Shiloh's hurt leg, torn open right to the bone, the bites around Shiloh's neck, and the ripped ear. I turn my head away and sniffle some more.

"I'll do what I can," Doc says. "The thing we got to worry about now is infection. That leg wound is going to take twenty . . . thirty stitches. What happened?"

I figure Dad will answer for me, but he don't — just turns to me. "Marty?"

I swallow. "Big old German shepherd chewed him up."

Doc Murphy goes over to the sink and washes his hands. "Baker's dog? Every time that shepherd gets loose, there's trouble." He comes back to the table and takes a big needle out of his bag, fills it full of something. Something to make Shiloh numb, maybe. "This your dog, son?"

I shake my head.

"No?" He looks at me, then at Dad. Dad still won't say nothing, makes me do the talking. While the doc leans over Shiloh and slowly inserts the needle in his side, I get up my nerve.

"It's Judd Travers's," I tell him. I got to start practicing the truth sometime.

"Judd *Travers's*? This the dog he's missing? How come you brought it in?"

"I had him," I say.

Doc Murphy sucks in his breath, then lets it out a little at a time — *huh, huh, huh.* "Whew!" he says, and goes on about his work.

Don't know how long we're there in Doc's kitchen, Dad standing over against the wall, arms folded, me with my hands

cupped over Shiloh's head while Doc Murphy washes the wounds, dresses them, and starts stitching the skin back up. Once or twice I feel Shiloh jerk, like it hurts him, but when he lays too still, I don't know if it's because he's numb or if he's dying.

"The next twenty-four hours, we'll know if this dog's going to live," the doc says. "You check with me tomorrow evening; we'll have some idea then. I can keep him here for a day or two, Ray. Then, if he makes it, you can take him on home."

I put my face down near Shiloh's again, my mouth next to his ear. "*Live*, Shiloh, *live!*" I whisper.

Hardest thing in the world is to leave Shiloh there at Doc Murphy's, the way his eyes follow me over to the doorway, the way his muscles move, like he's trying to get up when he sees me leaving. Second hardest thing is to crawl in the Jeep with Dad afterward.

There isn't a word passed between us till we get home. Once Dad turns the motor off, though, and I'm all set to get out, he says, "Marty, what else don't I know?"

"What?" I ask.

"You keeping Judd's dog up there on our hill — got a place for him all built, never letting on. What else you keeping from me?"

"*Nothing*, Dad!"

"How do I know that's not another lie?"

"'Cause it's not."

"You saying so don't make it true."

I know then what Ma meant. But it's not all so black and white as Dad makes it out to be, neither. And sometimes, when I get mad, it clears my head.

"You would have thought more of me if I'd let that dog wander around till Judd found it again, kick the daylights out of 'im?" I ask. "That what you want me to do, Dad?"

"I want you to do what's right."

"What's right?"

For once in my eleven years, I think I have my dad stumped. Leastways, it seems to be thirty . . . forty seconds before he answers:

"You've got to go by the law. The law says a man that pays money for a dog owns that dog. You don't agree with the law, then you work to change it."

"What if there isn't time, Dad? Shiloh could be dead by the time somebody looked into the way Judd treats his dogs."

Dad's voice is sharp: "You think Judd Travers is the only one around here hard-hearted toward his animals? You think he's the only one who starves 'em or kicks 'em or worse? Open up your eyes, Marty. *Open your eyes*!" Now Dad half turns in his seat, back resting against the door, facing me: "How many times have you walked to the school bus and seen a chained-up dog in somebody's yard? How many times you ever put your mind to whether or not it's happy, its ribs sticking out like handles on the sides? Suddenly you're face-to-face with a dog that pulls at your heart, and you all at once want to change things."

I swallow. "There's got to be a first time," I answer.

Dad sighs. "You're right about that," he says.

I'm pushing my luck, I know. "If Doc Murphy don't tell Judd about Shiloh, can we bring him back here and keep him? I could build him a better pen. Make the fence high enough so the shepherd can't get in."

Dad opens the Jeep door on his side. "No," he says, and gets out.

I get out, too. "Just till Shiloh's better, then? You know how Judd treats anything that don't work right. He'll shoot Shiloh, Dad! I found a dog once before over near Judd's place with a bullet hole in his head. We could at least get Shiloh well. I'm going to pay Doc Murphy's bill. I promise you that. You get all my can money for the next three years, and I'll deliver the county paper, too, if I get the chance. Honest! I promise!"

Dad studies me. "You can keep him here till he's well, that's all. Then we're taking him back to Judd." And he goes in the house.

My heart starts pounding again. *Thumpity thump. Thumpity thump.* There's still time, I'm thinking. Shiloh's still alive, and I ain't licked yet.

Unleash Yourself

Contact Your Local ASPCA

Find out the location of the closest animal rescue shelter. Contact it either by phone or mail, and ask for information about the services they provide. Will they, for example, come between an animal and its owner in a situation like the one in this story? Do they offer stray dogs for adoption? Are there laws protecting animals from mistreatment? What are the penalties? If possible, place a poster or a brochure about the shelter in your school or local library.

Discuss Options

What Can Marty Do?

What are Marty's choices at this point in the story? With a partner or a small group, brainstorm all the choices you think he has. Then circle the one or two that you think are the best and explain why. Compare your list to that of another pair or group.

Compare Selections

Be an Illustrator

I Can Picture . . .

Jo Ellen McAllister Stammen has illustrated eight moments of this story, but as you read, you may picture many more. Imagine that you've been hired as an illustrator and asked to create at least two more illustrations for the story. Include a caption for each. Choose two moments that you consider most important, most vivid.

Think About Right and Wrong

In this story and in "The Wrong Lunch Line," the main characters struggle with ideas about right and wrong. In both stories, the lines between right and wrong are not clearly drawn. Make a chart for both stories with the headings WHAT'S RIGHT? WHAT'S WRONG? WHO'S RIGHT? and WHO'S WRONG? Show your chart to another reader. Do you both agree?

TALKING PEACE

A VISION FOR THE NEXT GENERATION

by Jimmy Carter

▲ President Carter, newly elected in 1976, greets a young supporter at the White House.

One big question you may have is *Why me?* Why do I need to know about the people at war in Africa or Asia, so far away, living in cultures so different from my own? As we have discussed, the world is getting smaller in a very real sense. What we do in this country impacts people in other nations — and vice versa. You may have had a friend or relative who fought in the Persian Gulf War. You may know someone who was injured in the Los Angeles riots — or someone who was killed by violence in your own neighborhood. As an active American citizen, you can help shape your own life, your community, your city, and even the policies of your national government.

492

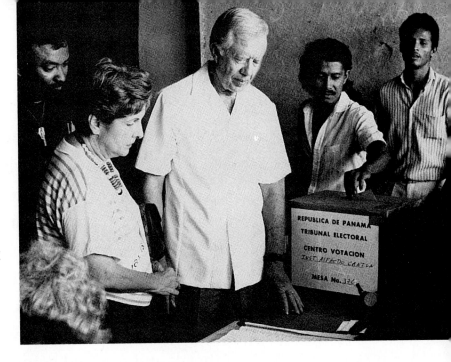

Examining the voter registration list at a polling site during the 1989 elections in Panama, Central America ▶

Soon you will cast your first vote. With that ballot, you will help to choose the leaders of the most powerful country in the world. Your decision will have an impact on millions of lives and on the fate of the environment as well. Remember, too, that many local leaders are elected, as well as your state government representatives. Too few Americans pay attention to these smaller, less-glamorous races, yet the men and women who fill these offices may have the greatest impact on our daily lives. They regulate housing, the police force, municipal garbage and recycling programs, public transportation

Why do I need to know about the people at war in Africa or Asia, so far away, living in cultures so different from my own?

systems, juvenile courts, and schools, among many other things. Your vote should be an educated one. Elections are the key to unlocking all of what is best about democracy and individual freedoms.

Besides voting, there is a lot that citizens can do to influence the programs of the people elected to office. One young student eventually convinced the major American fast-food chains to alter packaging habits that were damaging the

environment. A young girl's letter to a Soviet leader, expressing her fears about nuclear war, helped inspire him to conduct disarmament talks. A twelve-year-old in New Jersey petitioned state officials and testified before the legislature to get a shocking series of racist television commercials pulled off the air. Just the names of Prime Minister Begin's grandchildren reminded him to persevere in the Camp David negotiations. Young people *can* have an effect.

▲ In 1978, Israel's prime minister Menachem Begin, President Carter, and Egyptian president Anwar Sadat stand together for the U.S. national anthem. Thanks to President Carter, Israel and Egypt later signed a peace treaty — the Camp David Accord.

A young girl's letter to a Soviet leader, expressing her fears about nuclear war, helped inspire him to conduct disarmament talks.

After a close friend was injured while playing in the street, nine-year-old James Ale (*center*) made a plan and successfully campaigned for a playground in his neighborhood in Davie, Florida. Mayor Joan Kovac said, "This kid could teach a lot of adults I know how to lobby elected officials. He just didn't give up." ▶

494

Mia Robinson is standing in the Old Senate Chamber in the United States Capitol, Washington, D.C. At ten, Mia joined the Youth Task Force to Stop the Violence. As a Task Force member, she spoke in Washington's tough neighborhoods, encouraging kids to avoid violence. Because of her work, Mia has been invited to speak at important ceremonies and has appeared on radio and television shows. ▶

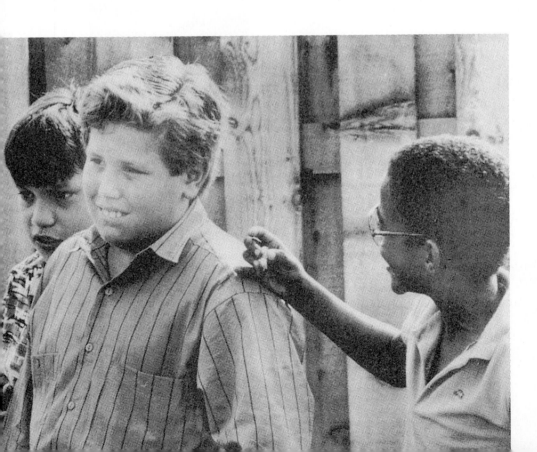

Join the Swim Team!

Persuasion by Nicholas Douville

Participating in a sport is a good way to meet people from other places and different backgrounds who share a common interest. Nicholas uses this reason and others to try to persuade his fellow students to join the swim team.

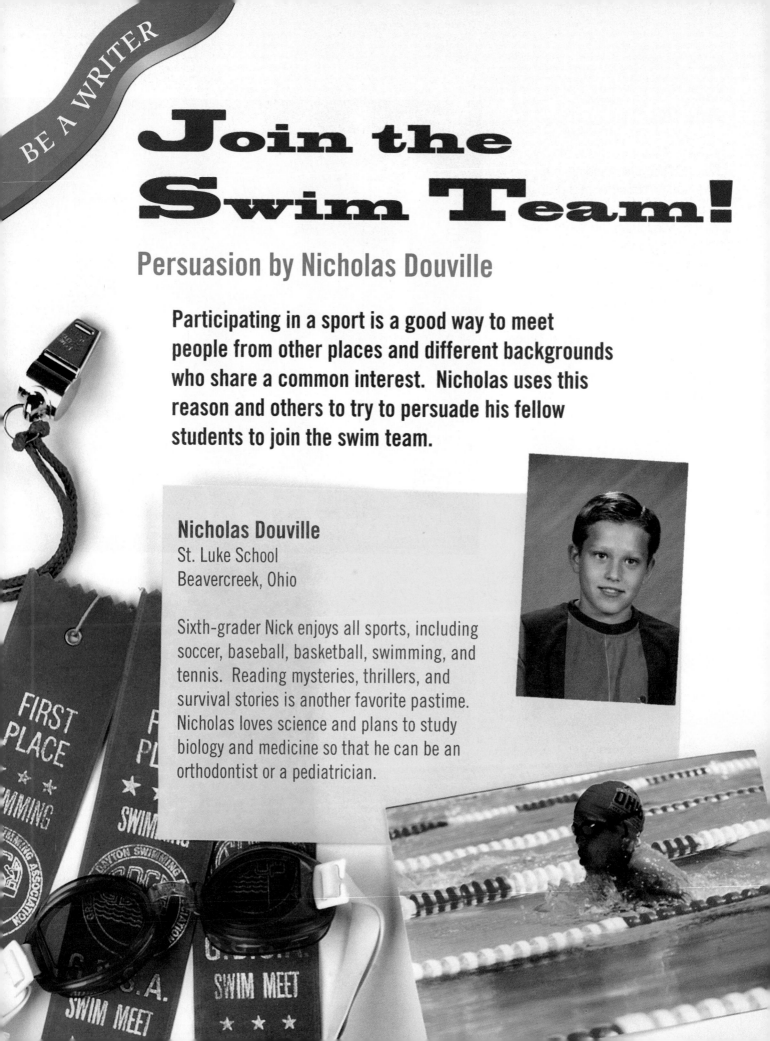

Nicholas Douville
St. Luke School
Beavercreek, Ohio

Sixth-grader Nick enjoys all sports, including soccer, baseball, basketball, swimming, and tennis. Reading mysteries, thrillers, and survival stories is another favorite pastime. Nicholas loves science and plans to study biology and medicine so that he can be an orthodontist or a pediatrician.

Join the Swim Team!

Because swimming can build up strength, teach self-discipline, and improve social skills, I hope you will realize that swimming can be a valuable sport that can provide you with skills and experiences that will help you the rest of your life. I hope you will join the swim team.

Swimming helps build up strength. It can also help with other sports and help you score higher in national fitness contests. Throwing the medicine ball and using pull buoys, stretch cords, and paddles build up triceps. Kicking and running improve quadriceps.

Swimming can also teach you self-discipline because you have to push yourself every day to go to practice. Even when you feel that your arms can't move another stroke, you have to force

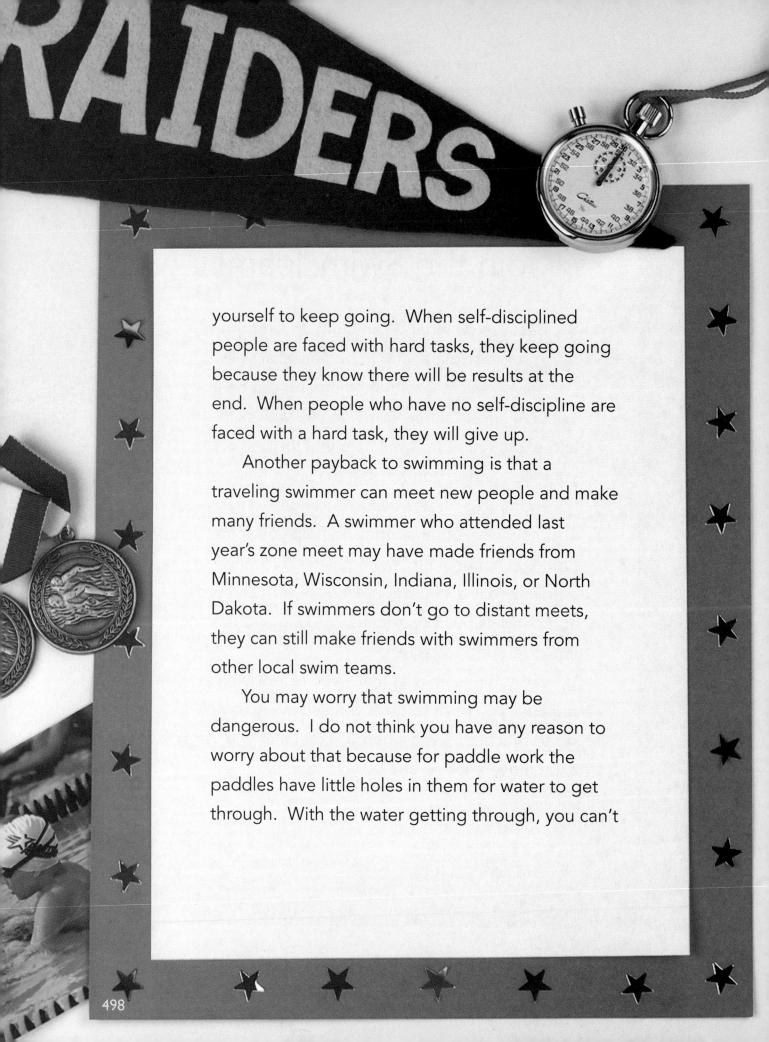

yourself to keep going. When self-disciplined people are faced with hard tasks, they keep going because they know there will be results at the end. When people who have no self-discipline are faced with a hard task, they will give up.

Another payback to swimming is that a traveling swimmer can meet new people and make many friends. A swimmer who attended last year's zone meet may have made friends from Minnesota, Wisconsin, Indiana, Illinois, or North Dakota. If swimmers don't go to distant meets, they can still make friends with swimmers from other local swim teams.

You may worry that swimming may be dangerous. I do not think you have any reason to worry about that because for paddle work the paddles have little holes in them for water to get through. With the water getting through, you can't

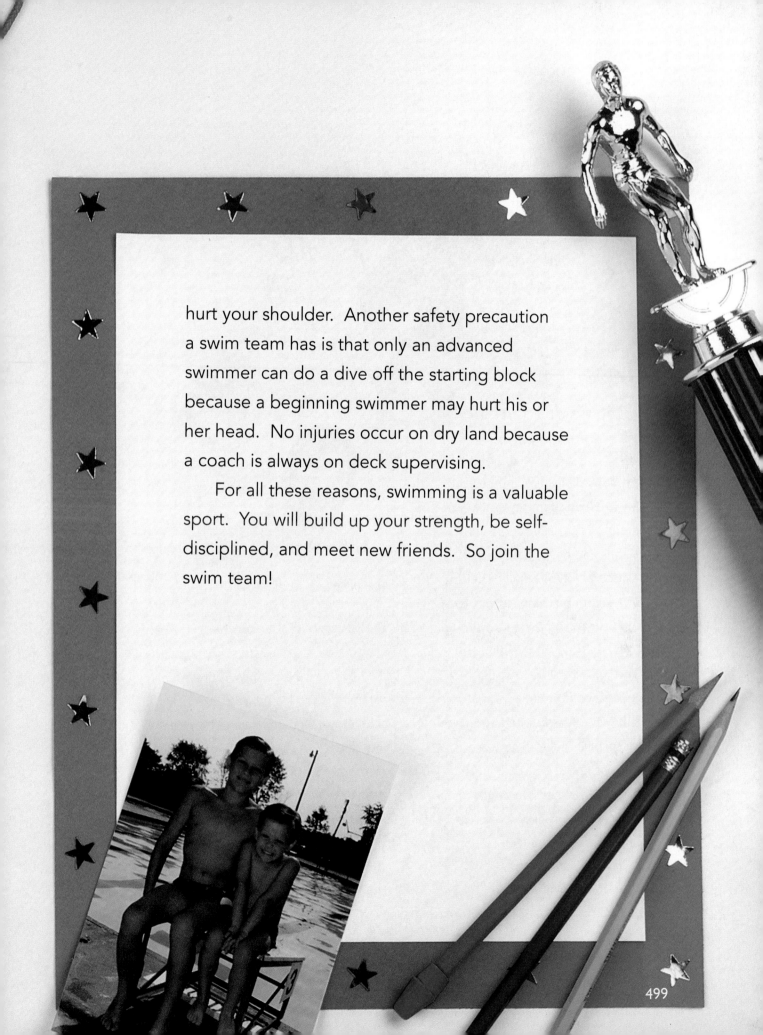

hurt your shoulder. Another safety precaution a swim team has is that only an advanced swimmer can do a dive off the starting block because a beginning swimmer may hurt his or her head. No injuries occur on dry land because a coach is always on deck supervising.

For all these reasons, swimming is a valuable sport. You will build up your strength, be self-disciplined, and meet new friends. So join the swim team!

Meet the Author

When **Betsy Byars's** children were younger and still living at home, she always asked them to read her manuscripts. They offered useful suggestions and never held back their criticisms. On the night before her son's eighth birthday, he was too excited to sleep. Coming into the room where Byars was writing, he said, "You know, maybe it would help me get to sleep if I read some of your failures." Byars agreed, handing him the specific "failure" he wanted. "He read for about three minutes," Byars recalls, "yawned, went into his room and fell fast asleep. It was a humbling moment."

Meet the Illustrator

The youngest of four brothers, **Francisco X. Mora** says, "As a kid I liked to doodle and draw. I drew family portraits when I was about five years old." Mora, who grew up in Mexico City, adds, "On weekends, we would visit my mother's hometown, Uruapan, which means 'bowl of flowers.' I loved the beautiful displays in the market, the smells, and the people. These colors and smells became inspiration for my paintings and helped me to become an artist/illustrator." Now in Wisconsin, Mora enjoys playing the guitar, listening to music, and visiting art galleries and museums.

One summer, two boys and a girl

are sent to live in a foster home.

Harvey, Thomas J, and Carlie, the girl,

are welcomed by Mrs. Mason, their new foster mother.

But Carlie isn't about to accept anything,

even a welcome, from anybody!

Carlie had been suspicious of people since the day she was born. She swore she could remember being dropped on the floor by the doctor who delivered her.

"You weren't dropped," her mother had told her.

"All right then, why is my face so flat? Was I *ironed*?"

Carlie also claimed that when she was two months old a baby-sitter had stolen a golden cross from around her neck.

"No baby-sitter stole a gold cross from you," her mother had told her.

"All right then, where is it?"

Carlie believed everyone was out to do her in, and she had disliked Mrs. Mason, the foster mother, as soon as she had seen her standing in the doorway.

"I knew she'd have on an apron," Carlie said to the social worker. "She's trying to copy herself after Mrs. Walton — unsuccessfully, I might add."

"Maybe she has on the apron because she was cooking, Carlie."

"*I* should be the social worker. I'm not fooled by things like aprons."

She also didn't like the Masons' living room. "This is right out of 'Leave It to Beaver,'" she said. She especially distrusted the row of photographs over the fireplace. Seventeen pictures of — Carlie guessed — seventeen foster children.

"Well, my picture's not going up there," she grumbled to herself. "And nobody better snap me when I'm not looking either." She sat.

Mrs. Mason waited until "Young and Restless" was over and then she said, "Carlie?"

"I'm still here."

"Well, come on and have some lunch. Then afterward you can help me get the boys' room ready."

Carlie turned. She looked interested for the first time. "The boys?" she asked. "There's going to be some boys here?"

"Yes, two boys are coming this afternoon — Thomas J and Harvey."

"How old?"

"Eight and thirteen."

"Oh, boo, too young." Carlie got up from the footstool. "What's wrong with them?"

"Wrong with them?"

"Yeah, why do they have to be here? I'm here because I got a bum step-father. What's their trouble?"

"Well, I guess they'll have to tell you that."

Carlie lifted her hair up off her neck. "How about the thirteen-year-old?" she asked. "What's he like? Big for his age, I hope."

"He has two broken legs. That's about all I can tell you."

"Well," Carlie said, "that lets out dancing."

Carlie was sitting in front of the television when Harvey arrived. He had to be carried in because of his legs. They set the wheelchair down by Carlie's footstool.

She looked around. "What happened to your legs?" she asked. She was interested in medical matters.

He said, "Nothing."

"Well, *something* must have happened. They don't just put casts on your legs for the fun of it. In fact they *won't* put casts on your legs unless you've had a real accident. I know, because a friend of mine tried to get a cast put on her ankle so she wouldn't have to be in Junior Olympics, and they wouldn't do it." She waited, then she said, "So what happened?"

There was a long pause. Harvey looked down at his legs. In his mind the shiny Grand Am lunged over him again. He felt sick. He said, "If you must know, I broke my legs playing football."

He wished it had happened that way. A boy at school had broken his ankle playing football, and everyone in school had autographed his cast.

Girls had even kissed the cast and left their lipstick prints.

Harvey's casts were as white as snow. He wished he had thought to forge some names on them. "Love and kisses from Linda." "Best wishes to a wonderful English student from Miss Howell."

Carlie was still looking at him, eyeing the casts, his toes sticking out the end. Then she glanced up at his face.

"What position were you playing?"

Harvey hesitated. "Quarterback," he said.

Carlie snorted. "You're no quarterback. I've seen Joe Namath in person." She looked him over. "If you were playing football at all, you were probably the ball."

Harvey kept looking at his legs.

Carlie decided to give him one more chance. "So what really happened?"

"I was playing football," he insisted.

"Listen," Carlie said. "This is one of my favorite shows, so if you're going to tell me a bunch of big lies about what happened to your legs, well, I'll just go back to watching my show."

"Go back to watching it," Harvey said.

Thomas J arrived after supper. He had been living with the Benson twins so long that he yelled everything. That was the only way he could be heard at the Bensons'. The twins were almost deaf.

"Where do I put my things?" he yelled at Mrs. Mason.

"Why, right back here, Thomas J. I'm putting you and Harvey in the same room so you can help him if he needs it."

"I'll be glad to," he yelled. He was used to helping people.

"If Harvey has any trouble in the night, you can call me."

"I'll call you."

"He's sure got the voice for it," Carlie said.

"Do I put my things in the drawer or just leave them in the suitcase?"

Carlie spun around on the footstool. "Will you keep your voice down. I can hardly hear the television."

"I'll be glad to," Thomas J yelled.

That night the three of them sat watching "Tony Orlando and Dawn."

"Now, this really is one of my favorite shows," Carlie said as soon as it was announced. She gave each of them a long hard look.

Thomas J nodded. Actually he would rather have watched something else. The show brought back sad memories. It had been one of the Benson twins' favorites. The twins had always liked anything that came in pairs — Doublemint-gum commercials brought them hobbling — and Dawn in their matching dresses looked like twins even though they weren't.

"Sing the song, girls," Tony Orlando said, stepping back on his high-heeled shoes.

Thomas J felt awful. He could remember the twins leaning forward on their canes, trembling a little as they squinted at Dawn. They had the oldest television set in Macon County, and they had to lean close to see anything.

He hoped there was a TV set at the hospital where they had been taken. They had both broken their hips on the same day. They had been coming in from the garden — Thomas J had been right behind them carrying a bushel basket of weeds — when one of them had slipped. She had grabbed the other for support, and they both had gone down on the path. One had broken her right hip; the other, her left.

It was not until they were being admitted to the hospital that Thomas J had learned their first names. For six years he had just called them both Aunt Benson. Their first names were Thomas and Jefferson. They had been named for their father's favorite president. That was how he had gotten the name Thomas J. He had been named for them.

"Don't worry, Thomas J," they had told him in the emergency room where they had lain on side-by-side tables, "we'll get over this, won't we, Sister?"

"*I* will."

"We *both* will because everybody in our family has lived to be at least ninety."

Thomas J had nodded. He knew their father had lived to be ninety-six. The father would have lived longer except that a limb fell off a tree and hit him on the head. The twins had kept the limb on the back porch for a long while, and the only time the twins had ever been angry at Thomas J was when he, not knowing the importance of the limb, had broken it up for firewood.

Andy Griffith was on the television now, telling a long joke. Carlie said, "Why doesn't he get off? Nobody wants to listen to him."

"I do," Harvey said.

Carlie glanced at him. "You would," she said.

Harvey felt a twinge in his right leg. It was the worst of the breaks. The bone had gone through the skin.

He looked at the back of Carlie's head. He would have liked to answer her back, to insult her, but he knew that Carlie could out-insult any-body he had ever met.

"He *gives* me a pain," Carlie said. She glanced around the room, taking in everyone present. "And he's not the only one."

Carlie entered her room slowly. It was the first time she had slept in a room by herself. At one time in her life she had slept with a cousin, her stepfather's two daughters and a half sister, all in one bed. She had spent her nights saying "Move over, will you?" and "Who do you think you are — Miss America?"

She walked slowly over to the dresser and looked at herself in the mirror. She had developed a way of smiling that hid her crooked lower teeth. She smiled at herself now, making sure she still had the technique.

Suddenly she heard a noise behind her. She swirled around. She didn't like anybody watching her when she was looking at herself. When she saw it was Thomas J, she could have stung him. "What are you staring at?"

"Nothing. I just wanted to tell you I found your earring." He came in with a small pleased smile. He was thin and walked as carefully as an old person. He held out the earring.

When Carlie had discovered one of her earrings was missing just after "Tony Orlando and Dawn," she had accused everyone in the house of stealing it. "I'm going to find that earring if I have to turn every one of you upside down and shake you," she had said. "That earring is pure gold."

"Now, now, Carlie, no one stole your earring," Mrs. Mason had said.

"All right then, where is it?"

"The earring was in the bathroom," Thomas J said, still smiling. "It was by the basin." He held it out. He had been as pleased when he found it as if it had been a gold nugget. He couldn't wait to bring it to her. Once when he had found the Bensons' father's gold watch, they had been so happy they had patted him. It was the only time the Benson twins had ever touched him on purpose. He could still remember their stiff old fingers tapping his head.

"Good boy," they had said. It had made him feel warm and happy. He had wanted them to lose the watch over and over again so he could keep finding it, the way a dog keeps fetching a stick.

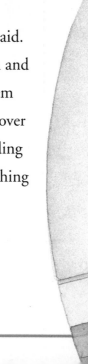

Also he wanted Carlie to like him. He admired her. Her long flowing hair — lion-colored — made him aware of his own scraggly head. The Benson twins always cut his hair together, one on each side, neither bothering to stop and check the other's work. As he came toward her, he smoothed his hair.

Carlie snatched the earring from him and looked at it suspiciously. "So you just *found* it, huh?"

He didn't get her meaning. "Yes, it was by the basin. I looked down and there it was. It was like the time the Benson twins lost their father's watch and I —"

"Huh, strange that you just *happened* to find it after I announced I was going to search everybody's room."

Now he got her meaning. "Oh, I didn't steal it. Really I didn't. I found it. It was by the basin. Honest." His voice got even louder. "You can ask Mrs. Mason if you don't believe me. She heard me find it."

Carlie put the earring back on her ear. "I tell you one thing. I'm having my ears pierced as soon as possible. That's the only way things are going to be safe around here."

"I found it, I tell you," Thomas J yelled. He took two steps backward. "I found it!"

"All right, all right, you found it," Carlie said. She glanced at the open door. "Keep your voice down." She turned back to the mirror. "I guess even a blind pig can come up with an acorn every now and then."

After Thomas J left, Carlie got into bed and stared up at the ceiling. Mrs. Mason passed by in the hall and stuck her head in the door. "Everything all right, Carlie?"

"What do you think?" Carlie said.

"Oh, I imagine things seem very wrong tonight."

"*Seem*?" Carlie said.

Mrs. Mason came in and stood by the bed. She patted Carlie's arm. "The first night is always the hardest."

Carlie was silent.

Mrs. Mason sat on the edge of the bed. "And I know how you feel."

"How do you know? Have you ever been in a foster home?"

"I've had a lot of kids staying with me — seventeen, not counting you three — and all seventeen told me that the first night was the worst. They all said they just felt sick." She kept her hand on Carlie's arm. "I guess 'home sickness' is a very real kind of illness, like measles or mumps."

"Too bad there's not a vaccine."

"Yes."

"Only the people that give money for vaccines, they want to give for heart diseases and polio, stuff *their* kids might get. Nobody worries about us."

"Yes, they do, Carlie."

"Anyway the only reason I came was because Russell — that's my step father — threatened to cut off all my hair. And it took me since fourth grade to grow this hair!" She yanked the sheet up higher on her shoulders. "Now I wonder if it was worth it."

"Carlie, did you see the pictures of the kids in the living room?"

"How could I miss?"

"Well, all of those kids have gone on into the world. Two of them are in college now. They write me letters. One has his own service station. Some are back with their families. It all works out somehow." She smiled. "Even without a vaccine."

She waited for a moment and patted Carlie's arm again. Then she rose from the bed. "Things'll be better tomorrow. You'll see."

"They better be," Carlie answered as Mrs. Mason left the room. She turned her face to the wall. She thought, I can always run away.

B⦿unce These

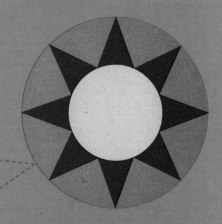

Knowing and Not Knowing

Sometimes what you don't know about a character is more important than what you do know. You might feel that's true about Carlie, Harvey, and Thomas J. For each, list three things you do know. Then list three things you don't know. Circle the thing you consider most important about each one. Share your lists with another reader.

What's a Pinball?

With a partner or small group, discuss the title of the story. First, brainstorm associations, facts, and ideas you have about pinballs. Then use these ideas to guess why the author chose this image as the title for her novel. How are these kids like pinballs? Do you think the image is a good one? Why or why not?

Ideas Around

Dramatize a Scene

Make Characters' Voices Come to Life

Read some dialogue from this selection with another student as if you were doing a play. You might choose the scene between Carlie and Mrs. Mason (502–504), the one between Carlie and Harvey (504–507), or the one between Carlie and Thomas J (510–511). Perform the scene for your classmates. Make your voices clear and different; try to capture the two personalities involved.

Compare and Contrast Characters

Finding Common Ground

Use the last line of the story, "I can always run away," as a way to compare and contrast other characters in this theme. Several characters would like to escape their situations, especially when they become most afraid, embarrassed, or confused. At what point in each story is the tension the highest? What do the characters do instead of running away? Discuss these similarities and differences with a partner or a small group.

515

Joey, age fourteen

by Jill Krementz

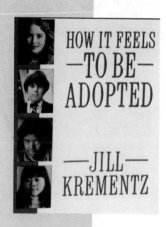

I lived with my mother until I was eleven, but it got to the point where she couldn't handle me and so she awarded me to the state — that's how I came to live at the orphanage. She kept my three sisters, but since she's no longer my mother, I don't think of them as my sisters anymore either.

Luckily, I only had to stay in the orphanage for about a year. What happened is that about two years ago, around Thanksgiving, a Catholic priest named Father Clements was trying to get his parishioners, who were mostly black, to adopt black kids who needed homes. No one was paying any attention to him, so he finally said, "Well, if you won't adopt, then I will!" Two weeks before Christmas he got a call from the director of the orphanage saying there was a twelve-year-old boy named Joey he might like to meet. Father Clements thought it would be nice to invite me to his house for Christmas dinner, but when he asked me I said I had to think about it because I had a lot of other invitations from family and friends. I was lying because I had too much pride to let him think I didn't have any place to go.

And it was my pride which actually impressed this priest and made him come back to see me again and again.

One day we went to the airport with his sister, who had to catch a plane somewhere, and while we were waiting she asked me to go and buy her a newspaper. Right there on the front page of the Chicago *Sun Times* was a picture of Father Clements and a story about his wanting to adopt a child. I was wondering if that kid might turn out to be me, but I didn't say anything — I just brought back the paper. On the way home Father Clements asked me if I had read it, and when I said "no," he pulled over to the side of the road. He put his arm around me and said that if we were going to have any kind of relationship at all, we had to begin by being honest with each other. So I admitted I'd read the story about him, and that's when he told me that he was going to adopt me. I started crying because I was so happy, and Father Clements thought I was crying because I didn't want him to adopt me, but we got everything straightened out and a few days later I moved in with him. It was two days before Christmas and I've been there ever since. That was the best Christmas I've ever had. The only part I didn't like was that all his relatives had gifts for me and I felt ashamed because I didn't have any for them.

There's been a lot of publicity about my being adopted by a priest, but it's hard for me to understand all the commotion — after all, what's the difference between having a priest for a father or having a doctor or a lawyer? As long as there's love and caring, that's all that matters. What's important is to get kids out of institutions and into homes. As far as I'm concerned, all homeless kids should be adopted by anyone who really wants them, regardless of race, color or creed or whether they're married or not. I know that whenever I used to dream about being adopted, all I hoped for was a loving home. Period. I just wanted to be adopted so I could start a new life for myself, and that's exactly what I've been able to do. Now I have someone to love and someone who loves me. We take care of each other and have those special feelings that are part of being a family. The way I see it, that's all that matters.

Mother to Son

by Langston Hughes

Well, son, I'll tell you:

Life for me ain't been no crystal stair.

It's had tacks in it,

And splinters,

And boards torn up,

And places with no carpet on the floor —

Bare.

But all the time

I'se been a-climbin' on,

And reachin' landin's,

And turnin' corners,

And sometimes goin' in the dark

Where there ain't been no light.

So, boy, don't you turn back.

Don't you set down on the steps

'Cause you finds it's kinder hard.

Don't you fall now —

For I'se still goin', honey,

I'se still climbin',

And life for me ain't been no crystal stair.

OCEAN QUEST

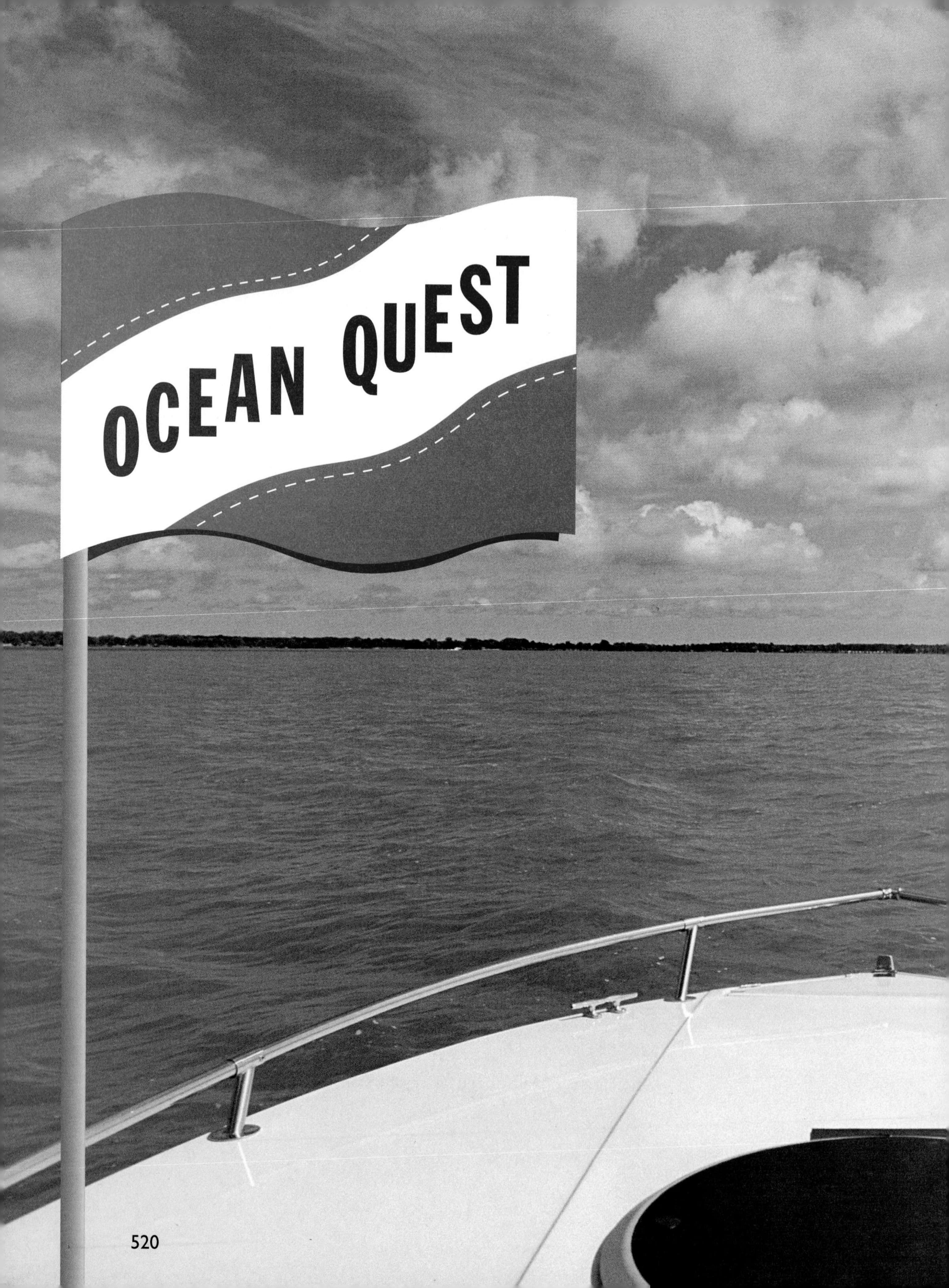

CONTENTS

OCEAN QUEST

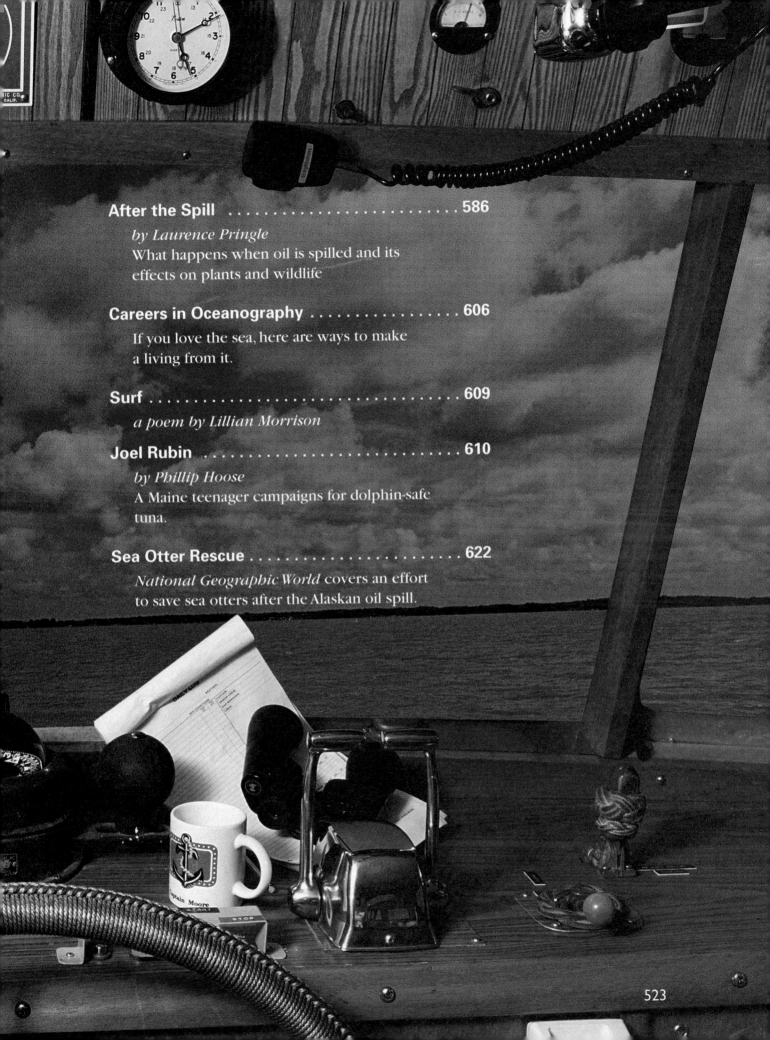

Read

On Your

Own

SHARKS
CHALLENGERS
OF THE DEEP

TEXT BY MARY M. CERULLO
PHOTOGRAPHS BY JEFFREY L. ROTMAN

PAPERBACK **PLUS**

Sharks: Challengers of the Deep
by Mary M. Cerullo
Discover the myths and realities
of the world of sharks.

In the same book . . .
more about how we see and think
about sharks.

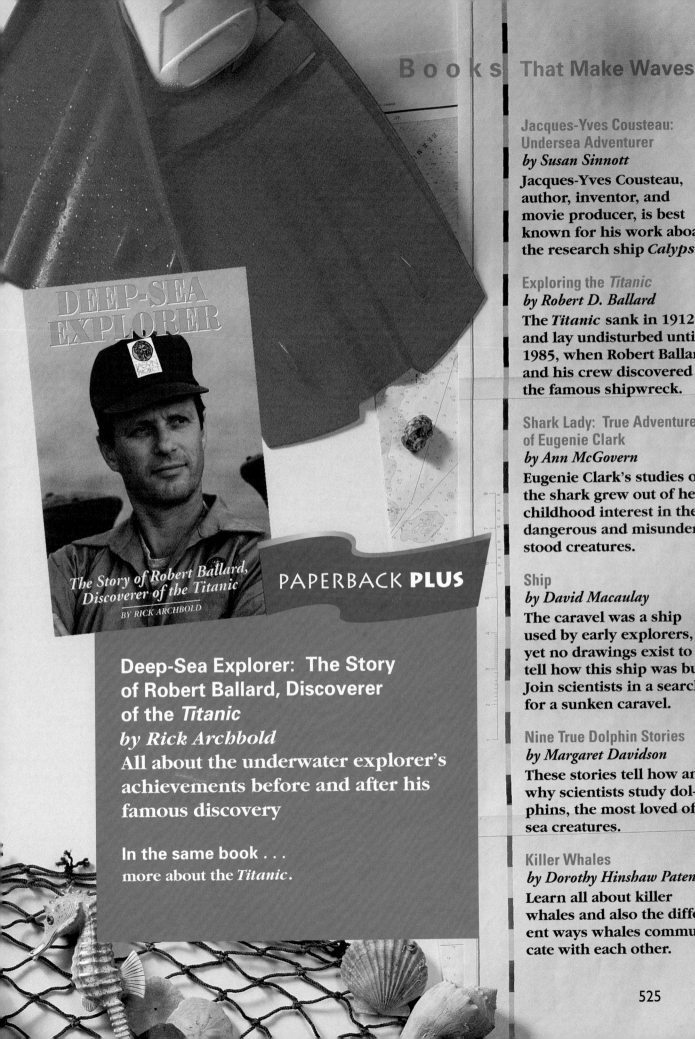

Books That Make Waves

DEEP-SEA EXPLORER

The Story of Robert Ballard, Discoverer of the Titanic

BY RICK ARCHBOLD

PAPERBACK PLUS

Deep-Sea Explorer: The Story of Robert Ballard, Discoverer of the *Titanic*
by Rick Archbold
All about the underwater explorer's achievements before and after his famous discovery

In the same book . . .
more about the *Titanic*.

Jacques-Yves Cousteau: Undersea Adventurer
by Susan Sinnott
Jacques-Yves Cousteau, author, inventor, and movie producer, is best known for his work aboard the research ship *Calypso*.

Exploring the *Titanic*
by Robert D. Ballard
The *Titanic* sank in 1912 and lay undisturbed until 1985, when Robert Ballard and his crew discovered the famous shipwreck.

Shark Lady: True Adventures of Eugenie Clark
by Ann McGovern
Eugenie Clark's studies of the shark grew out of her childhood interest in these dangerous and misunderstood creatures.

Ship
by David Macaulay
The caravel was a ship used by early explorers, yet no drawings exist to tell how this ship was built. Join scientists in a search for a sunken caravel.

Nine True Dolphin Stories
by Margaret Davidson
These stories tell how and why scientists study dolphins, the most loved of all sea creatures.

Killer Whales
by Dorothy Hinshaw Patent
Learn all about killer whales and also the different ways whales communicate with each other.

O C E

Meet Seymour Simon

When asked why he has written over a hundred books about science for young people, **Seymour Simon** answers, "It's very important to get kids to read science books from a very young age. . . . They have no fear at a young age, and they will stay familiar with science all of their lives." To get kids involved in his subjects, Simon often asks questions. "Sometimes I'll provide an answer, but more often I'll suggest an activity or an experiment that will let a child answer a question by trying it out."

ANS

Earth is different from any other planet or moon in the Solar System: It is the only one with liquid water on its surface. In fact, more than 70 percent of the earth's surface is covered by oceans. Although we speak of the Atlantic and Pacific as separate oceans, the world is really covered by a single body of water in which the continents are islands.

Echo soundings of the ocean floor show mountains more than twice as tall as Mt. Everest and canyons six times as deep as the Grand Canyon. A computer was used to produce this map of the land beneath the waves. Blues show the deepest spots and yellows the shallowest; the average depth is two-and-a-quarter miles.

The main features on the map are: the Mid-Atlantic Ridge (1), part of the longest mountain chain in the world; deep-ocean trenches (2, 3); and undersea mountains that rise above the waves to become islands (4, 5).

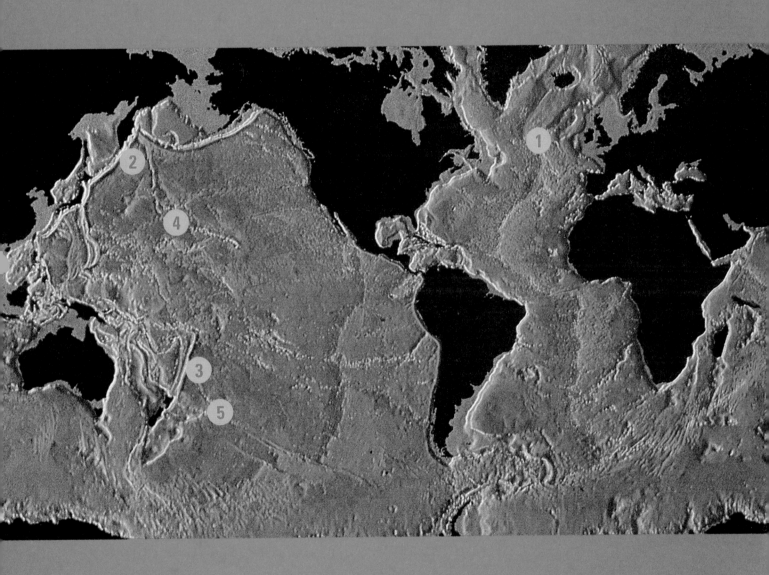

There is an enormous amount of water in the oceans, more than one-and-one-half quintillion (15 followed by 17 zeros) tons. That's 100 billion gallons for each person in the world. Yet the amount of water in the oceans has remained much the same for many millions of years. That is because most of the water that evaporates into the air returns to the sea in the form of rain or snow. Even the water that falls on land finally runs downhill in rivers and streams to the sea.

All this water is constantly in motion, driven by the sun's energy. The sun warms ocean waters, especially in the tropics, where the sun's rays are more direct. That warms the air at the surface of the waters, which then picks up moisture. Some of the moisture in the air condenses into clouds, releasing more heat into the atmosphere. The uneven heating causes winds that blow across the surface of the sea, producing waves and currents. These carry heat energy for thousands of miles from the warm waters around the equator to the colder waters of the polar regions.

The major ocean currents of the world flow in huge circular paths called gyres. This satellite photo shows a section of the warm Gulf Stream, part of the North Atlantic Gyre. The computer-generated colors show water temperatures from the warmest (red) to the coolest (blue). The Gulf Stream swirls up the east coast of North America and out into the Atlantic at a speed of up to one hundred miles a day. In the middle of the Atlantic, the Gulf Stream divides, and part of it becomes the North Atlantic Current. This flows past Northern Europe, making the climate warmer and milder than it might be otherwise. In the Pacific, the warm Japan Current becomes the North Pacific Current and then moderates the climate on the west coast of the United States and Canada.

Sometimes, the normal pattern of ocean currents changes and the results can be a disaster. One of the world's major fisheries is in the cool, nutrient-rich waters off the coast of Peru. Every few years, however, the cool water warms and the sea life disappears. This strange change is known as El Niño. These computer-generated maps show what happens: The blues are the coldest waters; reds, the warmest waters. The image on the left shows the warm currents (1) that produce normal weather in most years. The green area (2) shows the cool waters usually

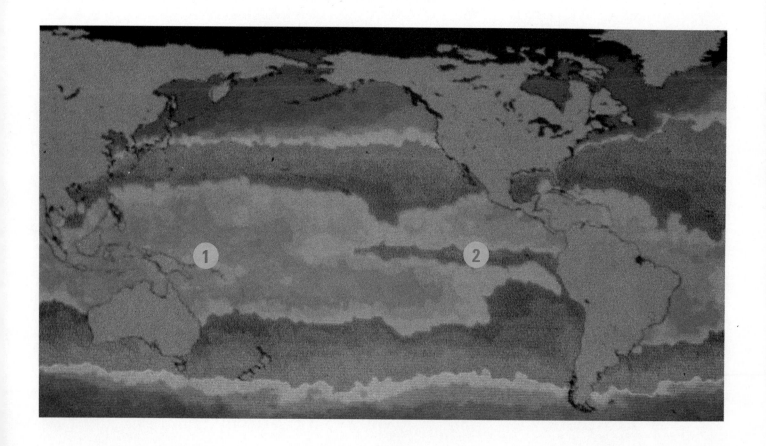

found off the coast of Peru. The image on the right shows that during El Niño, the warm currents have cooled (4) and the cool waters have warmed (3).

During the winter of 1982–1983 the biggest El Niño of the century was under way, and all around the Pacific, climates changed. Australia suffered the worst drought in two hundred years, causing immense dust storms and fires. On the west coast of South America, heavy rains up to three times above normal flooded the region, and in the United States, record snow fell in the Rocky Mountains, which resulted in heavy flooding in the spring.

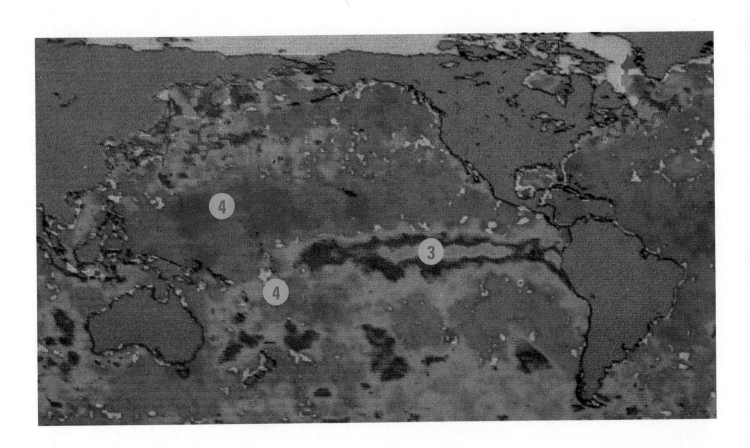

If you visit the shore, you'll soon notice the daily rise and fall of the water, which we call tides. Tides are caused by the gravitational pull of the moon and the sun. Even though the moon is much smaller than the sun, the moon is so much closer to the earth that its pull is much stronger. As the earth rotates, the ocean waters nearest the moon are pulled outward in a traveling bulge called high tide. There is also a traveling tidal bulge on the side of the earth opposite the moon. Here, the moon's pull on the waters is less, so there is a second high tide. Because of the double tidal bulges, most places on the coast have two high and two low tides every twenty-four hours and fifty minutes.

Twice a month, when the sun and the moon are lined up with the earth, their gravitational pulls combine and produce the biggest tides, called spring tides. The sun and moon also pull at right angles to each other twice a month. Then we get the smallest tides, called neap tides.

Even in places close together, tides do not always occur at the same time or have the same size. The time and size of the tides depend upon the shape of the shore and the width of the gulfs and bays. Think of an ocean as a kind of large, shallow pan of water sloshing back and forth. The water in the middle of the ocean moves up and down very little. The water at each end of the ocean moves up and down much more. Because of this, islands in the middle of the ocean, such as Hawaii, often have small tides compared to the lands around the edges of an ocean.

If a tide can spread out, such as in the wide Gulf of Mexico, it may rise and fall only a few inches a day. When the tide cannot spread out, the tides are much greater. The photos show an inlet in the narrow Bay of Fundy in Nova Scotia, where high tide may be fifty feet higher than low tide.

The waves commonly called tidal waves really have no connection with the daily tides. The name scientists use for this kind of wave is tsunami, pronounced SUE-nami, a Japanese word for sea wave. A tsunami is generated by a violent undersea earthquake or volcanic explosion. The shock forms a wave that can move across an ocean at five hundred miles per hour, as fast as a jet plane. In the open ocean, a tsunami is only two or three feet high and hardly noticeable; but when it approaches a shore, a tsunami may build up to a huge size and hit with the force of a runaway train.

These three photos show the arrival of a tsunami on the shores of the island of Oahu, Hawaii. The tsunami was generated by an earthquake 2,500 miles away in the Aleutian Islands, Alaska. This tsunami resulted in over fifty deaths and much property damage.

When the wind blows across the surface of ocean waters, little ripples form. As the wind continues to blow, the ripples grow into waves. The size of a wave depends upon the speed of the wind, how long it blows, and the fetch. The fetch is the distance over which the wave travels. The faster the wind, the longer it blows, and the greater the fetch, the bigger the waves.

In the open ocean, where the wind is blowing and making waves, the waves are all different sizes and shapes and go in different directions. As the waves move away from where they began, some travel faster than others and they form groups of about the same wavelength. The waves are now long and smooth and are called a swell.

Wave Energy

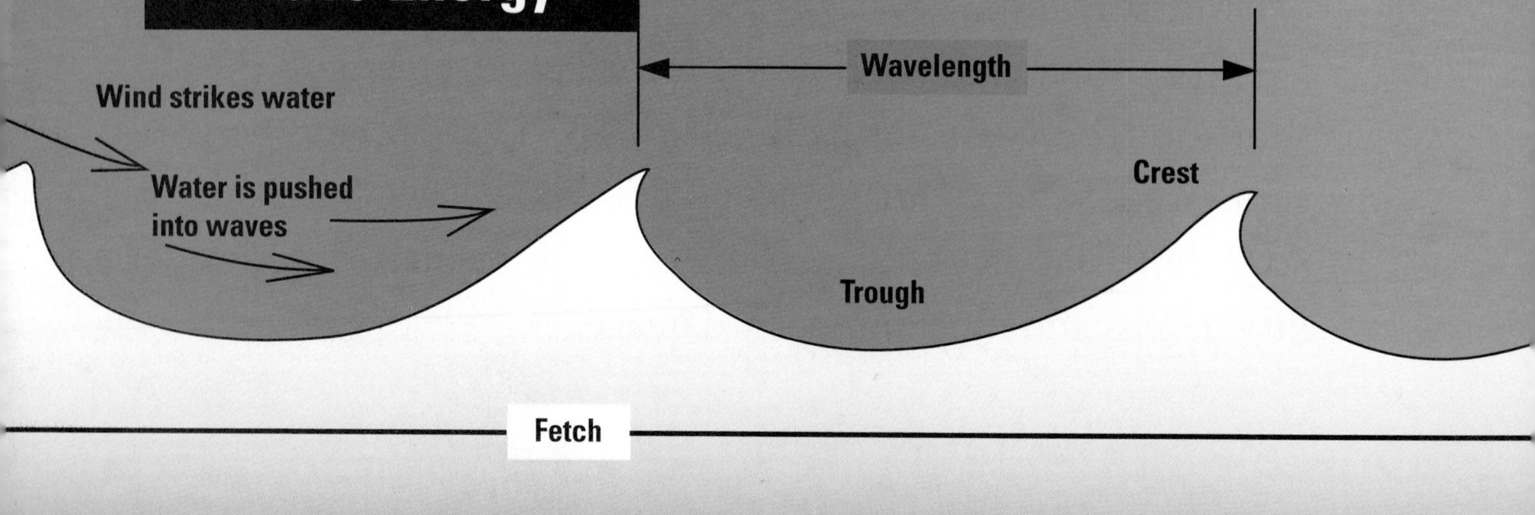

Wind strikes water

Water is pushed into waves

Wavelength

Crest

Trough

Fetch

Waves moving across the ocean carry the energy of the wind, but the ocean water does not move along with the wave. As the wave passes, the particles of water move up and down and around in a little circle. If you watch a stick floating on water as waves pass by, you'll see that it bobs up and down but stays in just about the same place. Only the energy of the waves moves forward.

The high spot of a wave is called a crest and the low spot is called a trough. The distance between two crests (or two troughs) is called the wavelength. The height of a wave is the distance from crest to trough.

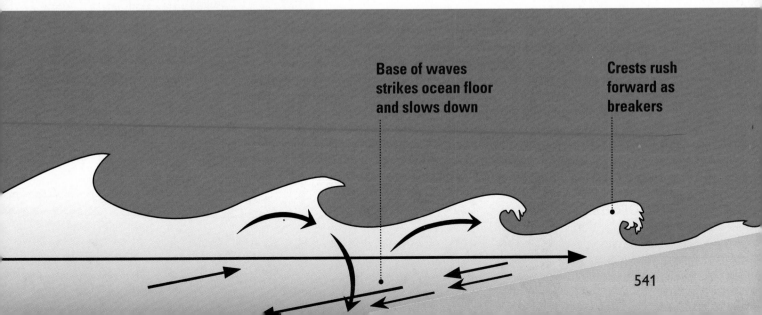

Base of waves
strikes ocean floor
and slows down

Crests rush
forward as
breakers

Storm-driven waves in the ocean can build up to great heights. The largest wave on record was 112 feet high, the height of a ten-story building. Oceangoing ships can ride over most waves. Small ships can ride up one side of a wave and down the other. Large ships can usually ride through waves without too much difficulty. During a hurricane or severe storm, however, a huge wave can dump hundreds of tons of water onto a ship in a few seconds, smashing it apart and sending it to the bottom.

When an ocean wave reaches the shallow water of shore, it begins to travel more slowly and its shape begins to change. Some people say that "the wave begins to feel the bottom." Waves begin to pile up and grow higher as those in the back come in faster than those in the front are moving.

As the waves slow down, the crest of the wave tries to continue at the same speed, until finally it topples over into the trough of the wave in front and becomes a breaker.

When waves break on the shore, the surf begins. Sometimes surf can break just a few yards from shore. However, if the shore is shallow, surf can form hundreds of yards out to sea. The waves on shallow beaches, such as this one in Hawaii, spill over slowly as they roll up the shore.

Even rocky coastlines are worn away by the power of the surf. The softer kinds of rock are worn away first, leaving rocky spires or platforms of harder rock. These, too, will eventually be worn down by the pounding of the waves. In other places, the incoming surf carries sand particles from one spot to another, slowly building up beaches and dunes. Every moment of every day, the sea is at work reshaping the land.

Millions upon millions of years ago, life began in the sea. Today, the sea is home to incredible numbers of living things, from microscopic plants and animals called plankton to giant whales larger than any dinosaur. Some animals are drifters, others swim freely, and still others spend their entire lives on the bottom of the sea.

One way or another, all sea animals depend upon the multitudes of tiny plankton plants, which drift in the surface waters of the ocean, using the energy of sunlight to produce food. The tiny plants are eaten by small fish and other animals, which are eaten by large animals, and which are eaten, in turn, by even larger animals. Many tons of sea animals of all kinds are eaten each day by people all over the world.

Throughout the ages, the sea has been the inspiration for art, music, and poetry, as well as a source of food and a highway to travel. The sea has also been used as the world's wastebasket for garbage and even radioactive wastes. Until now, the sea has always been able to renew itself, but we are reaching the limits of this vast ocean world. And without the sea, the earth would be a world without life.

ON YOUR

Write an Acrostic

O-C-E-A-N

Write the letters of a key word from this selection down the left side of a piece of paper. Then write a word, phrase, or sentence from *Oceans* that you considered important that begins with each letter. Include one statistic. Include one new word that you didn't know before.

Be an Editor

Boldface Words for Younger Readers

Imagine that you are an editor who has been asked to choose at least ten words (and no more than twenty) from this selection to bold-face for fourth graders. Provide your supervisor with a list of words and short, clear definitions that fourth graders will understand.

WAVELENGTH

Make a Bulletin Board

The Many Moods of the Ocean

This book shows that the oceans of the world have many moods, faces, and phases: angry and peaceful, hot and cold, high and low, choppy and smooth. Collect (or photocopy) photographs, drawings, and paintings and create a bulletin board that shows the variety of the oceans' moods. You might include captions using information from this selection.

Make an Outline

I, II, III and A, B, C

What subjects are covered in Simon's book? Make a traditional outline of this selection using Roman numerals for the major headings and capital letters for the sub-headings. For example:

I.
  A.
  B.
II.
  A.
  B.

When you're done, compare and contrast your outline with someone else's.

The sea has fascinated artists from all over the world. On these pages are works of art that look very different, but they have one thing in common. They were created by people who saw the sea and thought the best way to share it was through a picture. Can you see what these artists wanted to tell us through their work?

The Sea

David True (b. 1942; United States)
Wind and Geometry, 1978

Oil on canvas, 60" x 84"
Collection of Lilja Art Foundation,
Djursholm, Sweden

Katsushika Hokusai
(1760-1849; Japan)
*Great Wave of Kanagawa, from
the 36 Views of Mt. Fuji*
Woodcut, 9¾" x 12½"
Art Resource, NY

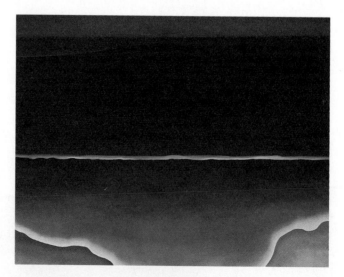

Georgia O'Keeffe
(1887-1986;
United States)
Wave, Night, 1928

Oil on canvas, 30" x 36",
1947.33
Gift of Charles L. Stillman
© Addison Gallery of
American Art,
Phillips Academy, Andover,
MA

in Art

Kenny Scharf
(b. 1958; United States)
Diatagua, 1994

Oil on canvas,
$122\frac{1}{2}$" × $76\frac{1}{2}$"
Tony Shafrazi Gallery,
NY

Amos Ferguson (b. 1920; Bahamas)
Untitled (mermaid), c. 1983

House paint on cardboard, $30\frac{3}{16}$" × $36\frac{1}{8}$"
International Folk Art Foundation
Collections in the Museum of International
Folk Art, a unit of the Museum of New Mexico, Santa Fe

Winslow Homer
(1836-1910; United States)
Maine Coast, 1896

Oil on canvas, 30" × 40"
The Metropolitan Museum of Art,
New York
Gift of George A. Hearn, in memory of
Arthur Hoppock Hearn, 1911
(11.116.1)

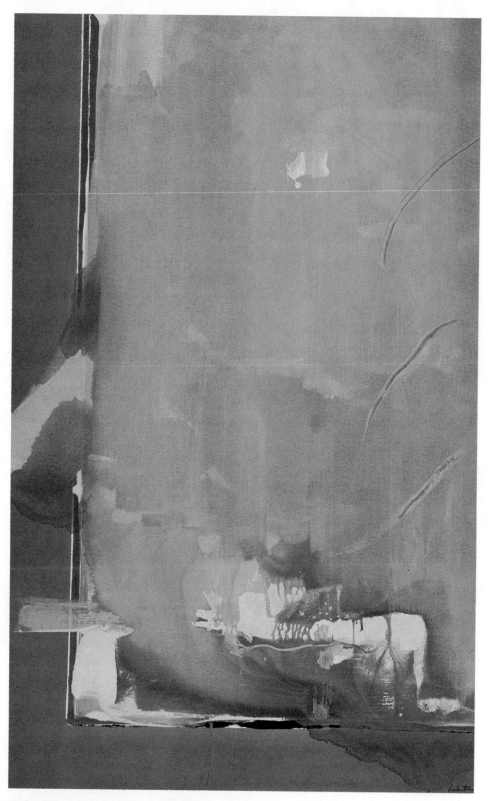

Helen Frankenthaler (b. 1928; United States)
The Strength of the Sea, 1987

Acrylic on canvas, 107 $\frac{1}{4}$" x 67"
Collection Beverly and Chester Firestein, Beverly Hills, CA
© Helen Frankenthaler 1996
Courtesy The André Emmerich Gallery, NY

THE SEA

The sea is a hungry dog,

Giant and gray.

He rolls on the beach all day.

With his clashing teeth and shaggy jaws

Hour upon hour he gnaws

The rumbling, tumbling stones,

And "Bones, bones, bones, bones!"

The giant sea-dog moans,

Licking his greasy paws.

And when the night wind roars

And the moon rocks in the stormy cloud,

He bounds to his feet and snuffs and sniffs,

Shaking his wet sides over the cliffs,

And howls and hollos long and loud.

But on quiet days in May or June,

When even the grasses on the dune

Play no more their reedy tune,

With his head between his paws

He lies on the sandy shores,

So quiet, so quiet, he scarcely snores.

James Reeves

Meet the Authors

Scott Kraus

Although Scott Kraus grew up inland and went to the beach only a few times as a child, he always wanted to be an oceanographer. "Maybe I just wanted to run away to sea," he admits. As an adult he finds his work endlessly interesting and surprising. "A scientist isn't a stiff person in a white coat. Science is a huge guessing game, especially when you study animals. The experiment keeps changing because animals always surprise you. This year you think you know something; next year everything's different. It takes a long time and a lot of discipline to make progress. You collect a lot of information, and each bit is like a little piece that falls into place in the puzzle."

Kenneth Mallory

When Kenneth Mallory got the idea of writing this book, he traveled up to the coast of Maine to see North Atlantic right whales firsthand. There he observed a group of right whales who were courting and oblivious of the human beings in their midst. "It was the most exciting encounter I've ever experienced," says Mallory. "The whales were under the boat and all around the boat, which was smaller than they were. Great casts of water from their flukes came over the boat, completely soaking us. I'll never forget it."

554

The Search for the
Right Whale

by Scott Kraus and Kenneth Mallory

It is a cold and breezy morning late in September 1991. More than ten miles off the coast of Nova Scotia, a dark shape breaks the surface of the North Atlantic Ocean. It makes a loud whooshing sound, like a fierce wind blowing across the opening of a large, wide pipe. Clouds of spray shoot up toward the sky in a watery mist.

A North Atlantic right whale named Stripe has just surfaced for a breath of air. At first, Stripe floats motionless and alone. Salt water washes over her back, making ripples and tiny waves. Seconds later, she is joined at the surface by another whale, this one half her size.

My name is Scott Kraus. As leader of a team of scientists from the New England Aquarium in Boston, Massachusetts, I am just 500 feet away, watching Stripe and her baby, called a "calf," with a pair of binoculars. At 30 feet long, our research boat, the **Nereid**, is only slightly longer than Stripe's calf.

We are surveying a small group of the rarest whale in the ocean, the North Atlantic right whale. The survey is part of a long-term study designed to obtain information that will ensure the survival of right whales. Together with other scientists, we are keeping track of as many individual whales as we can — trying to learn where they live, what they eat, and what can be done to protect them. By 1991, we have been following some whales for over ten years.

Stripe is one of our oldest friends. Her name comes from the long scar on the top of her head. We can only guess how Stripe got the scar. It may have been caused by a collision with a boat. Or she may have crashed into the bottom of the ocean while chasing food.

On Stripe's head, there are strange-looking patches of raised rough skin called **callosities**. Callosities provide a home for whale lice — tiny animals less than an inch long that look like crabs — but no one knows why right whales have the callosities. They look like gray and white islands against the whale's shiny black skin. Callosity patterns appear in the same places a person might have a mustache, a beard, and eyebrows.

These odd skin patches help researchers like me tell one right whale from another. The callosities on each individual whale form different patterns, like fingerprints. They remain more or less the same throughout the whale's life.

As we approach the two floating whales, our research team begins collecting data. Although it sounds like total confusion, it is, in fact, a carefully planned routine.

▼ Two views of the same whale, showing callosities on the *bonnet,* or top of the head, and on the lower lip.

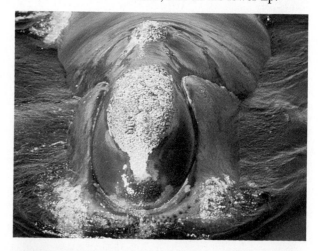

▼ Whale lice shown next to a centimeter ruler.

▲ Aboard the *Nereid,* Scott Kraus (center, with beard) and Amy Knowlton (on far right edge).

▲ Photographing a surfacing whale.

"Two islands right!" (Meaning: two callosity islands on the whale to the right.)

"CKS, twelve, frames three to seven!" ("CKS" are the observer's initials; "twelve" refers to film roll number 12; and "frames three to seven" are the numbers of the photographs taken by the observer.)

"Lips?" (Meaning: are there callosities on the lower lips?)

"Look, continuous post blowholes!" (The callosities are joined behind the blowholes.)

"Oh! Did you get that headlift?"

"Yes, ARK, ten, frames 21 through 26!"

"Any mud?"

"Aargh, I'm out of film!"

This apparent chaos provides the record keeper with information about the identifying features and photographs taken of each whale. Teamwork is essential.

▲ The mud on a whale's nose may be an indication of deep diving in search of food.

Another thing we notice is mud on Stripe's nose. It is evidence that right whales make deep dives to the ocean bottom in search of food. Sometimes Stripe gets so carried away she runs right into the ocean bottom and ends up with mud on her head.

While Stripe has been searching for something to eat, her young calf appears to have become bored. A tangled crown of seaweed is draped around his head like a brown and green beret. Right whale calves are no different from any other animal youngster: they love to play. Pushing a little seaweed around may give the calf something to do.

During our encounter with Stripe and her calf, we take photos, record behavior, and collect samples of skin using small darts shot from a crossbow. The pieces of skin and blubber help us determine how the whales are related to each other. They also tell us if the whale is healthy, since pollutants show up in the blubber.

We are excited to see Stripe swimming with a calf. From our own sightings and from earlier records made by other scientists, we know this is her sixth baby in the last 25 years. Later that day, as we drift with the *Nereid*'s engines turned off, we recognize one of Stripe's grownup calves, Stars, accompanied by a baby of her own. We met Stars as a newborn calf back in 1981. We gave her the name because the callosities on her head looked like clusters of stars. Stars' calf is her second, making Stripe a grandmother for the second time.

▼ A whale with a dart in its back. The line used to retrieve the dart can be seen trailing behind. The shot is painless. The inset shows three of the small darts used to collect blubber and skin from whales.

A week later, a third member of the family, Forever, appears swimming by herself. We first saw Forever as a newborn calf in the winter of 1984. She is Stripe's fourth calf, the next one after Stars. Forever doesn't have any easily identified features, so we broke with tradition: instead of naming her for distinctive markings, we named her so that together the names of the mother and her calves would have a special meaning. To us, the family of "Stars and Stripes Forever" symbolized our hopes for the rebirth of the North Atlantic right whale.

ABOUT THE RIGHT WHALE

The North Atlantic right whale, *Eubalaena glacialis*, ranges from 45 to 55 feet in length and can weigh up to 70 tons. Females usually grow larger than males. Both are black in color, often with patches of white on their throats and bellies. Their large heads, with narrow upper jaw and strongly bowed lower jaw, take up more than a quarter of their body length. Two widely separated blowholes make a distinctive V-shaped spout when seen from the front or back, making it easy to spot right whales from a distance. They have no dorsal fin, and their flukes, or tail fins, are broad and deeply notched. A closely related species, the southern right whale, *Eubalaena australis*, lives in the oceans of the southern hemisphere from Brazil to the Antarctic. Southern right whales are more numerous than North Atlantic right whales.

▲ An underwater photograph of a southern right whale. North Atlantic and southern right whales are very similar in looks and behavior. It is difficult to photograph North Atlantic right whales underwater because of murkier water in their habitat.

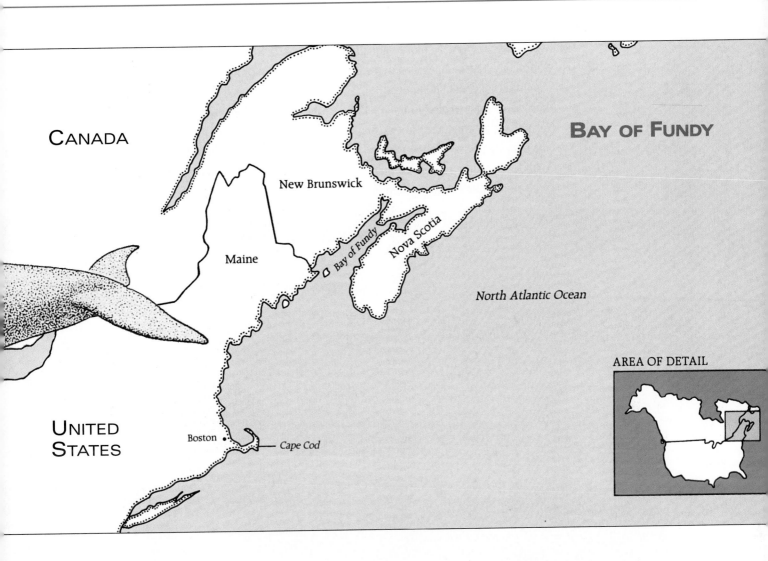

CANADA

BAY OF FUNDY

New Brunswick

Bay of Fundy

Nova Scotia

Maine

North Atlantic Ocean

UNITED
STATES

Boston •

Cape Cod

AREA OF DETAIL

Our study of the North Atlantic right whale began in 1980, when the New England Aquarium was asked to conduct a survey of the marine mammals in the Bay of Fundy, an area between New Brunswick and Nova Scotia. An oil company planned to place a refinery in the bay. They wanted to know what impact the building of a large tanker port might have on the surrounding wildlife. To our great surprise, we discovered 26 different right whales during our survey, including four mothers with their calves. Fortunately, the refinery was never built.

The Whale Fishery, a colored aquatint, shows the crew of an early nineteenth-century whale boat attempting to harpoon a right whale. In the background, other whalemen are raising the *blanket piece,* a large piece of blubber they have peeled from the body of the whale and attached to a blubber hook. It is raised onto the ship by pumping the *windlass,* a winch that was also used to raise and lower the anchor. The smoke comes from the giant-size pots of the *tryworks,* or on-deck furnace, where blubber cut into small pieces was rendered into oil.

The right whale got its name because it was the "right" whale for people who hunted whales. It swam slowly at the surface, so it was easy to catch and kill. Once killed, it floated — making retrieval easy — instead of sinking out of sight. And when it was boiled, the right whale's foot-thick layer of blubber produced as many as 70 barrels of lamp and lubricating oil.

For over 900 years, beginning about the year A.D. 1000, whaling nations from Europe and America hunted North Atlantic right whales until they had almost completely disappeared. By 1935, when they were given international protection as an endangered species, some scientists suspected there were fewer than 100 right whales left in the North Atlantic Ocean. Most thought the right whale was doomed to extinction.

Our discovery of a group of right whales that included calves was a sign of hope for the species. In the years that followed, research teams from the New England Aquarium returned to the Bay of Fundy each summer to study the whales. They learned that the bay is the summer and fall nursery ground for most right whale mothers and their new calves in the North Atlantic. There, strong tidal currents mix cold water and nutrients into a rich soup that supports large amounts of right whale food, including copepods, which are their favorite food. Copepods are tiny crab-like animals that live their entire lives drifting in the ocean currents. In the Bay of Fundy, swarms of these animals, each about the size of a grain of rice, form dense underwater clouds. The clouds are so thick that the right whales just open their gaping jaws to feast.

▼ Right whales in the Bay of Fundy. Head *(left)*, flukes *(center)*, and *breaching*, or leaping from the water *(right)*.

THE RIGHT FEEDING HABITS

A right whale does not use teeth to chew food but instead has a mouth full of long, finely fringed plates called *baleen*. The baleen plates are made of a substance similar to a person's fingernails. There are approximately 225 of them, each eight to nine feet long. When the whale swims with its mouth open, the *baleen* works like a strainer, collecting copepods, juvenile krill, and other tiny ocean creatures. To swallow, the whale probably licks the food off the baleen plates and into its throat by using its gigantic tongue. An adult right whale needs approximately 2,200 to 5,500 pounds of food each day. During feeding, it might dive from 8 to 12 minutes at one time.

▲ Baleen inside the mouth of a dead beached whale.

▲ A right whale feeding on surface, with baleen visible inside its open mouth.

Many different species of whale **migrate,** or travel, between winter breeding and calving grounds and summer feeding grounds. Migration is one way in which animals have adapted to changes in the seasons, and it is common in birds, herding mammals, whales, and many fishes. In whales, most summer migrations move into productive northern waters, where the food is abundant. In the winter, pregnant females move southward, so that when they give birth, their calves can spend their first weeks of life in warmer water.

Our discovery of right whales in the Bay of Fundy had shown us the northern, or "summer," end of the right whale's migration, but we still didn't know where the southern end might be. It took a look back over a hundred years to give us a clue.

In 1983, researchers Randy Reeves and Edward Mitchell found the missing piece of the puzzle. Searching through the logbooks of nineteenth-century whaling ships, they discovered that in the winter of 1876 a whaling schooner from New Bedford, Massachusetts, named **Golden City** had pulled into Brunswick, Georgia. It went there to remove its cargo, which included whale oil and whalebone (another name for baleen) from humpback whales taken near the Bahamas. But that year, instead of continuing farther north, as it usually did, the *Golden City* remained around Georgia for a couple of months. While it was there, the crew captured a single right whale.

They must have seen more because the following year a second whaling vessel appeared in Brunswick, and by 1880 five whaling vessels had made Brunswick their winter headquarters. Records showed that at least 25 to 30 right whales were killed there between 1876 and 1882.

In modern times, right whales had occasionally washed up dead along the coast of the southeastern United States, but there had been few sightings of live whales in the area. Even so, if right whales appeared off the coast of Georgia during the winters over a hundred years ago, as the whaling logs suggested, there was a chance they might still do so today. Perhaps Stars, Stripe, and the other right whales we had discovered in the Bay of Fundy traveled there during their seasonal migrations. But to prove it, we would need to survey the area — and we would need a way to recognize and follow individual right whales.

▲ This drawing from the inside cover of an old logbook kept during a voyage to the Indian and Pacific oceans between 1837 and 1839 aboard the whaling ship *Alexander Barclay* shows the harpooning of a whale. Whalers were sometimes pulled along at great speeds in their boats by the ropes attached to harpooned whales. Whalers called this a "Nantucket sleigh ride."

▲ Starry Night.

One of the most important tasks of our yearly surveys in the Bay of Fundy was to collect right whale "mug shots." Photographs and drawings showing callosities, scars, and other distinctive markings were combined to produce identification files for hundreds of individual whales. Together with other research teams studying whales, we began assembling a right whale catalog. The catalog would enable us to recognize individual whales and build up a picture of their movements.

Stars and Stripe were two of the earliest entries in the catalog. Snowball was another. A circular scar on the side of Snowball's head made him look as if he had been hit with a snowball. Stumpy, Droopy, Admiral, Smoothie, Starry Night, Kleenex, Necklace, Baldy, and Spitball were just a few of the other names we came up with in the beginning. Most names fit a feature of the whale that bore its name.

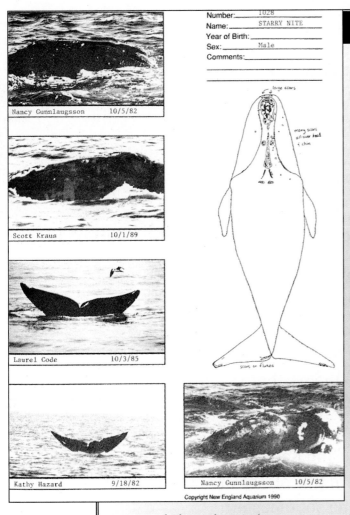

Number: 1028
Name: STARRY NITE
Year of Birth: _____
Sex: Male
Comments: _____

Nancy Gunnlaugsson 10/5/82

Scott Kraus 10/1/89

Laurel Code 10/3/85

Kathy Hazard 9/18/82

Nancy Gunnlaugsson 10/5/82

Copyright New England Aquarium 1990

THE RIGHT WHALE CATALOG

Information about North Atlantic right whales has been continually collected over the last few decades by scientists at Woods Hole Oceanographic Institution in Massachusetts, Marineland of Florida, the University of Rhode Island, the Center for Coastal Studies in Provincetown, Massachusetts, and the New England Aquarium. In 1986, these researchers established the North Atlantic Right Whale Consortium. Their goal was to consolidate their research and integrate their photographic collections to create one unified catalog of identified individual right whales. The catalog now contains more than 320 individual whales. The whales, identified by their natural markings, or callosities, and sometimes by their scars, are described in a diagram and by reference photographs taken by researchers. The catalog entry shown here is for Starry Night, the whale pictured on the opposite page. Scientists are not the only contributors to the right whale catalog. Sailors on commercial ships, fishermen, and people in sailboats and other recreational vessels send photographs of right whales to the New England Aquarium. There, three researchers working independently compare the sighting photographs with the catalog entries. If all three match the photograph with the same catalog entry, then the sighting is "officially" recorded in the catalog.

The catalog gave us our breakthrough in solving the puzzle of the right whale migrations. In 1983, at the end of a summer observing right whales in the Bay of Fundy, volunteer Kathy Lindbergh was reviewing a film we had received from the Georgia Department of Natural Resources. The film, taken the previous winter, showed a mother right whale and her calf swimming off the shores of Brunswick, Georgia.

Trying to match whales' faces in photos or film is often tedious and difficult work. But that day we were lucky: in the film, Kathy saw a whale we had seen that summer off the coast of Maine. It was the first time a right whale had been identified in both the northern feeding grounds off the Bay of Fundy and in the area off the coast of Georgia.

The findings in the whaling records and Kathy's match between Georgia and Maine were two pieces of evidence that the warm waters along the southeastern United States coast were the right whales' winter calving grounds. We decided to carry out a full-scale survey of the area to see if right whales were calving there.

Dave Mattingly *(third from left)* with fellow volunteer pilots.

As luck would have it, in the fall of 1983, Dave Mattingly, a professional airline pilot, called my office to volunteer his services. He was able to organize a group of pilots with private aircraft and flying time to carry out the survey off the coasts of Georgia and Florida. Most people thought we were crazy. No one had searched for right whales in the area since whalers left the region nearly 100 years earlier. When Dave told his friends he was looking for right whales off the coast of Georgia, people looked at him as if he had said he was going to downtown Atlanta to look for dinosaurs.

A pontoon plane lands on the water for a closer look at a whale spotted by a crew member. *Inset:* One of the survey planes above the Florida coast.

The survey took place in February 1984. Each plane had four people on board. One person flew the plane, one took notes, and the other two acted as observers, whose jobs were to find whales. We flew in a pattern that crossed back and forth in lines, or "tracks," over a section of the ocean, as if we were mowing a lawn. If there were any whales to be seen, this method would increase our chances of finding them.

It wasn't until the second day that we saw anything except turtles and sharks. Halfway through that day's flights, pilot Jon Hanson tapped me on the shoulder to say he had spotted something in the distance. When we flew in for a closer look, it turned out to be a mother and a baby right whale.

By the end of three days of flying, we had counted 13 right whales, including three mothers with their newborn calves. They were all swimming in coastal waters near the border of Georgia and Florida. One of the mother whales was our old friend Stripe. With her was her fourth calf, Forever. From her size, Forever might have been about two months old.

Since that first survey, our research team and the volunteer pilots have repeated surveys every winter but one. Based on this work and on searches carried out by boat, we know that the coastal waters of Georgia and Florida are the primary calving ground for the entire North Atlantic right whale population.

With the help of the right whale catalog, we have made many photographic matches between whales in the calving grounds and whales seen in the Bay of Fundy and in other places along the North American coast. These matches and surveys, combined with the work of other researchers in Massachusetts and Rhode Island, have begun to provide a picture of the yearly movements of the right whales along the Atlantic coast.

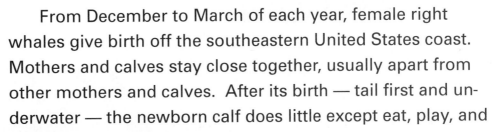

▼ Spitball, photographed off the coast of the southeastern United States.

◀ A southern right whale mother and calf underwater. The calf is between one and three months old.

From December to March of each year, female right whales give birth off the southeastern United States coast. Mothers and calves stay close together, usually apart from other mothers and calves. After its birth — tail first and underwater — the newborn calf does little except eat, play, and rest. It feeds from two nipples hidden in slits along its mother's belly. The milk provides all the nourishment the baby needs. Whale milk is so rich in fat that a newborn right whale may gain a ton — 2,000 pounds — in little over a month.

With the arrival of warmer weather and increasing daylight during the spring, mothers and calves begin a 1,400-mile journey north along the Atlantic coast. They stay close to each other because the calf is still very dependent on its mother's milk. But if they do get separated, we think they use underwater moos and squeals to help them keep in touch.

By April and sometimes earlier, the first of the right whale mothers and calves arrive in waters off the Massachusetts coast. Throughout the winter and during their journey north, the female whales have been living off the fat they store in their blubber. But as they reach cooler waters, they begin to feed. Researchers have observed right whales feeding in the Great South Channel — a deep water passage between the tip of Cape Cod and a productive underwater fishing bank 60 miles to the east called Georges Bank — and in Massachusetts Bay. By the end of July they reach the Bay of Fundy and continue their feast. The whales we have observed in the Bay of Fundy remain there for as long as three months.

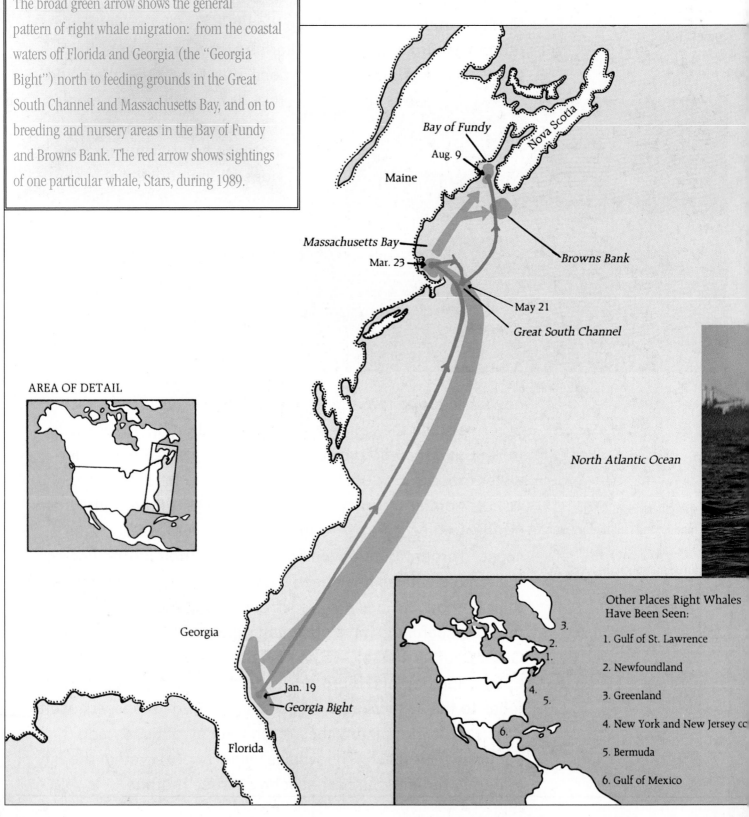

RIGHT WHALE MIGRATION

The broad green arrow shows the general pattern of right whale migration: from the coastal waters off Florida and Georgia (the "Georgia Bight") north to feeding grounds in the Great South Channel and Massachusetts Bay, and on to breeding and nursery areas in the Bay of Fundy and Browns Bank. The red arrow shows sightings of one particular whale, Stars, during 1989.

AREA OF DETAIL

Bay of Fundy

Aug. 9

Maine

Nova Scotia

Massachusetts Bay

Mar. 23

Browns Bank

May 21

Great South Channel

North Atlantic Ocean

Georgia

Jan. 19

Georgia Bight

Florida

Other Places Right Whales Have Been Seen:

1. Gulf of St. Lawrence

2. Newfoundland

3. Greenland

4. New York and New Jersey co

5. Bermuda

6. Gulf of Mexico

The whales need a lot of luck to make the 1,400-mile journey successfully. They travel the same route north as cargo vessels and passenger ships. We know of at least six right whale deaths since 1970 because of collisions with ships. The whales also have to contend with fishing nets. At least three right whales have become entangled in fishing gear and drowned in the last 20 years. Another 11 right whales — including Stars — have been observed swimming with ropes and nets from fishing gear trailing off them. Furthermore, over half the population have scars from entanglements — causing us to wonder if more deaths have occurred than we've heard about.

▲ The scar on this whale was probably caused by a ship's propeller.

By the summer of 1986, six years after our discovery of right whales in the Bay of Fundy, we had solved part of the puzzle of the right whale's migration.

 Stars, with fishing gear caught in her baleen.

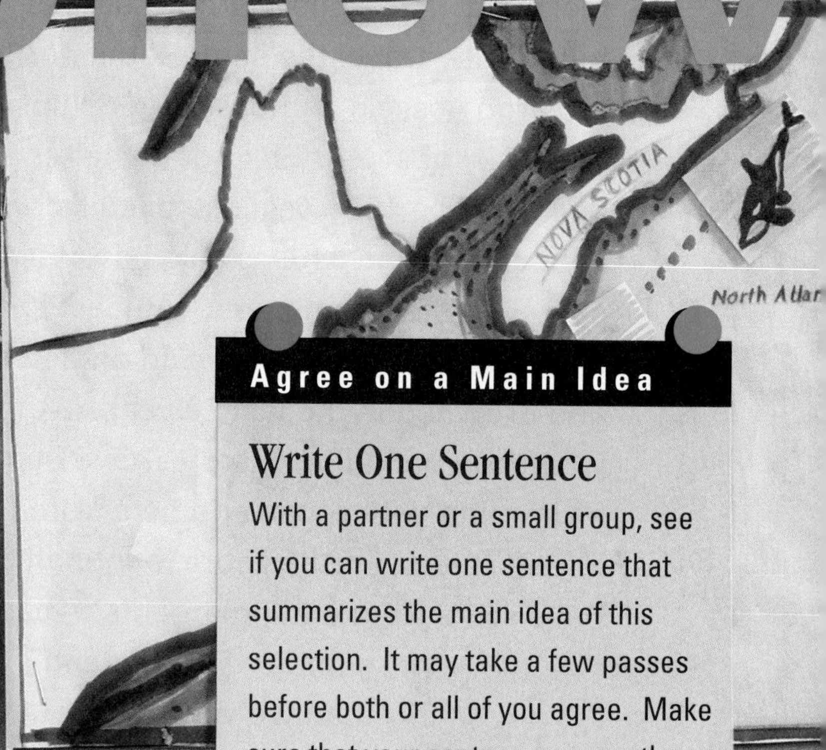

Make a Poster

Whales, Whales, Whales

Using information and illustrations from this selection and other resources about whales, make a poster or bulletin board for your classroom or library that shows all the different kinds of whales. For each, provide a picture or drawing and a short caption. Which species live nearest you?

Agree on a Main Idea

Write One Sentence

With a partner or a small group, see if you can write one sentence that summarizes the main idea of this selection. It may take a few passes before both or all of you agree. Make sure that your sentence covers the whole article, not just part of it. When you've reached an agreement, read your sentence to another pair or group and listen to theirs.

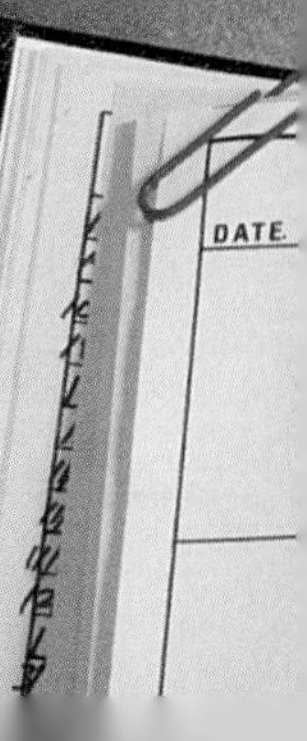

Your Ideas

Debate an Issue

Whaling: Right or Wrong?

Humans have used whales for lamp oil, strapping, stuffing, wigs, and meat. Is this right? Is it okay for humans to kill ocean animals to use their body parts for food and other necessities? With a partner, debate either side of this question for fifteen minutes, using as much evidence from this selection as you can. Then, in your journal, write your own opinion and give your reasons.

Look Back at *Oceans*

The Bay of Fundy

Use the previous selection, *Oceans*, to find out more about the Bay of Fundy, the right whales' summer habitat. How deep is it? Are there mountains in it? How warm is it? Is it affected by any currents such as the Gulf Stream or the North Atlantic Current? What other bodies of water is it near? How far is it from the equator?

RECORD OF SIGHTINGS

I.D.# NAME, AGE, GENDER

OBSERVATIONS AND COMMENTS

A Sandcastle on the Beach

A Description by Mariadeliz Camacho

Words can help you imagine places that you have never been. Let Mariadeliz's description transport you to a familiar scene at an ocean beach near her home.

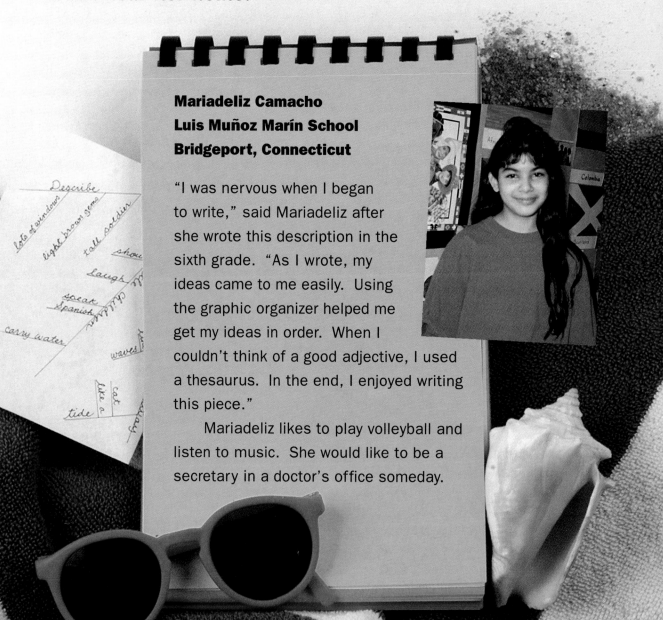

Mariadeliz Camacho
Luis Muñoz Marín School
Bridgeport, Connecticut

"I was nervous when I began to write," said Mariadeliz after she wrote this description in the sixth grade. "As I wrote, my ideas came to me easily. Using the graphic organizer helped me get my ideas in order. When I couldn't think of a good adjective, I used a thesaurus. In the end, I enjoyed writing this piece."

Mariadeliz likes to play volleyball and listen to music. She would like to be a secretary in a doctor's office someday.

580

A Sandcastle on the Beach

The sparkling sandcastle stands like a tall soldier on the beautiful shiny shore. The castle is a dream come true. It has open windows that welcome the warm sunlight. The front of the castle shines like sparkling brown gems.

Laughing children play near the castle. The castle is surrounded by white scalloped shells that shield it from the threatening tide. Little girls carry water in orange buckets to the castle. They speak to each other, giggling, in Spanish. They laugh and shout because speckled crabs nip at their feet. The girls' long brown hair bounces in the wind as they run toward the sparkling blue water. The sun is warm, but the breeze is chilly. It tickles like a long soft feather. The salty ocean spray sprinkles briny perfume in the air.

The girls play without a care until the warm sun starts its fading journey to rest on the ocean's surface. The glorious day comes to an end. The tide slowly rolls in like a sneaky cat. Its waves are like claws scratching at the castle's walls. The castle is no longer the tall soldier that the girls built. The strong waves turn it into a soft pile of sand. The tide continues to flatten it like a soft blue-green blanket.

The girls go home, and the beach is left alone with the glittering stars to watch it during the long, lonely night.

Extremely WEIRD Sea

Gorgon's Head Sea Star *(Gorgonocephalus arcticus)*

Text by Sarah Lovett

Most people look up when they think of stars, but down on the bottom of the ocean, thousands of species of sea stars can be found. Whether they live just below the tide line or 20,000 feet below the surface, sea stars (a.k.a. starfishes) are bottom dwellers. They come in a festive variety of colors — yellow, orange, blue, green, pink, red, purple — and range in size from $\frac{1}{2}$ inch to 3 feet across.

Sea stars usually have five flattened arms that resemble the rays of a star. But close relatives of sea stars, the five-armed brittle stars (also called serpent stars), look more like exotic flowers or snakes than stars. Brittle stars are energetic critters, and they can break off body parts when they are disturbed. Later, they grow new parts to replace the broken ones.

Like all sea stars, brittle stars have a mouth on the underside of their body. They use it to feed on whatever particles happen to be on the sea floor.

The gorgon's head sea star is an extremely odd brittle star that is known as a basket star because its arms branch. The gorgon's head thrives in deep water, and its body may grow to be 4 inches wide while its arms branch again and again to a length of more than one foot each.

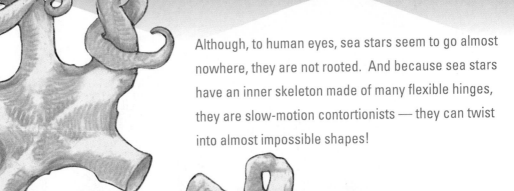

Although, to human eyes, sea stars seem to go almost nowhere, they are not rooted. And because sea stars have an inner skeleton made of many flexible hinges, they are slow-motion contortionists — they can twist into almost impossible shapes!

Creatures

"Echinoderm" comes from two Greek words: *echinos* means spiny, and *derma* means skin. Starfishes, sea urchins, sea cucumbers, and sand dollars are among the 6,000 animal species who belong to the prickly "spiny skin" phylum, echinoderms.

Headless Mop

Sea Cucumber *(Thelemota ananas)*

As the sausage-shaped sea cucumber creeps inch by inch, centimeter by centimeter, across the shallow seabed, it seems like a walking meal. Actually, when it comes to protecting itself from predators, the slow-motion sea cucumber has some very special defenses.

Some species have a poisonous skin to discourage hungry predators. If a predator persists, the sea cucumber tightens its muscles and squirts water from its body. An extremely upset cucumber will turn itself inside out and spew out its innards, including its respiratory organs and intestines. The attacker is caught in a tangled mop of organs, and the sea cucumber escapes. It takes about six weeks before the sea cucumber is able to fully regenerate the spewed organs.

Sea cucumbers live in all oceans.

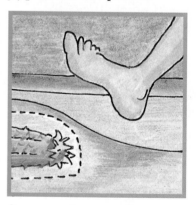

Sea cucumbers are also known as "water pickles." They are very shy critters who like to bury themselves in mud where they are out of a beachcomber's reach.

Wrinkled, flabby, leathery, and punchy as pudding, sea cucumbers are no beauties.

584

When you're beachcombing, look for the burrows of lugworms. These animals live in U-shaped burrows; telltale signs include two holes several inches apart with a pile of sand next to one.

Female fireworms are flashy critters; they produce a substance that glows like — you guessed it — fire! When they are not glowing, fireworms are a greenish gold color, and their many parapodia (paired outgrowths from the side of each segment of the animal) are red and white. All fireworms have another hot trick. When humans or other animals touch the fireworm's thick tufted bristles, they get an "on-fire" feeling. This is caused by tiny poisonous, breakable hooks in the bristles.

Fireworms live in sandy Mediterranean seabeds where they create U-shaped burrows. When they are burrowed in, they wiggle their bodies to stir things up and to circulate fresh water. As the water passes over their gills, they extract the oxygen they need to live.

Fireworms are only one species out of 8,000 that belong to the class Polychaetes. All members of this group are segmented worms. Their long bodies are made of many parts, each separated by partitions, instead of joints.

Some fireworms reach a length of 12 inches!

Hot Foot

585

After

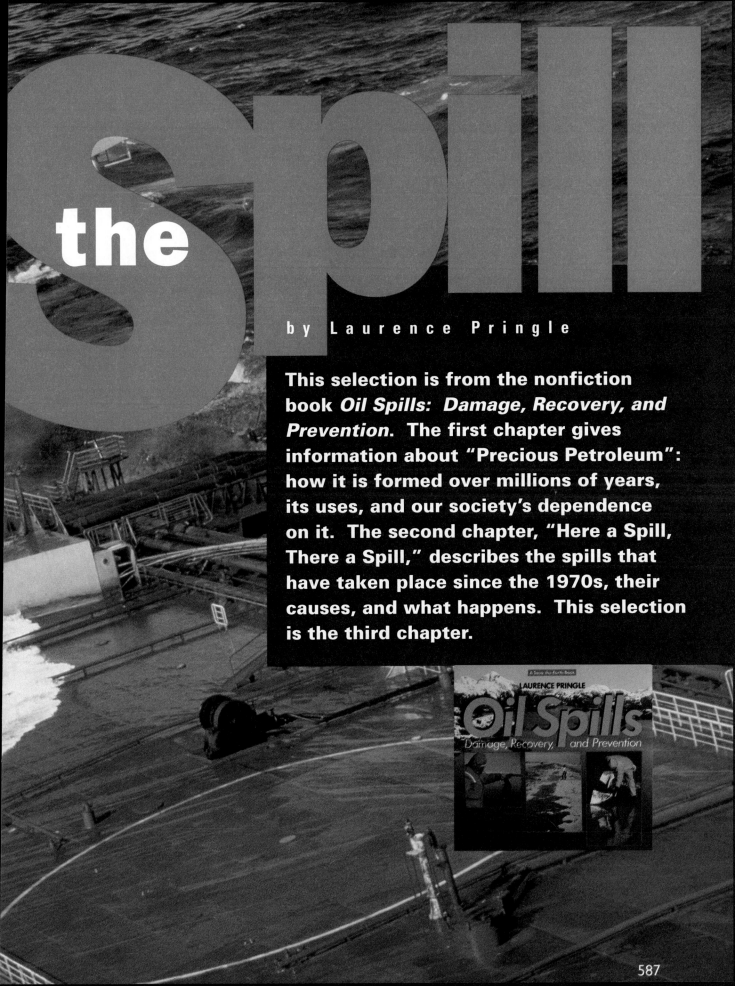

the Spill

by Laurence Pringle

This selection is from the nonfiction book *Oil Spills: Damage, Recovery, and Prevention*. The first chapter gives information about "Precious Petroleum": how it is formed over millions of years, its uses, and our society's dependence on it. The second chapter, "Here a Spill, There a Spill," describes the spills that have taken place since the 1970s, their causes, and what happens. This selection is the third chapter.

A Save-the-Earth Book

LAURENCE PRINGLE

Oil Spills
Damage, Recovery, and Prevention

ANATOMY OF A SPILL

News media and the general public view a major oil spill as a disaster for sea life. The oil industry has a different view. Here is how it was expressed in a 1977 issue of *Exxon Today:*
"Though manmade oil spills are unattractive and wasteful, they are not inevitably harmful to life in the sea . . . Most spills cause little damage to biological elements of the oceans."

The truth lies somewhere between these views. Spilled oil *can* cause great damage, but what effects oil has when it is spilled depend on many factors. Harm to living things depends not only on the amount of petroleum spilled, but also on what kind is spilled. For example, is it crude petroleum or gasoline? It also depends on where and when a spill occurs; and on the season, weather, and many other conditions after it happens.

The differing effects of two small oil spills along the coast of Maine illustrate this point. In 1971, five thousand gallons of jet fuel and heating oil leaked from storage tanks on land and leached into Long Cove at Searsport, Maine. This was a small, underground, invisible oil spill. It was discovered because it killed a population of soft-shell clams that had thrived in Long Cove.

In the summer of 1972, the *Tamano,* a Norwegian tanker, grazed an underwater ledge and spilled forty thousand gallons of fuel oil into Casco Bay. Thousands of boats had to be cleaned, sea plants and clams died, and the state closed contaminated areas to clam digging.

(inset) Smoke billows from burning oil on the sea around the U.S. tanker *Torrey Canyon* off Land's End, England.

(above) The 61,263-ton *Torrey Canyon* after it split in two on the Seven Stones Reef, spilling oil toward the beaches of southwest England.

A decade later, Dr. Edward Gilfillan of Bowdoin College compared the two sites. He said, "At Casco Bay now, you'll have to look hard for signs of the *Tamano*. Visibly and biologically, there has been excellent recovery.

"In Searsport, there has been practically no recovery. With that clay sediment in Long Cove holding that oil in place, there has hardly been any change in almost ten years. The clam population just hasn't come back." But eventually, like a wound healing, Long Cove did recover.

Even though oil spills at sea vary greatly, the study of several spills has given us a general picture of what happens when crude oil is released. "Weathering" is the term that scientists use to describe how an oil spill is affected by winds, waves, sunlight, and other factors in the environment. Weathering changes oil both physically and chemically.

Oil is lighter than water, so spilled oil at first stays at, or rises to, the surface. Then it begins to spread — the first step in the weathering process. The speed and pattern of its spread depends on the water temperature, currents, and the direction and speed of winds. Of course, the amount of oil spilled also affects how far oil spreads over the surface. In 1976, the *Argo Merchant* dumped nearly eight million gallons of heavy industrial oil off Nantucket, Massachusetts. At first, this spill formed a thick slick covering just a square mile. Eventually, it spread out in a thin, oily sheen that covered more than eleven thousand square miles.

Oil pollution on
the ocean's surface

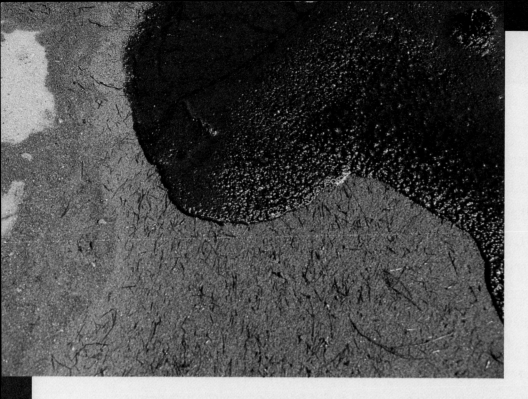

An oil-spill polluted
beach

As soon as spilled oil is exposed to air, parts of it begin to evaporate. The most
lightweight compounds of petroleum, which include benzene and other poisonous
hydrocarbons, evaporate first. They usually enter the atmosphere within a few hours
of a spill. As the process of evaporation continues, slightly heavier fractions enter the
air. Over a span of one to two weeks, as much as half of an oil spill may escape into
the air. (Spilled gasoline, jet fuel, or kerosene may evaporate completely.) As evaporation removes the lightest hydrocarbon compounds, the remaining oil becomes more
dense and heavy. Tar balls and floating mats of heavy hydrocarbons may form.

Waves mix oil and water, dispersing oil droplets below the water surface. Over
time, dispersion spreads oil compounds underwater even farther than the sheen of oil
that can be seen on the surface.

In mixing oil and water, waves and winds often cause water droplets to become
trapped within oil. This sticky, pudding-like mixture is called an emulsion. Water-in-
oil emulsions are brown-colored and are called chocolate mousse, or just mousse.
This emulsion slows the weathering process. Mousse may persist for as long as two
years after an oil spill.

Sunlight also affects spilled oil in a process called photooxidation. Solar energy
causes some petroleum compounds to mix with oxygen and form such compounds as
peroxides, ketones, and alcohols. These substances are more likely to dissolve in
water, and to harm living things, than their "parent" hydrocarbons.

Usually, some spilled oil settles to the ocean bottom, or is washed onto beaches. As an oil spill weathers and loses more and more of its lightest hydrocarbons, the remaining oil tends to sink. When ocean waters contain bits of soil, especially clay, the particles of earth stick to oil droplets. The more sediments that are mixed in the water, the more oil that is eventually deposited on the ocean bottom. Along beaches, storms also may carry oil-laden sand offshore and deposit it on the bottom.

Throughout the weathering process, bacteria and fungi play an important role in changing hydrocarbon compounds and removing them from the environment. This biodegradation of oil, as it is called, begins within hours after oil is spilled. The process of breaking down hydrocarbons by microscopic organisms (microbes) goes on at the surface, underwater, on beaches, and in sediments on the ocean bottom. It works best in warm waters that contain abundant oxygen, as well as such nutrients as nitrogen and phosphorus.

Under the best of circumstances, however, biodegradation is a slow process. Microbes have a difficult time breaking down tar balls and deposits of oil on the ocean bottom or along shores.

Oil lasts longest in protected coves and marshes, where there is little or no wave action. In contrast, along "high-energy" shores — where powerful waves scour the rocks and sand — the weathering process is speeded up.

(left, above) A salt marsh in Cypremort Point, Louisiana

(left, below) An oil-spill polluted marsh tideland

(right) The rocky coast of Maine

Scientists learned a lot about the oil weathering process after the 1978 *Amoco Cadiz* spill off the coast of Brittany, France. Not only did the huge loss of 223,000 tons of crude oil attract international scientific interest, but the accident also occurred near several ocean research laboratories. Soon after the accident, scientists began collecting water and oil samples. *Amoco Cadiz* remains one of the best-studied oil spills in history.

High waves whipped some of the *Amoco Cadiz's* cargo into a frothy mousse. Of the oil spilled, 30 percent evaporated and about 14 percent dispersed into the water. Another 4 percent was consumed in the open sea by microbes. Eight percent of the oil was deposited in sediments on the ocean bottom, and 28 percent washed into the intertidal zone of the shore.

Oil fouled nearly two hundred miles of Brittany's coast, including sandy beaches, rocky coves, and salt marshes.

This disaster occurred in March, migration time for many birds. More than 3,200 dead birds of thirty species were recovered; scientists believed that this was only 10 to 15 percent of the real kill. High concentrations of oil were found two feet underground in some tidal areas. The oil caused massive kills of clams, sea urchins, crabs, and other marine life. Brittany's oyster-raising industry was harmed, and its fishing and tourism business suffered.

A blue crab

(right) Dead baby crabs in oil-polluted marsh tideland

The *Amoco Cadiz*
sinking and spewing
oil off the coast of
Brittany, France

Crude oil spreads from
the Liberian tanker
Ocean Eagle at the
entrance to San Juan
Harbor, Puerto Rico.

Within a year, however,
catches of crabs, lobsters, and
most fishes returned to normal.
In one bay, three years passed before oil pollution lessened enough
for oysters to survive. Microbes
and weathering continued to rid
habitats of oil. Nevertheless, a
decade after the 1978 spill some
heavily-oiled marshes still had
harmful levels of hydrocarbons.

Although oil tankers have broken apart and even exploded
in the open seas, most oil spills occur closer to shore. On any given day,
about fifty tankers carrying 450 million gallons of oil enter American harbors. Coastal oil spills can be a threat to beach resorts and commercial
fishing. They may foul salt marshes and estuaries, which are nurseries
for young ocean fish.

Even if a spill fails to wash ashore, petroleum released anywhere
over continental shelves can do harm. Compared with the open sea,
water over the shelves, which may extend several hundred miles from
continental shores, is shallow. It is also rich with the nutrients needed
by the tiny plankton that are the base of many food chains. The upper
few feet of these waters are home to a wealth of life, including fish
eggs, fish larvae, and also crab and lobster larvae. And this precious
layer, the ocean's skin, is exactly the area over which an oil spill spreads.

The effects of petroleum on living things have been studied at the sites of spills and in laboratories. We know more about oil's effects on saltwater life than on freshwater organisms, because the biggest oil spills occur at sea, not on rivers or lakes. In either environment, hydrocarbons can kill plants and animals. Low doses can have "sublethal" effects; for example, not killing a fish directly, but harming its vision, its growth, or its ability to reproduce. A very low concentration of oil (five parts of oil in a million parts of water) affects fishes' sense of smell, and so impairs their ability to hunt.

Small-scale laboratory experiments may underestimate the harm done by oil pollution. Several of such studies, for example, showed little damage to coral reefs by oil. Then, in 1986, more than two million gallons of crude oil spilled from a refinery storage tank into the sea on the Caribbean coast of Panama. The area was already well-known to scientists at the nearby Smithsonian Tropical Research Institute, and they began studying the oil's effects soon after the spill.

The oil affected about fifty miles of shoreline habitats, seriously damaging the plant and animal life of mangrove forests, seagrass beds, and

(bottom left) A coral reef and its inhabitants in the Caribbean Sea

(inset) A closer look at coral

Sea urchins and coral
off Grand Cayman of
the Cayman Islands

coral reefs. Some reefs
were killed outright.
Others suffered from sub-
lethal effects, as algae and other organisms invaded their
injured skeletons. Five years after the spill, just five percent of the reef was alive, and it had little chance of with-
standing the eroding action of the sea.

Many forms of life are exposed to small amounts
of oil in their natural environment. They usually appear
unharmed, but may be affected by petroleum's sublethal
effects. Chronic, low-level exposure to hydrocarbons
occurs in many harbors and other coastal habitats where
small oil spills happen. It occurs in estuaries, where oil
carried by river waters mixes with sea water. It occurs
near natural seeps of oil from cracks in the ocean floor.

Divers among coral reefs

An Atlantic
Blue Reef fish
(*Chromis cyaneus*)

Chronic oil pollution also occurs in the Persian Gulf. Before the Desert Storm conflict of 1991, the Gulf was considered the world's most oil-polluted body of water. It is a shallow sea with only a narrow outlet, and pollutants tend to be trapped in its basin. However, the warmth of its water speeds the evaporation of oil and its breakdown by microbes. The buoyancy of its highly salty water also tends to keep oil from sinking to the bottom.

Despite chronic oil pollution in its waters, the Persian Gulf supported a thriving fish and shrimp industry, and an abundance of wildlife, including dolphins, whales, sea turtles, dugongs (relatives of manatees), and many species of seabirds. All of this life existed despite oil spills that average at least a million barrels annually.

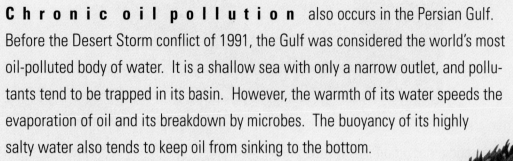

Searching for seabirds trapped by an oil spill off Abu Ali Island, Saudi Arabia

(below) Examining a pool of oil on a Saudi Arabian beach

(right) An oil burnoff in Libya

Crude oil from the Persian Gulf spill coats the feathers of a cormorant in northern Saudi Arabia.

Iraq's deliberate oil spill in 1991 totaled an estimated six million barrels. It was the largest oil spill in history. The oil threatened life in the western Gulf, where the water is most shallow and marine life is most abundant. Fish, algae, sea grass, mangroves, shrimp, and many other plants and animals that had survived long exposure to low levels of hydrocarbons died in great numbers.

In 1992, a team of scientists sponsored by the United Nations began assessing the damage. In Saudi Arabia, they found more than a hundred miles of beaches and shallow tidal zones covered by thick mats of tar. They found dead and dying coral reefs. In some areas of deep water, however, they found little apparent damage from the oil.

The scientists looked for signs that the life of the Persian Gulf could recover. "Some of the damage is permanent," said Dr. Sylvia Earle, then chief scientist of the National Oceanic and Atmospheric Administration (NOAA). "Life in the Gulf will recover, but it will be different."

SURVIVING A SPILL

O v e r a l l ,   w i l d l i f e   populations and their habitats eventually do recover from oil spills. Each spill is unique, however, and some pose a threat to endangered species. Oil from the Ixtoc-I well in the Gulf of Mexico moved toward the coasts of Mexico and Texas. Along the Texas coast there are seven national wildlife refuges, including the Aransas refuge, which is the winter home of the rare whooping crane. Oil did blacken some Texas beaches, but did not reach any of the major refuge areas.

(above) An oil-covered Red Necked Grebe found on Knight Island, thirty-five miles from the *Exxon Valdez* spill

Ixtoc-I's greatest threat was to the Atlantic Ridley sea turtle, which lays its eggs on beaches near Rancho Nuevo, Mexico. Baby turtles hatch in the summer, then swim northwest in the Gulf. In order to protect a generation of this endangered species, biologists caught about nine thousand hatchlings and airlifted them to the open sea beyond the oil slick.

Ever since the 1969 oil-well blowout off Santa Barbara, wildlife biologists and environmentalists have worried about the impact of an oil spill on seals and sea otters. This concern had grown since 1977, when oil fields were first tapped in Alaska and tankers began carrying crude petroleum along the West Coast of the United States and Canada.

(above) A Ridley sea turtle emerges from its nest.

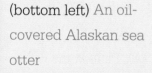

(bottom left) An oil-covered Alaskan sea otter

(bottom right) Healthy sea otters swimming in Prince William Sound

(above) Cleaning a Common Murre in the Bird Rescue Center in Valdez, Alaska

(left) A sea otter gets cleaned up at the rescue center in Valdez, Alaska.

Some aquatic mammals, including whales, do not seem to be harmed by swimming through an oil slick. However, the same oil may doom aquatic mammals with fur, including sea otters, river otters, and fur seals. Oil on their fur reduces its insulating qualities. Sea otters, in particular, depend on their fur to keep warm. Their fur must be groomed frequently in order to be effective. Grooming is a key to their survival, but it can also seal their doom. In the process of licking their fur, they can swallow a lethal dose of oil. Badly oiled fur drives sea otters into a frenzy of grooming, which only makes matters worse.

Oil spills in several places have killed sea otters, and, along a coast in Scotland, river otters. Autopsies showed that they had died from damage to their livers, kidneys, lungs, or nervous systems. Since sea otters spend so much time feeding, grooming, and resting on the water surface, they may inhale benzene and other toxic hydrocarbons that usually evaporate soon after an oil spill. Sea otters have also died from exposure after their fur lost its insulating quality, and perhaps from eating oil-contaminated clams and other shellfish. These mollusks filter petroleum from the sea and cannot excrete it. They store hydrocarbons, and for weeks or months after an oil spill are a lingering threat to any animal that eats them.

EXXON VALDEZ

The 1989 *Exxon Valdez* oil spill killed more than a thousand sea otters. These were known deaths; biologists believe that many others sank to the bottom without a trace. Before the accident, however, the otter population of Prince William Sound was estimated to be between twelve thousand and fifteen thousand. In time, barring further massive oil spills, the otter population will recover. Nevertheless, the *Exxon Valdez* spill showed how deadly an oil spill can be for sea otters. A spill of similar dimensions occurring along the California coast might wipe out a separate, much smaller sea otter population entirely.

The full extent of the harm done by the *Exxon Valdez* oil spill may never be known. Years after the first massive loss of seabirds, bald eagles, sea otters, and other life, scientists continued to study the area.

The *Exxon Valdez* awaiting repairs after hitting a reef

(right) A crew cleaning the rocks on the beaches of Naked Island, Alaska

(above) Cleaning up on Knight Island after the spill

(left) The cleanup on Latouche Island, Alaska

(left) Cleanup
on Knight Island

They feared that the damage would be long-lasting. Oil had coated nearly twelve hundred miles of coastline, and many square miles of bottom sediments. (Had the spill occurred on the eastern coast of the United States, it would have stretched from Cape Cod, Massachusetts, to North Carolina.) In a warm climate, most of this oil would break down quickly, except in sheltered coves where waves were small. However, oil weathering is a slow process in the subarctic climate of Prince William Sound. In limited sunlight and cold water, microbes break down oil molecules very slowly.

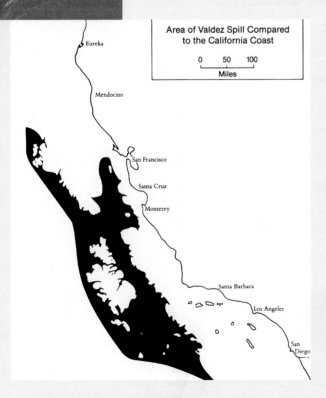

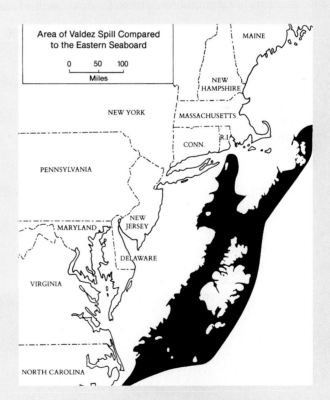

(left) Area of *Valdez* spill compared to the California coast

(right) Area of *Valdez* spill compared to the Eastern Seaboard

Two years after the spill, the United States government announced the results of some studies. Scientists had found many abnormal young herrings, and few or no salmon eggs and young in some salmon-breeding streams that flow into the sound. Some seabird colonies had lost nearly three-quarters of their populations. These colonies were located on islands where oil still persisted, and scientists feared that the birds could be completely wiped out.

Government scientists said that environmental damage at Prince William Sound would last much longer than they had originally thought. Some scientists predicted that recovery would take twenty or more years. In response, a spokesman for the Exxon Corporation, owner of the *Exxon Valdez* and its cargo, said, "Everything we are seeing suggests the biological community is healthy and thriving."

About **Laurence Pringle**

As a child growing up in rural New York State, Laurence Pringle loved to observe and photograph wildlife. Today he is the author of dozens of books about nature for young people. Pringle sees his career both as a way to explore the subjects that interest him and a way to help the environment. Why does he write for kids? "Perhaps we [children's writers] feel that it is too late to influence most adults, but that everything that touches a child's life, including magazine articles and books, can make a difference in the future of that child, and in the future of the world."

The *Exxon Valdez* in Prince William Sound

Damage Control

Make a Graph

How Big Is a Big Spill?

This selection includes the sizes, in gallons, of several important oil spills:

- Searsport, Maine, 1971
- *Tamano*, 1972
- *Argo Merchant*, 1976
- Panama spill, 1986
- Iraq's deliberate spill, 1991

Make either a bar graph or a picture graph that shows their relative sizes.

Write About Your Reaction

What Do I Think and Feel?

Does the information in "After the Spill" arouse any strong feelings in you? For example, is there any fact that makes you angry? Proud? Curious? Disbelieving? Awestruck? Hopeful? Choose one specific fact or story from the selection and write your personal reaction to it. Share what you've written with another reader.

Write Definitions

Make a Bulletin Board

Based on your reading, write and illustrate definitions of the following terms: *petroleum, oil spill, weathering, emulsions, biodegradation, hydrocarbons, habitat, environmentalists.* Choose two more words from the article that you think students might be curious about. Combine and display your definitions on a bulletin board in your school.

Debate an Issue

How Responsible Are We?

In pairs or small groups, use the information in this selection, and in *Oceans,* and in *The Search for the Right Whale* to prepare to debate one of the opinions below. Hold a debate with a pair or group of students who have researched the opposing viewpoint.

1 If human beings aren't careful, they will destroy the earth's oceans.

2 The earth's oceans go through natural phases and changes; they will endure no matter what humans do.

605

Careers in Oceanography

Combine your interests in science and the sea by becoming an **oceanographer**. Oceanographers work on research vessels at sea, along the shoreline, and in land-based laboratories. This career is rewarding in many ways, but it requires years of study. There are only a few thousand oceanographers in the United States today, each working in a specialty. What is your special interest?

(above) Sylvia Earle, who made the deepest solo dive in a submersible, gets into her Jim suit for another possible conquest.

(left) Illustrious oceanographer Jacques Cousteau in front of his research vessel *Calypso*

(right) Robert Ballard, discoverer of the wreck of the *Titanic*, gets ready to take the plunge with his underwater mobile camera.

(below) Studying a core sample from the bottom of Lake Erie to test for pollution

Take the Career Test...

☞ **Are you** curious about sharks, seaweed, dolphins, or plankton**?**
Be a *marine biologist*, and study the plants and animals of the oceans.

☞ **If you are fascinated** by hurricanes and waterspouts, become an *atmospheric oceanographer*, also called a *marine meteorologist*.

☞ **Do waves** make you wonder**?**
A *physical oceanographer* examines waves, currents, and tides, and studies how energy moves through the ocean.

☞ **Do you like** to get to the bottom of things**?**
A *geological oceanographer* studies the ocean floor. Some geological oceanographers work for oil companies, guiding the search for oil below the sea.

☞ **Are you** a hands-on problem solver**?**
As an *oceanographic engineer*, you might develop the systems and devices that other scientists use in marine research. Oceanographic engineers also design offshore oil rigs.

☞ **If you want to solve** the problems of ocean pollution, consider a career as a *chemical oceanographer*. Examine the chemicals in seawater and the chemical reactions that occur there.

You might prefer to become an **oceanographic technician**, assisting oceanographers with equipment and research. Plan on studying high school math and science. Then earn an associate's degree from a two-year college or from a trade school. Or earn a bachelor's degree in marine science at a four-year college.

If you have a deep desire to work underwater, consider becoming a **commercial diver**. You will need not just scuba-diving skills, but also training in other technologies — and the courage to work under dangerous, murky conditions. As a commercial diver, you might repair pipelines, lay cables, and maintain sewage lines. You might find work on harbor construction, dredging, demolition, and salvage projects. You might even find opportunities in the glamorous business of underwater photography.

Professional deep-sea divers explore inner space the same way astronauts aim for the stars.

One way to train for a career as a commercial diver is to attend a college that offers a two-year associate's degree in marine diving technology. Diving training can also be part of service in the United States Navy.

Fishing in the future will depend on the knowledge of **fish culturalists**, who have been trained in the fishery sciences. Fish culturalists may manage hatcheries and fish farms. They must understand the life cycles and habitats of the fish they are raising. To become an assistant or a technician, earn a degree in fisheries science or fisheries biology at a two-year or four-year college. To become a fisheries biologist, you will probably need a doctoral degree.

Waves want
to be wheels,
They jump for it
and fail
fall flat
like pole vaulters
and sprawl
arms outstretched
foam fingers
reaching.

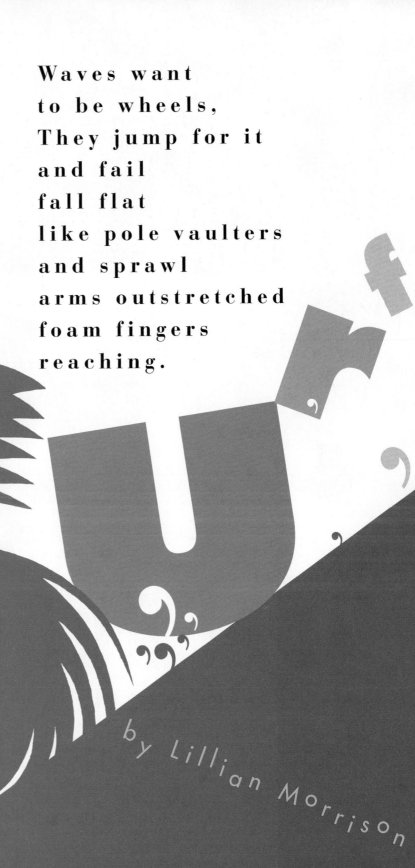

Surf

by Lillian Morrison

Joel Rubin

BY PHILLIP HOOSE

Joel Rubin, fifteen, found a way to influence a huge
multinational corporation to change the way it catches
tuna in the Pacific Ocean in order to keep dolphins
from being killed. His strategy was direct, personal,
and hard-hitting. As he put it, "You don't always have
to be polite."

One Sunday afternoon, Joel Rubin, a fifteen-year-old tenth-grader from Cape Elizabeth, Maine, slumped into a chair in the family rec room and snapped on the TV. He flipped around on the cable channels for a while, then locked onto a show about dolphins.

At first there were scenes of dolphins in family groups. They seemed amazingly like humans: intelligent, friendly, and playful. Through something like radar, they beamed out sounds that let them talk to one another.

Then the scene changed to a large tuna fishing boat in the eastern Pacific. The boat was specially equipped with large drift nets to haul in hundreds of tuna at once. The narrator said that dolphins and yellowfin tuna swim together. The dolphins swim above the tuna, leaping out of the water from time to time to breathe. That makes them perfect markers for tuna fishers.

"The tuna ship sent out helicopters to spot dolphins," Joel remembers. "Then the pilot would radio back to the ship, and suddenly speedboats would zoom out to surround the dolphins. They wanted to make the dolphins stay in one place so the tuna below wouldn't move. That way they could get nets around all the tuna."

As Joel watched, horrified, boat pilots hurled small bombs at the male dolphins who led the group and tried to run over them with their boat propellers. The sea was soon smeared with blood. The tuna ship steamed into the picture, and fishermen on deck hurriedly cast out a mile-long net. One edge was held up on the surface by a line of floats, while the other edge sunk down several hundred feet into the water.

The workers on the tuna boat closed up the net by cranking cables, as if they were pulling the drawstrings on a giant purse. Underwater cameras showed dolphins, trapped among hundreds of tuna, frantically trying to thrash their way out of the net before they ran out of oxygen. Then the giant net, bulging with writhing fish and dolphins, was hoisted high above the ship and dropped about forty feet down onto the deck. It landed with a crash that shook the camera.

Joel and his sister Kara swimming with dolphins

Joel sank back into his chair. He had never been an emotional person, but now he was nearly paralyzed with shock. "Those pictures did something to me," he remembers. "I had never felt that way before. It was the most disgusting thing I had ever seen. I had never tried to change anything before, but I had to do something about this."

WHAT COULD ONE STUDENT DO?

In the winter of 1990, many students throughout the U.S. were feeling the same way Joel did. They were forming environmental action groups and writing to their political representatives, demanding laws to save the dolphins.

Some were boycotting the companies who bought tuna that had been captured in drift nets. Thousands of students were refusing to pack tuna fish sandwiches in their lunch boxes. Others protested against tuna in their school cafeterias. One Colorado high school student named Tami Norton organized a boycott that forced her entire school system to remove tuna from lunchroom menus.

But Joel Rubin didn't know about the tuna boycotts that were going on elsewhere. He kept asking himself, what can I do? He called the producers of the TV show, the Earth Island Institute, and asked for more information. When a package arrived, the information made him even angrier: he learned that ten million dolphins had died at the hands of tuna fishers since 1960.

He also learned that the tuna fishers didn't have to use the drift nets; there were nets available that could open to release dolphins trapped inside.

Joel went to Dr. Hackett, his biology teacher, and told him about the show. Dr. Hackett was Joel's favorite teacher, an energetic, fast-talking man who seemed to spill over with ideas. They brainstormed together each day after class. After about two weeks, an idea began to take form. "We came up with the idea of starting a message-writing campaign aimed at a big company that buys tuna from the fishing boats using the drift nets. It started out really loose, but each day we worked out more details."

Joel figured the U.S. companies who bought the tuna were deserving targets. After all, they had the power to refuse to buy tuna caught in drift nets. If they did, the people who caught the fish would have to change their ways or lose business.

Joel decided to try to convince his schoolmates to write hundreds of messages to the H. J. Heinz Company. Joel had always thought of Heinz as a ketchup maker, but he had learned that Heinz also owned the world's biggest tuna company, Star-Kist. At the time, Star-Kist bought some of its tuna from fishers like those in the TV show.

Joel made a presentation to every science class in his school. "I asked their teachers to let me talk to the students. I needed their help. I told them what was going on with the dolphins and the facts I had learned. It was the first time most of them had heard about it. Most were as disgusted as I was."

Joel asked for volunteers to write personal messages to the Heinz Company. "I told them I didn't want anyone who didn't honestly want to work on this to be in on it. It had to be honest. Not a single student turned me down."

GETTING PERSONAL

After talking more with Dr. Hackett, Joel decided the best strategy would be to send postcards to the homes of the H. J. Heinz Company's executives. Postcards would work better than letters, he thought, since family members would notice them and read the messages. "I imagined the kids of these people showing the

> "If we just wrote letters to the company," says Joel, "they would just get thrown in a pile by a secretary. We wanted to have the postcards waiting at home each night after a day at the office."

cards to their parents when they came home from work and asking, 'What's this?' I thought that would help make the executives think about what they were doing."

And home was more personal than the office. "If we just wrote letters to the company," says Joel, "they would just get thrown in a pile by a secretary. We wanted to have the postcards waiting at home each night after a day at the office."

How many executives should they send cards to? Not just one, since one could just throw all the cards away and no one else in the company would know. Not too many, either, since they wanted a few targeted individuals to feel responsible. Three sounded about right.

Next Joel and Dr. Hackett went to the library to try to find out whom to send the cards to. The reference librarian brought out a book called *Standard and Poor's Register of Corporations, Directors and Executives*. It listed the names of the top executives in most of the big companies in America. *Volume Two: Directors and Executives* told a little bit about each boss.

They picked the president of the company, the head of the fish division, and the head of public relations — the person who is responsible for the company's public image.

Now they needed to find home addresses. The company headquarters was in Pittsburgh, so they found a copy of the Pittsburgh telephone directory

"I am in favor of animal rights as well as human rights. It is the way of a whole human being."

— Abraham Lincoln

Joel Rubin enjoys a swim with a friend.

616

in the library. They found addresses for three people with the right names, including their middle initials.

Dr. Hackett had a friend who lived in Pittsburgh. The friend called the three houses and asked if there was someone there who worked for the Heinz Company. Bingo.

They bought postcards of Maine, and the next day at school Joel passed them out in the science classes. He asked each student to write three postcards, one to each executive's address, and return them to him. He hadn't decided yet whether to send them all at once or a few each day.

And just to be fair, before he sent them, Joel wrote a letter to Anthony O'Reilly, the president of the Heinz Company, asking him to stop buying tuna caught in drift nets. "I explained to him what we were prepared to do and why," Joel says. "I didn't give away the details. I gave him two weeks to reply. He never answered."

Joel decided to mail six cards a day to each of the three executives. He figured that was just about the right amount so that each card would get read. When O'Reilly's deadline passed, Joel took the first six to the mailbox and dropped them in.

Two weeks later, Joel received an angry reply from one of the executives. "He was really upset," Joel says. "He wrote: 'I believe it is inappropriate to be mailing business correspondence to people's homes. I resent this as it crosses the border from professional to personal life. . . . I expect that I will not be hearing from you again.'"

Joel took the letter to school and passed it around the science classes. "We had a little celebration in class that day," Joel says, "because it showed we were getting somewhere. As for getting too personal, we felt very personally about the death of thousands of dolphins. We kept right on mailing to his home."

About a month later, in April of 1990, Heinz suddenly gave in. Anthony O'Reilly announced at a press conference that Heinz would start buying only tuna that were caught in nets that allowed dolphins to escape. Star-Kist tuna cans would say "Dolphin Safe" so that shoppers would know that no dolphins had been killed.

On the same day, two other big tuna companies, Bumble Bee and Van Camp, announced that they would do the same. Together, those three companies bought about seven out of every ten cans of tuna sold in the United States. It was an amazing victory.

In explaining why Star-Kist was making the change, Mr. O'Reilly held up several postcards from high school students in Cape Elizabeth, Maine. One read: "How can you sleep at night knowing your company is doing this?" O'Reilly said that even his own children had been urging him to stop killing dolphins.

Joel Rubin was on vacation with his family in California while O'Reilly was speaking. He happened to be at the Earth Island Institute, hoping to get more information, when he heard the news. The staff gathered around to congratulate him for inspiring the powerful postcards. In its own way, the news was almost as shocking as the television show had been a few months before. "It was an unbelievable feeling to know that I had something to do with helping to solve a big environmental problem," he says.

A clipping from the May 15, 1990, issue of The Star *magazine*

HOW HIGH SCHOOL TEEN SAVED THE DOLPHINS

Joel's army of kids battled tuna giants — and won

"I was disgusted," says Joel Rubin, who blitzed the giant Heinz company after seeing a film showing dolphins being slaughtered by tuna fishermen.

DOLPHI
SAFE

618

What was it that made the postcard campaign so effective? Joel believes several factors were key:

- *We believed deeply in what we were doing. It really came from our hearts.*
- *We made the campaign personal. We tried to find the people most responsible for the problem and tell them we expected them to change it.*
- *The messages were very simple. Some of the best postcards just said, "Why are you doing this?" or "How can you sleep at night?" They got right to the point.*
- *We weren't scared of a big company. I learned that you don't always have to be polite. The company wasn't polite to dolphins, so why should we beg, "Oh, please, please, would you stop doing that?"*
- *We assumed we would succeed. We didn't even think about failing.*
- *We took chances and were ready to change plans.*
- *We gave our target a chance to do the right thing before we started. We tried to be fair.*

"What happened is amazing," Joel says. "It just goes to show that if you really try, and plan, you can make a difference."

"*What happened is amazing,*" *Joel says.* "*It just goes to show that if you really try, and plan, you can make a difference.*"

ABOUT
PHILLIP HOOSE

While growing up in Indiana, Phillip Hoose was skinny, uncoordinated, and wore thick glasses. "Things weren't working out for me," he says. Then his seventh-grade teacher praised an essay he wrote about a baseball player. "First I was shocked, and then I thought, 'Whoa, maybe I really CAN write well.'" Hoose got the idea for *It's Our World, Too!* from his daughter's class having an art auction for the homeless. Besides writing books, magazine articles, and songs, Hoose is a conservationist and a long-distance runner.

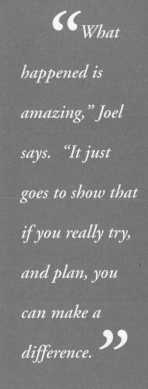

SET YOUR Ideas

Create a Brochure

Joel Rubin Wants You

Joel Rubin made presentations about the dolphins to science classes. He also needed volunteers to help him with his campaign. What kind of help do you think he was looking for? Write and design a campaign brochure that describes the kinds of volunteers Joel Rubin might have needed.

Make a Time Line

From Broadcast to Press Conference

Make an illustrated time line of the events in this nonfiction narrative. Begin with the TV program about dolphins that spurred Joel Rubin into action, and end with the press conference in which Anthony O'Reilly announced his plan for change. Include every small step along the way. Circle the three steps that you consider most important.

The Ocean World of Jacques Cousteau **Window In the Sea**

THE SEA LIFE NATURE LIBRARY

RESTLESS OCEANS

Dear Joel

Write a postcard to Joel Rubin that expresses your thoughts and feelings about what he accomplished. Like the ones described in this selection, make your message "simple" and "right to the point." When you're done, exchange yours with a partner to write a reply Joel Rubin could have written.

What Can We Do?

With a partner, a small group, or your whole class, brainstorm a list of things that you can do to keep the oceans and their creatures safe from harm. Use all of the selections from this theme as sources of ideas. Choose the twelve strategies you think are best and use them to make a poster or bulletin board called "Ocean Quest."

Sea Otter

R E S C U E

Taking it easy, sea otters swim on their backs in Prince William Sound. The otters seemed at home in the areas where they were freed.

Warning of disaster came just before midnight. On the supertanker *Exxon Valdez* a lookout noticed a flashing red light off to the ship's right. That meant the ship was dangerously off course. The seaman alerted the officer in charge.

The officer ordered a turn to the right. The ship did not respond. He called down to the captain: "I think we're in serious trouble." Moments later the tanker shuddered to a halt. Loaded with crude oil, it had run into a reef in Alaska's Prince William Sound. The thick, smelly cargo began gushing to the surface from gashes in the ship's hull.

A view of the *Exxon Valdez* oil spill in Prince William Sound, Alaska

The accident happened at 12:04 a.m. on March 24, 1989. Confusion and lack of training and equipment caused delays in responding. Twelve hours passed before the oil stopped gushing. By then the damage had been done. Eleven million gallons of crude oil had leaked into the sound. The oil drifted some 550 miles and fouled 1,200 miles of shoreline. For the people and animals of the sound, the event spelled catastrophe.

Oil spills are especially dangerous to sea otters. Otters spend most of their time on the water's surface, where the oil lies. Soon after the spill people began finding large numbers of dead or dying otters. The mucky oil was matting their fur. The cold water then could reach their skin, causing the otters to freeze to death. Otters were also dying from poisoning. The animals groom frequently, licking their fur. They were swallowing the poisonous goo they licked off.

Exxon USA pledged whatever money was needed to rescue the otters and other wildlife. The company hired animal-rescue experts from all over the United States. It built three rescue centers and hired fishermen to bring in oiled otters.

Paid staff and volunteers worked round the clock to save the otters. They cleaned them, fed them, and doctored the animals. Finally, in August, the otters that were judged fit were released. Workers put them in parts of the sound unspoiled by oil. The animals seemed content. They stayed in their new surroundings.

Exxon spent 18 million dollars on the rescue. About 220 of the 357 otters brought in recovered. "Saving the otters was worth it," says a local fisherman. "They're our neighbors."

1. Covered with oily gunk, an otter trudges along the shoreline. The oil makes its fur clump together, letting water reach the skin. Without help the animal will die of cold or of poisoning from the oil it licks off its coat.

2. Rub-a-dub-dub. A rescued sea otter gets a soaping at an otter rescue center in Valdez, Alaska. Tranquilizers keep it calm. Washing and rinsing a badly oiled otter might take four people two hours.

3. During a cleaning workers pause to let veterinarian Tom Williams check an otter. Each otter was tagged with a number so people could identify and keep track of it.

4. In the final cleaning step an otter gets blown dry and fluffed. Three rescue centers took in 357 oiled otters. Many survived and were later set free in unpolluted waters. Orphaned babies went to aquariums.

Some of the words in this book may have pronunciations or meanings you do not know. This glossary can help you by telling you how to pronounce those words and by telling you the meanings with which those words are used in this book.

You can find out the correct pronunciation of any glossary word by using the special spelling after the word and the pronunciation key that runs across the bottom of the glossary pages.

The full pronunciation key opposite shows how to pronounce each consonant and vowel in a special spelling. The pronunciation key at the bottom of the glossary pages is a shortened form of the full key.

Full Pronunciation Key

Consonant Sounds

b	**b**i**b**	l	**l**id, need**le**	th	**th**in
ch	**ch**ur**ch**	m	**m**u**m**	*th*	**th**is
d	**d**ee**d**, mill**ed**	n	**n**o, sudd**en**	v	**v**al**ve**
f	**f**i**fe**, **ph**ase, rou**gh**	ng	thi**ng**	w	**w**ith
g	**g**a**g**	p	**p**o**p**	y	**y**es
h	**h**at	r	**r**oa**r**	z	**z**ebra, **x**ylem
hw	**wh**oop	s	**s**au**ce**	zh	vi**s**ion, plea**s**ure,
j	**j**u**dge**	sh	**sh**ip, di**sh**		gara**ge**
k	**k**i**ck**, **c**at, pi**que**	t	**t**igh**t**, stopp**ed**		

Vowel Sounds

ă	p**a**t	îr	d**ear**, d**eer**, p**ier**	ŭ	c**u**t
ā	p**ay**	ŏ	p**o**t	ûr	**ur**ge, t**er**m,
âr	c**are**	ō	t**oe**		f**ir**m, w**or**d,
ä	f**a**ther	ô	c**augh**t, p**aw**, f**or**		h**ear**d
ĕ	p**e**t	oi	n**oi**se	ə	**a**bout, it**e**m,
ē	b**ee**	o͞o	t**oo**k		edibl**e**, gall**o**p,
ĭ	p**i**t	o͞o	b**oo**t		circ**u**s
ī	p**ie**, b**y**	ou	**ou**t	ər	butt**er**

Stress Marks

Primary Stress ′	Secondary Stress ′
bi•ol•o•gy [bī **ŏl′** ə jē]	bi•o•log•i•cal [bī′ə **lŏj′** ĭ kəl]

Pronunciation key © 1994 by Houghton Mifflin Company. Adapted and reprinted by permission from *The American Heritage Student Dictionary*.

amputate

*The word **amputate** comes from the Latin word* amputāre, *meaning "to cut around." The word is derived from the Latin* ambi-, *"around" +* putāre, *"to cut."*

anxiously

*Derived from **anxious,** which comes from the Latin* ānxius, *from the verb* angere, *"to torment." Tormenting people will cause them to behave anxiously.*

amateur

autopsy

*The word **autopsy** developed from the Greek word* autopsia, *which means "seeing for oneself."*

---

ab•sent•ly (ăb′sənt lē) *adv.* As if lost in thought or not paying attention: *The director stared **absently** out the window during the performance.*

ab•sorbed (əb sôrbd′ or əb zôrbd′) *adj.* Completely interested in; taken up by: *The scientist was **absorbed** in her work, finding little time to eat or sleep.*

ab•stract (ăb străkt′or ăb′străkt′) *adj.* **1.** In art, concerned with designs or shapes that do not show a person or thing realistically: *The **abstract** painting uses bold colors and irregular shapes to express feelings of love.* **2.** Hard to understand: *The speaker's topic was so **abstract** that the students could not follow his arguments.*

ac•cu•ra•cy (ăk′ yər ə sē) *n.* Exactness; precision: *The new computer allows for much greater **accuracy** in our test results.*

am•a•teur (ăm′ ə tûr or ăm′ ə choŏr′ or ăm′ ə tyoŏr) *n.* A person who does something without professional training or skill: *The leaky roof had been put on by **amateurs.***

---

am•pu•tate (ăm′pyoō tāt′) *v.* **am•pu•tat•ed, am•pu•tat•ing, am•pu•tates.** To cut off a part of the body, especially by surgery: *The man's foot was badly infected and had to be **amputated.***

anx•ious•ly (ăngk′shəs lē or ăng′ shəs lē) *adv.* **1.** In an uneasy or worried way. **2.** In an eager and earnest way: *We waited **anxiously** for the recess bell to ring.*

ar•chae•ol•o•gist or **ar•che•ol•o•gist** (är′kē ŏl′ə jĭst) *n.* A person who studies the remains of past human activities: *For years, the **archaeologist** had sifted through the ruins of the ancient city.*

ar•ti•fact (är′tə făkt′) *n.* A handcrafted object of archaeological interest: *Pottery, jewelry, and other **artifacts** were exhibited in the museum.*

au•top•sy (ô′tŏp′ sē) *n., pl.* **au•top•sies.** A medical examination of a dead body to determine the cause of death: ***Autopsies** were performed on the disaster victims.*

ă p**a**t / ā p**ay** / âr c**are** / ä f**a**ther / ĕ p**e**t / ē b**e** / ĭ p**i**t / ī p**ie** / îr p**ier** / ŏ p**o**t / ō t**oe**

B

bound•a•ry (**boun'**də rē *or* **boun'**drē) *n.* A border or limit; a dividing line that marks the area of a place: *The stone wall marks the northern **boundary** of their property.*

boy•cott (**boi'**kŏt') *v.* **boy•cott•ed, boy•cott•ing, boy•cotts.** To join together to refuse to buy or use something, usually as part of a protest: *By **boycotting** tuna fish, students helped bring about dolphin-safe tuna fishing.*

C

cal•cu•la•tion (kăl'kyə **lā'**shən) *n.* The result of using mathematics to determine an answer: *Our **calculations** enabled us to improve the design of the aircraft.*

cam•paign (kăm **pān'**) *n.* Activity organized to reach a certain social, political, or commercial goal: *The group organized a **campaign** to save the lives of dolphins.*

can•yon also **ca•ñon** (**kăn'**yən) *n.* A steep and narrow valley cut into the earth by running water: *The walls of the **canyon** rose high above the river banks.*

chafe (chāf) *v.* **chafed, chaf•ing, chafes.** To irritate or make sore by rubbing: *The constant **chafing** of his poorly darned sock had caused a blister.*

chron•ic (**krŏn'** ĭk) *adj.* Lasting for a long time or recurring frequently: *A **chronic** infection kept him indoors for most of the winter.*

claim (klām) *v.* **claimed, claim•ing, claims.** To state to be true: *Dan **claimed** that he had found the gold necklace in the locker room.*

claus•tro•pho•bic (klô' strə **fō'** bĭk) *adj.* Suffering from claustrophobia; uncomfortably confined or hemmed in: *Working in the crawlspace, the plumber began to feel **claustrophobic**.*

cleft (klĕft) *n.* A crack or crevice: *My compass fell into a **cleft** in the rock.*

com•po•si•tion (kŏm'pə **zĭsh'**ən) *n.* The arrangement of parts forming a whole, as in an artistic work: *The artist rearranged the objects on the table to form a more pleasing **composition**.*

---

boycott

Charles Boycott was an English land agent in Ireland. When Boycott refused to lower rents on his properties, his tenants refused to work for or trade with him. Their action came to be known as **boycotting.**

calculations

The ancient Romans used small pebbles to help them add and subtract. From the Latin word for pebble, calculus, *we get* **calculate** *and* **calculations.**

claustrophobic

Claustrophobic *is derived from the word* **claustrophobia,** *which developed from the Latin word* claustrum, *meaning "enclosed place," plus the Greek word* phobos, *meaning "fear."*

cleft

ô p**aw** / oi b**oy** / ou **ou**t / o͞o t**oo**k / o͞o b**oo**t / ŭ c**u**t / ûr **ur**ge / th **th**in / *th* **th**is / hw **wh**oop / zh vi**s**ion / ə **a**bout

condensed

contamination

data

con•dense (kən **dĕns′**) v. **con•densed, con•dens•ing, con•dens•es.** To change from a gas to a liquid or solid: *Water vapor in the air **condenses** and falls as rain.*

con•fi•dent (**kŏn′**fĭ dənt) adj. Feeling or showing confidence; being sure of oneself: *Since I have studied all weekend, I am **confident** that I will pass the test.*

con•sol•i•date (kən **sŏl′**ĭ dāt′) v. **con•sol•i•dat•ed, con•sol•i•dat•ing, con•sol•i•dates.** To combine into one; unite: *We can **consolidate** the various study groups into one re-search team.*

con•tam•i•nate (kən **tăm′**ə nāt′) v. **con•tam•i•nat•ed, con•tam•i•nat•ing, con•tam•i•nates.** To pollute or make unclean by contact or mixture: *The spilled oil **contaminated** the sea-water, killing animal and plant life.*

con•vey (kən **vā′**) v. **con•veyed, con•vey•ing, con•veys.** To express or communicate; to make known: *My images and stories **convey** my feelings about my family.*

corpse (kôrps) n. A dead body: *The police photographer took pic-tures of the **corpse** before the′ ambulance arrived.*

cringe (krĭnj) v. **cringed, cring•ing, cring•es.** To shrink back in apprehension or fear: *The old dog **cringed** when the child reached out to pet it.*

cul•ture (**kŭl′**chər) n. The arts, beliefs, customs, and institutions of a people at a particular time: *Many **cultures** were represented in the festival.*

cur•rent (**kûr′**ənt or **kŭr′**ənt) n. **1.** A mass of liquid or gas that moves: *Ocean **currents** are like giant rivers flowing through the sea.* **2.** A flow of electricity through a wire: *When a tree fell across the wires, the maintenance crew had to turn off the current to make the re-pairs.*

D

da•ta (**dā′**tə or **dăt′**ə) pl. n. Information used as the basis for a decision: *Scientists are collecting and analyzing **data** on the effects of the new safety procedures.*

de•ceit•ful (dĭ **sēt′**fəl) adj. Deceptive; intentionally misleading: *The company was fined for using **deceitful** claims in their advertisements.*

ă p**a**t / ā p**ay** / âr c**are** / ä f**a**ther / ĕ p**e**t / ē b**e** / ĭ p**i**t / ī p**ie** / îr p**ier** / ŏ p**o**t / ō t**oe**

de•com•pose (dē′kəm **pōz′**) *v.*
de•com•posed, de•com•pos•ing,
de•com•pos•es. To decay, rot,
or break down: *The leaves had*
decomposed *and were ready to*
be used for compost.

ded•i•cate (**dĕd′**ĭ kāt′) *v.*
ded•i•cat•ed, ded•i•cat•ing,
ded•i•cates. To devote oneself
fully to something: *Our team was*
dedicated *to baseball; we did all we*
could to improve our game.

de•fi•ant•ly (dĭ **fī′**ənt lē′) *adv.*
Boldly resistant; in open opposition:
The crew **defiantly** *ignored the cap-*
tain's orders.

de•ject•ed•ly (dĭ **jĕk′**tĭd lē)
adv. In a depressed or low-spirited
way: *After losing the tennis match,*
the boy walked home **dejectedly.**

des•o•late (**dĕs′**ə lĭt) *adj.*
1. Having few if any inhabitants; deserted: *The* **desolate** *island has few*
visitors. **2.** Having little if any vegeta-
tion; barren: *They passed through a*
desolate *stretch of desert.* **3.** Dreary
or dismal: *Rain and fog made this a*
desolate *day.*

de•spair (dĭ **spâr′**) *v.* **de•spaired,**
de•spair•ing, de•spairs. To lose
all hope: *Delayed by the storm, we*
despaired *of arriving before the*
program ended.

des•per•ate (**dĕs′**pər ĭt) *adj.*
Driven by a great need for something: *My paper was due, and I was*
desperate *for a good idea.*

dig•ni•ty (**dĭg′**nĭ tē) *n.* Poise and
self-respect: *Although she had been*
falsely accused, she responded with
dignity.

di•men•sion (dĭ **mĕn′**shən *or*
dĭ **mĕn′**shən) *n.* **1.** The measure-
ment of a length, width, or thickness: *The dimensions of the window*
are 2 feet by 4 feet. **2.** Aspect; element: *The old photographs in the*
book add a human **dimension** *to*
the historical narrative.

dis•may (dĭs **mā′**) *n.* A sudden loss
of confidence or courage: *The child*
was filled with **dismay** *when he real-*
ized he was lost.

dis•per•sion (dĭ **spûr′**zhən *or* dĭ
spûr′shən) *n.* The process of scat-
tering in different directions: *Wind*
and waves cause the **dispersion** *of*
spilled oil into an ever-wider area.

dis•tinc•tive (dĭ **stĭngk′**tĭv)
adj. Serving to identify or set apart
from others: *We recognized the*
whale by her **distinctive** *white*
stripe.

ô p**aw** / oi b**oy** / ou **ou**t / o͞o t**oo**k / o͞o b**oo**t / ŭ c**u**t / ûr **ur**ge / th **th**in / th **th**is /
hw **wh**oop / zh vi**s**ion / ə **a**bout

drift

dis•tract (dĭ **străkt'**) *v.* **dis•tract•ed, dis•tract•ing, dis•tracts.** To draw the attention away from something: *The driver lost control of the car when he was* **distracted** *by a wasp.*

dis•trust (dĭs **trŭst'**) *v.* **dis•trust•ed, dis•trust•ing, dis•trusts.** To doubt or lack confidence in; suspect: *Though we had helped him many times, he still* **distrusted** *our motives.*

drift (drĭft) *v.* **drift•ed, drift•ing, drifts. 1.** To be carried about on a current of water or air: *The canoe* **drifted** *downstream as we rested.* **2.** To move slowly and aimlessly: *She* **drifted** *from one task to another.*

E

em•balm•er (ĕm **bäm'**ər) *n.* A person who treats a dead body with preservatives in order to prevent decay: *The good condition of the mummy is the result of skilled* **embalmers.**

es•sen•tial (ĭ **sĕn'**shəl) *adj.* Of the greatest importance; necessary: *In basketball, teamwork is* **essential.**

es•ti•mate (ĕs'tə māt') *v.* **es•ti•mat•ed, es•ti•mat•ing, es•ti•mates.** To calculate roughly or approximately: *I* **estimate** *that the meeting will last for about an hour.*

et•i•quette (ĕt'ĭ kĕt' *or* ĕt'ĭ kĭt) *n.* Rules or customs of proper or formal behavior: *Good* **etiquette** *requires you to thank someone for a gift or a favor.*

e•vap•o•rate (ĭ **văp'**ə rāt') *v.* **e•vap•o•rat•ed, e•vap•o•rat•ing, e•vap•o•rates.** To change from a liquid into a vapor or gas: *In the hot sun, the water* **evaporates** *and the pavement dries.*

ev•i•dence (ĕv'ĭ dəns) *n.* Thing or things that help one make a judgment or come to a conclusion: *Stone axes and arrowheads were* **evidence** *that hunters had used the cave in ancient times.*

ex•e•cute (ĕk'sĭ kyo͞ot') *v.* **ex•e•cut•ed, ex•e•cut•ing, ex•e•cutes. 1.** Perform: *The dancer* **executed** *the move gracefully.* **2.** To put (usually a criminal) to death: *The prisoners had been told that they would be* **executed,** *but they were rescued.*

ă p**a**t / ā p**ay** / âr c**are** / ä f**a**ther / ĕ p**e**t / ē b**e** / ĭ p**i**t / ī p**ie** / îr p**ier** / ŏ p**o**t / ō t**oe**

ex•pec•ta•tion (ĕk′spĕk tā′shən) *n.*
1. The act of expecting. **2.** Anticipation: *The profits from
the bake sale exceeded our
expectations.*

ex•po•sure (ĭk **spō′**zhər) *n.* Being
subjected to a situation, condition, or
influence: *The campers' exposure
to the wilderness helped them appreciate the hardships of pioneer life.*

fa•tal (**fāt′**l) *adj.* **1.** Capable of
causing death: *Many fatal accidents
occur on our highways.* **2.** Causing
ruin or destruction; disastrous: *The
player's lack of attention proved to
be fatal to the team.*

gla•cier (**glā′**shər) *n.* A large mass
of ice that accumulates over many
years and moves very slowly down
mountains and through valleys:
*Glaciers can be thought of as huge
rivers of ice.*

grav•i•ta•tion•al (grăv′ĭ **tā′**shən
əl) *adj.* Having to do with the force
that attracts and tends to draw together any two objects in the uni-
verse: *The gravitational pull of the
moon causes ocean tides.*

her•i•tage (**hĕr′**ĭ tĭj) *n.* Something
other than property that is passed
down from one generation to the
next: *An interest in quilts and quilt-
making was part of the family's
heritage.*

hes•i•tate (**hĕz′**ĭ tāt) *v.*
**hes•i•tat•ed, hes•i•tat•ing,
hes•i•tates.** To pause or wait briefly
due to uncertainty: *Jake hesitated,
trying to decide how to answer the
question.*

hu•mil•i•ate (hyo͞o **mĭl′**ē āt′) *v.*
**hu•mil•i•at•ed, hu•mil•i•at•ing,
hu•mil•i•ates.** To lower the pride,
dignity, or self-respect of a person:
*I was humiliated by their rude
laughter.*

glacier

ô p**aw** / oi b**oy** / ou **ou**t / o͞o t**oo**k / o͞o b**oo**t / ŭ c**u**t / ûr **ur**ge / th **th**in / *th* **th**is /
hw **wh**oop / zh vi**s**ion / ə **a**bout

I

im•age (ĭm′ĭj) *n.* The concept of a person or thing that is held by the public, especially as a result of advertising or publicity: *The ads create the* **image** *of a company that cares about the environment.*

im•pul•sive•ly (ĭm **pŭl′**sĭv lē) *adv.* In a sudden or wishful manner: *A few minutes after meeting the Smiths, we* **impulsively** *invited them to dinner.*

in•stinct (ĭn′stĭngkt′) *n.* **1.** An inborn pattern of behavior that is characteristic of a given species: *Birds′* **instincts** *determine their migration patterns.* **2.** A powerful impulse: *We didn't know what made the noise, but our* **instincts** *told us to run at once.*

in•te•grate (ĭn′tĭ grāt′) *v.* **in•te•grat•ed, in•te•grat•ing, in•te•grates.** To bring all the parts together to form a whole: *The scientists will* **integrate** *the separate findings into one report.*

L

leg•a•cy (lĕg′ ə sē) *n., pl.* **leg•a•cies.** Something handed down to those who come later; heritage: *The great writers and artists of the past have left us a rich cultural* **legacy.**

M

man•u•script (măn′yə skrĭpt′) *n.* The form of a book, paper, or article as it is submitted for publication: *I had sent* **manuscripts** *to several magazines before one was finally published.*

med•i•ta•tion (mĕd′ĭ tā′shən) *n.* The process of thinking deeply and quietly: *A few moments of quiet* **meditation** *will help you relax before a game.*

me•di•um (mē′dē əm) *n., pl.* **me•di•a** (mē′dē ə) or **me•di•ums.** **1.** A technique, material, or means of expression used by an artist: *Although his paintings were famous, sculpture was his favorite* **medium.** **2.** A substance in which scientists grow bacteria or other microorganisms: *The researcher learned that some organisms grow best when the* **medium** *is kept evenly moist.*

ă p**a**t / ā p**ay** / âr c**are** / ä f**a**ther / ĕ p**e**t / ē b**e** / ĭ p**i**t / ī p**ie** / îr p**ier** / ŏ p**o**t / ō t**oe**

mi•crobe (**mī'**krōb') *n.* A disease-causing organism so small that it can only be seen under a microscope; a bacterium: ***Microbes*** *living in the sea slowly break down spilled oil.*

mim•ic (**mĭm'**ĭk) *v.* **mim•icked, mim•ick•ing, mim•ics. 1.** To copy or imitate another's speech, expression, or gesture: *The monkey **mimicked** the trainer's gestures.* **2.** To imitate in order to ridicule or mock: *He **mimicked** his brother's whining tone of voice.*

mis•treat (mĭs **trēt'**) *v.* **mis•treat•ed, mis•treat•ing, mis•treats.** To treat badly or inconsiderately; to abuse: *We should never **mistreat** animals.*

mod•er•ate (**mŏd'**ə rāt') *v.* **mod•er•at•ed, mod•er•at•ing, mod•er•ates.** To make less extreme: *The warm Gulf Stream **moderates** our climate in winter.*

mum•my (**mŭm'**ē) *n., pl.* **mum•mies.** The body of a person or animal embalmed after death: *Inside the ancient coffin was a **mummy.***

non•cha•lant•ly (nŏn'shə **länt'**lē) *adv.* In an unconcerned or carefree way: *Not wanting to seem embarrassed, I strolled **nonchalantly** down the street.*

o•blige (ə **blīj'**) *v.* **o•bliged, o•blig•ing, o•blig•es.** To make indebted or grateful: *I am **obliged** to you for your hospitality.*

pa•tient•ly (**pā'**shənt lē) *adv.* Enduring trouble, hardship, annoyance, or delay in a calm and uncomplaining manner: *For over three hours, I waited **patiently.***

per•sist (pər **sĭst'**) *v.* **per•sist•ed, per•sist•ing, per•sists.** To insist or repeat stubbornly: *Although I wouldn't answer her question, she **persisted** in asking it.*

Phar•aoh also **phar•aoh** (**fâr'**ō or **fā'**rō) *n.* A king of ancient Egypt: *The **pharaoh** was seated on a throne of gold.*

microbes

microbes

Microbes *are tiny life forms. The word come from the Greek mikro-, "small" and bios "life."*

mimic

The word **mimic** *has retained its basic meaning through the centuries. It comes from the Greek words mimikos and mimos, meaning "imitator" or "mime."*

patiently

The Latin verb form patiēns meant "enduring." So if you are **patient,** *you endure pain, boredom, or other difficulty without complaining.*

ô p**aw** / oi b**oy** / ou **out** / ͞oo t**oo**k / ͞oo b**oo**t / ŭ c**u**t / ûr **ur**ge / th **th**in / th **th**is / hw **wh**oop / zh vi**s**ion / ə **a**bout

prehistoric

prac•ti•tion•er (prăk **tĭsh'**ə nər) *n.* A person who practices an occupation, sport, or other activity: *Several **practitioners** of judo were working out in the gym.*

pre•his•tor•ic (prē'hĭ **stôr'**ĭk *or* prē hĭ **stŏr'**ĭk) *adj.* Of or belonging to a time before things or events were recorded in writing: *Scientists have discovered the remains of many **prehistoric** animals, such as dinosaurs.*

pres•en•ta•tion (prĕz'ən **tā'**shən *or* prē'zən **tā'**shən) *n.* Something presented to an audience, such as a lecture, demonstration, or performance: *In my **presentation** to the class, I explained several causes of water pollution.*

pre•serve (prĭ **zûrv'**) *v.* **pre•served, pre•serv•ing, pre•serves.** To keep in perfect or unchanged condition or form; to maintain intact: *The museum specimens were **preserved** in climate-controlled rooms.*

prim•i•tive (**prĭm'**ĭ tĭv) *adj.* Basic, simple, or crude: *The child drew several **primitive** stick figures to represent his family.*

rapids

pri•va•cy (**prī'**və sē) *n.* Seclusion; freedom from the presence or view of others: *I wrote my journal entry in the **privacy** of my room.*

pro•cras•ti•nate (prə **krăs'**tə nāt') *v.* **pro•cras•ti•nat•ed, pro•cras•ti•nat•ing, pro•cras•ti•nates.** To put things off until later; to delay: *Because of her constant **procrastinating**, the job was never finished.*

pros•pect (**prŏs'**pĕkt') *n.* Something expected or foreseen: *I was encouraged by the **prospect** of warm weather and good company.*

pro•test (prə **tĕst'** *or* **prō'**tĕst') *v.* **pro•test•ed, pro•test•ing, pro•tests.** To express strong objections to (something), as in a formal statement or public demonstration: *People **protested** the killing of dolphins by tuna boats.*

public relations (**pŭb'**lĭk rĭ **lā'**shənz) *pl. n.* (*used with a singular verb*). The art or science of establishing and promoting a favorable relationship with the public: *To improve **public relations**, the company invited the townspeople to tour the new plant.*

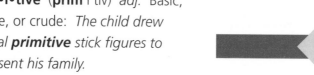

rap•id (**răp'**ĭd) *n.* A part of a river where water flows swiftly over a steep descent in the riverbed. Usually used in the plural: *The hikers de-*

ă pat / ā pay / âr care / ä father / ĕ pet / ē be / ĭ pit / ī pie / îr pier / ŏ pot / ō toe

cided not to cross the river because of the dangerous **rapids.**

rav•en•ous•ly (răv′ə nəs lē) *adv.* Greedily; in an extremely hungry manner: *The crew ate **ravenously** at the end of the long shift.*

re•as•sur•ance (rē′ ə shoor′əns) *n.* The act of restoring confidence: *My teacher's positive words gave me the **reassurance** that I needed to finish the story.*

re•lieve (rĭ lēv′) *v.* **re•lieved, re•liev•ing, re•lieves.** To free from pain, worry, or distress: *The medicine will **relieve** her discomfort.*

re•sign (rĭ zīn′) *v.* **re•signed, re•sign•ing, re•signs.** To give up or quit one's job or position: *The officer will **resign** from duty next week.*

re•sort (rĭ zôrt′) *v.* **re•sort•ed, re•sort•ing, re•sorts.** To have recourse; to turn to for help: *I could not reach him by telephone, so I had to **resort** to writing a letter.*

re•vi•sion (rē vĭzh′ən) *n.* A new or edited version of a piece of writing: *After many **revisions,** the author was finally satisfied with her story.*

rid•i•cule (rĭd′ĭ kyōōl′) *n.* Words or actions intended to cause laughter at or scorn of a person or thing: *His silly antics earned the **ridicule** of his classmates.*

ro•tate (rō′tāt) *v.* **ro•tat•ed, ro•tat•ing, ro•tates.** To turn on or around an axis or center: *The earth **rotates** once every 24 hours.*

ru•in (rōō′ĭn) *n.* The remains of something that has been destroyed or has fallen apart from age. Often used in the plural: *The explorers discovered the **ruins** of an ancient city.*

S

sa•cred (sā′krĭd) *adj.* Revered as a religious symbol, object, or place: *Archaeologists study **sacred** objects to learn about ancient religions.*

sar•coph•a•gus (sär kŏf′ə gəs) *n. pl.* **sar•coph•a•gi** (sär kŏf′ə jī′) or **sar•coph•a•gus•es.** A stone coffin, often inscribed with words or ornamented with sculpture: *The ancient **sarcophagus** found at the burial site weighed several tons.*

ruin

ô p**aw** / oi b**oy** / ou **ou**t / ōō t**oo**k / ōō b**oo**t / ŭ c**u**t / ûr **ur**ge / th **th**in / *th* **th**is / hw **wh**oop / zh vi**s**ion / ə **a**bout

seep (sēp) *v.* **seeped, seep•ing, seeps.** To pass slowly through a small opening; to leak: *Cold air was **seeping** in under the door.*

sheer (shîr) *adj.* Extremely steep; almost perpendicular: *We had to climb down a **sheer** cliff to reach the river.*

shroud (shroud) *n.* The cloth used to wrap a body for burial: *The king's body had been wrapped in a **shroud** of fine linen.*

sig•nif•i•cance (sĭg nĭf′ĭ kəns) *n.* **1.** Importance: *We understood the **significance** of the court's decision.* **2.** Implied meaning: *Although she said nothing, we grasped the **significance** of her frown.*

site (sīt) *n.* The place where something was, is, or will be located: *This was the **site** of the original courthouse.*

skirt (skûrt) *v.* **skirt•ed, skirt•ing, skirts.** To pass around something rather than across or through it: *The runners **skirted** the large puddle in the path.*

slink (slĭngk) *v.* **slunk** or **slinked, slink•ing, slinks.** To move in a quiet and stealthy way: *I saw the cat **slinking** toward the birds that were hopping about under the tree.*

som•ber•ly (sŏm′bər lē) *adv.* **1.** In a melancholy manner: *"I really miss my old home," he said **somberly**.* **2.** Seriously; gravely: *The honor guard filed **somberly** onto the stage, carrying their flags.*

sta•bi•lize (stā′bə līz′) *v.* **sta•bi•lized, sta•bi•liz•ing, sta•bi•liz•es.** To hold steady; to make stable or firm: *The new tail helped **stabilize** the glider during turns.*

sup•press (sə prĕs′) *v.* **sup•pressed, sup•press•ing, sup•press•es.** To hold back or keep in: *The student **suppressed** his relief when the bell rang just as the teacher called on him to answer.*

sur•vey (sər vā′ or sûr′vā′) *v.* **sur•veyed, sur•vey•ing, sur•veys.** To inspect or study carefully: *Scientists are **surveying** the harbor to see how many different types of fish live there.* —*n.* (sûr′vā′). A detailed study or investigation: *The **survey** lists every type of fish in the bay.*

sus•pi•cion (sə spĭsh′ən) *n.* The act of suspecting something on little evidence or without proof: *Her **suspicions** were aroused when she saw that the dog would not look at her directly.*

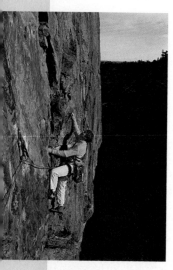

sheer

---

stabilize

This came from the Latin word stabilis, *"firm," which traveled through Old French to become the English* **stable** *and* **stabilize**. *The Latin* stabulum, *"standing place," is the source of the other English meaning of* **stable**: *"the place where domestic animals stand."*

slink

ă pat / ā pay / âr care / ä father / ĕ pet / ē be / ĭ pit / ī pie / îr pier / ŏ pot / ō toe

sys•tem•at•ic (sĭs′tə **măt′**ĭk) *adj.* Done in an orderly, step-by-step way: *A* **systematic** *check of every wire led the electricians to the problem.*

T

tar•get•ed (tär′gĭt ĭd) *adj.* Identified as the person or group intended to be influenced by an action or event: *The* **targeted** *group was young women, and the ads were aimed at them.*

tech•nique (tĕk nēk′) *n.* An established method or procedure for accomplishing a task: *Researchers are working to develop new* **techniques** *for preventing disease.*

te•di•ous (tē′dē əs) *adj.* Tiresome because slow, dull, or long; boring: *Computers are now used to carry out complicated and* **tedious** *mathematical calculations.*

tomb (tōom) *n.* **1.** A place of burial; a grave. **2.** A chamber or vault for the burial of the dead: *Many beautiful objects were buried with the king in his* **tomb.**

tour•na•ment (tōor′nə mənt *or* tur′nə mənt) *n.* A contest in which players compete in a series of games or matches: *I won two of my three matches in the karate* **tournament.**

tra•di•tion (trə dĭsh′ən) *n.* A set of customs or practices handed down from generation to generation: *We follow our family* **tradition** *and attend a reunion each summer.*

trail•head (trāl′hĕd′) *n.* The place where a trail or path begins: *The hikers gathered at the* **trailhead** *to form teams and distribute supplies.*

U

un•ex•pect•ed•ly (ŭn′ĭk spĕk′tĭd lē) *adv.* In a way that is not expected; without warning; suddenly: *The answer to my question came* **unexpectedly** *in a dream.*

V

veer (vîr) *v.* **veered, veer•ing, veers.** To swerve or change course or direction: *She* **veered** *sharply to avoid running into the bicycle.*

tomb

tournament

In the Middle Ages, French knights enjoyed torneiement, *a sport in which they used swords and lances to knock each other off their horses. Fortunately, most* **tournaments** *today aren't so rough!*

tradition
The word **tradition** *comes from the Latin* trīdere, *which means "to hand over, deliver, or entrust."*

trailhead

ô p**aw** / oi b**oy** / ou **ou**t / o͞o t**oo**k / o͞o b**oo**t / ŭ c**u**t / ûr **ur**ge / th **th**in / *th* **th**is / hw **wh**oop / zh vi**s**ion / ə **a**bout

wilderness

wil•der•ness (**wĭl′**dər nĭs) *n.* An area left in its natural condition; unsettled and uncultivated land: *The campers checked their supplies before setting out to explore the* **wilderness.**

wist•ful•ly (**wĭst′**fəl lē) *adv.* In a way full of wishful longing: *The hungry dog looked* **wistfully** *at the refrigerator door.*

wrong•do•ing (**rông′**do͞o′ĭng *or* **rŏng′**doo ing) *n.* An act that is considered to be unethical or immoral: *He had never cheated, and was surprised when the referee accused him of* **wrongdoing.**

ă pat / ā pay / âr care / ä father / ĕ pet / ē be / ĭ pit / ī pie / îr pier / ŏ pot / ō toe

ACKNOWLEDGMENTS

For each of the selections listed below, grateful acknowledgment is made for permission to excerpt and/or reprint original or copyrighted material as follows:

Selections

"After the Spill," from *Oil Spills*, by Laurence Pringle. Copyright © 1993 by Laurence Pringle. Reprinted by permission of Morrow Junior Books, a division of William Morrow & Company, Inc.

"Anne of Green Gables," by Lucy M. Montgomery, adapted by Jamie Turner, from April 1987 *Plays: The Drama Magazine for Young People.* Copyright © 1987 by Plays, Inc. Reprinted by permission of *Plays: The Drama Magazine for Young People.*

From *Bearstone*, by Will Hobbs. Copyright © 1989 by Will Hobbs. Reprinted by permission of Atheneum Books for Young Readers, an imprint of Simon & Schuster Children's Publishing Division. Cover reprinted by permission of Avon Books.

From *Betsy Byars The Moon And I*, by Betsy Byars. Copyright © 1991 by Betsy Byars. Reprinted by permission of Julian Messner, a division of Simon & Schuster.

"Coming Here, Going There," by Katie Monagle, from November 1991 *Scholastic Update*. Copyright © 1991 by Scholastic Inc. Reprinted by permission.

From *Dig This! How Archaeologists Uncover Our Past*, by Michael Avi-Yonah. Copyright © 1993 by Runestone Press, a division of Lerner Publications Company. Reprinted by permission.

Selections from *Extremely Weird Sea Creatures*, by Sarah Lovett. Copyright © 1992 by John Muir Publications. Reprinted by permission.

From *Faith Ringgold*, by Robyn Montana Turner. Copyright © 1993 by Robyn Montana Turner. Reprinted by permission of Little, Brown and Company.

"How Old Is It?" by Alison S. Brooks from March 1991 *Faces* magazine. Copyright © 1991 by Cobblestone Publishing, Inc., 7 School St., Peterborough, NH 03458 Reprinted by permission.

"Hypothermia," by Franklyn M. Branley from February 1993 *Cricket* magazine. Copyright © 1984 by Franklyn M. Branley. Reprinted by permission of the author. Cover copyright © 1993 by Leo and Diane Dillon. Reprinted by permission of the artists.

The Iceman, by Don Lessem. Copyright © 1994 by Don Lessem. Reprinted by permission of Crown Publishers, Inc.

From *Into the Mummy's Tomb*, by Nicholas Reeves. Copyright © 1992 by Nicholas Reeves and The Madison Press Limited. Reprinted by permission of The Madison Press Limited.

From *Island of the Blue Dolphins*, by Scott O'Dell. Copyright © 1960 by Scott O'Dell. Reprinted by permission of Houghton Mifflin Company. All rights reserved.

"Joel Rubin," from *It's Our World, Too!: Stories of Young People Who Are Making a Difference,* by Phillip Hoose. Copyright © 1993 by Phillip Hoose. Reprinted by permission of Little, Brown and Company.

"Joey, age fourteen," from *How It Feels to Be Adopted,* by Jill Krementz. Copyright © 1982 by Jill Krementz. Reprinted by permission of Alfred A. Knopf, Inc.

From *Last Summer with Maizon*, by Jacqueline Woodson. Copyright © 1990 by Jacqueline Woodson. Reprinted by permission of Bantam Doubleday Books for Young Readers.

From *Maniac Magee*, by Jerry Spinelli. Copyright © 1990 by Jerry Spinelli. Reprinted by permission of Little, Brown and Company, Inc.

"Meet . . . George Lucas: Setting the Scene for Adventure," from October 1992 National Geographic *World*. Copyright © 1992 by National Geographic *World*. *World* is the official magazine for Junior Members of the National Geographic Society. Reprinted by permission.

"Mummy Making: The Why and the How," from June 1990 National Geographic *World*. Copyright © 1990 by National Geographic *World*. *World* is the official magazine for Junior Members of the National Geographic Society. Reprinted by permission.

"The New Wave in Feature Animation," by James Gates, from January 1995 *Animation Magazine*. Copyright © 1994 by *Animation Magazine*. Reprinted by permission.

"The No-Guitar Blues," from *Baseball in April and Other Stories*, by Gary Soto. Copyright © 1990 by Gary Soto. Reprinted by permission of Harcourt Brace & Company.

Oceans, by Seymour Simon. Copyright © 1990 by Seymour Simon. Reprinted by permission of Morrow Junior Books, a division of William Morrow & Company, Inc.

From *Pacific Crossing*, by Gary Soto. Copyright © 1992 by Gary Soto. Reprinted by permission of Harcourt Brace & Company.

From *The Phantom Tollbooth*, by Norton Juster. Copyright © 1961, 1989 by Norton Juster. Reprinted by permission of Random House, Inc.

From *The Pinballs*, by Betsy Byars. Copyright © 1977 by Betsy Byars. Reprinted by permission of HarperCollins Publishers.

The Pyramids of Egypt, edited by Stella Sands, from premier issue 1992 of *Kids Discover* magazine. Copyright © 1991 by *Kids Discover* magazine. Reprinted by permission.

Quotes by di Suvero, Grooms, Oldenburg, from *The Sculptor's Eye*, by Jan Greenberg and Sandra Jordan. Delacorte, 1993.

"Rain at the Koster Dig," by Gerry Armstrong from November 1990 *Cricket* magazine. Copyright © 1990 by Gerry Armstrong. Reprinted by permission of the author.

"Subway Rush Hour," from *Montage of a Dream Deferred*, by Langston Hughes. Copyright © 1951 by Langston Hughes. Copyright renewed 1979 by George Houston Bass. Reprinted by permission of Harold Ober Associates Inc.

"Summer's Bounty," from *In Other Words*, by May Swenson. Copyright © 1987 by May Swenson. Reprinted by permission of Alfred A. Knopf, Inc.

"Surf," by Lillian Morrison from *The Sidewalk Racer and Other Poems of Sports and Motion*. Copyright © 1965, 1967, 1968, 1977 by Lillian Morrison. Reprinted by permission of Marian Reiner for the author.

"Twelve Below," from *Letters from Maine*, by May Sarton. Copyright © 1984 by May Sarton. Reprinted by permission of W.W. Norton & Company, Inc.

Special thanks to the following teachers whose students' compositions are included in the Be a Writer features in this level:
Julie Welch, Kane School, Lawrence, Massachusetts; Joyce Hansen, Charles R. Drew Intermediate School 148, Bronx, New York; Miki Hayes, Kamehameha Schools, Honolulu, Hawaii; Cathi Elsbree, Gertrude Scott Smith School, Aurora, Illinois; Jeanne Duell, St. Luke School, Beavercreek, Ohio; Deborah Broccoli, Luis Muñoz Marín School, Bridgeport, Connecticut

CREDITS

Illustration 18–29 Scott Nash; 37–53 John Patrick; 61, 64, 69 Jerry Pinkney; 78–97 Josée Morin; 126–127 Marty Blake; 134–143 Celina Hinajosa; 150–167 Lambert Davis; 172–179 Michael Steirnagle; 186–201 Simon Ng; 234 Jack McMaster/Margo Stahl; 246–247 Rob Wood-Wood Ronsaville Harlin, Inc.; 250–261 Sandra Speidel; 264–265 Brian Callanan; 267 John Baxter; 268–273 Rob Wood-Wood Ronsaville Harlin, Inc.; 294–296 Rubin De Anda; 306–307, 312 Marie Muscarnera; 313 Bryn Barnard; 314–316 Marie Muscarnera; 318–320 Bryn Barnard; 324, 326–327 Marie Lessard; 334–355 Will Terry; 397 Vaishali Nandé; 420 Susan Leopold; 436–449 Hui Han Liu; 458–467 Rosanne Kaloustian; 472–489 Jo Ellen McAllister Stammen; 502–513 Francisco X. Mora; 564–565, 578 Maps: Anne Diebel; 564 Sarah Landry; 609, 610–612 Vaishali Nandé; 612 Pat Rossi

Assignment Photography 124–125, 182–183, 184–185, 222, 358–359 (t), 360–361 (t), 362–363 (t, bl), 386 (bm), 388 (b), 389 (tm), 398–399, 496–497, 498–499, 500–501, 580–581 Banta Digital Group; 298 (inset), 522–523, 548–549 Kindra Clineff; 128–129, 130–131, 132–133, 144–145, 148, 168–169, 170–171, 180–181, 182–183, 184–185, 202–203, 205 (tl), 222, 224–225, 226–227, 228–229, 230–231, 262–263, 298–299, 322–323, 325, 328–329, 330–331, 333, 384–385, 421, 468, 490–491, 524–525, 578–579, 620–621 Tony Scarpetta; 204, 205, 386 (bl), 387 (tl), 388 (br), 450–451 Tracey Wheeler

Photography 1 Griffith Institute Ashmolean Museum 2 Griffith Institute Ashmolean Museum (tl); Stuart Westmorland/Tony Stone Images (tr) 18 Carolyn Soto/Courtesy of Gary Soto 53 Courtesy of Will Hobbs (b); Courtesy of John Patrick 54–55 Candace Cochrane/Positive Images 56 Rod Planck/Tony Stone Images 57–59 Letraset (background) 58 REI (ml) 59 Mosbys First Responder 60 Courtesy of Jerry Pinkney; Simon Spicer/University of South Dakota Photo Service (tl) 62-63 Tom & Pat Leeson/Photo Researchers 70 Bryan F. Peterson/The Stock Market 71 Paul Steel/The Stock Market (background); Bryan F. Peterson/The Stock Market 75 ©Pedigo/Custom Medical Stock Photo (t); Van Bucher/Science Source/Photo Researchers (m); ©Ken Eward/ Science Source/Photo Researchers (b) 76 Pierre Perrin/Liaison International (l); George D. Dodge/ Bruce Coleman Inc (m) 77 O.Y. Lehtikuva/Westlight (t); Keith Gunnar/Bruce Coleman Inc (m); Christopher Arneson/Tony Stone Images/Chicago Inc (m); Dallas & John Heaton/Westlight (b); Phillipe Achache/Tony Stone Images/Chicago Inc (bl) 78 Courtesy of Scott O'Dell (t); Courtesy of Josee Morin (b) 98-99 Sue Bennett; John Barr/Liaison International (background) 100 Phillip Warrick/FPG International (m) 105 Sandra Reus/Liaison International (r) 107 Shonna Valensky 109 Courtesy of Erik Ibell Jr. 110 M. Elaine Adams/Little, Brown & Co. (tl); Courtesy of Phil Boatwright (mr) 130 Lawrence Migdale/Tony Stone Images/Chicago Inc (ml); Bill Bachman/Sipa Press (bl) 134 Carolyn Soto/ Courtesy of Gary Soto (t); Courtesy of Celina Hinajosa (b) 146-147 Ronald C. Modra/Sports Illustrated (m) 147 Flint Journal Photo (tr) 148 Philip Saltonstall/Sports Illustrated for Kids (cover) 150 Photo by Marion Roth/Courtesy of Jacqueline Woodson 179 Courtesy of Michael Steirnagle/ Munro Goodman 185 Courtesy of Tara Bonaparte 186 Courtesy of Simon Ng (l); K. Yep/ Courtesy of Laurence Yep (m) 206-7 Prince Edward Island Public Archives and Records Office 209, 210-211, 214, 215, 216-217 Barrett & Mackay 218 George Wotton Photographer (bl); S.J.A. De Janos/Confederation Centre of The Arts (tl, tr, m) 219 Barrett & Mackay (br) 221 Barrett & Mackay; Prince Edward Island Public Archives and Records Office (t) 224 ©Shelley Grossman /Woodfin Camp and Associates (l) 225 ©Robert Frerck/Woodfin Camp and Associates (br); Nathan Benn/©National Geographic Society (m) 230 Claire Reeves/Nicholas Reeves 232 Ronald Sheriden/Ancient Art and Architecture 233 Griffith Institute Ashmolean Mus (l) 234-235 Robert Harding Picture Library (m) 236 Griffith Institute Ashmolean Mus (r) 237 Robert Harding Picture Library (r) 238 Nicholas Reeves (t); Robert Harding Picture Library (l) 239 Griffith Institute Ashmolean Mus (r) 240 Lee Boltin Library (l); Griffith Institute Ashmolean Museum 241 The Mansell